Advanced Introduction to International Human Rights Law

Elgar Advanced Introductions are stimulating and thoughtful introductions to major fields in the social sciences and law, expertly written by some of the world's leading scholars. Designed to be accessible yet rigorous, they offer concise and lucid surveys of the substantive and policy issues associated with discrete subject areas.

The aims of the series are two-fold: to pinpoint essential principles of a particular field, and to offer insights that stimulate critical thinking. By distilling the vast and often technical corpus of information on the subject into a concise and meaningful form, the books serve as accessible introductions for undergraduate and graduate students coming to the subject for the first time. Importantly, they also develop well-informed, nuanced critiques of the field that will challenge and extend the understanding of advanced students, scholars and policy-makers.

Titles in the series include:

International Political Economy
Benjamin J. Cohen

The Austrian School of Economics
Randall G. Holcombe

Cultural Economics
Ruth Towse

International Conflict and Security Law
Nigel D. White

Comparative Constitutional Law
Mark Tushnet

International Human Rights Law
Dinah L. Shelton

Advanced Introduction to

International Human Rights Law

DINAH L. SHELTON

Manatt/Ahn Professor of International Law (emeritus),
George Washington University Law School, USA and former member
of the Inter-American Commission on Human Rights (2010–2014)

Elgar Advanced Introductions

Edward Elgar
Cheltenham, UK • Northampton, MA, USA

Published by
Edward Elgar Publishing Limited
The Lypiatts
15 Lansdown Road
Cheltenham
Glos GL50 2JA
UK

Edward Elgar Publishing, Inc.
William Pratt House
9 Dewey Court
Northampton
Massachusetts 01060
USA

A catalogue record for this book
is available from the British Library

Library of Congress Control Number: 2014938767

10 07472865

MIX
Paper from
responsible sources
FSC   FSC® C013056
www.fsc.org

ISBN 978 1 78254 521 7 (cased)
ISBN 978 1 78254 523 1 (paperback)
ISBN 978 1 78254 522 4 (eBook)

Typeset by Servis Filmsetting Ltd, Stockport, Cheshire
Printed and bound in Great Britain by T.J. International Ltd, Padstow

Contents

Preface

The aim of this volume is to provide an overview of the development, contents and challenges of international human rights law, which can serve to inform those new to the topic and also be of benefit to those seeking to further their knowledge of particular aspects of that law. The subject of human rights is increasingly complex as it enters its eighth decade of development since the end of the Second World War. New rights are emerging or being proposed, existing rights have been expanded or reformulated. Nearly all global and regional intergovernmental organizations now engage in standard-setting and monitor to a greater or lesser extent the human rights actions of their members. Those organizations that have not incorporated human rights considerations in the exercise of their mandates are increasingly criticized for failing to do so by the ever-growing number of civil society organizations dedicated to the promotion and protection of human rights. At the same time, debate continues over how to reconcile and balance human rights concerns with what may appear to be competing primary mandates of organizations dedicated to other matters, such as trade, environment or economic development.

No doubt remains that the observance of human rights is a matter of international concern, but in part as a consequence of this development many human rights bodies created within international organizations struggle to meet expanded expectations, new functions and a growing caseload. At the same time, human rights bodies often encounter resistance to compliance with norms and decisions, and nearly all human rights institutions function at less than peak potential due to a lack of adequate financial resources and personnel. The risk of backsliding, including denunciation of human rights treaties, is ever-present in an international system that is largely consensual. The expanding power of non-State actors also presents difficulties for an international system that was designed to respond to the excesses and abuses of powerful governments, and not those of failed States and weak State institutions unable to ensure the effective enjoyment of human rights for those within the State's territory and jurisdiction. These are all challenges to the survival and strengthening of international human rights law.

An advanced introduction cannot cover every topic in depth. In order to ensure an adequate discussion of the global and regional institutions, norms and procedures that have emerged in the field of human rights law, national institutions and constitutional law are not addressed. In addition, it has been necessary to omit any detailed discussion of the overlapping, but still separate fields of international humanitarian law and international criminal law.

I would like to thank Herb Somers of the George Washington University law library for his assistance in obtaining materials and sources for the preparation of this volume, Jannat Majeed for her research assistance, and the law school for the leave of absence that enabled me to meet the contractual date set for completion of this volume. I also benefitted greatly from the experience of serving from 2010 to 2014 on the Inter-American Commission on Human Rights. The invaluable insights gained from four years of participation in one of the institutions discussed in this volume contributed greatly to generating new reflections on the critically important topic of international human rights law.

Abbreviations

ACMW	ASEAN Committee on the Implementation of the Declaration on the Protection and Promotion of the Rights of Migrant Workers
ACWC	ASEAN Commission on the Promotion and Protection of the Rights of Women and Children
ADRDM	American Declaration of the Rights and Duties of Man
Af. Ct. HR	African Court of Human Rights
Afr. Comm. HPR	African Commission on Human and Peoples Rights
AICHR	ASEAN Inter-Governmental Human Rights Commission
AICHR TOR	Terms of Reference of the ASEAN Intergovernmental Commission on Human Rights
ASEAN	Association of Southeast Asian Nations
AU	African Union
BIT	Bilateral Investment Treaty
CAT	Convention against Torture and Other Cruel Inhuman and Degrading Treatment or Punishment
CEDAW	Convention on the Elimination of All Forms of Discrimination against Women
CERD	Convention on the Elimination of All Forms of Racial Discrimination
CESCR	Committee on Economic, Social and Cultural Rights
COE	Council of Europe
COM	Committee of Ministers of the Council of Europe
CPMW	Convention on the Protection of the Rights of All Migrant Workers and Members of their Families
CRC	Convention on the Rights of the Child

CRPD	Convention on the Rights of Persons with Disabilities
CSCE	Conference on Security and Cooperation in Europe
CSW	Commission on the Status of Women
DPIL	UN Declaration on Principles of International Law
ECHR	European Convention on Human Rights
ECJ	European Court of Justice
ECOSOC	UN Economic and Social Council
ECOWAS	Economic Community of West African States
ECRI	European Commission against Racism and Intolerance
EHRR	European Human Rights Reports
ESC	European Social Charter
ETS	European Treaty Series
EU	European Union
Eur. Ct. HR	European Court of Human Rights
FAO	Food and Agriculture Organization
FRA	Fundamental Rights Agency
HCNM	High Commissioner on National Minorities
HFA	Helsinki Final Act
HRC	UN Human Rights Committee
I-A	Inter-American
I-A CPPT	Inter-American Convention to Prevent and Punish Torture
I-A Ct. HR	Inter-American Court of Human Rights
IACHR	Inter-American Commission on Human Rights
ICCPR	International Covenant on Civil and Political Rights
ICESCR	International Covenant on Economic, Social and Cultural Rights
ICISS	International Commission on Intervention and State Sovereignty
ICJ	International Court of Justice
ICRC	International Committee of the Red Cross
ICTY	International Criminal Tribunal for the Former Yugoslavia
ILC	International Law Commission
ILO	International Labour Organization
ILOAT	International Labour Organization's Administrative Tribunal

NEPAD	New Partnership for Africa's Development
NGO	Non-governmental organization
OAS	Organization of American States
OAS TS	Organization of American States Treaty Series
OAU	Organization of African Unity
OECD	Organisation for Economic Co-operation and Development
OHCHR	Office of the High Commissioner for Human Rights
OPCAT	Optional Protocol to the Convention against Torture
OSCE	Organization for Security and Cooperation in Europe
OUP	Oxford University Press
PACE	Parliamentary Assembly of the Council of Europe
PAHO	Pan American Health Organization
PCIJ	Permanent Court of International Justice
PSC	Peace and Security Council of the African Union
R2P	responsibility to protect
SADC	South African Development Community
SPT	Subcommittee for the Prevention of Torture
TRIMs	Trade-Related Investment Measures
UDHR	Universal Declaration of Human Rights
UN	United Nations
UNDRIP	United Nations Declaration on the Rights of Indigenous Peoples
UNESCO	United Nations Educational, Scientific and Cultural Organization
UNTS	United Nations Treaty Series
US	United States
VCLT	Vienna Convention on the Law of Treaties
WBG	World Bank Group
WHO	World Health Organization
WTO	World Trade Organization

1 Concepts and foundations

The concept of human rights involves consideration of what "rights" a person possesses by virtue of being "human", that is, rights that human beings have simply because they are human beings, independent of the infinite variety of individual characteristics and human social circumstances. What is the essence of "human" that inevitably gives right to rights, if it does? It is also necessary to consider the meaning of "rights" and the variety of legal relationships encompassed within the term. Approaches to these issues vary widely, and some scholars claim that efforts to define human rights are futile because they involve self-evident moral judgments that are not further explicable. Those who are instrumentalist in approach are more concerned with the consequences of having human rights than with a theoretical justification of rights. Many persons concerned with this topic, however, consider it useful to understand the foundations that support human rights law.

A "right" may be defined in relation to a duty of another, an immunity from having a legal status altered, a privilege to do something or a power to create or alter a legal relationship.[1] One limited concept of human rights is a claim against a government to refrain or abstain from certain acts, such as torture and infringement of individual liberties. This claim may stem from a metaphysical concept such as the nature of humanity, or from a religious belief such as a divine spark inherent in each person. Alternatively, a claim of right may be based on certain interests such as the common good deriving from social contract, requiring a determination of the common good, along with the need to balance it against other societal interests. International legal texts such as the Preambles to the Universal Declaration of Human Rights

---

1 Wesley Newcomb Hohfeld, *Some Fundamental Legal Conceptions as Applied in Judicial Reasoning* (1913) 23 YALE LJ 16; WESLEY NEWCOMB HOHFELD, FUNDAMENTAL LEGAL CONCEPTIONS AS APPLIED IN JUDICIAL REASONING AND OTHER LEGAL ESSAYS (Walter Wheeler Cook ed., Yale UP 1919); HLA HART, THE CONCEPT OF LAW (2nd edn, OUP, 1961).

(UDHR)[2] and the International Covenants on Human Rights partly reflect a utilitarian approach in mentioning that "recognition of the inherent dignity and of the equal and inalienable rights of all members of the human family is the foundation of freedom, justice and peace in the world", but the Covenants add that "these rights derive from the inherent dignity of the human person".[3] Part of the complexity in identifying the foundations of human rights is the need "to confront conflicts between utilitarian and anti-utilitarian philosophy, between values of equality and liberty, between absolute and relativist conceptions of rights, all issues of moral justification".[4]

Understanding the foundations of human rights can help clarify issues of universality, the scope of protection available, the permissibility and limits of derogations or exceptions, the balancing or priorities afforded to various rights, and similar problems. The justifications for human rights that affect the responses to these and similar issues are considered in this chapter.

1.1   Foundations

1.1.1   Religion

A central tenet of most religions is that every human being has a sacred spark conferred by a transcendental creator. It is deemed to follow from this belief that divine authority establishes the equal and inherent value of each person. Such common and unique humanity means that every human has a high moral standing that requires appropriate consideration. While the sacred texts of major religions do not speak of human rights per se, they address ethical obligations and responsibilities towards others. The rationales underlying these duties – equality, human dignity and the sacredness of life – provide a foundation for the concept of human rights.[5] Indeed, some scholars believe that the moral

---

2 Universal Declaration of Human Rights, GA Res 217A, UN GAOR, 3d Sess, Pt I, at 71, UN Doc A/810 (10 Dec 1948).

3 International Covenant on Civil and Political Rights, GA Res 2200A, (XXI), 19 Dec 1966, 999 UNTS 171, 1057 UNTS 407, 6 ILM 368 (1967); International Covenant on Economic, Social and Cultural Rights, 19 Dec 1966, 993 UNTS 3.

4 Jerome J Shestack, *The Philosophical Foundations of Human Rights*, in HUMAN RIGHTS: CONCEPTS AND STANDARDS (Janusz Symonides ed., Ashgate 2000) 31, 33.

5 See generally LEONARD SWINDLER, RELIGIOUS LIBERTY AND HUMAN RIGHTS: IN NATIONS AND IN RELIGIONS (Ecumenical Press, Hippocree Books, 1986); ROBERT TRAER, FAITH IN HUMAN

foundation for human rights comes exclusively from religious ethics, that nothing outside of religious precepts can support the ethical platform of human rights law.[6]

According to the eminent scholar Paul Gordon Lauren, "all of the major religions of the world seek in one way or another to speak to the issue of human responsibility to others".[7] Among the ancient religions of the East, Hindu texts address the necessity for moral behaviour, the importance of duty (*dharma*) and good conduct towards the suffering of others. Adherents are taught to practise charity and compassion for the hungry, sick, homeless and unfortunate because all life is sacred, to be loved and respected. "Noninjury (*ahimsa*) is not causing pain to any living being at any time through the actions of one's mind, speech or body" (*Veda*).[8] Buddhism, too, encompasses respect for all life and duties of compassion and charity; it urges renunciation of differences of caste and rank in favour of universal brotherhood and equality. The Confucian *Analects, Doctrine of the Mean*, and *Great Learning* express the belief that harmony and cooperation exist when duty and responsibility are exercised towards others, which leads to considering all human beings as having equal worth and recognizing that "within the four seas, all men are brothers".[9] The fundamental teaching here, as in nearly all religions, is "Do not impose on others what you yourself do not desire".[10] Another well-known epigram links individuals together in the creation of a just global society: "If there be righteousness in the heart, there will be beauty in the character. If there is beauty in the character, there will be harmony in the home. If there is harmony in the home, there will be order in the nation. If there be order in the nation, there will be peace in the world".[11]

RIGHTS: SUPPORT IN RELIGIOUS TRADITIONS FOR A GLOBAL STRUGGLE (Georgetown UP 1991); RELIGION AND HUMAN RIGHTS: AN INVITATION (John Witte, Jr and M Christian Green eds, OUP 2011).

6 Michael J Perry, *The Morality of Human Rights: A Problem for Non-Believers?*, 133 COMMONWEAL, 14 July 2006, at 16.

7 PAUL GORDON LAUREN, THE EVOLUTION OF HUMAN RIGHTS: VISIONS SEEN (3rd edn, University of Pennsylvania Press 2011).

8 ARVIND SHARMA, HINDUISM AND HUMAN RIGHTS: A CONCEPTUAL APPROACH (OUP 2004).

9 Joseph CW Chan, *Confucianism and Human Rights* in RELIGION AND HUMAN RIGHTS: AN INVITATION (n. 5), 92.

10 *Analects*, XV, 23. Similar expressions can be found in Judaism (Leviticus 9:13, 15, 18) and Christianity ("Do unto others as you would have them do unto you" Galatians 3:28; 5:14). See JUDAISM AND HUMAN RIGHTS (Milton R Konvitz, ed, 2nd edn, Transaction 2001).

11 *Great Learning*, cited in HUSTON SMITH, THE RELIGIONS OF MAN (Harper & Row, 1958), 181.

The monotheistic religions that emerged from Western Asia all ground the dignity and worth of human beings in the divine spark of creation with which each person is imbued. In Judaism, the sacredness of the individual, endowed with equal worth and value, is important. Isaiah 58:6–7 teaches all to "undo the tongs of the yoke, let the oppressed go free[,] . . . share your bread with the hungry, and bring the homeless poor into your house". The ethics of the Torah contain "the principle that in the eyes of the law all people are equal" (Leviticus 19:15) and that every person can demand his rights and that "justice must be extended to all alike".[12] Christianity preaches a message of equality and respect for others.[13] In Islam, one of the pillars of belief is charity or lifting the burdens of those less fortunate. The Qur-an speaks to justice, the sanctity of life, freedom, mercy, compassion and respect for all human beings. Racial equality and religious tolerance should be guaranteed by giving Jews and Christians in equality the right to practise their religion as freely as the Muslims.[14]

1.1.2   Philosophical traditions

In addition to the religious doctrines that shaped many societies, moral and political philosophers developed theories of the just society and good governance. As early as the fifth century before the present era, Chinese philosopher Hsün-tzu wrote that "[i]n order to relieve anxiety and eradicate strife, nothing is as effective as the institution of corporate life based on a clear recognition of individual rights".[15] Greek philosophy developed the idea of natural law including equal respect for all citizens, equality before the law, equality in political power and suffrage, and equality of civil rights. The Roman jurist Cicero opined that natural law and universal justice bind all human society together and apply to all without distinction.[16] Each person has unique dignity which imposes on all the responsibility to look after others. This natural law is eternal and unchangeable and valid for all nations and all times.

---

12 SAMUEL BELKIN, IN HIS IMAGE: THE JEWISH PHILOSOPHY OF MAN EXPRESSED IN RABBINIC TRADITION 87 (Abelard-Schuman 1960).
13 "There is neither Greek nor Jew, nor slave nor free, nor man nor woman, but we are all one in Christ". Galatians 3:28.
14 IRENE OH, THE RIGHTS OF GOD: ISLAM, HUMAN RIGHTS, AND COMPARATIVE ETHICS (Georgetown University Press 2007).
15 Hsun Tse, *Enriching a Country*, quoted in LIANG CHI-CHAO, HISTORY OF CHINESE THOUGHT DURING THE EARLY TSIN PERIOD 64 (Kegan Paul 1930); UNESCO, BIRTHRIGHT OF MAN 303.
16 MARCUS TULLIUS CICERO, THE REPUBLIC AND THE LAWS (Niall Rudd, tr., OUP 1968), 68–9.

Enlightenment thinkers such as John Locke in his *Second Treatise of Government* (1690) argued that every individual person in the state of nature is born in a state of perfect equality and possesses certain natural rights prior to the existence of any organized government. Societies and governments are formed to preserve these rights, not to extinguish them. Jean-Jacque Rousseau similarly posited that man is born free with intrinsic worth. Olympe de Gouge (nom de plume of Marie Gouze) extended this to women, declaring that "woman is born free and remains equal to man in her rights".[17] The same year she proclaimed the rights of women, Thomas Paine introduced the expression "human rights" in his best seller *The Rights of Man* (1791). In sum, in political theory a social contract in the relationship of the individual to the State provides the foundation of human rights, in which the State's role is to protect and guarantee individual rights.[18]

1.1.3   Science

More recent approaches to determining why human rights exist have emerged from science, in particular from evolutionary biology, sociology and psychology.

The theory of evolution through natural selection suggests that characteristics of competition and tendencies to dominate, on the one hand, and altruism and compassion on the other hand, have a basis in biology.[19] Evolutionary theory posits that individuals compete with one another for limited resources in their environment; those with traits providing them greater ability to obtain necessary resources and respond to threats in that environment will be more likely to survive and reproduce. Competition leads to individuals striving for dominance over other individuals to gain greater access to resources, such as food, sleeping sites and mates. Nonetheless, humans live in social groups and need to cooperate with one another for many aspects of survival, including finding sources of food and defending territory against other groups. This necessitates helping fellow group members and providing assistance and protection to the most vulnerable members of the

---

17 Declaration of the Rights of Woman and Citizen (France 1791). One year later, Mary Wollstonecraft published A VINDICATION OF THE RIGHTS OF WOMEN (1792).

18 JOHN LOCKE, SECOND TREATISE OF GOVERNMENT (1690); JEAN-JACQUES ROUSSEAU, DISCOURSE ON INEQUALITY (1754); THE SOCIAL CONTRACT (1762).

19 Chris A Robinson, *Biology* in OXFORD HANDBOOK OF HUMAN RIGHTS LAW (D Shelton, ed, OUP 2013); ORIGINS OF ALTRUISM AND COOPERATION (Robert W Sussman and C Robert Cloninger, eds, Springer 2011).

group. This tension, between inter-individual competition to maximize individual success, and cooperation among individuals within groups to maximize group success, is part of the evolutionary history of humans. It has resulted in humans possessing biological predispositions towards both selfish/dominant and altruistic behaviours.

Sociologists have posited related foundations for human rights, based on several assumptions: about the vulnerability of human beings as embodied agents; the resulting dependency of humans on each other, especially during childhood and old age; the general reciprocity and social interconnectedness of the world; and the need for, but fragility of, social institutions.[20] Rights also presuppose autonomous and aware agents, capable of rational choice and moral deliberation, and thus capable of being held responsible for their actions. Such agents must also engage in the basic act of mutual recognition of shared moral agency, and thereby accept the rights claims of others. From this, in order to protect themselves from shared threats, humans create and sustain social institutions to provide for their collective security. Such institutions are vulnerable, however, to corruption and abuse and must be restrained in their exercise of power through establishing agreed limits, often expressed as inalienable rights. This idea of a shared ontology is seen to overcome assertions of cultural relativism and provide a justification for universal human rights.

Psychologists have begun to focus on the human capacity to identify and respond to concepts of rights and duties.[21] A growing literature suggests that humans have some innate moral psychological capacities, just as they have innate capacities for language.[22] Analysis of how such capacities function involves integrating social and cognitive psychology with philosophical constructs and evolutionary theory. The analysis finds distinctive ways that human beings reason about rights and the distinctive relations that thoughts about rights have to a more primary set of thoughts about interpersonal obligation. These capacities result in distinctive forms of human social life and interaction. The origin and function of these special psychological capacities are understood from an evolutionary perspective, as they appear func-

---

20 BRYAN S TURNER, VULNERABILITY AND HUMAN RIGHTS (Pennsylvania State University Press 2006).

21 Robin Bradley Kar, *Psychology* in OXFORD HANDBOOK OF HUMAN RIGHTS LAW (n. 19).

22 See, for example, RICHARD JOYCE, THE EVOLUTION OF MORALITY (MIT Press 2006); Robin Kar, *The Deep Structure of Law and Morality* (2006) 106 TEX L REV 877.

tionally designed to enable humans to resolve in a flexible manner the recurrent problems of cooperation that are often referred to as "social contract problems".

From these various approaches, it may be posited that human rights exist because human beings exist with goals and the potential for personal development based upon individual capacities which contribute to that personal development. This can only be accomplished if basic needs which allow for existence are met and if other persons refrain from interfering with the free and rational actions of the individual. Recognition of the fact that there are rational and legal limits to individual, corporate or State conduct that would interfere unreasonably with the free aims and life projects of others is a basic idea underlying contemporary understanding of human rights.

1.2 Basic concepts: dignity and equality

"Human dignity is one of the most fundamental concepts of international human rights law, appearing in nearly all human rights instruments and applied by human rights bodies regularly".[23] At the same time, human dignity can be understood in multiple ways that diverge from and sometimes contradict one another. Many scholars support reliance on the idea of human dignity and its greater use in judicial interpretation[24] while critics object that it has no stable meaning or content.[25]

Human dignity in international human rights law refers both to a foundational premise of human rights and to a principle having an impact on the methods of interpretation and application of specific human rights. Human dignity is understood, first, as an affirmation that every human being has an equal and inherent moral value or status. Interrelated with this status claim is the idea of human dignity

---

23 Paolo Carozza, *Human Dignity* in Oxford Handbook of Human Rights Law (n. 19).
24 For example, Jeremy Waldron, "Dignity, Rank, and Rights: The 2009 Tanner Lectures at UC Berkeley" (2009) *NYU School of Law, Public Law & Legal Theory Research Paper Series Working Paper No 09-50* <http://ssrn.com/abstract=1461220> accessed 3 February 2013; Christopher A Bracey, *Dignity in Race Jurisprudence* (2005) 7 U Pa J Const L 669, 719.
25 Justin Bates, *Human Dignity – An Empty Phrase in Search of Meaning?* (2005) 10 JR 165; Mirko Bagaric and James Allen, *The Vacuous Concept of Dignity* (2006) 5 JRH 257; Neomi Rao, *On the Use and Abuse of Dignity in Constitutional Law* (2008) 14 Colum J Eur L 201; Christopher McCrudden, *Human Dignity and Judicial Interpretation of Human Rights* (2008) 19 EJIL 655.

as a normative principle affirming that all human beings are entitled to have other persons and institutions respect this status.

Among international instruments the UDHR contains five references to human dignity. The drafters of the UDHR aimed to reach agreement on the articulation of specific human rights, without necessarily attaining consensus about the origins of those rights.[26] Jacques Maritain commented that it was possible to agree about the rights, "but on condition that no one asks us why. It is with the 'why' that all the disagreements begin".[27] In this context, human dignity emerged from different cultural and legal traditions, which despite their diversity affirmed the equal moral worth of all human persons.

Subsequent international treaties and declarations on human rights have consistently adopted the UDHR reliance on dignity as a basic concept. The two International Covenants (International Covenant on Civil and Political Rights (ICCPR) and International Covenant on Economic, Social and Cultural Rights (ICESCR)) both recognize that "these rights derive from the inherent dignity of the human person" and each refers to dignity in relationship to certain specific rights (ICCPR, Art. 10; ICESCR, Art. 13). The preamble to the 1984 Convention against Torture similarly affirms that human rights "derive from the inherent dignity of the human person". The 1965 Convention on the Elimination of all Forms of Racial Discrimination mentions dignity three times in its preamble,[28] as does the 1979 Convention on the Elimination of All Forms of Discrimination against Women,[29] while the 1989 Convention on the Rights of the Child has eight separate references to human dignity (Preamble and Arts 23, 28, 37, 39, 40).[30] The 2006 Convention on the Rights of Persons with Disabilities speaks of human dignity nine times.[31]

---

26 MARY ANN GLENDON, A WORLD MADE NEW: ELEANOR ROOSEVELT AND THE UNIVERSAL DECLARATION OF HUMAN RIGHTS (Random House 2002) 175; JOHANNES MORSINK, THE UNIVERSAL DECLARATION OF HUMAN RIGHTS: ORIGINS, DRAFTING AND INTENT (University of Pennsylvania Press 1999).

27 Jacques Maritain, *Introduction* in UNESCO, HUMAN RIGHTS: COMMENTS AND INTERPRETATIONS (Greenwood Press 1949) 9.

28 Convention on the Elimination of All Forms of Racial Discrimination, 21 Dec 1965, 660 UNTS 195, 5 ILM 352 (1966).

29 Convention on the Elimination of All Forms of Discrimination against Women, 18 Dec 1979, GA Res 34/180, 1249 UNTS 13.

30 Convention on the Rights of the Child, Nov 20, 1989, 1577 UNTS 3, GA Res 44/25.

31 Convention on the Rights of Persons with Disabilities, UN Doc A/61/611 (30 Mar 2007).

Among regional instruments the European Convention on Human Rights (ECHR) is the only major treaty to omit the word. The ECHR is, however, expressly based on the UDHR. Moreover, the idea of dignity is an integral part of European human rights jurisprudence; the European Court has in fact declared that "the very essence of the Convention is respect for human dignity".[32] The African Charter, uniquely, links dignity to certain collective rights and interests in addition to individual ones, by referring in its Preamble to the goal of "the total liberation of Africa, the peoples of which are still struggling for their dignity and genuine independence".[33] The preamble to the revised Arab Charter begins by affirming faith in the dignity of the human person and the human right to a life of dignity based on freedom, justice and equality.[34] Article 3 explicitly refers to the equal dignity of men and women while Article 17 calls for protecting the dignity of any child charged with an offence. Article 20 provides that all persons deprived of their liberty shall be treated with humanity and with respect for the inherent dignity of the human person. States are also to ensure to persons with mental or physical disabilities a decent life that guarantees their dignity (Art. 40). The 2012 ASEAN Declaration similarly refers to the equal dignity of all persons.[35]

Beyond having a foundational role underpinning human rights, dignity has been used as a principle to interpret specific rights, in particular the right to physical and personal integrity. ICCPR Article 10(1) requires that all persons deprived of liberty "be treated with ... respect for the inherent dignity of the human person". The American Convention on Human Rights uses virtually identical language,[36] while Article 5 of the African Charter of Human and Peoples' Rights refers to "the dignity inherent in a human being" in reference to the prohibition of "slavery, slave trade, torture, cruel, inhuman or degrading punishment and treatment". Other treaties, including the Convention on the Rights of the Child (Arts 28, 37) and the International Convention on the

---

32 *Goodwin v United Kingdom* [GC] (2002) 35 EHRR 18 at para. 90; *Pretty v United Kingdom*, App 2346/02 (2002) 35 EHRR 1 (29 Apr) para. 65; *VC v Slovakia*, App 18968/07, judgment of 8 Nov 2011, Rep Judgements and Decisions 2011, para. 105.

33 African Charter on Human and Peoples' Rights, OAU Doc CAB/LEG./67/3/Rev 5 reprinted in 21 ILM 59 (1982).

34 Revised Arab Charter on Human Rights, May 22, 2004, unofficial English trans 12 INT'L HUM RTS REPS 893.

35 ASEAN Declaration on Human Rights, 18 Nov 2013, www.asean.org/news/asean-statement-communiques/item/asean-human-rights-declaration.

36 American Convention on Human Rights, 22 Nov 1969, 1144 UNTS 123, OAS TS 36.

Protection of the Rights of All Migrant Workers and Members of Their Families (Art. 17),[37] similarly call for respecting dignity in contexts where persons are deprived of their liberty or subjected to detention of any sort.

Human rights tribunals have made use of dignity in developing jurisprudence on the prohibition of cruel, inhuman and degrading treatment. The European Court of Human Rights (Eur. Ct. HR) did so first in the 1978 decision *Tyrer v United Kingdom*, which found the corporal punishment of a child in school to be a violation of Article 3.[38] Since that case, the European Court has emphasized that treatment or punishment is "considered to be 'degrading' when it humiliates or debases an individual, showing a lack of respect for, or diminishing, his or her human dignity".[39]

The Inter-American Court of Human Rights (I-A Ct. HR) similarly holds that cruel, inhuman and degrading treatment violates persons' human dignity.[40] Beyond affirming that "persons detained have the right to live in prison conditions that are in keeping with their dignity as human beings",[41] the Court has held that prolonged isolation and deprivation of communication are a violation of a detainee's "inherent dignity as a human being",[42] while excessive force in controlling inmate behaviour "constitutes an assault on the dignity of the person".[43] Dignity is compromised also by prohibiting persons in detention from using their native language[44] and by forcing prison inmates to be naked for extended periods.[45]

---

37 Convention on the Protection of the Rights of All Migrant Workers and Members of Their Families, 18 Dec 1990, adopted by GA Res 45/158 reprinted in 30 ILM 1517 (1991).

38 *Tyrer v United Kingdom* (1978) 2 EHRR 1 at para. 30.

39 *MSS v Belgium and Greece* App no 30696/09 at para. 220 (ECtHR, 21 Jan 2011). See also *Peers v Greece* 2001-III ECHR at para. 75; *Kuznetsov v Ukraine* App no 39042/97 at para. 126 (ECtHR, 29 Apr 2003); *Ramirez Sanchez v France*, App 59450/00 45 EHRR 49 (4 Jul 2007), Rep Judgments and Decisions 2006-IX, at para. 119; *Ribitsch v Austria* App no 18896/91 at para. 38 (ECtHR, 4 Dec 1995); *Wiktorko v Poland* App no 14612/02 at para. 54 (ECtHR, 31 Mar 2009).

40 See, for example, *Cabrera García and Montiel Flores v Mexico* and *Maritza Urrutia v Guatemala* (Merits, Reparations and Costs), I-A Court HR Ser C, No 103 (2003).

41 *Juvenile Reeducation Institute v Paraguay* (Preliminary Objections, Merits, Reparations, Costs) I-A Court HR, Ser C, No 112 (2 Sep 2004).

42 *Velásquez-Rodríguez v Honduras* (Merits) I-A Court HR, Ser C, No 4 (29 Jul 1988).

43 *Loayza Tamayo v Peru* (Merits) I-A Court HR, Ser C No 33 (17 Sep 1997).

44 *López-Álvarez v Honduras* (Merits, Reparations and Costs) I-A Court HR, Ser C No 141 (1 Feb 2006).

45 *Case of the Miguel Castro-Castro Prison v Peru*, (Merits, Reparations and Costs), I-A Court HR, Ser C, No 160 (25 Nov 2006).

The General Comments of the Committee on Economic, Social and Cultural Rights (CESCR) have, in general, argued that the principle of human dignity requires an expansive interpretation of a whole range of Covenant rights.[46] The right to adequate food, according to the Committee, "is indivisibly linked to the inherent dignity of the human person and is indispensable for the fulfilment of other human rights enshrined in the International Bill of Human Rights",[47] as is the right to the highest attainable standard of health.[48] The Committee describes the right to work as "an inseparable and inherent part of human dignity",[49] and the right to social security as being "of central importance in guaranteeing human dignity for all persons when they are faced with circumstances that deprive them of their capacity to fully realize their Covenant rights".[50] The CESCR has also made an explicit link between dignity of individuals and the (collective) right to culture.[51]

Similarly, the Inter-American Court has attached a robust notion of dignity to its interpretation and application of the right to life that allows that right to include a guarantee of the minimal socio-economic conditions for a life lived with dignity.[52]

The principle of dignity also touches on notions of human freedom generally, but there is no consensus on how far dignity protects individual autonomy. In *Pretty v United Kingdom*, the European Court explicitly rejected a claim that Article 2 of the ECHR implies a right to choose the time and manner of one's death, even while acknowledging the centrality of dignity to the meaning and content of the Convention as a whole. Yet, patients have autonomy to make their own medical decisions, based on a respect for human dignity.[53] The Committee

---

46 UN Committee on Economic, Social and Cultural Rights (CESCR), *General Comment No 4: The Right to Adequate Housing (Art 11(1) of the Covenant)*, 13 Dec 1991, UN Doc E/1992/23 [7].

47 CESCR, *General Comment No 12: The Right to Adequate Food (Art 11)*, 12 May 1999, UN Doc E/C.12/1999/5 [4].

48 CESCR, *General Comment No 14: The Right to the Highest Attainable Standard of Health (Art 12)*, 11 Aug 2000, UN Doc E/C.12/2000/4.

49 CESCR, *General Comment No 18: The Right to Work*, 6 February 2006, UN Doc E/C.12/GC/18 [1].

50 CESCR, *General Comment No 19: The Right to Social Security (Art 9)*, 4 Feb 2008, UN Doc E/C.12/GC/19 [1].

51 CESCR, *General Comment No 21: Right of Everyone to Take Part in Cultural Life (Art 15, Para. 1a of the Covenant on Economic, Social and Cultural Rights)*, 21 Dec 2009, UN Doc E/C.12/GC/21 [1], [40].

52 *Indigenous Community Yakye Axa v Paraguay* (Merits, Reparations and Costs) I-A Court HR, Ser C No 125 (2005).

53 *VC v Slovakia* (n. 32), para. 105.

on the Elimination of All Forms of Discrimination against Women has also recognized that human dignity provides the basis of the right to choose a spouse and enter freely into marriage.[54] In contrast, the Human Rights Committee upheld a French judicial judgment forbidding dwarf throwing as a violation of the human dignity of the participants, notwithstanding their free consent.[55]

Equality is the second major overarching principle in human rights law, linked to dignity as reflected in Article 1 of the UDHR. Human rights law recognizes and celebrates human diversity by aiming to ensure the conditions necessary for each person to exercise individual self-determination in realizing her or his goals and potential as fully as possible, consistent with other persons' self-fulfilment. The law emphasizes the shared attributes and inherent nature of human beings. Thus, everyone is entitled to the same freedoms to speak, learn, think, vote, express opinions, hold office, marry and have children, and choose a religion. The physical and mental integrity of each person is guaranteed along with equal access to public services, medical care, justice, education and employment. Equality and nondiscrimination are implied in the fact that human rights instruments guarantee rights to "all persons", "everyone" or "every human being". In fact, the right to be free from discrimination and to enjoy equality in the exercise of rights has been called "the most fundamental of the rights of man . . . the starting point of all other liberties".[56]

In jurisprudence, in *Cyprus v Turkey*, the Eur. Ct. HR emphasized that "special importance" should be attached to racial discrimination because to publicly single out a group of persons for differential treatment on the basis of race "might, in certain circumstances, constitute a special affront to human dignity".[57] The European Court has made the same point with respect to discrimination against sexual minorities.[58] The Inter-American Court has affirmed, as essential aspects of human nature, the connection between equality and dignity. In an early Advisory Opinion, the Court declared that "the notion of equality

---

54 CEDAW, *General Recommendation No 21: Equality in Marriage and Family Relations*, (1994) UN Doc A/49/38 [16].

55 *Wackenheim v France*, UN Doc CCPR/C/75/D/854/1999 (15 Jul 2002).

56 SIR HERSCH LAUTERPACHT, AN INTERNATIONAL BILL OF THE RIGHTS OF MAN (Columbia University Press 1945), 115.

57 *Cyprus v Turkey* (2001) App no 25781/94, ECHR 2001-IV at paras 306, 309.

58 *Goodwin v United Kingdom* (n. 32) at paras 90, 91; concerning ethnic minorities, see *Nachova and Others v Bulgaria* App nos 43577/98 and 43579/98 at para. 145 (ECtHR, 6 Jul 2005).

springs directly from the oneness of the human family and is linked to the essential dignity of the individual".[59] A later Advisory Opinion on migrant workers went so far as to describe the equal protection of the law as a peremptory norm of international law "linked to the essential dignity of the individual".[60]

1.3   Rights and duty holders

If human rights law involves claims against others, there should be a corresponding and identifiable duty holder required to respect or fulfil those claims. This requirement has led some critics to assert that economic and social rights are merely a statement of aspirations rather than rights, because it is not obvious that governments or any other duty holder can be identified as obligated to provide food, shelter, medical care and a healthy environment.[61] Nonetheless, the ICESCR sets forth a set of obligations on States Parties, which have been further elaborated by the CESCR in a General Comment[62] premised on the view that in general, all human rights law imposes duties on States whose governments are formed for the purpose of protecting and ensuring the rights of those within the States' jurisdiction.

Although the focus of human rights law is on the responsibilities of States, some international instruments also impose duties on individuals and groups. In 1948 the United Nations adopted the Convention on the Prevention and Punishment of the Crime of Genocide.[63] It was the first convention (and remains one of only two) to declare the acts referred to as "crimes under international law" for which individuals may be held accountable. The other convention to use such terminology is the Convention against Apartheid.[64] Neither convention establishes an international system for the prosecution and punishment of

---

59 See also *Atala Riffo and Daughters v Chile*, IACHR Case 1271-04, Report no 42/08, OAE/SerL/V/II130 Doc 22 rev1 (24 Feb 2012) (discrimination on the basis of sexual orientation).

60 *Juridical Condition and Rights of the Undocumented Migrants*, Advisory Opinion OC-18/03, I-A Court HR Ser A, No 18 (2003).

61 David Beetham, *What Future for Economic and Social Rights?* (1995) 43 POLITICAL STUDIES 41.

62 CESCR, *General Comment No 3, The Nature of States Parties Obligations (Article 2)* (1990), UN Doc E/1991/23, Annex II.

63 Convention on the Prevention and Punishment of the Crime of Genocide, 9 Dec 9 1948, 78 UNTS 277.

64 Convention on the Suppression and Punishment of the Crime of Apartheid, 30 Nov 1973, GA Res 3068 (XXVIII).

offenders but leaves these matters to national courts and legal systems. The trials of Nazi war criminals at Nuremberg provided a precedent for international criminal prosecution of the most serious violations of human rights, but it was a precedent not followed until 1993, when the UN Security Council created an ad hoc tribunal for the former Yugoslavia, followed one year later by a similar tribunal to prosecute acts of genocide in Rwanda. In 1998 the principle of individual responsibility for the most serious violations of human rights and humanitarian law became generalized at the international level with the adoption of the Rome Statute of the International Criminal Court.[65] Many issues of accountability remain debated, however, such as the relationship between civil and criminal responsibility and customary immunities for diplomats and heads of State. Current discussions also centre on issues of corporate responsibility, whether civil or criminal, and the required remedies, including rehabilitation and compensation for victims. The nature and scope of the obligations of duty holders are addressed in more detail in Chapter 6

---

65 Rome Statute of the International Criminal Court, 17 Jul 1998, 2187 UNTS 90.

2   Historical overview

The extensive legal protection for human rights that currently exists in national and international law is the product of millennia of struggle by individuals concerned with justice and human well-being. Many of these advocates acted out of religious belief and duty, as suggested in Chapter 1; others contributed out of compassion or a sense of responsibility, or in response to their own suffering at the hands of repressive regimes. Each of those involved endeavoured to convert the theories of human rights into positive law.

Those advocating for human rights have been confronted consistently with powerful opponents seeking to retain privilege, hierarchy, hereditary rule, property, dominance and caste. Thomas Paine was hung in effigy in English cities; Voltaire's writings were banned. Conservative authors referred to the "monstrous fiction" of human equality.[1] Jeremy Bentham rejected the idea of natural law, calling it "simple nonsense" and labelling human rights "nonsense on stilts". People should know "their proper place".[2] These theories reflected the widespread practices of the time. The notion of divine right of rule continued in many countries until recently. Ruling elites aimed and still aim to maintain power and invoke cultural traditions subordinating, inter alia, women, children, minorities and workers. Throughout much of history slavery has been widespread, often justified by distorted theology, and torture has been a prevalent method of investigation and punishment. Even now, executions sometimes are held in public places and capital punishment is imposed for a wide variety of offences, although no State now continues the once common practice of holding criminally responsible children above the age of seven. In many countries, educational opportunities are limited to the rich, and a few landholders dominate the numerous landless poor. Theories seeking to justify discrimination and

---

1 EDMUND BURKE, REFLECTIONS ON THE REVOLUTION IN FRANCE (1790).
2 JEREMY BENTHAM, ANARCHICAL FALLACIES (written 1791–1795, published 1816).

repression, often based in racist ideologies, have by no means disappeared from society.

2.1   Legal texts and traditions

The Code of Hammurabi (1795–1750 BCE), the oldest legal compilation available today, represented a codification and development of the customary law of the region.[3] While many aspects of the Code are incompatible with modern views of human rights (in particular the punishments imposed), other portions established basic human rights principles such as equal protection of the law and remedies for the mistreatment of prisoners. Persia's Great Charter of Cyrus guaranteed liberty and security, freedom of movement and religious belief, the right to property, and other economic and social rights. In ancient Egypt, the Laws of the Pharaohs commanded: "Make sure that all is done according to the law, that custom is observed and the right of each man respected".[4]

Throughout South Asia, the Edicts of Asoka (300 BCE) guaranteed freedom of religion and other rights. Indian customary law had already developed humanitarian laws of war, protecting all places of religious worship, civilian houses and property against attack. The Law of Manu applied the wartime principle of discrimination in prohibiting the killing of anyone who is sleeping; without his armour; naked; deprived of his weapons; not engaged in the fighting, or engaged in fighting with another person. The law also mandated humane treatment of prisoners of war, the sick and the wounded.[5]

Some traditional African societies operated on democratic principles, allowing all members of the group to participate in the decision-making process.[6] Many communities gave paramount place to rights

---

3 See Leon R Yankwich, *The Cultural Background and Some of the Social Phases of the Code of Hammurabi*, 4 S CAL L REV 20 (1930); Frank L Fetzer, *The Code of Hammurabi: The Oldest Known Legal Code* (1930) 35 COM LJ 726.

4 PAUL GORDON LAUREN, THE EVOLUTION OF HUMAN RIGHTS: VISIONS SEEN (3rd edn, University of Pennsylvania Press 2011).

5 See ZAKONY MANU, LAWS OF MANU 134–5 (1992), quoted in Olga Butkevych, *The History of Ancient International Law: Challenges and Prospects* (2003) 5 J HIST INT'L L 189, 207.

6 John Beattie, *Checks on the Abuse of Political Power in Some African States: A Preliminary Framework for Analysis* (1959) 9 SOCIOLOGUS 97, reprinted in COMPARATIVE POLITICAL SYSTEMS 355, 361–73 (R Cohen and J Middleton eds, University of Texas Press 1967).

to life and personal security.[7] The concept of rights often had a group aspect, reflecting egalitarian aspirations and economic benefit sharing[8] and some communities "took pride in according respect and human rights to women, children and old persons".[9]

Within Europe, legal texts began guaranteeing some rights as early as the twelfth century. In Spain, the Kingdom of Leon in 1188 confirmed the rights of the Assembly, the right of an accused to a trial, and the inviolability of life, honour, home and property.[10] In England a series of foundational texts, including the Magna Carta (1215), Petition of Right (1628) and Habeas Corpus Act (1679) claimed broadly applicable civil rights and established the rule of law: "no freeman shall be arrested, or detained in prison or deprived of his freehold . . . except by the lawful judgment of his peers or by the law of the land".[11] In Hungary, the Golden Bull (Aranybulla, 1222) created the framework for an annual meeting of the Diet. Like the Magna Carta, the Golden Bull was issued at the insistence of the nobility, largely to safeguard their rights, but its final provision assures the right of individuals to disobey royal acts not conforming to the law.

The colonial origins of the United States saw the emergence of govern-ance structures based on popular consent that begin to entail rights. The Plymouth Constitution of 1620 (popularly known as the Mayflower Compact) contains a provision for the application of "equal Laws". In 1638 Maryland passed one of the earliest US statements on religious freedom in An Act for Church Liberties. The 1640 Massachusetts Body of Liberties, adopted by the Massachusetts General Court, contained seven of the 26 rights contained in the US Bill of Rights, including due process, equality before the law, freedom of assembly, and freedom of expression. The 1650 Connecticut Code of Laws contains similar due process rights. Even more rights are contained in the 1682 Charter of

---

7 SBK Asante, *Nation Building and Human Rights in Emergent African Nations* (1969) 2 CORNELL INT'L LJ 72, 73–4.

8 FO AWOGU, POLITICAL INSTITUTIONS AND THOUGHT IN AFRICA (Vantage Press 1975), 83.

9 EMMANUEL G BELLO, AFRICAN CUSTOMARY HUMANITARIAN LAW (Oyez Publishing [for the] International Committee of the Red Cross 1980), 29.

10 See generally LYNN HUNT, INVENTING HUMAN RIGHTS: A HISTORY (WW Norton 2007), 112–204.

11 Magna Carta, 25 Edw 1 (1297), cap 29, reprinted in 1 STATUTES AT LARGE 1, 7 (Owen Ruffhead ed., 1763). The subsequent English Bill of Rights of 1689 included a right to free elections and guaranteed freedom of speech in Parliament. It also prohibited cruel and unusual punishment. Much of the Bill of Rights remains in force.

Liberties and Frame of Government of the Province of Pennsylvania and the New York Charter of Liberties and Privileges of 1683.[12]

As the United States moved towards independence, the Virginia Declaration of Rights of 1776 proclaimed: "all men are by nature equally free and independent, and have certain inherent rights". The national Declaration of Independence placed rights in the framework of religious belief, "that all men are created equal, that they are endowed by their Creator with certain unalienable rights, that among these are life, liberty and the pursuit of happiness". The Declaration continues, moreover, to insist that the very purpose of government is "to secure these rights" based on the consent of the governed; thus, "whenever any form of government becomes destructive of those ends, it is the right of the people to alter or to abolish it, and to institute new government". In 1791 the federal Bill of Rights received the necessary ratifications and became the first ten amendments to the US Constitution, guaranteeing inter alia freedoms of religion, expression and assembly; the right of petition; due process and trial by jury; and freedom from cruel and unusual punishment. Later constitutional amendments banned slavery and guaranteed equal protection of the law, as well as the right to vote without discrimination based on race or sex.

France's Declaration of the Rights of Man and Citizen (1789) enumerated a series of rights based on the understanding that "[a]ll are born and remain free and equal in rights" which are "natural and imprescriptible". The Declaration, which remains a cornerstone of the French Constitution,[13] guarantees political rights, including the right to vote and to participate in politics, as well as civil rights such as the right to equality before the law, the right to be protected against arbitrary arrest or punishment, the right to be presumed innocent until proven guilty, the right to hold personal opinions and religious beliefs, the right of freedom of expression, and the right to possess property.

---

12 The documents referred to in the paragraph are collected and reprinted in COLONIAL ORIGINS OF THE AMERICAN CONSTITUTION: A DOCUMENTARY HISTORY (Donald S Lutz ed., Liberty Fund 1998).

13 The Constitution of the Fifth Republic of France, adopted on 4 October 1958, refers to the Declaration of Rights in the preamble.

2.2   International law before the twentieth century

The idea that human rights in general is a matter of legitimate international concern did not take root until the twentieth century, but specific issues about the treatment of individuals and groups were topics of international agreement as far back as there is an historical record.

2.2.1   Diplomatic protection

The first guarantees contained in early international agreements imposed a duty on rulers to protect merchants, diplomats and others travelling within their realms. International travel has always been hazardous and throughout history individuals have been vulnerable to robbery, murder, enslavement or impressment. Privateers or pirates frequently looted ships at sea and killed or sold their crews. The loss of a national was and still is seen as the loss of a valuable asset belonging to the sovereign, whether prince or State. Those who caused harm to foreign nationals diminished the wealth of the sovereign to whom such nationals were deemed to belong.

Through protests, reprisals, interventions and other State practice the rule emerged that a State was responsible for abusive acts committed against foreign nationals within the State's territory and by its nationals on the high seas. The ruler and the State itself were deemed to be collectively responsible for the damage caused to the foreign citizen. The victim's ruler could authorize the victim, his family or commercial partners to use self-help against the other country and its citizens. Letters of marque and reprisal authorized the capture of vessels or cargoes belonging to the State whose nationals were responsible for the wrong. Obviously, such actions could lead to further conflict and thus, over time, several procedural prerequisites emerged to limit reprisals. Most importantly, those wronged had first to seek justice from the government of the country in which the damage occurred or whose citizens inflicted the injury. Reprisals were only authorized after a denial of justice.[14] Secondly, reprisals had to be proportional to the wrong done; some countries required strict accounting to the government for the execution of reprisals. By the nineteenth century, reprisals for injuries to aliens were removed from private hands and became

---

14 Treaties requiring exhaustion of local remedies can be found as early as the ninth century (for example, Treaty between Naples and Benevent of 836; Treaty between Lothar I and Venice of 840).

the prerogative of the State; by the middle of that century the concept arose of peaceful, third party settlement of disputes by arbitration or a claims commission. In presenting such claims, the petitioning State was deemed to be asserting its own right to ensure that its subjects were not mistreated in violation of international law. As the law of diplomatic protection evolved, several legal doctrines developed that have been incorporated into human rights law, particularly with respect to exhaustion of local remedies, the concept of denial of justice, and the law of reparations and redress.

In rare instances, a State would claim the right to intervene not only for the protection of its own nationals, but on behalf of oppressed minorities. In 1860 the major European powers authorized France to intervene to protect the Christian population in Lebanon against massacres by the Druses.[15] Russia similarly intervened in Bulgaria in the 1870s.[16] Weaker States rightly objected to the selectivity and self-interest that motivated many so-called humanitarian interventions, and controversy remains today about the use of force to halt human rights violations, as discussed in Chapter 9.

2.2.2 Religious liberty

The religious divisions that accompanied the Crusades and the later Reformation in Europe provoked widespread impoverishing wars together with religious persecution, forced conversions and massacres of religious minorities. The conflicts eventually led to the inclusion of guarantees of freedom of religion in peace treaties, in an effort to remove one of the main causes or pretexts for war. On 24 October 1648 the Articles of the Treaties of Peace signed at Munster and Osnabrück, in Westphalia, ended the Thirty Years War between Protestant and Catholic areas of Europe. The Treaty of Westphalia is often cited as the beginning of the nation-State system and modern international law, but the Treaty is also significant in containing provisions that today would be considered part of human rights law.[17] First, the Treaty declared an amnesty for all offences committed during the "troubles" (Art. II), and it provided for the restitution of property and ecclesi-

---

15 DAVID RODOGNO, AGAINST MASSACRE: HUMANITARIAN INTERVENTIONS IN THE OTTOMAN EMPIRE 1815–1915 (Princeton University Press, 2011), ch. 4.

16 WAR AND DIPLOMACY: THE RUSSO-TURKISH WAR OF 1877–1878 AND THE TREATY OF BERLIN (M Hakan Yavuz and Peter Sluglett, eds, University of Utah Press (2012).

17 Treaty of Westphalia, 24 Oct 1648, http://avalon.law.yale.edu/17th_century/westphal.asp.

astical or lay status (Arts VI–XXXIV). Second, freedom of contract was enforced by annulling contracts procured by duress or threats. Freedom of movement, freedom of commerce and the right to legal protection were also included. Article XXVIII further provides for restitution of church property and for the free exercise of religion.[18] The Westphalian Treaty of Osnabrück with Sweden contained similar provisions. Pope Innocent X promptly declared null and void the articles in the treaties of Westphalia relating to religious matters, but the principle of religious liberty was established, as was the link between peace and respect for rights and liberties.

2.2.3   Abolition of the slave trade and slavery

Slavery has existed throughout history and across the world, but it changed fundamentally in the sixteenth century with the transatlantic slave trade. The numbers alone exceeded any past practice. Moreover, slavery came to focus on Africa and led to the emergence of ideologies of racism, apartheid and segregation. From the sixteenth to the nineteenth century, the international slave trade flourished and slavery was legally practised in many countries of the world, particularly in the Western hemisphere.

Almost from the beginning of this trafficking in humans, a vocal minority expressed its determined opposition to slavery[19] and slaves themselves engaged in uprisings. Many abolitionists began to organize the world's first non-governmental organizations, through which they published articles and pamphlets, preached and taught against slavery, and organized active campaigns of protest. Many of the most outspoken opponents of slavery were former slave traders or slave owners. They saw and used the gap between the practice of slavery and the proclamations of rights, especially in the UK, the US and France, as well as the high ideals of religion and philosophy that rested on the moral value of each human being. They were thus able to draw strength from the general proclamations of human rights. New economic interests that did not rely on slavery joined the movement.

---

18 *Treaty of Westphalia*, in 1 MAJOR PEACE TREATIES OF MODERN HISTORY (Fred L Israel ed., 1967). 7.

19 See Jenny S Martinez, *The Anti-Slavery Movement and the Rise of Non-governmental Organizations*, in OXFORD HANDBOOK OF HUMAN RIGHTS LAW (D Shelton ed., OUP 2013).

Throughout the first part of the nineteenth century, public pressure grew. In 1807 public opinion led to the US Act to Prohibit the Importation of Slaves, matched by the British Act for the Abolition of the Slave Trade. Both Acts made it illegal to trade in, purchase, sell, barter or transport any human cargo for the purpose of slavery. Neither of these laws could be effective, however, without international measures of enforcement and the agreement of other nations, because slave traders could simply move their operations to those countries where it remained legal. Anti-slavery activists thus turned to international measures, urging action by the Congress of Vienna (1814–1815). The public pressure led the delegates to establish a special committee on the international slave trade and to signing a final agreement, the Eight Power Declaration, which acknowledged that the international slave trade was "repugnant to the principles of humanity and universal morality" and that "the public voice in all civilized countries calls aloud for its prompt suppression".[20]

The Eight Power Declaration did not make slave trading a crime, sanction the arrest of slavers or provide machinery for enforcement, but treaty language soon followed. Even during the Congress, a Treaty signed on 20 November 1815 between Britain, Russia, Austria, Prussia and France included a pledge to consider measures "for the entire and definitive abolition of a Commerce so odious and so strongly condemned by the laws of religion and nature".[21] The Treaty of Peace and Amity signed at Ghent by the United States and Britain the same year declared traffic in slaves "irreconcilable with the principles of humanity and justice".[22] By 1882 a network of more than 50 bilateral agreements permitted the search of suspected slave ships on the high seas, without regard to flag.

Anti-slavery societies continued their pressure and in 1840 organized the first World Anti-Slavery Conference. Internally, States slowly emancipated their slaves in response to public pressure. Britain did so in 1833, France in 1848, and most Latin American countries did so as they became independent. Cuba and Brazil were the last countries in the Western hemisphere to abolish slavery, in the late 1880s.

---

20 Congress of Vienna, ACT No XV, Declaration of the Powers, on the Abolition of the Slave Trade, 8 Feb 1815, English trans in Hansard, *The Parliamentary Debates from the Year 1803 to the Present Time*, Vol 32. 1 Feb to 6 Mar 1816, TC Hansard, 1816, 200–201.
21 See William L Chew III, *The Second Peace of Paris*, in 2 THE HISTORICAL ENCYCLOPEDIA OF WORLD SLAVERY 570 (Junius P Rodreguez ed., ABC-CLIO 1997).
22 Treaty of Peace and Amity (Ghent), US–UK, 24 Dec 1814, 8 Stat 218, 12 TIAS 47.

By 1890 governments were prepared to take effective international action. They negotiated the 1890 General Act for the Repression of the African Slave Trade, which referred to the "crimes and devastations engendered" by trafficking in humans.[23] The convention required signatories to take actions to suppress the slave trade at sea and along inland caravan routes, to prosecute and punish slave traders, and to liberate captured slaves. Further agreements on abolition of slavery and repression of the slave trade were concluded in 1919, 1926 and 1956. Recent efforts have turned to modern forms of slavery, including human trafficking.[24]

2.2.4 Humanitarian laws of war

As early as the fourth century BCE, Chinese military theorist Sun Tzu wrote in *The Art of War* that an obligation exists to care for the wounded and prisoners of war. Yet, for the most part mutually acceptable rules limiting the actions of soldiers did not appear until the Industrial Revolution, when weaponry began an ongoing evolution of increased destructiveness and armies became more professional and larger, with the practice of conscription spreading during and following the Napoleonic Wars. The emergence of the press and increased literacy, together with the invention of photography, also had an impact, as they brought home the horrors and atrocities perpetrated during conflicts. The confluence of these factors led to growing concern regarding the conditions of war, the treatment of wounded and sick, and the protection of civilians.

The US Civil War and the Crimean War in Europe brought public attention forcefully to bear on wartime conditions. The United States produced the Lieber Code, the first Western written regulation of armed conflict.[25] In Europe in 1859 Henry Dunant witnessed the Battle of Solferino, where 300,000 troops battled for 15 hours, leaving a

---

23 General Act for the Repression of the African Slave Trade, 2 July 1890, reprinted in 3 AJIL 29 (1909).

24 See, for example, Convention on Action against Trafficking in Human Beings, 16 May 2005, ETS No 197; IACHR, Captive Communities of the Guarani Indigenous People and Contemporary Forms of Slavery in the Bolivian Chaco, OAS Doc OEA/SerL/V/II, Doc 58, 24 Dec 2009; Anne Gallagher, The International Law of Human Trafficking (CUP 2010).

25 Francis Lieber, *Instructions for the Government Armies of the United States in the Field*, which was issued by the War Department (as revised) as General Orders No 100, *reprinted in* Richard Shelly Hartigan, Lieber's Code and the Law of War (Precedent Publishing 1983) 45–71.

battlefield of wounded among the dead. Dunant's account of the battle aroused public opinion which led to offers of support for Dunant in an effort to create an international relief society which would care for the wounded as individuals, without regard to nationality, class or race. An organizing committee invited governments to send representatives to Geneva in order to make the proposal a reality. The Geneva International Conference met in 1863 and by its conclusion had created a private international organization, the International Committee of the Red Cross (ICRC).

The ICRC, led by Dunant, organized a second conference of government representatives within the year. They negotiated the 1864 Geneva Convention for the Amelioration of the Condition of the Wounded in Armies in the Field, the first international agreement to protect individuals in times of war. The treaty required all signatories to acknowledge and respect the neutrality or immunity of military hospitals and their staffs, and to protect them from attack. Red Cross societies and volunteers quickly emerged and became visible in every subsequent conflict.

By 1899 the Hague Peace Conference concluded a broad Convention on the Laws and Customs of War on Land that explicitly spoke of the "rights" of the wounded to receive medical treatment, of prisoners of war to be given food and clothing and protection under the law, of individuals to be considered inviolable when surrendering, and of civilians to be protected from unlimited warfare.[26] In 1907 the Hague Peace Conference extended humanitarian law by concluding new agreements on land and marine warfare. In the so-called Martens Clause, the agreements expressed the consensus of participants that the means and methods of warfare are not without limits, but instead are governed by "usages established among civilized peoples, from the laws of humanity, and the dictates of the public conscience".[27]

---

26 Convention Respecting the Laws and Customs of War on Land, Hague IV, 18 Oct 1907, www.icrc. org/ihl/52d68d14de6160e0c12563da005fdb1b/1d1726425f6955aec125641e0038bfd6.

27 Convention Respecting the Laws and Customs of War on Land, Hague IV, 18 Oct 1907; and Convention for the Adaptation to Maritime Warfare of the Principles of the Geneva Convention, Hague X, 18 October 1907, Pmbls. For discussion of the current relationship between human rights and humanitarian law, see, for example, RESEARCH HANDBOOK ON HUMAN RIGHTS AND HUMANITARIAN LAW (Robert Kolb and Gloria Gaggioli eds, Edward Elgar 2013); Oona A Hathaway et al., *Which Law Governs during Armed Conflict? The Relationship between International Humanitarian Law and Human Rights Law* (2012) MINNESOTA LAW REVIEW 1883–1943.

2.3   Early twentieth century precedents

Although the specific topics discussed in the previous section became matters of international concern, human rights generally continued to be considered as exclusively within the domestic jurisdiction of States. Oppenheim's *Treatise on International Law*, written at the beginning of the twentieth century, insisted that "the so-called rights of man" could not enjoy any protection under international law because that law is concerned solely with the relations between States and cannot confer rights on individuals.[28] Yet, the exceptions already carved out revealed that there was nothing inherently internal about matters of human rights. Human rights specifically or generally would become topics of international law when States so decided.

On the regional level, consideration of human rights matters increased throughout the nineteenth and early twentieth century. The effort to create a confederation of Latin American States in 1826, including as one of its aims the abolition of slavery, led to a series of regional meetings to discuss mutual defence and other forms of cooperation. Prior to 1890, these meetings or Congresses of American States were convoked in response to specific problems or needs, but they became institutionalized after the First International American Conference in Washington DC in 1889–90, and the participating States created a secretariat referred to as the Pan American Union. The Conferences met in regular sessions until 1938 and re-emerged a decade later as the Organization of American States. The Conferences took up human rights issues early, adopting a Convention relative to the Rights of Aliens in 1902,[29] conventions on asylum in 1928 and 1933, and a convention on nationality in 1933.

This same period saw a wave of globalization with technological advances in communications (telephone and telegraph) and transportation (rail networks, steamships) accompanied by increasing mobility of wealth through movements of capital and labour as a consequence of the Industrial Revolution. Non-governmental organizations increased in number and variety. States formed the first permanent intergovernmental organizations, beginning with the International Telegraph Union (1865), the International Postal Union (1874) and the

---

28 Lassa Oppenheim, International Law: A Treatise (1923, reprinted Nabu Press 2010), sections 289–92.

29 Convention Relative to the Rights of Aliens, 1902.

International Meteorological Organization (1878). The International Office of Public Health, created in 1907, advocated a global right to health.

2.3.1 Economic and social rights

In the nineteenth century many countries abolished serfdom, but the emergence and development of the Industrial Revolution led to a rapid expansion in the numbers of exploited workers, including young children in urban centres primarily in Europe and North America. The average factory work week in Europe in the mid-nineteenth century was 84 hours. Poverty, starvation, epidemics and crime were rampant. The obvious social injustices provoked reform movements within countries and eventually on the international level.

Workers fought to create the first trade unions and to take action against abuses. The Catholic Church took up the issue of social justice, most famously in Pope Leo XIII's 1891 encyclical *Rerum Novarum*, which focused on "the natural rights of mankind", including the right of everyone to procure for themselves and their families the basic needs of life. The text insisted on preferential treatment for the poor:

> Human rights must be religiously respected wherever they are found; and it is the duty of the public authority to prevent and punish injury and to protect each one in the possession of his own. Still, when there is question of protecting the rights of individuals, the poor and helpless have a claim to special consideration. The richer populations have many ways of protecting themselves.

The revolutions that came to Mexico, Russia and Ireland in the early twentieth century drew the attention of all governments to the dangers of denying economic, social and cultural rights. Riots and strikes occurred in Germany, Russia, Austria and Italy. The 1910 Mexican Revolution resulted in the first modern constitution containing guarantees of economic, social and cultural rights.

Even before the revolutions and the Great War (1914–1918), some governments realized the necessity of international action in order to avoid distortions in competition and improve low labour standards. They met to form the International Association for the Protection of Labour, with an International Labour Office. In 1906 they concluded two conventions for the protection of workers.[30] Following the end of the War, pressed by labour unions, governments created a Commission on International Labour Legislation comprised of labour representatives. The Commission produced a draft convention for the establishment of a permanent organization for international labour law, to promote "lasting peace through social justice". The proposal envisaged a membership of States represented by a unique tripartite structure of government, labour and business. The Commission also produced a Statement of general principles, including the principle that "labour should not be regarded merely as a commodity or article of commerce", and therefore human beings are entitled to "a reasonable standard of life". Other principles called for adoption of an eight-hour working day, abolition of child labour, rights of association and equal pay for men and women for equal work.

Many of the principles were combined with the draft convention to become the constitution of the International Labour Organization (ILO),[31] an organization founded on human rights principles whose subsequent work has elaborated various aspects of economic and social rights.[32] The mandate of the ILO was echoed in the Covenant of the League of Nations in which all members pledged themselves "to secure and maintain fair and humane conditions of labour for men, women and children, both in their own countries and in all countries to which their commercial and industrial relations extend".[33] They agreed to support enforcement of agreements to combat traffic in women and children, and to take public health measures to prevent and control disease.

By 1933 the ILO had adopted 40 conventions, covering hours of work, maternity leave, unemployment, conditions of labour at night for women and children, equality of pay, minimum age at sea, forced labour and freedom of association.

---

30 Convention Respecting the Prohibition of Night Work for Women in Industrial Employment, Berne, 26 Sep 1906; Convention on the Prohibition of the Use of White Phosphorus in the Manufacture of Matches, Berne, 26 Sep 1906.

31 Constitution of the International Labour Organization, 15 UNTS 35, UKTS 47 (1948), UKTS 59 (1961), UKTS 110, 203 (1975).

32 On the foundations of the ILO, see Janelle Diller, *Social Justice, Rights, and the International Labor Movement*, in OXFORD HANDBOOK OF HUMAN RIGHTS LAW (n. 19).

33 Covenant of the League of Nations, 28 Jun 1919, 34 LNTS.

2.3.2   The minorities treaties and the League of Nations

At the conclusion of the Great War, President Woodrow Wilson's Fourteen Points promised to support liberty, the right of self-determination and equality of rights across borders.[34] Negotiations at the Paris Peace Conference ultimately redrew the borders throughout Europe, creating a host of new minorities in new States. In order to protect these minorities, a series of minorities treaties provided human rights guarantees.[35] Poland, Czechoslovakia, Yugoslavia, Romania and Greece, as a condition of their creation or expansion as States, had to assure full and complete protection of life and liberty to all of their inhabitants without distinction based on birth, nationality, language, race or religion. The treaties specified equal protection of the law, equal civil and political rights, language rights and the rights of minorities to establish their own schools and cultural institutions. Specific protection was afforded to Jewish and Muslim minorities. To reinforce the treaties, each contained a provision stating that "the stipulations in the foregoing articles, as far as they affect persons belonging to racial, religious, or linguistic minorities, constitute obligations of international concern and shall be placed under the guarantee of the League of Nations".[36]

The Covenant of the League of Nations itself contained some references to economic rights, but other proposals made during the drafting failed to be adopted, such as one recognizing "religious persecution and intolerance as fertile sources of war" and another promising that member States "will make no law prohibiting or interfering with the free exercise of religion and that they will in no way discriminate, either in law or in fact, against those who practice any particular creed, religion or belief". Japan and China, the two Asian countries at the conference, sought to include a reference to racial equality but ran into profound opposition by colonial powers. When the majority of delegates voted in favour of including the reference, the chairman discovered a rule requiring unanimity and the proposal was defeated.[37] The obvious unwillingness of the great powers to accept the same rules

---

34 THE MESSAGES AND PAPERS OF WOODROW WILSON, VOL. 1, (Albert Shaw, ed., Review of Reviews, 1924), 475.

35 See, generally Peter Kovacs, *The Protection of Minorities under the Auspices of the League of Nations*, in OXFORD HANDBOOK OF HUMAN RIGHTS LAW (n. 19).

36 Société des Nations/League of Nations, Document CL 110, 1928.

37 Lauren (n. 4).

for themselves that they were imposing on others gave rise to lasting animosity.

In practice, the League came to consider respect for minority rights as a condition of membership for new States. The League also encouraged members to sign bilateral agreements protecting minority rights and expressed its desire in a resolution adopted 21 September 1922

> that the States which are not bound by any legal obligations to the League with respect to minorities will nevertheless observe in the treatment of their own racial, religious, or linguistic minorities at least as high a standard of justice and toleration as is required by any of the Treaties and by the regular action of the Council.

In a decision as important as the substantive guarantees it adopted, the League created supervisory machinery and procedures to monitor compliance with the minority treaties' obligations. The most innovative procedure allowed those who asserted that their rights had been violated to file petitions with the League. If the League's Secretary-General considered a claim meritorious, he could recommend to the Council that it appoint an ad hoc Minorities Committee to investigate the matter and try to reach a mutually acceptable settlement. If this friendly settlement effort failed, the complaint could be sent to the Council as a whole or to the Permanent Court of International Justice (PCIJ). The PCIJ received two requests for advisory opinions from the League on minority matters. In the first case, the *Rights of Minorities in Upper Silesia*, the PCIJ held that the application of racial, linguistic or religious criteria for admission to school was unacceptable.[38] In *Minority Schools in Albania*, a 1935 Advisory Opinion, the Court insisted on the necessity of maintaining equality in fact as well as in law in educational institutions.[39]

The League of Nations' system of protection functioned well for 15 years, but it ultimately failed. Those subject to it objected that they were bound by laws the major powers would not adhere to themselves. Further, the United States' refusal to join the League of Nations undermined its effectiveness, as did the requirement of unanimity before the Council could act. Nonetheless, the legacy of laws, institutions and

---

38 *Rights of Minorities in Upper Silesia*, Judgment no 12 of 26 April 1928 15 PCIJ (Ser A) (1928).
39 *Minority Schools in Albania*, Advisory Opinion of 6 April 1935, PCIJ Ser A/B no 64 (1935).

procedures constructed in the framework of the League of Nations has had a lasting impact on modern human rights law.

2.3.3   Civil and political rights for women

Many of the women who became leaders in the struggle for women's rights began as abolitionists in the anti-slavery campaigns of the nineteenth century.[40] They learned effective techniques of organizing and protesting. They also learned the importance of the moral claim of equality. Through their efforts, changes began in national law, with women obtaining the right to vote in Finland and Australia in 1906, and Norway in 1913. The revolutionary feminist Qui Jin organized the first women's association in China and advocated equal rights for women.[41] Similar organizations and efforts appeared in Egypt, Great Britain, France, Iran, India, Indonesia, Japan, Korea, the Philippines, Sri Lanka, Turkey, the United States and Vietnam.[42] Women soon moved to cooperate internationally by forming NGOs and international federations of trade unions such as the International Ladies' Garment Workers' Union.

Many of the international efforts to guarantee rights for women took place in the regional meetings of the Pan American Union. A 1933 Convention on the Nationality of Women (1933)[43] was followed by the Inter-American Convention on the Granting of Political Rights to Women (1948)[44] and the Inter-American Convention on the Granting of Civil Rights to Women (1948),[45] both preceding UN treaty action. In addition to the treaties, American Conferences adopted resolutions on the rights of women, the first in 1923. The 1928 Conference recommended that States adopt legislation on maternity leave and non-discrimination in employment.

In sum, the first half of the twentieth century saw the list of international human rights concerns grow, to encompass economic, social

---

40 Martinez (n. 19).

41 Lauren (n. 4).

42 See Kumari Jayawardena, Feminism and Nationalism in the Third World (Zed Books 1986).

43 Convention on the Nationality of Women, 26 Dec 1933, OAS TS No 4, 38.

44 Inter-American Convention on the Granting of Political Rights to Women, 2 May 1948, OAS TS No 3.

45 Inter-American Convention on the Granting of Civil Rights to Women, 2 May 1948, OAS TS No 23.

and cultural rights and the rights of minorities and women. Global and regional institutions not only engaged in standard-setting but also created the first international petition procedures. The transboundary dimensions of economic issues perhaps made it easier for States to accept international regulation of workers' rights. The issue of national minorities was so closely linked to the onset of the First World War that the link between peace and human rights appeared undeniable, although international legal theory still proclaimed that a State's treatment of its own citizens was a matter of exclusive domestic jurisdiction. What happened during the Second World War emphatically overturned this theory.

2.4   The post-war human rights revolution

In August 1941 the Allies' Atlantic Charter proclaimed the Four Freedoms President Roosevelt had enunciated at the beginning of the year: freedom of speech and expression, freedom of religion, freedom from fear and freedom from want.[46] The Charter also proclaimed the right of self-determination. These principles were reaffirmed in the Declaration of the 26 United Nations on 1 January 1942. Conferences of the American States also became increasingly vocal about human rights prior to and during the Second World War, expressing their concern through resolutions such as those on Humanization of War (1936), Defence of Human Rights and Persecution for Racial or Religious Motives (1938) and International Protection of the Essential Rights of Man (1945).

2.4.1   The United Nations Charter and early actions

The UN Charter contains more than a dozen references to human rights.[47] The very purposes of the UN include cooperation in promoting respect for human rights and fundamental freedoms for all. Among the Charter's provisions, particular importance is given to Article 55, which states that the UN shall promote "respect for, and observance of, human rights" and the pledge of member States in Article 56 to take action separately and with the UN to achieve this aim.[48] These

---

46 6 Jan 1941, Eighth Annual Message to Congress.

47 Charter of the United Nations, 26 Jun 1945, 1 UNTS XVI, 59 Stat 1031, TS 993, 3 Bevans 1153.

48 See David Weissbrodt, *Human Rights: An Historical Perspective*, in HUMAN RIGHTS (Peter Davies ed., Routledge 1988), 1–20.

articles, with other provisions, have been called a "golden thread" running through the Charter,[49] which establish human rights as a matter of international concern in which State action is constrained by binding legal obligations.

Non-governmental organizations and smaller States, especially those of Latin America, were insistent on the inclusion of human rights provisions in the Charter. The original Dumbarton Oaks proposals for the UN, prepared by the great powers, contained only one general mention of human rights. Even after the human rights provisions were added to the Charter, many governments contended that the guarantees were too weak, and they urged the conclusion of an international bill of rights as soon as possible.

The provisions of the UN Charter had an immediate effect on colonial peoples, who seized on the language concerning human rights, self-determination and non-discrimination to demand decolonization.[50] By 1960, the Declaration on the Granting of Independence to Colonial Countries and Peoples directly called for ending colonial governance, based on the right of peoples to self-determination.[51] A decade later, in the Declaration of Principles of International Law, the UN General Assembly affirmed that any subjection of peoples to alien domination and exploitation constitutes not only a violation of the principle of self-determination but a denial of fundamental human rights and a violation of the Charter. Throughout much of its history the UN has placed considerable emphasis on the right of peoples to self-determination.

The UN Charter's references to equality and non-discrimination similarly allowed NGOs and governments to speak out immediately and repeatedly against systematic discrimination.[52] During the first session of the UN General Assembly, India criticized segregation in the United States, and the latter reciprocated by pointing to the caste system in India.[53] Egypt, supported by Latin American States, introduced a resolution, which passed unanimously, to condemn racial and religious

---

49 John P Humphrey, *The International Law of Human Rights in the Middle Twentieth Century*, in The Present State of International Law and Other Essays (Maarten Bos ed., Kluwer 1973), 75, 83.

50 See Lauren (n. 4) 206–7.

51 Declaration on the Granting of Independence to Colonial Countries and Peoples, GA Res 1514 (XV), at 66, UN Doc A/4684 (14 Dec 1960).

52 See Lauren (n. 4) 207; see also the discussion in Chapter 5.

53 See Lauren (n. 4).

persecution.[54] India then sought a resolution to condemn South Africa for its policies of racial discrimination, accusing the government of gross and systematic human rights violations in breach of the principles and purposes of the Charter.[55] The resolution passed with the required two-thirds majority, despite opposition from Australia, Great Britain, Canada and the United States, each of which had its own racial policies that contravened the Charter's guarantees.[56]

In subsequent General Assembly sessions, specific allegations of human rights violations were brought against Bulgaria, Romania, Hungary[57] and the Soviet Union.[58] Member States also pressed for action on sex discrimination: the Economic and Social Council (ECOSOC) voted to create the Commission on the Status of Women,[59] and the General Assembly urged States to grant political rights to women.[60] In 1949 the General Assembly declared that measures taken by the Soviet Union to prevent the wives of citizens of other nationalities from leaving in order to join their husbands was not in conformity with the UN Charter.[61] In 1959, 1961 and 1965 the General Assembly condemned violations of human rights in Tibet.[62] By the 1980s, the General Assembly was discussing human rights violations in Kampuchea,[63] Guatemala,[64] Chile,[65] El Salvador[66] and Afghanistan.[67] Indeed, human rights issues have been a consistent topic on the agenda of the General Assembly, its committees, and ECOSOC.

---

54 GA Res 103 (I), at 200, UN Doc A/RES/1031 (19 Nov 1946).

55 Letter from the Indian Delegation to the Sec'y Gen of the United Nations, UN Doc A/149 (22 Jun 1946).

56 See GA Res 44(I), at 69, UN Doc A/64/Add1 (8 Dec 1946). The issue of South Africa's racial policies remained on the agenda of the UN in every session until the end of apartheid.

57 See UN GAOR, 3d Sess, Annex, at 31, UN Doc A/820 (16 Mar 1949); UN GAOR 3d Sess, Annex, at 31–2, UN Doc A/821 (19 Mar 1949); UN GAOR, 3d Sess, Annex, at 35–6, UN Doc A/829 (9 Apr 1949); UN GAOR, 4th Sess, Annex, at 1 (21 Sep 1949).

58 GA Res 285 (III), at 34, UN Doc A/900 (25 Apr 1949).

59 ECOSOC, *Resolution Establishing the Commission on the Status of Women*, UN Doc E/RES/2/11 (21 Jun 1946).

60 GA Res 56 (I), at 90, UN Doc A/64/Add1 (11 Dec 1946).

61 See GA Res 285 (III) (n. 58) 58.

62 GA Res 1353 (XIV), at 61, UN Doc A/4354 (21 Oct 1959); GA Res 4723 (XVI), at 66, UN Doc A/5100 (20 Dec 1961); GA Res 2079 (XX), at 3, UN Doc A/6014 (18 Dec 1965).

63 GA Res 38/3, at 14, UN Doc A/RES/38/3 (27 Oct 1983).

64 GA Res 38/100, at 203, UN Doc A/RES/38/100 (16 Dec 1983).

65 GA Res 38/102, at 205, UN Doc A/RES/38/102 (16 Dec 1983).

66 GA Res 38/101, at 204, UN Doc A/RES/38/101 (16 Dec 1983).

67 GA Res 37/37, at 25, UN Doc A/RES/37/37 (29 Nov 1982).

During the first decades of the UN, those States that were targets of censure often asserted that the topics being raised were matters of exclusive domestic jurisdiction; that assertion became increasingly implausible over time and States shifted to claiming that the UN members were applying a double standard when examining human rights issues. UN Charter Article 2(7), which prohibits "intervening" in matters "essentially within the domestic jurisdiction" of States, is rarely invoked today because States acknowledge that the inclusion of human rights throughout the UN Charter made the topic a matter of international concern.

Usually, governments that raise human rights issues are motivated by strategic and political considerations or historic rivalries. This does not necessarily undermine the results of the process; politically motivated criticisms can still point to real human rights problems. At the same time, such motivation may create suspicion about the accusation, thereby undermining any call to action. It also may make the target State more intransigent. For this and other reasons, States are often reluctant to make human rights the centrepiece of foreign policy, which constitutes only one of many matters of international concern for them.

2.4.2   Regional organizations

While the UN was emerging as the pre-eminent global institution, regional bodies also engaged in developing human rights law, drawing inspiration from the human rights provisions of the UN Charter and the UDHR. Europe had been the theatre of the greatest atrocities of the Second World War and felt compelled to press for international human rights guarantees as part of European reconstruction. Faith in Western European traditions of democracy, the rule of law and individual rights inspired belief that a regional system could be successful in avoiding future conflict and in stemming post-war revolutionary impulses supported by the Soviet Union.[68] The Congress of Europe meeting at The Hague in May 1948 announced its desire for

---

68 See JG Merrills, *The Council of Europe (I): The European Convention on Human Rights*, in R HANSKI AND MARKKU SUKSI, AN INTRODUCTION TO THE INTERNATIONAL PROTECTION OF HUMAN RIGHTS (Institute for Human Rights, Åbo Akademi University 1997), 221 ("Many Statesmen of the immediate post-war epoch had been in resistance movements or in prison during the Second World War and were acutely conscious of the need to prevent any recrudescence of dictatorship in Western Europe"). Merrill also views the emergence of the East–West conflict as a stimulus to closer ties in Western Europe.

"a Charter of Human Rights guaranteeing liberty of thought, assembly and expression as well as the right to form a political opposition" and "a Court of Justice with adequate sanctions for the implementation of this Charter". The European system began with the creation of the Council of Europe by ten Western European States in 1949.[69] It has since expanded to include Central and Eastern European countries, bringing the total membership to 47 States. Article 3 of the Council's Statute provides that every member State must accept the principles of the rule of law and of the enjoyment by all persons within its jurisdiction of human rights and fundamental freedoms. Membership in the Council is de facto conditioned upon adherence to the 1950 ECHR,[70] the first human rights treaty of the post-war period,[71] followed by the European Social Charter in 1961,[72] both of which have been supplemented by protocols.[73]

Following the creation of the Council of Europe and adoption of the ECHR in 1950, European States began founding and joining other regional entities, the most prominent of which are the European Union (EU) and the Organization for Security and Cooperation in Europe (OSCE). The EU is the smallest of the European regional groupings, with 28 participating States, all of them also members of the Council of Europe and the OSCE. The OSCE is the largest organization and includes the United States and Canada among its 56 participating States, making it more of an Atlantic than a European body. The EU is a supranational body with legislative powers over its Member States; the OSCE lacks a treaty basis and did not even become an "organization" until two decades after its participating States began meeting.

The original treaties establishing what has become the European Union aimed at economic integration of Member States through the elimination of internal barriers to the free movement of goods, services,

---

69 The Statute of the Council of Europe was signed in London on 5 May 1949 on behalf of Belgium, Denmark, France, Ireland, Italy, Luxembourg, Netherlands, Norway, Sweden and the United Kingdom.

70 Convention for the Protection of Human Rights and Fundamental Freedoms, 4 Nov 1950 as amended by Protocol No 11, ETS No 5, 213 UNTS 221.

71 See Committee of Ministers, Declaration on Compliance with Commitments Accepted by Member States of the Council of Europe, adopted on 10 November 1994, *reprinted in* Council of Europe, Information Sheet No 35 (Jul–Dec 1994)(1995), Appendix I, 146.

72 European Social Charter, 18 Oct 1961, ETS No 35.

73 European Social Charter, Additional Protocol Providing for a System of Collective Complaints, 9 Nov 1995, ETS No 158.

capital and people. The treaties were virtually silent on the protection of human rights. As the powers of the institutions created by the treaties expanded over time in order to achieve the aim of the founders, EU legislative and administrative activities increasingly affected the rights of individuals and companies. Observers expressed concern that there might be no remedy against human rights violations because neither the ECHR nor Member State constitutional guarantees applied to EU institutions. Responsive developments occurred initially through judicial decisions of the European Court of Justice. In 1969, in *Stauder v City of Ulm*, the Court stated in *dicta* that it must ensure the observance of "the fundamental rights of the individual enshrined in the general principles of Community law and protected by the Court".[74] The Court's approach relied on the provision of Article 164 of the EEC Treaty which requires the Court to "ensure that in the interpretation and application of the Treaty the law is observed".

In *Nold v Commission*, the Court went one step further and, in addition to the common constitutional traditions of the Member States, drew inspiration from "international treaties for the protection of human rights on which the Member States [had] collaborated or of which they [were] signatories", especially the ECHR.[75] The Court's approach to the ECHR was expressly ratified by the 1977 Joint Declaration on Fundamental Rights and by the 1987 Single European Act, amending the EEC Treaty, which mention the ECHR as one of the sources of the fundamental rights recognized by the European Community. Formal treaty status was given to the ECHR in Article F(2) of the Common Provisions of the Treaty on European Political Union, signed at the Maastricht Summit of December 1991. Finally, the Member States proclaimed the Charter of Fundamental Rights of the European Union in Nice on 7 December 2000 and later incorporated the Charter into the basic Treaty of Lisbon of the European Union,[76] giving the EU its own Bill of Rights.[77]

In 1975 33 European nations, the United States and Canada signed the Helsinki Final Act (HFA) to conclude the Conference on Security

---

74 *Stauder v City of Ulm*, Case 29/69 [1969] ECR 415, 9 CMLR 112 (1970).

75 *Nold Kohlen und Baustoffgro Bhandlung v Commission*, Case 4/73 [1974] ECR 491.

76 The Treaty of Lisbon amended the Treaty on the European Union (Treaty of Maastricht) and the Treaty on the European Community (Treaty of Rome), without replacing either. The Treaty of Lisbon, which entered into force on 1 December 2009, incorporates the Charter of Fundamental Rights, making it binding on all EU Member States pursuant to Article 6 Treaty of Lisbon, amending the Treaty on the European Union, entry into force 13 Dec 2007, OJ C 306/01.

77 Charter of Fundamental Rights of the European Union, 7 Dec 2000, OJ C 364.

and Cooperation in Europe (CSCE). With the end of the Cold War, the membership of the CSCE expanded to more than 50 nations, including Albania and the former Soviet Republics in Europe and Central Asia. In 1994 the CSCE became the OSCE. The OSCE's human rights system consists of a catalogue of human rights and duties and various supervisory institutions that have evolved over time. This evolution was possible because of the manner in which the HFA was drafted and because of the follow-up mechanism it established. The HFA was not concluded as a treaty, and it was not intended by the participating States to create binding legal obligations. A State's failure to comply with any of the HFA commitments thus has political but not legal consequences. The history of the HFA suggests that its political character has not proved detrimental to its normative content nor to objectives it was designed to achieve. Also important was the creative decision to link human rights and security concerns, giving human rights an important place on the political agenda of East–West relations.

The HFA and subsequent human rights texts have set standards that have been invoked in the international arena and in national contexts to improve human rights. The HFA itself consists of four chapters, or so-called baskets. Human rights issues are addressed primarily in the Guiding Principles proclaimed in Basket I and to some extent in Basket III. Two of the ten Guiding Principles deal with human rights. Principle VII concerns "Respect for human rights and fundamental freedoms, including the freedom of thought, conscience, religion or belief". In Principle VII the participating States undertake to "respect human rights and fundamental freedoms" and to "promote and encourage the effective exercise of civil, political, economic, social, cultural and other rights and freedoms". Principle VII also deals with freedom of religion, rights of individuals belonging to national minorities, and the right of the individual to know and act upon his rights and duties in this field. The last paragraph of Principle VII commits the participating States to act in conformity with the purposes and principles of both the Charter of the United Nations and the Universal Declaration of Human Rights and to fulfil their obligations as States Parties to other international human rights agreements.

HFA Basket IV established a follow-up process that has been instrumental in the long-term success of the OSCE. Participating States periodically convene intergovernmental conferences to undertake "a thorough exchange of views . . . on the implementation of the provisions of the Final Act". These follow-up conferences provide a forum to review compliance with human rights commitments and to expand the human rights catalogue through amplification, reinterpretation and extensive revision of the HFA. The meetings also have been used to focus public attention on the failure of certain States to live up to their human rights commitments. The normative evolution referred to has been accomplished by the consensus adoption at each conference of a "concluding document" in which the participants proclaim new OSCE commitments or expand, modify or interpret the scope and meaning of existing ones. In this respect, the OSCE pioneered a holistic approach to human rights that emerged subsequently in other human rights settings.

In the Western hemisphere, the Americas had a long tradition of regional approaches to international issues, including human rights, growing out of hemispheric solidarity developed during the struggle for independence. The Pan American Conferences took action on several human rights matters well before the creation of the UN. In 1907 several Central American States created the first human rights tribunal, the Central American Court of Justice. The court had jurisdiction over cases of denial of justice between a government and a national of another State.

The Inter-American system as it exists today began with the transformation of the Pan American Union into the Organization of American States (OAS). All 35 independent States of the Americas are member States of the OAS, although the Cuban government was suspended from participating in the OAS in 1962 and has not re-engaged with the organization. The 1948 Charter made few references to human rights, but one important provision was Article 3(j), now Article 3(l), wherein "the American States proclaim the fundamental rights of the individual without distinction as to race, nationality, creed, or sex" to be among the principles to which they are committed.[78] Human rights also appeared in Article 13, now Article 17, which declared that "each State has the right to develop its cultural, political and economic life freely and naturally", but that "in this free development, the State shall respect the rights of the individual and the principles of universal morality". The Charter did not define "the fundamental rights of the individual" to which Articles 3 and 17 referred, nor did it create any institution to promote their

---

78 Charter of the Organization of American States, 30 Apr 1948, 2 UST 2394, UNTS 48.

observance. However, the same diplomatic conference that con-cluded the OAS Charter also proclaimed the American Declaration of the Rights and Duties of Man (ADRDM), some seven months prior to the UN's adoption of the UDHR.[79] The ADRDM provides an extensive catalogue of human rights that define the Charter's general reference to human rights.

The OAS Charter has been amended by the Protocol of Buenos Aires, adopted in 1967, and by the Protocols of Cartagena de Indias (1985), Washington (1992) and Managua (1993). The role of human rights in the OAS has been strengthened by provisions in some of these amendments. For example, the Protocol of Buenos Aires called for the conclusion of a treaty on human rights and made the Inter-American Commission on Human Rights (IACHR) an organ of the OAS. In 1992 the OAS Permanent Council convened the Sixteenth Special Session of the General Assembly to examine proposed OAS Charter amendments concerning, first, suspension of governments in case of anti-democratic coups and, second, provisions on the issue of extreme poverty in the region. The Protocol of Washington adopted on 14 December 1992 provides for the suspension of any member State whose democratically constituted government has been overthrown by force. The Protocol also added eradication of extreme poverty to the organization's purposes and principles, calling it "an obstacle to the full democratic development of the peoples of the hemisphere".

In Africa, the Organization of African Unity (OAU), founded in 1963, aimed to rid the continent of the remaining vestiges of colonization and apartheid; to promote unity and solidarity among African States; to coordinate and intensify cooperation for development; to safeguard the sovereignty and territorial integrity of member States; and pro-mote international cooperation within the framework of the UN. As a continental organization, the OAU provided a forum for member States to adopt coordinated positions on matters of common concern in international forums and to defend the interests of Africa. The OAU Coordinating Committee for the Liberation of Africa worked to forge an international consensus in support of the liberation struggle and the fight against apartheid. While the OAU's Charter recognized and upheld the principles enshrined in the Charter of the United Nations and the Universal Declaration of Human Rights, the OAU itself was

---

79 American Declaration of the Rights and Duties of Man, Adopted by the Ninth International Conference of American States, Bogota, 30 Mar–2 May 1948, OAS Res XXX.

firmly rooted in the doctrine of non-interference in the newly independent States. The Charter thus emphasized sovereign equality and
the territorial integrity of member States, principles reinforced in 1964
when the OAU adopted a resolution declaring the commitment of all
member States "to respect the borders existing on their achievement
of national independence".[80] Although the Charter required OAU
members to have due regard to the rights set forth in the Universal
Declaration, it did not create a human rights organ.

On 9 September 1999 the OAU Heads of State and Government
issued the Sirte Declaration calling for the establishment of an African
Union (AU) to replace the OAU and accelerating the process of integration within the continent, thereby enabling the African States to
play a stronger role in the global economy, while at the same time
addressing the continent's social, economic and political problems.
The AU Constitutive Act, subsequently adopted, gives a prominent
place to human rights.[81] Member States express that they are "determined to promote and protect human and peoples' rights, consolidate
democratic institutions and culture and to ensure good governance
and the rule of law". The AU Objectives (Art. 3) and Principles (Art.
4) include the need to "promote peace, security and stability on the
continent" with a recognized need to "encourage international cooperation, taking due account of the Charter of the United Nations
and the Universal Declaration of Human Rights" and to "promote and
protect human and peoples' rights in accordance with the African
Charter on Human and Peoples' Rights and other relevant human
rights instruments". Thus States should promote gender equality and
have "respect for democratic principles, human rights, the rule of law
and good governance, respect the sanctity of life and condemn unconstitutional changes of government".

Africa is also the seat of sub-regional organizations concerned with
human rights. The treaty establishing the Economic Community of
West African States (ECOWAS)[82] was signed in Lagos on 28 May
1975 with the stated aim to promote economic, social and cultural

---

80 OAU Assembly, *Border Disputes Among African States*, Res 16(I), Doc No AHG/Res16(1), 2
    (1964).

81 Constitutive Act of the African Union, 11 July 1981, 1520 UNTS I-37733.

82 Fifteen West African nations originally joined ECOWAS: Liberia, Nigeria, Togo, Ghana, Burkina
    Faso, Cote d'Ivoire, Guinea, Gambia, Benin, Niger, Sierra Leone, Guinea Bissau, Mauritania,
    Senegal, and Mali. The Republic of Cape Verde later joined, while Mauritania withdrew in 2002.
    Treaty Establishing the Economic Community of West African States (ECOWAS), 28 May 1975.

cooperation and integration, ultimately leading to the establishment of an economic and monetary union through the total integration of the national economies of member States. It also aims to raise the living standards of its peoples, maintain and enhance economic stability, foster relations among member States, and contribute to the progress and development of the African continent. A revised treaty of 1993 designated the achievement of a common market and a single currency as economic objectives, while in the political sphere it provided for a West African parliament, an economic and social council, and an ECOWAS court of justice with jurisdiction over human rights issues,[83] to replace a pre-existing tribunal. The fundamental principles of ECOWAS include "recognition, promotion and protection of human and people's rights in accordance with the provisions of the African Charter on Human and People's Rights".

The South African Development Community (SADC) also created a court that could hear cases alleging violations of human rights. SADC, like ECOWAS, is an intergovernmental organization. In *Campbell and Others v Republic of Zimbabwe*, the SADC Tribunal heard its first human rights matter, holding that land expropriations and invasions in Zimbabwe, as well as the denial of access to justice, violated the applicants' rights.[84] Following this judgment, the States Parties suspended operations of the court, causing concern about the degree of political support for strong and independent human rights institutions in the organization.

Egypt, Iraq, Jordan, Lebanon, Saudi Arabia and Syria founded the League of Arab States, generally referred to as the Arab League, with the adoption of the Pact or Charter of the League on 22 March 1945.[85] Yemen joined two months later. The Arab League has 22 members and four observers as of 2013. According to its Charter, the main goal of the League is to "draw closer the relations between Member States and co-ordinate collaboration between them, to safeguard their independence and sovereignty, and to consider in a general way the affairs and interests of the Arab countries". The Charter does not mention

---

83 A Protocol creating the Community Court of Justice was signed on 6 July 1991, and entered into force on 5 Nov 1996. The Court is the principal organ of the Community and its decisions are binding on the member States, on the institutions of the Community, and on individuals and corporate bodies appearing before it. The member States of ECOWAS, pursuant to Article 3 of the Protocol, appoint the seven members of the Court.

84 *Campbell and Others v Republic of Zimbabwe* S Afr Dev Trib Case 2/2007 (2008).

85 Pact of the League of Arab States, 22 Mar 1945, 70 UNTS 237.

human rights, but the organization was formed and its founding agreement concluded before the UN Charter put promotion and protection of human rights on the international agenda. Over time, the League initiated and then augmented a concern with human rights. On 12 September 1966 the Council of the League of Arab States adopted its first resolution on human rights, calling for the establishment of a steering committee to elaborate a programme for the celebration of Human Rights Year in 1968. The Committee recommended the establishment of a permanent Arab Committee on Human Rights and the convening of an Arab Conference on Human Rights. In 1968 the Council of the League created the Arabic Commission of Human Rights, but it was not until 1994 that the League of Arab States approved an Arab Charter on Human Rights.[86] The Charter was heavily criticized for failing to reflect global human rights standards; the League replaced it in 2004 with a "modernized" version more consistent with international norms.

Finally, the Association of Southeast Asian Nations (ASEAN) was formed on 8 August 1967 by Indonesia, Malaysia, the Philippines, Singapore and Thailand, the region's non-communist countries. Some 30 years later the organization expanded with the successive entries of Vietnam, Laos, Myanmar and Cambodia. ASEAN was created as a forum for cooperation on matters of peace, stability, progress and prosperity in the region. Over the years, the members of ASEAN agreed on some common values and principles, as set forth in a series of declarations. To make further progress towards its aims, ASEAN member States formalized their association in a binding Charter, signed 20 November 2007.[87] By the end of 2008, all ten member States had ratified the Charter. The new ASEAN Charter declares that the organization's purposes include strengthening democracy, promoting the rule of law, and protecting human rights and fundamental freedoms. The Charter further states that among the key principles governing the conduct of ASEAN and its member States are "respect for fundamental freedoms, the promotion and protection of human rights, and the promotion of social justice" and "adherence to the rule of law, good governance, the principles of democracy and constitutional government".

In sum, the constituting texts of the large majority of global and regional organizations have made respect for human rights by their

---

86 Arab Charter on Human Rights, 22 May 2004 reprinted in (2005)12 INT'L HUM RTS REP 893.
87 ASEAN Charter, 20 Nov 2007, www.asean.org/archive/publications/ASEAN-Charter.pdf.

member States a part of their aims and principles. The nearly eight decades that have passed since the formation of post-war institutions have seen further evolution in human rights law, from the inclusion of new rights and adoption of new means of monitoring and enforcement, to the proliferation of institutions with a wide range of functions and powers. The next chapter surveys these institutions and the scope of their mandates.

3 International institutions

Human rights law requires institutions and procedures to monitor the promotion and protection of internationally guaranteed rights. The relative youth of human rights as a branch of international law means that the current institutions and procedures remain works in progress, repeatedly reformed, challenged and reconsidered. Moreover, human rights bodies and organs generally function within international institutions whose mandates are not limited to human rights issues. The treaties that create these institutions may in fact place primary emphasis on other matters, such as economic integration or maintaining international peace and security, creating a constant tension in the efforts to balance or reconcile various mandates and priorities. The status accorded human rights among the purposes and functions of each organization is an important factor in the potential effectiveness of the organization's human rights programme. Even in organizations that purport to place high priority on human rights, the entities and their mandates are created and maintained by States that are not always eager to have strong institutions scrutinizing their compliance with human rights norms.

The main global entity concerned with human rights is the UN system, including its main and subsidiary organs and the specialized agencies affiliated with it. Other global organizations, including international financial bodies and the World Trade Organization (WTO), touch on human rights matters in their work but the topic is not mentioned in their founding documents. Numerous regional human rights institutions and systems have also emerged, particularly since the end of the Cold War. This chapter introduces the global and regional human rights institutions and organs, their commonalities, differences and present challenges.

3.1   The United Nations

Taken as a whole, the UN system has played a central role in creating and monitoring modern human rights law. The provisions in the UN Charter contributed to enshrining human rights on the global agenda. Articles 55 and 56 create binding if general obligations for all member States and a mandate for the organs of the UN to promote human rights and fundamental freedoms for all. The UN organs have exercised this mandate within the competence and powers granted to each of them, including by adopting a set of detailed human rights treaties and other instruments and creating subsidiary monitoring bodies.

3.1.1   The main UN organs

The mandates of all the principal UN organs include the issue of human rights. The General Assembly, the plenary body of the UN, may discuss any matter within the UN Charter and is authorized to initiate studies and make recommendations "to assist in the realization of human rights and fundamental freedoms" (Art. 13(1)(b)). The General Assembly receives annual reports of UN Charter-based institutions and human rights treaty bodies that contribute to the fulfilment of its functions. Throughout its history the General Assembly has engaged in standard-setting and discussion of violations of human rights. This has resulted in a *corpus juris* clarifying the obligations of member States with respect to human rights. In particular, it is now accepted that a State engaged in a consistent pattern of gross and systematic violations of human rights is in breach of its UN Charter obligations.

The Security Council's primary responsibility over peace and security includes jurisdiction to take action under Chapter VII in response to any situation it concludes is a threat to the peace, a breach of the peace, or an act of aggression, including when such a situation is due to violations of human rights. Decisions taken under the authority of Chapter VII of the UN Charter are binding, but require nine votes to be adopted and are subject to the exercise of a veto by any of the five permanent members. The first human rights matters that gave rise to Security Council action were the declaration of independence by a white minority government in the former British colony of Rhodesia and the apartheid regime in South Africa. The Security Council has since responded to human rights violations occurring in Rwanda, the former Yugoslavia, the Sudan, Democratic Republic of the Congo and Syria, among others.

The UN Economic and Social Council is authorized by Charter Article 62 to make recommendations to promote respect for and observance of human rights and to draft treaties on the topic. The Charter also instructs ECOSOC to establish "commissions in economic and social fields and for the promotion of human rights". Exercising this authority, ECOSOC created the UN Commission on Human Rights in 1946. The Commission grew as membership in the UN increased and eventually was composed of 53 States elected to three-year terms by ECOSOC. The General Assembly voted to replace the Commission in 2006 with the Human Rights Council.[1]

The UN Secretary-General carries out a number of human rights activities both directly and through the Office of the High Commissioner on Human Rights (OHCHR). The General Assembly created the post of High Commissioner[2] and the OHCHR in 1994, after many years of debate. The Office of the High Commissioner provides secretariat services to the Human Rights Council, the UN special procedures, and the treaty-monitoring bodies. In recent years, the Office has expanded its activities to gather and disseminate information on human rights, and to provide technical and advisory services to member States, in part by expanding the number and resources of its field offices. The work of the field offices began as primarily promotional, although the field presences increasingly have taken on the role of on-site monitoring.

The High Commissioner on Human Rights is an independent official with a mandate to act on behalf of the UN and to administer the OHCHR. The High Commissioner is empowered "to play an active role in removing the current obstacles and in meeting the challenges to the full realization of all human rights and in preventing the continuation of human rights violations throughout the world". This broad language permits the High Commissioner to be proactive in addressing any contemporary human rights issue. The High Commissioner and other senior members of the secretariat often make public statements on human rights situations and issues of concern, including apparent violations of rights. The Charter guarantees independence for the

---

1 GA Res 60/251, UN Doc A/RES/60/251 (3 Apr 2006).
2 GA Res 48/141 of 7 Jan 1994, UN Doc A/RES/48/141 (20 Dec 1993).

secretariat working under her administration,[3] but outside political pressure is not unknown.[4]

Finally, the 15 judges of the International Court of Justice (ICJ), the "principal judicial organ of the United Nations" in the words of the Charter, have jurisdiction to decide inter-State cases and issue advisory opinions at the request of the UN and its specialized agencies, including on matters of human rights law. Litigating States have insisted on the human rights obligations contained in the UN Charter.[5] Only States may be parties to cases before the ICJ. The ICJ has pronounced on important issues of human rights law,[6] including reservations to human rights treaties,[7] questions concerning apartheid,[8] the independence and immunities of human rights experts,[9] the relationship between human rights law and international humanitarian law,[10] and the right of self-determination.[11]

3.1.2 The Human Rights Council

The UN Commission on Human Rights was replaced in 2006 largely due to criticism that the political character of the Commission had affected its work when it came to deciding on which governments to condemn for human rights violations and what topics to

---

3 UN Charter Art. 100.

4 See Iain Guest, Behind the Disappearances (University of Pennsylvania Press 1999).

5 See, for example, Memorial of United States; *United States Diplomatic and Consular Staff in Tehran* (US v Iran), 1980 ICJ Pleadings 182 (12 Jan 1980).

6 See Ludivoc Hennebel, *La Cour internationale de Justice face au droit international des droits de l'homme*, Liberae Cogitationes: Liber amicorum Marc Bossuyt (Andre Alen et al, eds, Intersentia 2013), 299.

7 *Reservations to the Convention on the Prevention and Punishment of the Crime of Genocide*, 1951 ICJ Rep 15 (28 May).

8 See *International Status of South–West Africa*, 1950 ICJ Rep (Advisory Opinion of 11 July); *South West Africa Cases (Liberia v South Africa, Ethiopia v South Africa)*, Second Phase, Judgment 1966 ICJ 6 (18 July); *Legal Consequences for States of the Continued Presence of South Africa in Namibia (South West Africa) notwithstanding Security Council Resolution 276 (1970)*, Advisory Opinion 1971 ICJ 16 (21 Jun).

9 See *Applicability of Article VI, Section 22, of the Convention on the Privileges and Immunities of the United Nations*, 1998 ICJ 177, 200 (15 Dec); *Difference Relating to Immunity from Legal Process of a Special Rapporteur of the Commission on Human Rights*, 1999 ICJ 62 (26 Apr).

10 *Legal Consequences of the Construction of a Wall in the Occupied Palestinian Territory*, Advisory Opinion 2004 ICJ 136 (9 July).

11 ICJ, *International Status of South-West Africa*, (n. 8), 12; ICJ, *Western Sahara*, Advisory Opinion of 16 October 1975, ICJ Reports 1975, 20; *Case concerning East Timor (Portugal v Australia)*, 1995 ICJ 92 (Judgment of 30 June 1995).

examine.[12] The Secretary-General's High Level Panel on Threats, Challenges and Change noted that States had sometimes sought membership on the former Commission not to strengthen human rights but to protect themselves against criticism or to criticize others.[13] Indeed, the election of States with egregious human rights records sometimes allowed them to escape condemnation and contributed to the perception of a double standard. While there is some merit to the claims of political decision making, the Commission was the first and principal forum to confront governments with allegations of violations that demanded response. It is also noteworthy that despite all the criticisms of the Commission as a political body, UN member States decided to create a Council similarly composed of State representatives, rather than one of independent experts.[14]

General Assembly resolution 60/251, which created the Human Rights Council, elevated its status by having it report directly to the General Assembly rather than to ECOSOC. The Council consists of 47 States elected by the General Assembly according to the principle of "equitable geographic distribution". The General Assembly added criteria to guide States in voting for the member States seeking to sit on the Commission, but these criteria are not particularly stringent. Nonetheless, the candidate States are expected to make voluntary pledges and commitments to contribute to the promotion and protection of human rights. The Council is authorized to meet three times a year for ten weeks but can also hold special sessions, which it has done relatively frequently during its early years. The Council's mandate is to "be guided by the principles of universality, impartiality, objectivity and non-selectivity, with a view to enhancing the promotion and protection of all". The Council can also consider and make recommendations on situations of human rights violations.

The General Assembly required the Council to scrutinize the human rights record of every member of the UN in addition to addressing

---

12 See Joint NGO Statement on UN Reform – Presented to the 61st Session of the UN Commission on Human Rights (12 Apr 2005), available at http://hrw.org/english/docs/2005/04/12/global10463_.htm.

13 Chairman, *Report of the High-Level Panel on Threats, Challenges, and Change*, 282–3, delivered to the General Assembly, UN Doc A/59/565 (2 Dec 2004).

14 GA Res 60/251. On 13 November 2013 the General Assembly elected Algeria, China, Cuba, France, Maldives, Mexico, Morocco, Namibia, Russian Federation, Saudi Arabia, South Africa, the former Yugoslav Republic of Macedonia, United Kingdom and Viet Nam to serve three-year terms beginning on 1 January 2014.

gross and systematic violations, based on "objective and reliable information", ensuring "universality of coverage and equal treatment" of
all States.[15] This peer review process in effect expands the periodic
reporting system used by UN treaty bodies to all member States. It is
intended to be fair, transparent and effective, but its workings largely
depend on the composition of the Council and whether it has the
time and resources to review comprehensively the record of each
State.

Specific States and human rights situations that require attention
remain on the agenda of the Human Rights Council, as well as the
agendas of the General Assembly and Security Council, but the principles that guide the Council's programme of work, including, inter
alia, universality, impartiality, non-selectiveness, constructive dialogue
and cooperation, indicate a preference among a majority of members
to avoid country-specific resolutions. The Council's framework asks
States to secure the broadest possible support for country-specific resolutions, preferably at least 15 members. Not surprisingly, there have
been fewer country-specific resolutions introduced or adopted since
the demise of the former Commission.

3.1.3   Other subsidiary UN Charter-based bodies

All of the main UN organs concerned with human rights, except
the OHCHR and the ICJ, consist of governmental representatives
of the member States. Among subsidiary human rights bodies, the
Commission on the Status of Women (CSW), created in 1946, today
consists of 45 governmental representatives. The CSW mandate
includes the preparation of studies, reports and recommendations on
human rights and related issues affecting women. In the early 1980s
ECOSOC empowered the CSW to undertake a limited review of communications charging specific violations of women's rights. These
communications have served as a source of information for studies
rather than as the foundation of a true complaints procedure. In resolution 1996/6, ECOSOC further augmented the CSW role by asking it
to identify emerging issues, trends and new approaches to issues affecting equality between women and men.

The former Human Rights Commission created a subsidiary body of
independent experts in 1947, known as the Sub-Commission on the

---

15 GA Res 60/2561, Art. 5(e).

Prevention of Discrimination and Protection of Minorities (renamed in 1999 the Sub-Commission on the Promotion and Protection of Human Rights). The experts were nominated by States and elected by the Human Rights Commission. The decision to transform the Human Rights Commission into the Council was coupled with the demise of the Sub-Commission, a decision that concerned many observers because much of the standard-setting and many other human rights actions originated in the independent Sub-Commission. The decision to form the present Human Rights Council included the creation of an advisory committee to which some members of the former Sub-Commission have been elected, but the advisory committee lacks the power of initiative exercised by the earlier body.

Other subsidiary entities are independent, most importantly the network maintained by the Human Rights Council of working groups and rapporteurs with thematic or country mandates, together known as the "special procedures". The first such body, the five-member Working Group on Enforced or Involuntary Disappearances, was created in 1980, followed in 1982 by the Special Rapporteur on Extrajudicial, Summary or Arbitrary Executions, and rapporteurships concerning Torture (1985) and Religious Intolerance (1986). The number of mandates has continued to grow, with 37 thematic and 14 country rapporteurships in operation at the end of 2013. The topics chosen for thematic rapporteurships generally address either serious violations occurring in a number of countries, such as torture, or new topics that may benefit from additional standard-setting, such as human rights and the environment. The independent experts are appointed for a term of three years and mandate holders are normally limited to two terms. The functions assigned to these special procedures vary, with some mandates extending to investigations and receipt of complaints; most rapporteurs make on-site visits to countries in the exercise of their functions.

Following the Vienna Conference in 1993, the special rapporteurs, representatives, independent experts and chairpersons of working groups of the special procedures of the Human Rights Council began holding annual meetings, in order to provide better coordination of their work. The result has been an increasing number of joint communications and Statements. Overall, the special procedures have originated and developed a considerable body of human rights law.

3.1.4   UN treaty bodies

The UN refers to nine "core" human rights treaties: the International Covenant on Economic, Social and Cultural Rights (ICESCR); the International Covenant on Civil and Political Rights (ICCPR); the Convention on the Elimination of All Forms of Racial Discrimination (CERD); the Convention on the Elimination of All Forms of Discrimination against Women, (CEDAW); the Convention against Torture and Other Cruel, Inhuman or Degrading Treatment or Punishment (CAT); the Convention on the Rights of the Child (CRC); the Convention on the Protection of the Rights of All Migrant Workers and Members of their Families (CPMW); Convention on the Rights of Persons with Disabilities (CRPD); and the Convention on the Protection of All Persons from Enforced Disappearance.[16] All but the last-mentioned treaty, which is not in force, establish a monitoring body to supervise compliance by States Parties. States have been notably reluctant, however, to include measures that amount to enforcement or allow binding judgments to be taken or sanctions imposed for non-compliance. Nonetheless, some of the treaty-monitoring mechanisms have been strengthened through the adoption of additional protocols, such as those that supplement the CAT and CEDAW.

The critical aspect of all treaty bodies, compared to the Charter-based mechanisms and UN main organs, is that the treaty bodies are composed of a relatively small number of independent experts elected by States Parties to serve in their individual capacity and maintain their independence and autonomy during their term of office (usually four years). The number of independent experts for each committee ranges from ten to 25. Except in the case of the Subcommittee for the Prevention of Torture (SPT) and CRPD, whose members are eligible for re-election once if re-nominated, the treaties impose no limit on the number of times a member's term may be renewed, and some members have served for long periods. In choosing experts, most treaties refer to criteria of high moral standing and competence in the field, along with consideration being given to equitable geographical distribution and to the representation of the different forms of civilization as well as the principal legal systems. Only the CPRD adds the additional consideration of "balanced gender representation and participation of

---

16 Convention for the Protection of All Persons from Enforced Disappearance, UN Doc A/61/488 (6 Feb 2007).

experts with disabilities" as factors to be taken into account in nomi-nating and electing experts. The quality of the elected individuals, in respect to both independence and expertise, while important to the credibility and integrity of the treaty bodies, does vary.

The first of the UN core treaties to enter into force, the CERD, estab-lished an 18-member committee of independent experts to ensure the implementation of the obligations by States Parties.[17] CERD con-ferred three main functions on the CERD Committee; in doing so it established a model that has been followed in most of the subsequent UN treaties. The Committee examines periodic reports (Art. 9); con-siders inter-State communications (Arts 11–13); and considers indi-vidual communications (Art. 14).[18] The first two of these procedures are mandatory for all States Parties. The CERD Committee almost immediately used its Article 9 power to "request further informa-tion from the States Parties" to establish reporting guidelines[19] and to invite representatives of the reporting State to attend the relevant meetings of the Committee.[20] The invited States appeared before the Committee and set a precedent for the practice of other UN treaty bodies.

CERD Article 9(2) provides that the CERD Committee may "make sug-gestions and general recommendations based on the examination of the reports and information received from the States Parties". As one of the Committee's original members has commented, "[t]he interpre-tation of this provision has caused significant Committee debate",[21] not only about the sources of information the CERD Committee can access, but also about the legal weight of its concluding suggestions and recommendations. CERD was the first UN treaty to include a reference

---

17 CERD, Art. 8(1). See, KJ Partsch, *The Committee on the Elimination of Racial Discrimination*, in THE UNITED NATIONS AND HUMAN RIGHTS: A CRITICAL APPRAISAL (P Alston, ed., Clarendon 1992), 339, 340–41.

18 CERD, Arts 8, 11–13, and 14. A fourth function, to aid other UN bodies in reviewing petitions from trust and other non-self-governing territories, has diminished with the gradual independ-ence of trust and colonial territories. See CERD, Art. 15.

19 "Communication to States Parties", CERD/C/R/12 and A/8027 (1970), Annex IIIA.

20 In fact, the General Assembly recommended that CERD invite representatives of States Parties to be present for the discussions of their reports. GA Res 2783 (XXVI) (1971). The practice was adopted in 1972. A/8718 (1972), para. 37, Dec 1(V). It has been followed by all subsequent UN treaty bodies in the examination of State reports.

21 Partsch (n. 17) at 351. See also Legal Opinion of the UN Office of Legal Affairs to the Assistant Secretary-General for Inter-Agency Affairs, 1972 UN Judicial Yearbook 164 (1974) (asserting that the provisions of CERD do not limit the sources available to the Committee).

to the power of its Committee to make suggestions and general recommendations.[22] The phrase was added late in the drafting process, just
a month before the Convention was adopted.[23] A few States proposed
deleting either the word "suggestions" or the word "general" but the
overall power of the committee to adopt comments was neither controversial nor much discussed.[24]

Turning to the Covenants, Part IV of the ICCPR sets out the composition, status, functions and procedures of its 18-member Human
Rights Committee (HRC). The competence and duties of the HRC are
similar to those of the CERD Committee, with the exception that the
individual communication procedure is set forth in the first Optional
Protocol to the Covenant rather than appearing in an optional clause
in the treaty itself. The text makes clear that the HRC monitors implementation of the ICCPR by States Parties, but the lengthy drafting process for the treaty included considerable disagreement among States
over the precise role and powers of the HRC.[25] That disagreement
continued in the early years of the Committee, leading to a general
discussion in 1980.[26] Consensus was reached on the need for the HRC
to issue general comments on matters of common interest to the States
Parties in addition to specific concluding observations with respect
to individual States' periodic reports. Subsequently, the Committee
issued a restrained statement on the duties of the HRC under Article
40 of the Covenant.[27] Since then, General Comments have become a
significant source of legal commentary on the rights and obligations in
the ICCPR. The HRC has also strengthened its oversight through the
reporting system, established a follow-up procedure and a procedure
for examining the situation in States Parties that fail to file the required
reports. HRC members also now use information provided to them by
NGOs and receive shadow reports from civil society.

The ICESCR initially established a different oversight mechanism
and did not provide for a treaty body. The only monitoring procedure
foreseen was periodic State reporting. ECOSOC delegated review of
State reports to a working group of its members, which transmitted

---

22 CERD, Art. 9(2).

23 UN Doc A/C.3/L.1293 (1965), Art. VIII (bis).

24 UN Doc A/6181 (1965), paras 113–14.

25 See Torkel Opsahl, *The Human Rights Committee* in Alston (n. 17) at 371–2.

26 Report of the Human Rights Committee, A/35/40 (1980).

27 Statement on the duties of the Human Rights Committee under Article 40 of the Covenant
    adopted on 30 Oct 1980, in Report of the Human Rights Committee, A/36/40 (1981), Annex IV.

its general findings to ECOSOC, the UN HRC and specialized agencies concerned with economic, social and cultural rights. The inadequacy of this procedure led ECOSOC to adopt a series of resolutions on monitoring, which eventually led to establishment of a Committee on Economic, Social and Cultural Rights, composed of 18 experts elected in their personal capacities.[28] The procedures for selecting the CESCR Committee and its functions were derived from those initiated by CERD and the ICCPR. Like the other treaty bodies, the CESCR Committee has developed a robust State reporting system and issued important general comments. An Optional Protocol of 19 December 2008 further enhanced the monitoring of ESC rights by establishing a collective complaints procedure.[29]

The CEDAW Committee, established in 1981, originally had a surprisingly limited mandate, given the precedents of earlier UN human rights treaties. The treaty provided for no inter-State or individual communications. The 23 members of CEDAW were thus limited to issuing general comments and observations on State reports until the entry into force of an Optional Protocol to CEDAW on 22 December 2000.[30] The Protocol created a communications procedure as well as an inquiry procedure for grave or systematic violations (Arts 8, 9), but granted States Parties the discretion to opt out of the inquiry procedure. As with the ICCPR, the consideration of individual communications results in views and recommendations.

The CAT, which entered into force on 28 June 1987, established a ten-member independent monitoring body and procedures that involve State reporting and general comments, added to which are optional procedures for individual and inter-State complaints, as well as an optional inquiry procedure. The treaty confirms the practice initiated by other treaty bodies to address individual comments to each reporting State. The States Parties to CAT created another, new kind of treaty body with the SPT. The SPT has a purely preventive mandate and proactive approach to the prevention of torture and ill treatment. The SPT started its work in February 2007, after it was established pursuant to the provisions of the Optional Protocol to the Convention against

---

28 ECOSOC Res 1985/17 of 22 May 1985.
29 Optional Protocol to the International Covenant on Economic, Social and Cultural Rights, UN Doc A/63/435 (24 Sep 2009).
30 Optional Protocol to the Convention on the Elimination of All Forms of Discrimination against Women, 6 Oct 1999, 2131 UNTS 83.

Torture (OPCAT) adopted on 18 December 2002 by the General Assembly.[31] The SPT is composed of 25 independent and impartial experts elected by States Parties to the OPCAT for a four-year mandate, with the possibility of one re-election.

With the exception of the SPT, all UN treaty bodies receive and consider the periodic reports of States Parties on steps they have taken to implement the provisions of the relevant treaty and, in the case of CRC, its substantive protocols.[32] All of the core treaty bodies now are or will be entitled[33] to consider individual communications against those States Parties that have accepted this optional procedure, and four (CAT, CEDAW, CED and CRPD) may conduct inquiries into alleged violations of their treaty's provisions, where this procedure has been accepted by the State Party. Some treaty bodies (CAT, CED, CEDAW, CERD, CMW, ICESCR, HRC and eventually the CRC) may consider inter-State communications about alleged violations of the treaty by another State Party; the States must declare acceptance of this procedure, except in the case of CERD which provides that States Parties are subject to the procedure upon ratification or accession to the treaty.

The major human rights bodies have made broad use of their express power to issue General Comments or General Recommendations, adopting over 100 such texts.[34] This device is used to express a committee's considered legal opinion on the scope of a right or obligation contained in one of the provisions of the treaty it supervises; the issuing committee attaches considerable importance to the contents of General Comments and they are also cited by other global and regional treaty bodies as authoritative statements of human rights law.[35] The

---

31 Optional Protocol to the Convention against Torture and Other Cruel, Inhuman, or Degrading Treatment or Punishment, 18 Dec 2002, 2375 UNTS 237.

32 In 2002, two optional protocols to the CRC were adopted: the Optional Protocol to the Convention on the Rights of the Child on the involvement of children in armed conflict and the Optional Protocol to the Convention on the Rights of the Child on the sale of children, child prostitution and child pornography.

33 An Optional Protocol to the UN Convention on the Rights of the Child on a Communications Procedure (Third Optional Protocol) was adopted during the Sixty-sixth session of the UN General Assembly on 19 Dec 2011 and opened for signature and ratification on 28 Feb 2012. It was not in force as of the beginning of 2014.

34 The more than 100 general comments and recommendations are reproduced in the *Compilation of General Comments and General Recommendations adopted by Human Rights Treaty Bodies*, UN Doc HRI/GEN/1/Rev 9 (2 vols).

35 On the development of general comments, see, Philip Alson, *The Historical Origins of the Concept*

committees distinguish General Comments from the country-specific final observations made to individual countries, yet there is a clear interplay with views on individual cases and final observations on State reports. On the issue of extraterritorial application of the ICCPR, for example, the HRC has repeatedly taken the position that the ICCPR applies outside a State's territory in certain circumstances. It first said so in communications filed against individual States Parties, after which in 2004 it issued General Comment 31 to further elaborate its views.

A General Comment thus generally represents a distillation of the case law or jurisprudence of the treaty body. The HRC has asked States Parties to refer to General Comments in their periodic reports and some States do. In addition, some domestic courts have utilized General Comments in rendering judgments and decisions. The Constitutional Court of South Africa, for example, relied on the ICESCR General Comment 7 in its decision *Government of the RSA et al. v Grootboom*.[36] The African Commission on Human and Peoples Rights similarly used ICESCR General Comments 4, 7 and 14 in *SERAC v Nigeria*.[37] In sum, a General Comment is "one of the potentially most significant and influential tools available to each of the United Nations human rights treaty bodies in their endeavours to deepen the understanding and strengthen the influence of international human rights norms".[38] The fact that they are approved by consensus helps bolster their authority.

3.2 UN specialized agencies

The UN system extends beyond the main and subsidiary UN organs and treaty bodies established pursuant to UN human rights agreements, to include UN specialized agencies such as the ILO, the United Nations Educational, Scientific and Cultural Organization (UNESCO), the World Health Organization (WHO) and the Food and Agriculture Organization (FAO). Specialized agencies are autonomous UN-

---

of *"General Comments" in Human Rights Law*, in The International Legal System in Quest of Equity and Universility, Liber Amicorum Georges Abi-Saab (L Boisson de Chazournes and V Gowlland-Debbas eds, Brill 2001).

36 The applicants also presented arguments based on General Comment 3, the obligations of States parties, calling it "persuasive" authority for the Constitutional Court.

37 Comm 155/96, *Social and Economic Rights Center (SERAC) v Nigeria* [2001] AHRLR 60 (AfCHPR, 27 Oct 2001), paras 44, 63.

38 Alston (n. 17), 763.

affiliated intergovernmental organizations each governed by its own constitution, policy-making structure, and specific mandate set forth in its founding treaty. The most active of the specialized agencies in the field of human rights are the ILO, UNESCO, the FAO and the WHO. The expertise of each agency helps to de-politicize some human rights issues by rendering them more technical. With a few exceptions, such as the Pan American Health Organization (PAHO) most regional organizations have not created similar agencies.

The Constitution of the ILO begins its preamble by stating the drafters' belief that "universal and lasting peace can be established only if it is based on social justice". The mandate of the ILO, founded in 1919, includes human rights related to work and to working conditions, including the right to form trade unions, the right to strike, the right to be free from slavery and forced labour, equal employment and training opportunities, the right to safe and healthy working conditions, and the right to social security. The ILO also provides protections for vulnerable groups and has adopted standards on child labour, employment of women, migrant workers, and indigenous and tribal peoples. The ILO is unique among global organizations with respect to the composition of each member State's delegation, which includes not only representatives from the government, but also a delegate from the business sector and a delegate representing labour. This tripartite structure allows for formal participation of civil society in the activities of the ILO.

Standard-setting occurs at the annual General Conferences. In addition to concluding treaties and making recommendations, in 1998 the ILO adopted a Declaration of Fundamental Rights and Principles at Work, together with a follow-up procedure. The Declaration insists that all ILO member States, by virtue of joining the organization, have an obligation to ensure the protection of four areas of human rights or core labour standards: freedom of association and the right to collectively bargain; freedom from child labour; freedom from forced or compulsory labour; and non-discrimination in employment. Important ILO human rights conventions include the conventions on Forced Labour (No 29) of 1930, Freedom of Association and Protection of the Right to Organize (No 98) of 1949, Equal Remuneration (No 100) of 1957, Abolition of Forced Labour (No 105),[39] Discrimination (Employment and Occupation) (No 111) of 1958, Indigenous and Tribal Peoples (No

---

39 Convention Concerning the Abolition of Forced Labour (ILO No 105), 25 June 1957, 320 UNTS 291.

169) of 1989,[40] and the Worst Forms of Child Labour (No 182) of 1999. All member States must report annually if they have not ratified the relevant ILO conventions on these subjects, indicating the obstacles to ratification.

A 20-member independent ILO Committee of Experts monitors implementation of ILO conventions and recommendations. The Committee meets annually to examine State reports and may follow up with Direct Requests to governments and organizations of workers and employers in the State. The Committee may make observations to governments on any serious or persistent problem; these observations are published in the Committee's annual report to the plenary ILO Conference. The Conference appoints each year another subsidiary body, the Committee on the Application of Conventions and Recommendations, made up of representatives of government, employers and workers. This Committee utilizes the reports of the Committee of Experts to identify important situations to be discussed in the presence of the government, with a report then submitted to the Conference.

According to Article I(1) of its Constitution, UNESCO was established in 1945 with a purpose

> to contribute to peace and security by promoting collaboration among the nations through education, science and culture in order to further universal respect for justice, for the rule of law and for the human rights and fundamental freedoms which are affirmed for the peoples of the world, without distinction of race, sex, language or religion, by the Charter of the United Nations.[41]

Its aims include realizing gradually "the ideal of equality of educational opportunity without regard to race, sex or any distinctions, economic or social".[42] UNESCO thus may address the right to education, scientific freedom, freedom of expression, and the right to culture, including cultural property.[43] The organization adopts treaties and recommendations on these topics and promotes teaching and research on human

---

40 Convention Concerning Indigenous and Tribal Peoples in Independent Countries (ILO No 169), 17 June 1989 reprinted in (1989) 28 ILM 1382.

41 UNESCO Constitution, 16 Nov 1945, reprinted in UNESCO, Basic Texts (2012), http://unesdoc.unesco.org/images/0021/002161/216192e.pdf#page=7.

42 Ibid. at Art. I(2)(b).

43 See Stephen P Marks, *The UN Educational, Scientific and Cultural Organization*, in Guide to International Human Rights Practice (Hurst Hannum ed., 4th edn, Hotei Publishing 2004).

rights. Among the primary UNESCO treaties are the 1962 Convention against Discrimination in Education[44] and the 1954 Convention for the Protection of Cultural Property in the Event of Armed Conflict and its 1999 Second Protocol. In 1977 it adopted a Universal Declaration on the Human Genome and Human Rights, the first international instrument to address human rights and modern biotechnology and to reject the cloning of human beings. UNESCO has a non-judicial, non-confrontational communications procedure, which was established in 1978 and allows a victim or anyone with reliable knowledge about a human rights violation concerned with education, science or culture to submit a petition to UNESCO seeking a resolution of the matter by friendly settlement.

The FAO, one of the UN's largest specialized agencies, aims to ensure food security and alleviate hunger. In 2004 the FAO's Committee on World Food Security endorsed a set of voluntary guidelines to support the progressive realization of the right to adequate food in the context of national food security. The Guidelines are intended to integrate a human rights approach in the operational activities of States, UN bodies and civil society to ensure national food security. At the same time, the Guidelines indicate measures that States should adopt to implement the CESCR. The FAO Council approved the text in November 2004.[45]

The WHO Constitution expresses conviction that "[t]he enjoyment of the highest attainable standard of health is one of the fundamental rights of every human being without distinction of race, religion, political belief, economic or social condition".[46] The WHO Constitution defines health as a state of complete physical, mental and social well-being and not merely as the absence of disease or infirmity. The WHO considers the right to health to mean the right to access to facilities, goods, services and conditions necessary to enjoy the highest attainable standard of health. The WHO has established a global programme on HIV/AIDS, undertaking standard-setting on this topic. The WHO has also supported recognition of the right to safe drinking water and sanitation, and it has cooperated with the

---

44 UNESCO Convention against Discrimination in Education, 14 Dec 1960, 429 UNTS 93.
45 FAO doc CL 127/REP, appendix D.
46 Constitution of the World Health Organization, 22 July 1946, www.who.int/governance/eb/who_constitution_en.pdf.

Committee on the Rights of the Child to comment on child and adolescent health rights.

The main exceptions at the global level to the widespread practice of mentioning human rights within the mandates or purposes of international organizations created at the end of the Second World War are the treaties governing the international financial institutions, including the World Bank Group[47] and the International Monetary Fund. Similarly the 1994 Agreement establishing the World Trade Organization omits any mention of human rights. There is continuing controversy over the degree to which the financial and trade bodies should or must take human rights into consideration in developing and carrying out their programmes and policies. They are increasingly being pressed to do so. During the past decade, the World Bank has addressed social issues through the development of ten "Safeguard Policies" and through the work of the Inspection Panel established in 1993. In doing so, the Bank recognized the connection between economic issues and social issues.[48] In 1998 the Bank decided to reorganize its Operational Manual around related themes. This type of "mainstreaming" has been a recent goal of the UN and is considered essential to making human rights guarantees effective. The General Assembly has encouraged the integration of human rights concerns into economic and financial policies, particularly in the context of its considerable attention to the eradication of poverty as a human rights issue.[49] In addition, the former UN Commission on Human Rights suggested that multilateral financial and trade institutions must conform their policies and practices to international human rights norms.

---

47 Siobhán McInerney-Lankford, *Human Rights and Development: Regime Interaction and the Fragmentation of International Law* (2013) 4 THE WORLD BANK LEGAL REVIEW 123–59.

48 Key policies were grouped together, including Involuntary Resettlement (OP 4.12, Dec 2001), Indigenous Peoples (OD 4.20, Sep 1991), Cultural Property (OP 11.03, Sep 1986), Safety of Dams (OP 4.37, Sep 1996), International Waterways (OP 7.50, Oct 1994), and Projects in Disputed Areas (OP 7.60, Nov 1994). For a general overview of the Bank's approach to human rights, see IBRD/WORLD BANK, DEVELOPMENT AND HUMAN RIGHTS: THE ROLE OF THE WORLD BANK (1998), IBRD/World Bank, Development and Human Rights: The Role of the World Bank3IBRD/World Bank, Development and Human Rights: The Role of the World Bank2–4, 5–6, 8, 11, 12, 30.

49 See, for example, Report of the Independent Expert on the Question of Human Rights and Extreme Poverty, A/HRC/7/15, 28 Feb 2008.

3.3   Regional bodies

3.3.1   Europe

The Statute of the Council of Europe (COE) of 5 May 1949 articulates the values, principles and aims of the organization, including the importance of respect for human rights.[50] All the organs of the Council of Europe have roles with respect to human rights. The Committee of Ministers (COM), composed of the Foreign Affairs Ministers of all the Member States or their permanent diplomatic representatives, has the authority to invite European States to become members of the Council of Europe (Statute, Arts 4, 5 and 6). When the Committee of Ministers receives an official application for membership, it consults the Parliamentary Assembly of the Council of Europe (PACE), a group of 630 members (315 representatives and 315 substitutes) from the 47 national parliaments. The Parliamentary Assembly examines whether the candidate State fulfils all the necessary membership requirements, in particular those concerning human rights and the rule of law. This examination is done through an on-site visit by parliamentary committees and also by expert fact-finding missions. The Assembly may seek from the State specific commitments to undertake reforms and improvements in its domestic laws and practices. In addition, PACE's Committee on Human Rights adopts resolutions and declarations on key human rights issues, often leading to the conclusion of new treaties. The COM decides on membership after receiving the report of PACE. PACE also has the key role in the selection of judges to the Eur. Ct. HR.

The COM may suspend or terminate State membership, and it has the critically important function of supervising the execution of the judgments of the Eur. Ct. HR. In addition to supervising compliance with the Court's judgments, the COM undertakes thematic monitoring of human rights matters, pursuant to a 1994 declaration on compliance with commitments made by new Member States. A third major function of the Committee of Ministers is to approve protocols to the ECHR and other human rights treaties, which are then submitted to the Member States for ratification.

The European system was the first to create an international court for the protection of human rights and to create a procedure for individual

---

50 Statute of the Council of Europe, 7 May 1949, ETS No 1.

denunciations of human rights violations. The Eur. Ct. HR has changed considerably since its origin, becoming the only full-time international human rights body. According to Protocol No 11 to the ECHR, in force since 1 November 1998, the Eur. Ct. HR operates on a permanent basis and is made up of full-time professional judges resident in Strasbourg. The number of judges is equal to that of the High Contracting Parties. Protocol No 14 to the Convention instituted a single term of office of nine years for judges elected to the Court. The ECHR specifies that judges shall be of high moral character and must either possess the qualifications required for appointment to high judicial office or be jurisconsults of recognized competence. PACE elects the judges by a majority of votes cast from a list of three candidates nominated by the High Contracting Party.

The ECHR continues to be monitored primarily through a litigation-based system in which those who claim their rights have been violated file cases at the Court; however the need for institutions to undertake promotion of human rights and initiate actions has led the COE to create other bodies, like the European High Commissioner and the European Commission against Racism and Intolerance (ECRI). The COE created the post of Commissioner for Human Rights on 7 May 1999. The Commissioner is elected by the Parliamentary Assembly from a list of candidates drawn up by the Committee of Ministers and serves a non-renewable six-year term. The functions of the Commissioner are to serve independently and impartially as "a non-judicial institution to promote education in, awareness of and respect for human rights, as embodied in the human rights instruments of the Council of Europe". The functions are thus primarily promotional and preventive; the Commissioner has no power to accept communications from individuals or groups.

The ECRI was established pursuant to the Vienna Declaration of the Heads of State and Government of the Member States of the Council of Europe, signed 9 October 1993. The ECRI's mandate is to review Member States' legislation, policies and other measures to combat racism and intolerance and to propose further action at local, national and European levels. The ECRI monitors the situation in Member States through an in-depth study of the situation in each country followed by specific proposals designed to solve current problems or remedy deficiencies. Draft texts are communicated to national liaison officers to allow national authorities to respond with observations. After confidential dialogue, the ECRI adopts a final report and submits it to the State concerned through the Committee of Ministers. State reports are made public two months after transmission to the government unless the government expressly objects.

The European Commission for Democracy through Law, or Venice Commission, is the COE's advisory body on constitutional matters and works to uphold democracy, human rights and the rule of law. Among other functions, it gives advisory opinions on these issues. For example, on 20 February 2009 the Constitutional Court of Albania requested an amicus curiae opinion on the Albanian lustration law adopted at the end of 2008. The Albanian Court asked five specific questions of the Venice Commission. In its opinion CDL-AD (2009)044, the Commission determined that lustration may be applied by Albania, on condition that the constitution and rule of law are respected. The Commission found that the lustration law in question violated the Albanian constitution.

Finally, the Secretary General of the COE set up a Human Rights Trust Fund on 28 March 2008, funded in large part by the governments of Norway, Germany and the Netherlands, as well as the Council of Europe Development Bank. The Trust Fund has supported projects to enhance the effectiveness of the system by improving compliance with judgments of the Court.

In the EU, the Commission and Council must respect fundamental rights as guaranteed by the ECHR and the constitutional traditions common to the Member States. The European Court of Justice relies on the ECHR and jurisprudence of the Eur. Ct. HR in its judgments. The European Parliament has a Committee on Citizens' Freedoms and Rights, Justice and Home Affairs that monitors human rights within the EU and the implementation of rights policies. A separate Committee on Foreign Affairs, Human Rights, Common Security and Defence Policy devotes attention to human rights in the EU foreign policy. It has insisted on the inclusion of human rights provisions in agreements with other countries. It also produces an annual report on human rights in the world. Finally, the European Parliament established a Committee on Petitions in 1987, to which any natural or legal citizen or resident of the EU may have access for raising a human rights matter that affects them directly.

The EU established two further institutions that include human rights within their mandates. First, the Ombudsman of the EU hears complaints about maladministration by EU institutions. The Ombudsman especially seeks to ensure that the Charter of Fundamental Rights is upheld. The second institution is the Fundamental Rights Agency (FRA), created in 2007 in order to provide independent advice on fundamental rights. The agency's staff members include legal experts, political and social scientists, statisticians, and communication and networking experts. A Management Board defines the agency's priorities, approves its budget and monitors its work. The Management Board is comprised of independent experts, one appointed by each Member State, two European Commission representatives and one independent expert appointed by the COE.

The FRA engages in legal and social science research on practices concerning human rights within the EU, in part to identify areas where there are deficiencies in meeting internationally accepted standards. The FRA primarily refers to the Charter of Fundamental Rights of the European Union, which sets forth a binding list of rights for the EU and its Member States when interpreting and applying EU law, but the agency also refers to treaties and other instruments of the COE and the UN. FRA research typically covers all EU Member States, but some topics may be limited to a smaller number of EU Member States.

The largest of the European organizations, the OSCE, established the office of the High Commissioner on National Minorities (HCNM) in 1992 to

> provide early warning and, as appropriate, early action at the earliest possible stage in regard to tensions involving national minority issues which have not yet developed beyond an early warning stage, but, in the judgment of the High Commissioner, have the potential to develop into a conflict within the CSCE area, affecting peace, stability or relations between participating States, requiring the attention of and action by the Council [of Ministers of Foreign Affairs] or the CSE [Committee of Senior Officials].

The principal function of the HCNM is to address minority problems before they degenerate into serious conflicts. In all activities, the High Commissioner is to be guided by "CSCE principles and commitments". The HCNM is to "work in confidence and . . . act independently of all parties involved in the tensions". The High Commissioner has rendered mediating and advisory services to governments and national minorities in a number of countries, resolving potentially explosive conflicts or, at least, getting different groups together to seek solutions.

The useful work of the HCNM led the OSCE in 1997 to establish the post of Representative on Freedom of the Media in order to "address serious problems caused by, inter alia, obstruction of media activities and unfavourable working conditions for journalists".[51] The Media Representative acts as an advocate, observing relevant media developments in OSCE participating States and promoting compliance with OSCE principles and commitments regarding freedom of expression and free media. The Representative also aims to provide early warning on violations of freedom of expression, concentrating on rapid response to serious non-compliance with OSCE principles and commitments by participating States. Where problems arise, the Representative seeks direct contacts with the participating State and other parties involved, assesses the facts, and seeks to resolve the issue. The Representative collects and receives information on the situation of the media, including information about hate speech, from participating States, organizations or institutions, media and their representatives, and relevant NGOs. The Representative reports to the Permanent Council, recommending further action where appropriate.

3.3.2   The Americas

Within the Organization of American States, the Ministers of Foreign Affairs of the Member States decided in 1959 to create a seven-member autonomous body to promote and protect human rights.[52] The resolution conferred on the OAS Permanent Council the authority to determine the powers and functions of the new institution. The Council adopted a Statute for the resulting Inter-American Commission on Human Rights on 25 May 1960, granting it the power to make recommendations to the governments of the member States in general "if it considers such action advisable, for the adoption of progressive measures in favour of human rights within the framework of their domestic legislation and, in accordance with their constitutional precepts, appropriate measures to further the faithful observance of those rights" (Art. 9(b) of the 1960 Statute). In 1965 the Statute was amended to expand the functions of the IACHR, authorizing it to receive communications alleging violations of human rights committed by any of the OAS member States.

---

51 OSCE Permanent Council, Mandate of the OSCE Representative on Freedom of the Media, Decision No 193, 2 (5 Nov 1997).

52 Res VIII, OAS, Minutes of the Fifth Meeting of Consultation of Ministers of Foreign Affairs.

According to the Statute and the 1969 American Convention on Human Rights, the Commission is composed of seven members, who shall be persons of high moral character and recognized competence in the field of human rights, elected in a personal capacity by the OAS General Assembly from a list of candidates proposed by the governments of the member States. Each of those governments may propose up to three candidates, who may be nationals of the State proposing them or of any other OAS member State. When a slate of three is proposed, at least one of the candidates shall be a national of a State other than the one proposing the slate. The members of the Commission are elected for a four-year term and may be re-elected only once.

Unlike the European Court, the IACHR has a double mandate: to promote and protect human rights. As such, it holds hearings, undertakes on-site visits, publishes special country and thematic reports, issues guidelines and general recommendations, requests information of States, reviews periodic reports and hears cases. The Commission's country reports are often based on on-site visits to the subject countries, during which the human rights situation in the particular country is examined. The report includes an assessment and recommendations to the government. Country reports have been prepared on the Commission's own initiative and at the request of the country concerned. The Commission may also appoint special rapporteurs to prepare studies on hemisphere-wide problems.

The American Convention on Human Rights conferred the additional competence on the Commission to oversee compliance with the Convention. The Convention, which entered into force in 1978, also created the seven-member Inter-American Court of Human Rights. The Court has jurisdiction over contentious cases submitted against States that accept its jurisdiction. The Court may also issue advisory opinions at the request of the Commission or any OAS member State and order provisional measures to protect against the imminent threat of serious human rights violations. The I-A Court's advisory opinions have been important in developing human rights law in the Americas.

3.3.3 Africa

The African Charter on Human and Peoples' Rights establishes an African Commission on Human and Peoples' Rights of 11 independent members elected for a renewable period of six years. The African Charter confers four functions on the Commission: promotion of human and peoples' rights; protection of those rights; interpretation of the Charter; and the performance of other tasks which may be entrusted to it by the Assembly of Heads of State and Government. The Commission may undertake studies, conduct training and teaching, convene conferences, initiate publication programmes, disseminate information and collaborate with national and local institutions concerned with human and peoples' rights. As part of this promotional effort, the Commission may "give its views or make recommendations to Governments" (African Charter, Art. 45(1)(a)). The African Charter also provides for a State reporting procedure. Unlike the other systems, the African system envisages not only inter-State and individual communications procedures, but a special procedure for situations of gross and systematic violations. The Commission may bring to the attention of individual governments problem areas revealed by its studies as well as by its review of States' implementation reports. It has adopted a system of country rapporteurs and undertakes visits to individual countries. The Commission has also appointed special or thematic rapporteurs for summary and extra-judicial executions, prisons and conditions of detention, and the rights of women, and extractive industries.[53]

The African Commission exercises a type of advisory jurisdiction that allows it to "interpret all the provisions of the present Charter" when so requested by a State Party, an institution of the OAU or an African Organization recognized by the OAU. The Commission is empowered "to formulate and lay down, principles and rules aimed at solving legal problems relating to human and peoples' rights and fundamental freedoms upon which African Governments may base their legislations" (African Charter, Art. 45(1)(b)). The Commission thus may further develop regional human rights standards by preparing draft legislation and proposing legal solutions to disputes.

A major institutional change in the African regional human rights system came with the adoption on 8 June 1998 of an Additional Protocol to the Charter on the establishment of an African Court on Human and Peoples' Rights.[54] The African Court was inspired by, and modelled after, those in the European and American regional human rights systems. The Protocol on the court came into force in 2004,

---

53 See F Viljoen, *State Reporting under the African Charter on Human and Peoples' Rights: A Boost from the South* (2000) 44 J Afr L 110. J Harrington, *Special Rapporteurs of the African Commission on Human and Peoples' Rights* (2001) 1 Afr Hum Rts J 247.

54 See OAU/LEG/AFCHPR/Prot.III, reprinted at (2000)12 Afr J Int'l & Comp L 187.

and the 11 judges were sworn in on 2 July 2006. The African Union's Assembly has proposed to merge the human rights Court with the African Court of Justice. On 1 July 2008 the Heads of State approved a new protocol of merger for what is to be called "The African Court of Justice and Human Rights".[55] The Protocol requires 15 ratifications to enter into force; as of the end of 2013 only three States had approved it, and the human rights Court continues as a separate entity.

The African Court received more than two dozen matters between 2008 and 2013. Many of the applicants represented themselves; most of the petitions were declared outside the jurisdiction of the Court, because the States in question had not filed the requisite declaration accepting the right of individuals to sue. Other applicants had not exhausted local remedies, and the matter was deemed inadmissible. The Court issued its first judgment on the merits of a case in June 2013.[56]

A further proposed protocol on criminal jurisdiction would add a third chamber to the two previously mentioned, retaining the same broad subject matter competence as the existing human rights court, that is, over cases alleging any violation of a right guaranteed by the African Charter on Human and Peoples Rights, the Charter on the Rights and Welfare of the Child,[57] the Protocol to the African Charter on Human and Peoples' Rights on the Rights of Women in Africa, or "any other legal instrument relating to human rights ratified by the States Parties concerned".

3.3.4 The Arab League

The Arab League created an Arab Permanent Commission on Human Rights[58] as a result of an initiative begun by the UN in March 1967, when the UN Commission on Human Rights requested in resolution No 6 (XXIII) that the UN General Secretary inquire from regional organizations lacking permanent human rights commissions about the possibility of establishing such bodies. After an exchange of cor-

---

55 African Charter Protocol on the Statute of the African Court of Justice and Human Rights, 21 Jul 2008.

56 Afr Ct HPR, *Tanganyika Law Society/Legal and Human Rights Center v Tanzania*, App 009/211, *Mtikila v Tanzania*, App 011/211 (Consolidated cases), 14 Jun 2013.

57 African Charter on the Rights and Welfare of the African Child, 11 Jul 1990, OAU Doc No CAB/LEG/24.9/49.

58 See R Daoudi, *Human Rights Commission of the Arab States*, in 2 EPIL (Elsevier 1995).

respondence, the Council created the Arab Permanent Commission on Human Rights by resolution No 2243 on 3 September 1968 and the Commission held its first session from 3 to 6 March 1969. The Commission initially did not have its own statute, but until 2007, was governed by the rules applicable to the functional commissions of the League of Arab States.

The Permanent Commission is composed of representatives of the member States of the League of Arab States. Each country may nominate one or several persons to be its representative. The 2007 Rules of Procedure provide that the Arab States shall keep in mind, when nominating their representatives, the need for specialists in the field of human rights. The Permanent Commission meets in two regular sessions each year, and may hold special sessions at the request of the Council of the League of Arab States, the Secretary General of the League of Arab States, or three member States. Each member State in the Permanent Commission has one vote and the recommendations of the Commission are adopted by consensus if possible; if that is not possible recommendations are then adopted by the majority of the members present. The Arab Permanent Commission has engaged in standard-setting, participating in the preparation of the first, highly criticized Arab Charter on Human Rights 1994 and its revision in 2004.

The Secretary General of the League also may appoint a secretary in the League Secretariat to work on human rights. The resulting "Department of Human Rights", established by the Secretary General on 16 April 1992, helps the Arab Commission carry out its tasks.

The most significant change in Arab League human rights institutions came after the entry into force of the Arab Charter on Human Rights on 16 March 2008, following which the States Parties elected members of the Arab Human Rights Committee to oversee compliance with the Charter. The Committee is composed of seven "highly experienced persons" in the field of work of the Committee, who act in their personal capacity and perform their work "with full impartiality and integrity". Like the IACHR, the Arab Committee members serve for four years and may be re-elected only once. The primary activity foreseen is in reviewing periodic reports of the States Parties to the Charter, making recommendations, and reporting to the Council of the League. Submission and examination of individual or inter-State complaints is absent from the Arab Charter.

3.3.5   ASEAN

ASEAN's supreme policy-making body, the ASEAN Summit, takes decisions on key issues pertaining to the realization of the objectives of ASEAN and addresses any emergency affecting ASEAN. The ASEAN Coordinating Council, composed of the ASEAN Foreign Ministers, prepares the meetings of the Summit, coordinates with the various councils to enhance policy coherence and cooperation, and undertakes tasks enumerated in the ASEAN Charter.

ASEAN Charter Article 14, which calls for establishing an ASEAN human rights body, was implemented through the creation of the ASEAN Inter-Governmental Human Rights Commission (AICHR). Unlike those of other regional bodies, the AICHR members are not independent; instead, each serves at the pleasure of his or her government.[59] Member States are obliged to pay "due consideration to gender equality, integrity and competence in the field of human rights". In practice most Commissioners thus far have been current or former government officials. They must act by consensus and have limited powers conferred by the Terms of Reference.

The Terms of Reference of the ASEAN Intergovernmental Commission on Human Rights (AICHR TOR) lists the purpose of AICHR as follows: "To promote and protect human rights and fundamental freedoms of the peoples of ASEAN".[60] AICHR is also to uphold specific international standards contained in "international human rights instruments to which ASEAN Member States are parties". The promotion work is to be done "within the regional context, bearing in mind national and regional particularities and mutual respect for different historical, cultural and religious backgrounds, and taking into account the balance between rights and responsibilities". The "promotional" mandate and functions include enhancing public awareness of human rights, promoting capacity building, encouraging member States "to consider acceding to and ratifying international human rights instruments" and promoting implementation of "ASEAN instruments related to human rights". Although protection is mentioned, that mandate has not been spelled out through the grant of specific functions and powers. Notably, in late March 2010, during the AICHR's first formal session

---

59 AICHR TOR, Art. 5(2), (6).
60 Terms of Reference of the ASEAN Intergovernmental Human Rights Commission, 20 Jul 2009, www.refworld.org/docid/4a6d87f22.html.

in Jakarta, efforts by families of journalists massacred in Maguindanao, Philippines to have the Commission receive a formal complaint and investigate the incident were rejected, the Commission being unwilling to imply a power not formally granted in the TOR.

ASEAN also created a Commission on the Promotion and Protection of the Rights of Women and Children (ACWC) and a Committee on the Implementation of the Declaration on the Protection and Promotion of the Rights of Migrant Workers (ACMW).[61] Like the AICHR, these human rights bodies are composed of governmental representatives. On 18 November 2012 the Heads of State of ASEAN adopted the ASEAN Human Rights Declaration, further clarifying the mandate of the AICHR.[62] Importantly, the ASEAN Declaration is seen as a precursor to a formal treaty for the region, as has happened with human rights declarations at the UN and in other regional systems.[63]

3.4 Assessing the institutions

The texts establishing human rights bodies describe in very general terms the functions of promoting or protecting human rights. The regional courts are typical judicial bodies that hear and decide complaints filed by victims alleging human rights violations. They may also have advisory jurisdiction. In contrast, the UN treaty bodies and regional commissions have a wide variety of functions, generally grouped under the headings of promotion and protection of human rights. In general, regional bodies appear to have a greater range of functions and jurisdiction than UN bodies.

There are obviously some commonalities but also differences in the composition, functions and procedures of the existing commissions, committees and courts. The commonalities stem from the fact that

---

61 ASEAN Declaration on the Protection and Promotion of the Rights of Migrant Workers, 13 Jan 2007, www.asean.org/communities/asean-political-security-community/item/asean-declaration-on-the-protection-and-promotion-of-the-rights-of-migrant-workers-3.

62 On the drafting and contents of the Declaration, see Catherine Shanahan Renshaw, *The ASEAN Human Rights Declaration 2012* (2013) 11 Human Rights Law Review 3. ASEAN Declaration on Human Rights, 18 Nov 2013, www.asean.org/news/asean-statement-communiques/item/asean-human-rights-declaration.

63 For a discussion of the evolution with respect to human rights bodies in the Arab League, see Mohammed Amin Al-Midani, *Human Rights Bodies in the League of Arab States* (2012) 3 Jinan Hum Rts J 109–34; Daoudi (n. 58).

member States of the organization create the bodies and the States decide whether or not they are willing to accept scrutiny of their human rights practices, including through allowing victims to bring petitions or complaints against them, or whether they prefer to maintain maximum discretion and flexibility without accountability to or oversight from a strong monitoring body. Compliance is a concern in every human rights system; without the peer pressure of States in the organization, human rights bodies have little ability to ensure that their recommendations and decisions are implemented. Member States must have the political will to support an effective human rights mechanism and demonstrate that will in several key areas that determine the effectiveness of the institution.

First, the work of a human rights body is only as good as its membership; if decisions must be taken by consensus it will only be as good as its weakest member. Human rights bodies need a reputation for integrity, impartiality, independence and legitimacy to create respect for their decisions and pressure for compliance. If States choose to nominate unqualified or biased candidates who are then elected to serve on the body, the institution will be undermined. The smaller the body the more important it is to ensure that all members meet the qualifications to serve.

Second, human rights bodies should have adequate meeting time to carry out their functions. The only full-time human rights body currently is the Eur. Ct. HR. All other commissions and courts are organized as part-time bodies whose members then are employed elsewhere. This situation can make it difficult to schedule on-site visits and to take quick action outside the scheduled sessions, which may total only between six and nine weeks a year. Members may be geographically quite distant one from another and have difficulty maintaining close contact. Reliance on secretariats for maintaining the functioning of the system between sessions risks creating the impression – and even the reality – that the secretariats are the primary bodies responsible for deciding cases and fulfilling the mandates of the bodies. As long as membership on human rights bodies is a part-time position, some delegation of functions to the secretariats will be necessary, but will therefore also demand oversight and accountability.

Linked to the second factor, in most human rights systems the secretariat is supplied by the parent organization. Few human rights bodies have the power to select their own lawyers, registrar and other key personnel. In practice the head of the organization will often take into account the views of the human rights body, but there is always a risk of political appointments or other interference if the human rights body does not control the hiring and tenure of its staff, which must be professional, independent, expert and dedicated. The problem of having only short-term contracts, a problem linked to budgetary short-falls, undermines the ability to obtain and retain good staff. The size of the staff and the time for meeting, as well as the ability to make on-site visits, hold hearings, and fulfil the functions conferred on a human rights body depend entirely on the budget and financial contributions available to it. This is a matter of urgency and even crisis in nearly all human rights systems.

Adequate publicity is also important to the promotion and protection of human rights. Human rights bodies need a functioning and accessible website, regular publication of documents and decisions, a press office that can ensure press coverage, and regular meetings with the member States and civil society organizations.

Ultimately, the commitment to human rights of the member States is determinative. If the level of respect for human rights norms on the domestic level is low, and domestic institutions are not effective, the workload of human rights bodies becomes unmanageable and ineffective. Compliance may be assisted by issue linkage, sometimes more negatively referred to as conditionality. As the OSCE has shown, trade, communications, travel, security and other links between States Parties can help to elevate human rights and make possible the conditions to take enforcement measures in those cases where gross and systematic violations make them appropriate or necessary.

4   The law of human rights

The stated purpose of the UN and other intergovernmental organizations to promote respect for and observance of human rights depended on first reaching agreement on the meaning of the term human rights along with defining the corresponding obligations, followed by the construction of appropriate institutions and procedures to ensure compliance with the adopted international norms. The law-making process that helps develop these aspects of human rights law involves an array of participants interacting in complex ways; civil society organizations and other non-State actors are increasingly involved, but the international legal system continues to be one primarily comprised of laws made by, and governing the relations between, States.

4.1   Sources of human rights law

4.1.1   Treaties

The exercise of State sovereignty includes entering into binding agreements to act or refrain from acting according to the terms of the agreement: in other words, to limit by law the scope of discretion to exercise future State sovereignty. The Vienna Convention on the Law of Treaties (VCLT) largely codifies the customary law of treaties and is widely applied by national and international tribunals and human rights bodies.[1]

The VCLT Article 2 defines a treaty as "an international agreement concluded between States in written form and governed by international law, whether embodied in a single instrument or in two or more related instruments and whatever its particular designation". Human rights treaties carry various designations, including convention, covenant, protocol and treaty. The name is sometimes chosen to indicate

---

1 Vienna Convention on the Law of Treaties, 22 May 1969, 1155 UNTS 331, 8 ILM 679.

the degree of solemnity attached to the commitments, but the choice of name does not affect the legal status of the agreement, provided the parties agree that the contents are legally binding. Other names usually, but not always, reflect a non-binding status: declaration, memorandum of understanding, *modus vivendi*. The American and Universal Declarations of Human Rights, and the more recent ASEAN Declaration were adopted as non-binding texts. The Organization for Security and Cooperation in Europe (OSCE) functions largely on the basis of non-binding political commitments.

Multilateral human rights treaty practice includes a wide variety of drafting techniques designed to provide the flexibility necessary to encourage States to adhere to the final agreement, even if they have concerns with particular provisions. Among these techniques are optional clauses – often used for dispute settlement provisions – that require States to file an additional declaration in order to accept the obligation therein. The UN treaties and American Convention on Human Rights, for example, provide for States to file such a declaration to indicate acceptance of the jurisdiction of the UN treaty body and the I-A Ct. HR respectively. Another technique involves drafting a comprehensive set of provisions, from which the ratifying States must accept certain core provisions but may choose among the remaining provisions those additional obligations they are willing to undertake. The European Social Charter is an example of this type of treaty. Human rights agreements also frequently contain provisions that set forth the guaranteed right in a first paragraph, followed by a second paragraph that delineates the legal grounds and scope of State discretion to limit the exercise of the right contained in the article.

States may also modify, within limits, the obligations in a treaty through attaching one or more reservations at the time of their signature or ratification. According to the Vienna Convention on the Law of Treaties, Article 2(1)(d), a reservation "means a unilateral statement, however phrased or named, made by a State, when signing, ratifying, accepting, approving or acceding to a treaty, whereby it purports to exclude or modify the legal effect of certain provisions of the treaty in their application to that State". It therefore does not matter whether a State refers to its attached Statement as a reservation, declaration or understanding; the crucial test is the legal effect of the Statement. Some human rights treaties prohibit reservations; many other human rights treaties restrict the type or scope of reservations that may be submitted. Legal restrictions on the ability of a State to file reservations to human rights treaties has given rise to debate about the role of treaty bodies in monitoring or pronouncing on the legality of reservations to the treaty. Many human rights bodies have claimed jurisdiction to do so, although the procedure foreseen in the VCLT confers that authority on other States Parties to the treaty. Some States have objected to treaty bodies claiming the right to sever an illegal reservation from a State's acceptance of the treaty and impose the treaty as if the reservation had not been made.[2]

Treaties may provide for denunciation or termination with notification.[3] While most of the African human rights treaties have no such provision, European and Inter-American human rights conventions generally include denunciation clauses. The "core" UN human rights treaties differ on this point; some permit denunciation at any time while others allow denunciation only after the expiry of a certain period. Some treaties permit withdrawal from their procedural arrangements, and a few are silent on denunciation or withdrawal altogether. No treaty expressly prohibits a State from denouncing the agreement. If a treaty does not contain a provision on denunciation, the VCLT seems to create a presumption that it cannot be done. In 1998 the UN HRC declared that once inhabitants of a particular territory are accorded the protection of the rights contained in the ICCPR, "such protection devolves with the territory and continues to belong to them"[4] even if there is a change of government or the government attempts to denounce the treaty. Very few States have ever denounced a human rights treaty.[5]

4.1.2   Custom

Customary practices viewed as obligatory have been part of the interaction within and between societies throughout history. Until the twen-

---

2 See CCPR, General Comment 24 and the comments of the United Kingdom and the United States in the Report of the Human Rights Committee, Vol I, UNGAOR, 50th Sess, Supp No 40, A/50/40, 126–34. The European Court employed the doctrine of severability in the *Bellilos* case and the Inter-American Court did so in, for example, *Radilla-Pacheco v Mexico*, Judgment of 23 Nov 2009.

3 See VCLT Art. 56; American Convention, Art. 78. See also, Yogesh Tyegi, *The Denunciation of Human Rights Treaties* (2008) BRITISH YEARBOOK OF INTERNATIONAL LAW 79.

4 The Human Rights Committee developed this general comment in response to the purported denunciation of the ICCPR by the DPRK in 1997. See CCPR, General Comment 26 (61) on the "Continuity of Obligations under the International Covenant on Civil and Political Rights".

5 Trinidad & Tobago and Venezuela have denounced the American Convention on Human Rights; Jamaica denounced the Optional Protocol to the ICCPR, thereby removing the jurisdiction of the Human Rights Committee to receive communications against the State.

tieth century, custom was the primary source of international legal obligation. Bilateral treaties have long existed, but multilateral treaties were rare until the advent of international organizations. Important legal rules continue to find their source in custom, which is critical with respect to those States not parties to major international human rights agreements. The codification of custom in such treaties does not extinguish the customary norm, which retains its force as an independent source of obligation.[6]

The definition of custom contained in ICJ Statute Article 38(1) involves both an objective element (State practice) and a subjective element (*opinio juris sive necessitatis*, or the recognition that the content of the custom is legally binding and not a matter of courtesy or discretion). These criteria raise issues of what counts as practice, how long term and widespread a practice needs to be before it can be said to constitute custom, and whether, if a practice is sufficiently uniform over a long period of time, *opinio juris* can be inferred. Also important for human rights law is the question of whether, if there are strong expressions of legal obligation contained in non-binding texts and treaties, this can suffice to create custom in the absence of long-standing State practice.

Some scholars have claimed that the entire catalogue of rights in the UDHR now constitutes customary international law, but this claim lacks support in State practice. Still, a growing list of international human rights and obligations has been recognized in international and domestic tribunals as having reached the status of custom. This includes the right to be free from genocide, torture and prolonged arbitrary detention; the guarantee of equality and non-discrimination, and the right to life, including the prohibition on juvenile executions.[7]

4.1.3   General principles of law

Article 38 § 1(c) of the Statute of the ICJ refers to "the general principles of law recognized by civilized nations" as one of the sources of

---

6 *Military and Paramilitary Activities in and against Nicaragua (Nicaragua v United States of America)*, Merits, Judgment 1986 ICJ 14 (27 June).

7 The Restatement (Third) sec 702 of the Foreign Relations Law of the United States lists the following acts to violate customary international law: genocide, slavery, murder and forced disappearance, torture or other cruel, inhuman or degrading treatment or punishment, prolonged arbitrary detention, systematic racial discrimination, and consistent patterns of gross violations of internationally recognized human rights.

international law to be applied by the Court. General principles of law identified in the case law of international courts and arbitral tribunals, derived from commonly accepted domestic rules, include, inter alia, the principle of good faith, the obligation to make reparation for international wrongs, the principle of *res judicata*, the principle of estoppel, the principle of *jura novit curia*, equality of the parties to a dispute, the rights of the defence, and respect for fundamental rights. They have served to fill gaps in treaty law or customary obligation. A basic division is often made between principles of domestic law and principles of international law, considered distinct from norms of customary international law.[8]

General principles derived from national law, especially constitutional law, heavily influenced the drafting of the UDHR.[9] The initial text of the declaration drew on draft declarations submitted by governments and by NGOs.[10] The Secretariat compiled a "documented outline"[11] linking each of the rights in the draft to provisions contained in the constitutions of the then 55 member States of the UN. Numerous civil, political, economic, social and cultural rights appeared in a large number of these constitutions. Several Latin American States supported including the economic and social rights guaranteed by their constitutions in the UDHR.[12] The drafting history reveals that the enumerated rights in the constitutions of UN member States influenced their inclusion in the final text.

General principles play a role in human rights cases where the rights in question lack detailed treaty content as well as in those few instances where the treaties themselves refer to general principles. The text of the ICCPR refers to general principles in Article 15, guaranteeing the right of *nullum crimen nulla poena sine lege*. The Article adds that "[t]his article shall not prejudice the trial and punishment of any person for any act or omission which, at the time when it was committed, was criminal according to the general principles of law recognised by civi-

---

8 See Michael O'Boyle and Michelle Lafferty, *General Principles and Constitutions as Sources of Human Rights Law*, in OXFORD HANDBOOK OF INTERNATIONAL HUMAN RIGHTS LAW (D Shelton ed., OUP 2013).

9 See JOHANNES MORSINK, THE UNIVERSAL DECLARATION OF HUMAN RIGHTS: ORIGIN, DRAFTING & INTENT (U Pennsylvania Press 1999).

10 Ibid.

11 UNCHR "International Bill of Rights Documented Outline" (11 Jun 1947) UN Doc E/CN.4/AC.1/3/Add.1.

12 See Morsink (n. 9) 89, 130–33, 157, 191.

lised nations".[13] The ECHR replicates this provision in Article 7. The HRC and the European Court have referred to this principle without extensive discussion.

The European Court has drawn on the concept of general principles in order to interpret and apply several rights guaranteed by the Convention. In the early case of *Golder v United Kingdom*, citing Article 31 § 3(c) of the VCLT, the Court referred to the need to take into account any relevant rules of international law applicable between the parties, which in its view included general principles of law.[14] The court observed that during the drafting of the Convention, the Committee on Legal and Administrative Questions had foreseen that the Court "must necessarily apply such principles" in the execution of its duties; thus it considered it unnecessary to insert a specific clause to this effect in the Convention.[15] With this in mind, the Court in *Golder* found that the principle of access to justice for a civil claim ranked as one of the universally recognized fundamental principles of law and concluded that Article 6 § 1 had to be read in light of this principle.[16] Similarly, in *Vilho Eskelinen and Others v Finland*,[17] the Court found the judicial control of administrative action to be a general principle implicit in the constitutional traditions common to member States and reflected in Articles 6 and 13 (right to an effective remedy) of the ECHR.

The European Court regularly relies on the general principle of estoppel in rejecting preliminary objections relating to admissibility as well as the principle of *res judicata* as an element of legal certainty, inherent in the rule of law.[18] In *Murray v United Kingdom*, the court found that the right to remain silent and the privilege against self-incrimination are "generally recognised international standards . . . at the heart of the

---

13 Art. 7 § 2 of the Convention. See Art. 15 § 2 of the ICCPR. There are two other references in the ECHR. Art. 35 § 1 requires that all domestic remedies be exhausted "according to the generally recognised rules of international law". Art. 1 of Protocol No 1 protecting the right to property provides that "[n]o one shall be deprived of his possessions except in the public interest and subject to the conditions provided for by law and by the general principles of international law".

14 *Golder v United Kingdom* (1975) 18 ECHR (Ser A), 1 EHRR 52.

15 Consultative Assembly, "Working Paper No 93" (1950) vol III, 982.

16 *Golder* (n. 14) at paras 35–6.

17 *Vilho Eskelinen and Others v Finland*, App. no. 63235/00, 2007-II Eur. Ct. HR [GC] (9 Apr. 2007).

18 On estoppel, see *Markin v Russia*, App 59502/00 (ECtHR, 30 Mar 2006), para. 96. In *Brumarescu v Romania*, App 28342/95 (GC) (Merits), 1999-VII (28 Oct), it found a violation of Art. 6 (right to a fair trial) on the grounds that the Supreme Court of Justice had set aside a judicial decision that was irreversible under Romanian law. Para. 62.

notion of a fair procedure under Article 6".[19] In *Scoppola (no 2) v Italy*, the court found that where the penalty for a crime had been lowered since the commission of the offence, Article 7 § 1 of the Convention required by implication that the convicted person be given the benefit of the more lenient penalty.[20]

The Court's 2008 judgment in *Demir and Baykara v Turkey* reiterated its approach to interpreting the provisions of the Convention, quoting with approval its finding in the *Golder* case that the relevant rules of international law include "general principles of law recognised by civilised nations".[21] In concluding that civil servants are entitled to the guarantees of Article 11, the court drew support from the practice of European States, observing that all Member States of the Council of Europe recognize the right of such employees to join trade unions. As to whether civil servants enjoy the right to bargain collectively, the Court noted that such a right had been recognized as applicable to civil servants in the "vast majority" of the Member States, albeit subject to certain restrictions. This led the Court to conclude that such a right had become "one of the essential elements" of the right to form and join trade unions in Article 11.

4.2   Political commitments

In the international arena, just as at other levels of governance, law is one form of social control or normative claim, but basic requirements of behaviour also emerge from morality, courtesy and social custom reflecting the values of society. They form part of the expectations of social discourse; compliance with such norms may be expected and violations sanctioned. Thus, State practice in recent years, inside and outside international organizations, has often placed normative statements in non-binding political instruments such as declarations, resolutions, concluding texts of international conferences, and programmes of action, and has signalled that compliance is expected with the norms contained in these texts.

Commentators refer to these instruments as "soft law" and they debate whether or not the practice of adopting them constitutes evidence of

---

19 *Murray v United Kingdom*, App no 18731/91 at para. 45 (ECtHR, 8 Feb 1996).

20 *Scoppola (no 2) v Italy*, App 10249/03, [GC] (2010) 51 EHRR 403 (17 Sep). Article 7 § 1 is silent on this point.

21 *Demir and Baykara v Turkey* [GC] App no 34503/97 at paras 67, 71 (ECtHR, 12 Nov 2008).

new modes of international law making. States, however, appear clearly to understand that such soft law texts are political commitments that can lead to law, but they are not law, and thus give rise only to political consequences, which can be significant.[22] While there is no accepted definition of soft law, it usually refers to any written international instrument, other than a treaty, containing principles, norms, standards or other statements of expected behaviour. In some instances a given text may be hard law for States that choose to incorporate the norms into domestic law, while remaining soft law for others.

The UN frequently conducts studies, organizes global conferences such as the 1968 Teheran and 1993 Vienna conferences on human rights, and facilitates other meetings where standards may be elaborated. The UN General Assembly adopts normative resolutions that create expectations of compliance; in the area of human rights it has done so repeatedly since the 1948 UDHR. Whether or not such resolutions are law making cannot be answered without careful attention to the text and the context of each resolution.

In 1962 the UN Commission on Human Rights reported to ECOSOC on the impact of human rights declarations after debate arose in the Commission over the form of an instrument on freedom of thought, conscience and religion.[23] The Commission then requested a legal opinion on the difference between a recommendation and a declaration. The Office of Legal Affairs submitted a memorandum in which it said: "[i]n United Nations practice, a 'declaration' is a formal and solemn instrument, suitable for rare occasions when principles of great and lasting importance are being enunciated, such as the Declaration of Human Rights. A recommendation is less formal". The Legal Office added that although a declaration is not binding, "in view of the greater solemnity and significance of a 'declaration' it may be considered to impart, on behalf of the organ adopting it, a strong expectation that Members of the international community will abide by it".[24] The opinion also recognized that, in so far as the expectation is gradually

---

22 The exception is when the text expresses norms of customary international law. COMMITMENT AND COMPLIANCE: THE ROLE OF NON-BINDING NORMS IN THE INTERNATIONAL LEGAL SYSTEM (D Shelton ed., OUP 2000); C Tomuschat, *Obligations Arising for State Without or Against Their Will* (1993-IV) 241 RECUEIL DES COURS 191; P Weil, *Towards Relative Normativity in International Law?* (1983) 77 AJIL 413.

23 UN Doc E/3616/Rev.1, E/CN.4/832/Rev.1, Commission on Human Rights, Report of the Eighteenth Session, ECOSOC Supp No 8 (1962).

24 Ibid. at para. 105.

justified by State practice, a declaration may by custom become recognized as laying down rules binding upon States.

Human rights non-binding norms are often the precursor to treaty negotiations and sometimes stimulate State practice, leading to the formation of customary international law. Indeed, a non-binding normative instrument may do one or more of the following:

(1) codify pre-existing customary international law, helping to provide greater precision through the written text;

(2) crystallize a trend towards a particular norm, overriding the views of dissenters and persuading those who have little or no relevant State practice to acquiesce in the development of the norm;

(3) precede and help form new customary international law;

(4) consolidate political opinion around the need for action on a new problem, fostering consensus that may lead to treaty negotiations or further soft law;

(5) fill in gaps in existing treaties in force;

(6) form part of the subsequent State practice that can be utilized to interpret treaties;

(7) provide guidance or a model for domestic laws, without international obligation; or

(8) substitute for legal obligation when ongoing relations make formal treaties too costly and time consuming or otherwise unnecessary or politically unacceptable.

The interplay between soft law and custom is identified in the first three enumerations. Some soft law texts purport to do no more than set down in written form pre-existing legal rights and duties.[25] Other instruments may contain a combination of pre-existing law and new

---

25 The commentary to the UN *Basic principles and guidelines on the right to remedy and reparation for victims of gross violations of international human rights law and serious violations of international humanitarian law*, approved by the Commission on Human Rights in Res 2005/35 of 19 Apr 2005 and endorsed by the General Assembly in UNGA Res A/Res/60/147 of 16 Dec 2005,

developments. It is rare that a non-binding instrument is entirely codi-fication or innovation. Some texts are drafted to consolidate a trend towards changes in customary law or stamp with approval one among several conflicting positions on a legal issue. Conforming State practice is needed among States representing different regions and the major legal, economic and political systems in order for such soft law texts to become customary international law.

Using non-binding texts to give authoritative interpretation to treaty terms is particularly useful when the issues are contentious and terms are undefined in the treaty itself. Examples include the references to human rights in the OAS and UN Charters, undefined but authorita-tively interpreted by the Inter-American and Universal Declarations of Human Rights. Another example is the more recent ILO Declaration on Fundamental Principles and Rights at Work, which acts in relation to the ILO Constitution.

Non-binding instruments are generally faster to adopt, easier to change, and more useful for technical matters that may need rapid or repeated revision. In many instances, political divisions may limit the choice to having a soft law text or no text at all. Non-binding instruments are also useful in addressing new topics of regulation that require innovative means of rule making with respect to non-State actors, who generally are not parties to treaties or involved in the crea-tion of customary international law. The emergence of codes of con-duct reflects this development. The 2003 Norms on the Responsibilities of Transnational Corporations and Other Business Enterprises with Regard to Human Rights, adopted by the UN Sub-Commission on the Promotion and Protection of Human Rights, exemplifies such texts. Similarly, soft law texts may allow non-State actors to vote for or sign the instrument and participate in compliance mechanisms. The Voluntary Principles for Security and Human Rights in the Extractive Industries, for example, was negotiated between the US and UK gov-ernments, major human rights NGOs such as Amnesty International and Human Rights Watch, and oil and gas companies, including BP, Chevron/Texaco, and Royal Dutch/Shell.

In sum, non-binding norms often serve either as a precursor to legal regulation or as a supplement to a legal instrument. Non-binding

---

claims that the principles and guidelines contain no new norms, but instead reflect existing law scattered among a large number of treaties and widespread State practice.

instruments adopted subsequent to a treaty allow treaty parties to authoritatively resolve ambiguities in the binding text or fill in gaps.

4.3 Peremptory norms (*jus cogens*), obligations *erga omnes* and international crimes

In national legal systems, private agreements cannot derogate from the public policy of the community.[26] The international community remains somewhat divided over whether the same is true in the international legal system, but most States seem to accept, at least in theory, that a particular rule of custom or treaty law may be deemed so important to the international community of States as a whole that no one may derogate from it. Such rules are referred to as *jus cogens* or peremptory norms,[27] defined in Article 53 of the 1969 VCLT as rules "accepted and recognized by the international community of States as a whole as a norm from which no derogation is permitted and which can be modified only by a subsequent norm having the same character". VCLT Article 53 provides that a treaty will be void "if, at the time of its conclusion, it conflicts with a peremptory norm of general international law". Article 64 adds that the emergence of a new peremptory norm of general international law will render void any existing treaty in conflict with the norm. No clear agreement was reached during the VCLT negotiations, nor has one emerged since then about the content of *jus cogens*. No treaty has been invalidated for conflicting with a peremptory norm.

In practice, the concept of *jus cogens* has been invoked largely outside its original context in the law of treaties. The International Criminal Tribunal for the Former Yugoslavia (ICTY) was the first tribunal to mention *jus cogens*, declaring the prohibition of torture to be such a norm.[28] The issue had no bearing on the guilt or innocence of the person on trial, or on the binding nature of the law violated. It was not asserted that any treaty or local custom was in conflict with the customary and treaty prohibition of torture, so the discussion appeared aimed at emphasizing the importance of the norm in the view of the judges.

---

26 Art. 6 of the *Code Napoléon* is illustrative: "On ne peut déroger, par des conventions particulières, aux lois qui intéressent l'ordre public et les bonnes mœurs".

27 The terms *jus cogens* and peremptory norms are used interchangeably. VCLT Art. 53 is entitled "Treaties conflicting with a peremptory norm of general international law (jus cogens)".

28 *Prosecutor v Furundzija*, Judgment ICTY Trial Chamber Case no IT-95−17/1-T at para. 153 (1998).

In 2006, in its *Congo v Rwanda*[29] judgment, the ICJ for the first time affirmed both the existence of peremptory norms in international law and asserted that the prohibition of genocide is "assuredly" such a norm. In 2008 the Court was confronted directly with the question of whether or not peremptory norms override other norms of international law, when the Federal Republic of Germany filed an application against Italy at the ICJ, asserting that the Italian courts' exercise of jurisdiction over Germany in relation to claims of Second World War forced labour and other war crimes constituted a wrongful denial of sovereign immunity.[30] In its judgment of 3 February 2012, the Court and the parties agreed that immunity is governed by international law and is not a mere matter of comity, the Court noting that sovereign immunity holds an "important place" in international law, deriving from the principle of sovereign equality of States. Italy argued that Germany was not entitled to immunity because its acts in question involved "the most serious violations of rules of international law of a peremptory character for which no alternative means of redress was available".[31] The Court rejected all of Italy's arguments. Assuming without deciding that the alleged violations rose to the level of *jus cogens*, the Court held that there was no conflict between that determination and the rule demanding respect for sovereign immunity: "the two sets of rules address different matters", one substantive, one procedural. There could be no conflict between the two.

Human rights tribunals until recently avoided pronouncing on *jus cogens*. A Grand Chamber of the Eur. Ct. HR, in a 2002 judgment, first mentioned *jus cogens* in the context of a claim of immunity. By a vote of nine to eight, the Court called the prohibition of torture a peremptory norm, but like the ICJ denied that a violation of the norm could act to deprive a State of sovereign immunity.[32] The European Court found that it was "unable to discern" any basis for overriding State immunity from civil suit even where acts of torture are alleged. More

29 *Armed Activities on the Territory of the Congo (Democratic Republic of the Congo v Rwanda)*, Jurisdiction and Admissibility, Judgment 2005 ICJ 6 at para. 64 (19 Dec).

30 *Jurisdictional Immunities of the State (Germany v Italy)* 2008 (23 Dec) available at www.icj-cij.org/docket/files/143/14923.pdf.

31 Ibid. at para. 61.

32 *Al Al-Adsani v UK* [GC] (2001) ECHR 2001-XI, 34 EHRR 11; See also *Fogarty v UK* [GC] (2001) ECHR 2001-XI, 34 EHRR 12, and *McElhinney v Ireland and UK* [GC] (2001) App no 31253/96, ECHR 2001-XI, 34 EHRR 13 decided the same day as *Al-Adsani*.

recently, the European Court followed the ICJ in calling the prohibition of genocide a peremptory norm.[33]

The I-A Ct. HR referred to *jus cogens* with some frequency between its 2003 advisory opinion on the *Juridical Condition and Rights of Undocumented Migrants*[34] and 2008, but has done so far less often since then. In the 2003 advisory opinion, Mexico's fourth question to the I-A Court asked: "What is the nature today of the principle of non-discrimination and the right to equal and effective protection of the law in the hierarchy of norms established by general international law and, in this context, can they be considered to be the expression of norms *jus cogens*?" Mexico also asked the I-A Court to indicate the legal effect of a finding that these norms are *jus cogens*. The Court concluded that the non-discrimination norm is *jus cogens*, being "intrinsically related to the right to equal protection before the law", which, in turn, derives "directly from the oneness of the human family and is linked to the essential dignity of the individual". The Court added that the principle belongs to *jus cogens* because the whole legal structure of national and international public order rests on it and it is a fundamental principle that permeates all laws.

The I-A Court subsequently affirmed *jus cogens* norms in contentious cases, broadening the list to include the prohibition of torture,[35] access to justice,[36] the prohibition of forced disappearance, and the duty to prosecute violations of *jus cogens* norms.[37] The IACHR added the right to life to the list of *jus cogens* norms.[38]

---

33 *Jorgic v Germany* (2007) App no 74613/01, ECHR 2007-XI at para. 68.

34 *Juridical Condition and Rights of the Undocumented Migrants*, Advisory Opinion OC-18/03 I-A Court HR, Ser A, No 18 (2003).

35 See the I-A Court HR cases *Bayarri v Argentina* (Preliminary Objection, Merits, Reparations and Costs), I-A Court HR Ser C, No 187 at para. 81 (30 Oct 2008); *Martiza Urrutia v Guatemala*, para. 92; *Tibi v Ecuador* (Preliminary Objections, Merits, Reparations and Costs), I-A Court HR, Ser C, No 114 (7 Sept 2004) at para. 143 *Bueno-Alves v Argentina* (Merits, Reparations and Costs) I-A Court HR, Ser C, No 164 (11 May 2007) at para. 76; *Rochela Massacre v Colombia* (Merits, Reparations and Costs), I-A Court HR, Ser C, No 163 (11 May 2007) at para. 132; *Case of the Miguel Castro-Castro Prison v Peru*, (Merits, Reparations and Costs) I-A Court HR Ser C No 160 (25 Nov 2006). at para. 271.

36 *La Cantuta v Peru*, (Merits, Reparations and Costs) I-A Court HR, Ser C No 162 (2006) at para. 160.

37 Ibid. para. 157; *Ríos et al v Venezuela* (Preliminary Objections, Merits, Reparations, and Costs), I-A Court HR, Ser C No 194 (28 Jan 2009) at para. 91. See also *Perozo et al v Venezuela* (Preliminary Objections, Merits, Reparations, and Costs), I-A Court HR, Ser C No 195 (28 Jan 2009), citing *La Cantuta v Perú*, ibid. para. 157.

38 IACHR, *Victims of the Tugboat "13 de Marzo" v Cuba* Rep No 47/96, OEA/Ser.L/V/II.95/Doc.7, rev at 146–7 (1997).

Among other international organizations, the ILO report on a 1996 complaint against Myanmar for forced labour referred to *jus cogens* although the State had long been a party to ILO Convention (No 29) concerning Forced or Compulsory Labour.[39] The Report's Statement that the practice of forced labour violates a *jus cogens* norm appears intended mainly to invite the criminal prosecution of individuals using forced labour, labelling the systematic practice of forced labour a "crime against humanity".[40]

The Human Rights Committee addressed *jus cogens* in its General Comment No 29 on States of Emergency, issued 31 August 2001. According to the Committee, the list of non-derogable rights in Article 4(2) of the ICCPR is related to, but not identical with, the content of peremptory human rights norms. The Committee emphatically insisted that:

> States parties may in no circumstances invoke Article 4 of the Covenant as justification for acting in violation of humanitarian law or peremptory norms of international law, for instance by taking hostages, by imposing collective punishments, through arbitrary deprivations of liberty or by deviating from fundamental principles of fair trial, including the presumption of innocence.[41]

The concept of *jus cogens* norms has been asserted most strongly, though largely without success, in domestic courts when sovereign immunity has acted to shield defendants from civil lawsuits for damages or criminal prosecution. The issue has arisen most often in courts of the United States and the United Kingdom.[42] In both forums, lawyers have argued that the foreign sovereign immunity law must be interpreted to include an implied exception for violations of *jus cogens* norms. The argument posits that State agreement to elevate a norm to *jus cogens* status inherently results in an implied waiver of sovereign immunity because by definition no derogation is permitted from the

---

39 Convention Concerning Force or Compulsory Labour (ILO No 29), 28 Jun 1930, 39 UNTS 55.

40 *Report of the Commission of Inquiry on Forced Labour in Myanmar (Burma)* ILO Official Bulletin Special Supp Vol LXXXI (Ser B) at para. 538 (1998).

41 General Comment No 29, para. 11.

42 In the case of former Chilean leader, Augusto Pinochet Ugarte, the issue of *jus cogens* was pressed in response to his claim of immunity from criminal prosecution. The judgment ultimately did not rely on *jus cogens* to determine the issue, because the situation was controlled by treaty. *R v Bow Street Metropolitan Stipendiary Magistrate and others ex parte Pinochet Ugarte* [1999] 2 All ER 97, 179 (HL).

norm. Nearly every court thus far has rejected the argument and upheld immunity, although some judicial panels have split on the issue. Some of the US plaintiffs wrongly claim that the landmark decision *Filartiga v Peña-Irala* held torture to be a violation of international *jus cogens*. In fact, the federal appellate court in that case held that official torture constitutes a violation of the law of nations and never mentioned *jus cogens*.[43]

In regards to *erga omnes* obligations, the ICJ identified this category of obligations in *dicta* in the *Barcelona Traction* case. Unlike obligations arising with respect to specific injured States (for example, in the field of diplomatic protection), obligations *erga omnes* are owed to the international community as a whole. The broad scope of such obligations could be based on the fact that obligations *erga omnes* generally concern the internal behaviour of a State, as in the field of human rights, and thus no other State is likely to be injured by a breach. The principle of effectiveness thus supports broad standing, because without it violations could not be challenged. However, the rationale stated by the ICJ for recognizing obligations *erga omnes* appears more substantive: that "in view of the importance of the rights involved, all States can be held to have a legal interest in their protection".[44] This statement suggests that obligations *erga omnes* have specific and broad procedural consequences *because of* the substantive importance of the norms they enunciate. In addition, the fact that all States are deemed injured may make complaints more likely following commission of a wrongful act. It also suggests an important public interest in upholding the rule of law. The ICJ's examples of such obligations include the outlawing of aggression and genocide and the protection from slavery and racial discrimination. While all *jus cogens* obligations have an *erga omnes* character, the reverse is not necessarily true.[45]

Finally, the emergence of international criminal law has led to theories about the nature of international crimes and the relationship of this body of law to doctrines of *jus cogens* and obligations *erga omnes*.

---

43 *Filartiga v Peña-Irala* 630 F 2d 876 (2d Cir 1980).

44 *Barcelona Traction Light and Power Company Limited*, Second Phase, Judgment 1970 ICJ 3 (5 Feb); See also *East Timor (Portugal v Australia* 1995 ICJ 92 (Judgment of 30 Jun 1995), 90, para. 29; *Application of the Convention on the Prevention and Punishment of the Crime of Genocide (Bosnia-Herzegovina v Yugoslavia)* 1996 ICJ 595, para. 31 (11 Jul).

45 International Law Commission, Report of the Study Group on Fragmentation of International Law: Difficulties arising from the Diversification and Expansion of International Law, A/CN.4/l.676, 29 Jul 2005, paras 48, 50.

Similar to obligations *erga omnes*, international crimes are so designated because the acts they sanction are deemed of such importance
to the international community that individual criminal responsibility should result from their commission. Unlike obligations *erga
omnes*, international criminal norms can raise problems of relative
normativity. First, the question has been posed as to whether there
is a hierarchy among the crimes. Secondly, it has been clear since
the Nuremburg Trials that conforming to or carrying out domestic
law is no excuse for breach of international criminal law; it would
seem plausible as well, if unlikely to arise in practice, that a defence
would fail based on carrying out international legal obligations, such
as those contained in a bilateral treaty, if those obligations should
contradict the requirements of criminal law. In this respect, norms of
criminal law could be given supremacy over other international law
in practice.

The designation of international crimes and obligations *erga omnes*
does not involve a purported new source of law: crimes are created
and defined through the conclusion of treaties; obligations *erga omnes*
through treaty and customary international law. Secondly, it appears
logical that all international crimes are obligations *erga omnes* because
the international community as a whole identifies and may prosecute
and punish the commission of such crimes. The reverse is not the
case, however. Not all obligations *erga omnes* have been designated as
international crimes. Racial discrimination, for example, is cited as an
obligation *erga omnes*, but is not included among international crimes
except in its most extreme forms (genocide and apartheid). Among
those acts designated as international crimes, there appears to be no
hierarchy.[46]

4.4   The evolution of human rights law

4.4.1   UN standard-setting

The mandate of the UN to address human rights is stated in general terms in the Charter, leading the organization to place initial
emphasis on reaching agreement on the content of the rights the UN
should protect. In 1990 the Secretary-General of the United Nations

---

46 See *Prosecutor v Dusko Tadić*, Judgment in Sentencing Appeals ICTY Appeals Chamber Case no
IT–94–1–A at para. 69 (2000).

observed that the UN had "from its very inception . . . engaged itself in elaborating human rights instruments and establishing bench marks against which standards of behaviour can be measured".[47] Indeed, during its first decades, the UN devoted the majority of its time to drafting norms, beginning with the UDHR and continuing through the International Covenants and other core human rights instruments. Pre-war issues like labour rights and slavery continued to be addressed, along with new issues such as refugees, genocide, and discrimination against women and racial minorities. The process of reaching agreement was difficult, due to Cold War politics and decolonization, both of which gave rise to continuing debates over the universality of human rights. Throughout the process, UN member States, international organizations, civil society groups and individuals participated in creating the instruments that comprise modern human rights law.

When the San Francisco Conference ended without including in the UN Charter a listing of internationally guaranteed rights, a group of States remained insistent on the need to articulate a catalogue of the human rights to which the Charter referred. The Preparatory Commission of the UN recommended that ECOSOC immediately establish a Commission on Human Rights and direct it to formulate an "international bill of rights" and to prepare studies and recommendations which "would encourage the acceptance of higher standards in this field and help to check and eliminate discrimination and other abuses". The General Assembly approved this recommendation on 12 February 1946. Four days later ECOSOC created the Commission on Human Rights, subsequently conferring on the Commission the mandate to submit to the Council "proposals, recommendations and reports" regarding:

(a) an international bill of rights;

(b) international declarations or conventions on civil liberties, the status of women, freedom of information and similar matters;

(c) the protection of minorities;

(d) the prevention of discrimination on grounds of race, sex, language or religion; and

---

47 Secretary-General Rep on the Work of the Organization, UN GAOR 45th Sess At 15, UN Doc A/45/1 (1990).

(e) any other matter concerning human rights not covered by other items.

Standard-setting, in particular formulation of an international bill of rights, was thus the major focus of the Commission's work. The former Commission in fact completed the UDHR during two sessions over a period of less than 18 months and the General Assembly proclaimed it some six months later, on 10 December 1948.

Political and ideological differences over rights were evident from the beginning of the UDHR drafting process. States were divided between those who wanted a declaration only and those who sought binding obligations in a treaty or covenant. Ultimately, the two sides agreed that both types of instrument should be prepared and submitted to the General Assembly. Other problems were less amenable to compromise. The East–West divide over civil and political rights and economic, social and cultural rights came fully to the forefront during the process of converting the Declaration into binding treaty obligations.

Governments devoted nearly as much time debating the legal status of the Declaration as they did its contents. The Declaration refers to itself as "a common standard of achievement for all peoples and all nations" and today represents an agreed statement of the definition of "human rights" as that term is used in the UN Charter. The Declaration has been reaffirmed in global and regional treaties and in the UN Conferences on Human Rights held in Teheran (1968) and Vienna (1993). Reaching early agreement on the content of human rights had important consequences: it recast human rights policy as international law, making it more difficult for States to ignore human rights claims, and it served to refute assertions by some States that human rights was a matter of exclusive domestic jurisdiction.

Some observers assert that the UN's primary standard-setting activities occurred in the first half-dozen years (1947–54), but this view is not supported by an examination of the practice of the organization. In fact, the UN cannot avoid being continually engaged in standard-setting. As the International Commission of Jurists has noted, "... [l]aw-making, whether at the domestic or international level, is necessarily a never-ending process. Human rights law must keep pace with the changing nature of human needs and aspirations, and with new forms of rights violations and understandings reached about their causes".[48]

The UN began almost immediately developing the content of human rights law and mechanisms for compliance monitoring through the adoption of treaties. On 9 December 1948 the General Assembly adopted the Convention on the Prevention and Punishment of Genocide, and the following day the same resolution that approved the Universal Declaration gave the Commission a mandate to work on a binding treaty of human rights.

The Commission thereafter began negotiating what became the ICCPR and the ICESCR. The precedent this action set – of first adopting a declaration, then concluding a treaty on the same topic – was one followed with some consistency during the Commission's tenure.[49] The Commission initially devoted attention to a treaty containing only civil and political rights, but in 1950 the General Assembly determined that the treaty should include economic, social and cultural rights as well. Two years later, based on a proposal of India and Lebanon, supported by Belgium and the United States, the General Assembly decided to separate civil and political rights from economic, social and cultural rights and conclude two treaties with as many similar provisions as possible, including in both a right of peoples and nations to self-determination.

The Commission on Human Rights completed its work on the draft Covenants in 1954 and submitted them to ECOSOC. From there the Covenants went to the Third Committee of the UN General Assembly, where they were debated for more than ten years. It was only in 1966 that the General Assembly voted and approved the Covenants, one year after the adoption of the International Convention on the Elimination of All Forms of Racial Discrimination. Another ten years passed before the Covenants entered into force, with provision for mandatory periodic reporting by States Parties and an optional inter-State complaint process for the ICCPR. Individual communications were left to a separate optional protocol in the ICCPR; the General Assembly approved the establishment of a collective complaint pro-

---

48 International Commission of Jurists, *Reforming the Human Rights System: A Chance for the United Nations to Fulfill its Promise* (2005), 20.

49 On subjects of particular controversy, a declaration often proved to be the only text on which States could agree.

cedure through an optional protocol to the ICESCR only in 2008; the protocol entered into force in 2013.

CERD, adopted in 1965, was the first of a series of treaties addressing equal rights. It is not surprising that this issue was taken up even before the Covenants were concluded. The right to enjoy human rights without discrimination based on race, sex, language or religion is the only individual right mentioned in the UN Charter.[50] The struggle against colonialism, which was perceived as linked to racism and discrimination, also stimulated emphasis on this issue. The UN subsequently adopted treaties on the human rights of women (CEDAW), children (CRC), migrant workers (CPMW), and the disabled (CRPD), as well as a declaration on the rights of indigenous peoples.[51]

CEDAW sets international standards for achieving equality between men and women and prohibits discrimination against women. It covers civil, political, economic, social and cultural rights. Although the Convention has been widely ratified, it has suffered from a large number of reservations[52] and was originally very limited in its supervisory mechanisms. An optional protocol has strengthened the monitoring mechanisms and added a complaints procedure as well as an inquiry procedure with respect to grave or systematic violations.

In 1979 Poland introduced at the Commission a draft convention on the rights of the child. The process used to negotiate this convention, like that for the Torture Convention, involved creating a pre-sessional open-ended working group seeking consensus on each provision. The Children's Convention was completed and adopted in 1989, exactly 30 years after the Declaration on the same topic. While the length of the negotiations reflects the many difficult issues addressed, the process also helped create a consensus evidenced by the almost universal ratification of the agreement.

In addition to its standard-setting on equal rights for specific groups, the UN has also addressed prevention and accountability with respect

---

50 The Charter refers to the "principle" of self-determination rather than the right of self-determination.

51 Declaration on the Rights of Indigenous Peoples, GA Res 61/295, annex (13 Sep 2007).

52 See Rebecca Cook, *Reservations to the Convention on the Elimination of All Forms of Discrimination against Women* (1990) 30 VIRGINIA JOURNAL OF INTERNATIONAL LAW 643–716; Belinda Clark, *The Vienna Convention Reservations Regime and the Convention on Discrimination against Women* (1991) 82 AJIL 281–321.

to particularly egregious violations, adopting the Convention against Torture (CAT) in 1984 and a Convention for the Protection of All Persons from Enforced Disappearance in 2006. The CAT, which entered into force on 26 June 1987, was largely drafted by a Working Group of the Commission, but the origins are considerably more diverse. In 1973 Amnesty International began a campaign against torture, supported by the International Commission of Jurists, the ICRC, the Swiss Committee against Torture, and the World Council of Churches Commission on International Affairs. Two years later, the Fifth United Nations Congress on the Prevention of Crime and the Treatment of Offenders[53] recommended to the General Assembly a draft Declaration on the Protection of All Persons from Being Subjected to Torture and Other Cruel, Inhuman or Degrading Treatment or Punishment. The General Assembly approved the text in 1975; the Commission was not part of the process. In 1977 the General Assembly took further action on the subject by accepting a Swedish proposal to confer on the Commission the mandate to draft a treaty against torture. The Commission established an open-ended Working Group which met during the 1978 session, but made little progress. The Working Group had two drafts, one prepared by Sweden and the other submitted by the International Association of Penal Law. Both were referred to governments for comment. Working Group meetings were held before each Commission session. Experts from Amnesty International and the ICRC provided technical advice during the negotiations and made substantive proposals during the drafting. In 1984 a text with several provisions in brackets reflecting continued disagreements was sent to the Third Committee, which succeeded in finalizing the text by 10 December 1984. The Third Committee then approved, and the General Assembly adopted, the Convention.

Following this successful effort to enact detailed norms against torture, Amnesty International conducted a campaign against capital punishment. Taking up the issue, West Germany proposed that the Commission adopt a second optional protocol to the ICCPR. The

---

53 The United Nations congresses on crime prevention and criminal justice are one of the main periodic conferences of the United Nations. The policy-makers and practitioners from UN member States' criminal justice systems play a major role in international standard-setting and policy-making in crime prevention and criminal justice. Parliamentarians, individual experts from academia, representatives from civil society and the media also attend. The congresses have been held every five years since 1955. The first Congress adopted the landmark Standard Minimum Rules for the Treatment of Prisoners, widely considered to be the authoritative set of standards to be applied in the criminal justice system.

Commission, in Resolution 1985/46, referred the matter for study to an expert of the Sub-Commission, Marc Bossuyt, who prepared the draft of the protocol. It is one of the rare instances when the individual author of a UN agreement can be identified.

As the above history indicates, the process of elaborating standards has involved numerous actors, including States taking leadership on an issue, the Commission and Sub-Commission, specialized agencies, NGOs, the General Assembly (especially in the Third and Sixth Committees), and the Secretariat. In the process of drafting the Covenants, for example, the ILO addressed labour rights, UNESCO the right to education, and the WHO the right to health. The FAO succeeded in obtaining a reference to the "fundamental right to freedom from hunger". In sum, original authorship of UN human rights instruments normally can rarely be attributed to a single entity. The multiplicity of actors with different viewpoints participating in the drafting process has both a positive and a negative dimension. On the negative side, the desire for consensus sometimes has led to vague, weakened, and, some claim, inconsistent obligations. The Commission, like other UN bodies, preferred that resolutions be adopted by consensus. Sponsors sometimes accepted weakened statements of rights or obligations in order to obtain support. At the same time, the Commission was singularly unsuccessful in achieving consensus. Between 1979 and 1982, for example, some two-thirds of the resolutions were adopted by a divided vote. While the votes have often been viewed as reflecting the Cold War East–West divide, they also revealed North–South divisions. Proclamation of the New International Economic Order, the Convention on Apartheid, and resolutions on transboundary movement of hazardous wastes and products as a human rights violation, were all adopted by a divided vote, with "northern" States opposed or abstaining.

On the positive side, the process has served to invest States in the final product, often producing positive changes in national laws and practices even before the text has been adopted. At present, every UN member State has ratified at least one of the core human rights treaties.

The standard-setting process continues as member States place items on the agenda for action. Standard-setting will no doubt continue, because new problems arise. Although some observers express concern over a "devalued currency" with the proliferation of human rights instruments, the need to obtain a large majority if not consensus acts as a limitation in practice on the adoption of new texts. In this respect, it is important to examine the results. The nine core treaties, some of which are supplemented by optional protocols, are a small part of the total body of human rights law. The UN lists more than 90 other standard-setting instruments. There is clearly little reason to complain about the quantity of human rights standard-setting by the UN as a whole, especially if one adds the specialized agencies to the list.[54] In 1986 the General Assembly adopted a resolution to exercise some degree of quality control over the production of new standards.[55] Commentators also have examined UN standard-setting and proposed standards for the adoption of new standards.[56] In part the concern stems from the link between quantity and quality, with a fear that an increase in the former inevitably results in a decline in the latter. Another concern is with the capacity of States to comply with the multitude of norms and standards now in place. Arguably, the problem of normative proliferation is a consequence of too many standard-setting bodies. Numerous bodies throughout the UN system have been the source of human rights instruments. Overlapping jurisdiction and mandates can produce synergies, but can also mean repetitious or inconsistent norms, a lack of expert involvement, and a lack of continuity in the drafting process.

Another critique of the standard-setting process concerns the length of time involved in concluding normative texts, despite a decision by the Commission that "in most instances the established time-frame should in principle not exceed five years".[57] Some instruments required a decade or more to negotiate, becoming less demanding in the process. Examples include the Declaration on Human Rights Defenders,[58] the Declaration on the Protection of all Persons from Enforced

---

54 See Stephen P Marks, *Emerging Human Rights: A New Generation for the 1980s?* (1981) 33
RUTGERS L REV 435; Philip Alston, *Conjuring Up New Human Rights: A Proposal for Quality
Control* (1984) 78 AJIL 607; THEODOR MERON, HUMAN RIGHTS LAW-MAKING IN THE UNITED
NATIONS (Clarendon 1986).

55 GA Res 41/120, 4 Dec 1986, A/RES/41/120 recommends principles to guide States in developing
new international human rights instruments. They suggest that proposed new texts should (a) be
consistent with existing norms; (b) be "of fundamental character"; (c) be "sufficiently precise to
give rise to identifiable and practicable rights and obligations"; and (d) provide "realistic and effective implementation machinery". Ibid. at para. 4.

56 Theodor Meron, *Reform of Law-Making in the United Nations: The Human Rights Instance*, (1985)
79 AJIL 664 (1985); Bertram Ramcharan, *Standardsetting: Future Perspectives* in HUMAN RIGHTS:
THIRTY YEARS AFTER THE UNIVERSAL DECLARATION (Th. Meron, ed 1979), 107.

57 UN Commission on Human Rights, Decision 2000/109, Annex, para. 60.

58 GA Res 53/144, UN Doc A/RES/53/144 of 8 Mar 1999.

Disappearance,[59] the Declaration on the Rights of Persons Belonging to National or Ethnic, Religious and Linguistic Minorities,[60] and the Set of Principles for the Protection and Promotion of Human Rights through Action to Combat Impunity.[61] The Special Rapporteur on Human Rights and the Environment submitted a draft Declaration on the topic to the Commission in 1994 and it was still under study when the Commission ceased to function in 2006.

The lengthy process of negotiation may result in texts that are poorly drafted, inconsistent or overlapping with other normative texts. In the opinion of the government of Spain, the poor quality of texts is partly responsible for problems of implementation.[62] Of course, a level of generality may be necessary to achieve consensus. It also allows normative instruments to evolve in response to contemporary needs. The interpretive jurisprudence of human rights bodies can give guidance to States on the meaning of rights and the scope of their obligations, but it also shifts standard-setting away from States to small quasi-judicial expert bodies.

Undoubtedly, human rights standard-setting is a political activity, just as law making in every society is a political activity. One may disagree with the political choices made or question the neutrality of the law maker, but it is impossible to view law making as anything other than a political process. In the UN, the leadership of key States is important in the standard-setting process. One or several States may take the initiative, sometimes out of conviction or sometimes because of domestic political pressure after national reforms have been instituted to address particular problems.

In addition to State leadership, determined lobbying by NGOs and international civil servants working exclusively on human rights issues are a significant factor in agenda setting. Felice Gaer has called human rights NGOs the engine for virtually every advance made by the UN in the field of human rights since its founding.[63]

---

59 GA Res 47/133, UN Doc A/RES/47/133 of 18 Dec 1992.

60 GA Res 47/135, UN Doc A/RES/47/135 of 18 Dec 1992.

61 Commission on Human Rights, Res 2005/81, UN Doc E/CN.4/RES/2005/81 of 21 Apr 2005.

62 Review of the Multilateral Treaty-Making Process, UN Doc ST/LEG/SER.B/21 (1982), 43. See also Richard Lillich, *Civil Rights* in I HUMAN RIGHTS IN INTERNATIONAL LAW: LEGAL AND POLICY ISSUES (T Meron, ed., Clarendon 1984), 115, 121.

63 Felice D Gaer, *Reality Check: Human Rights NGOs Confront Governments at the UN*, in NGOs, THE UN AND GLOBAL GOVERNANCE (Thomas G Weiss and Leon Gordenker eds, Lynne Rienner 1996), 51, 51–3.

One example is Amnesty International's campaign on the death penalty, which led to the drafting of three treaties: the Second Protocol to the ICCPR, the Sixth Protocol to the ECHR, and the Inter-American Protocol to Abolish the Death Penalty.[64] NGOs have successfully aligned with medium and small powers to achieve considerable success. Groups representing torture survivors and other victims of abuse succeeded in obtaining provisions on victim compensation in the Statute of the International Criminal Court through alliance with key States, such as France and Canada.[65] In human rights negotiations, leadership of "repeat players", those with expertise and an impartial commitment to human rights, enhances coalition building.[66] Finally, the media plays a significant role in identifying human rights issues that need UN attention.[67] By documenting abuses, the media may generate public outrage that helps create coalitions of NGOs and others to mobilize action. Compelling media imagery can thus bring an issue forward.

Over time, UN bodies have developed a comprehensive *corpus juris* of human rights. The instruments adopted include general conventions, such as the Covenants, which contain a broad range of human rights. Second, other conventions aim to protect specific human rights, such as freedom from slavery, forced labour, torture and enforced disappearances. Another category establishes norms to protect particular groups of persons, such as women, children, refugees, migrants and indigenous peoples; some of these are directed in particular at eliminating discrimination.

4.4.2   Regional systems

Like the UN system, regional systems have engaged in human rights standard-setting throughout their existence. The European system is characterized by its evolution through the adoption of treaties and protocols, adopted under the aegis of the Council of Europe, to which texts of the EU and the OSCE may be added. The most significant texts of the Council

---

64 American Convention, Protocol to Abolish the Death Penalty, 8 Jun 1990, OAS TS No 73.

65 See generally Megan Hirst, *Victim Participation and Reparations in International Criminal Proceedings*, in ROUTLEDGE HANDBOOK OF INTERNATIONAL HUMAN RIGHTS LAW (Scott Sheeran and Nigel Rodley, eds, Routledge 2013) 683–707.

66 See Leon Gordenker and Thomas G Weiss, *Pluralizing Global Governance: Analytical Approaches and Dimensions*, in NGOs, THE UN, AND GLOBAL GOVERNANCE (n. 63), 17, 31.

67 See Dinah Shelton, *Human Rights*, in MANAGING GLOBAL ISSUES (PJ Simmons and Chantal de Jonge Oudraat eds., Carnegie Endowment for International Peace 2001), 439–40.

of Europe are the 1950 ECHR and its 16 protocols, the 1961 European Social Charter (ESC) with its Protocols, the European Convention for the Prevention of Torture and its Protocols,[68] the European Charter for Regional or Minority Languages,[69] the Framework Convention for the Protection of National Minorities,[70] and the Convention on Human Rights and Biomedicine with its Protocols.[71] Together these form a network of mutually reinforcing human rights protections in Europe.

Within the EU, the law-making powers of Community institutions included adopting directives and regulations prohibiting discrimination between citizens of the Member States and ensuring freedom of movement for workers and equal pay for equal work between men and women, as these topics are explicitly mentioned in the treaties. The general issue of human rights was not originally within the mandate of the EU, however, and much of the standard-setting in human rights initially came through litigation before the European Court of Justice (ECJ). The ECJ read a bill of rights into Community law notwithstanding the absence of reference to human rights within the EC Treaties.

In June 1999 the EU decided to draft a European Charter of Fundamental Rights to cover all rights that pertain to the Union's citizens, in effect combining the guarantees of the ECHR, the ESC and other human rights instruments. A working group consisting of representatives of the Member State governments as well as representatives of the Commission, the Parliament and national parliaments drafted the Charter. The Charter was not concluded as a treaty, due to lack of agreement among the Member States on this point, but was "proclaimed" at the meeting of the Council of the European Union in Nice on 18 December 2000. Thereafter, the Charter became binding upon entry into force of the Treaty of Lisbon.[72]

The Charter did not create new rights but drew together existing guarantees that were to be protected within the EU legal order. The Charter

---

68 European Convention for the Prevention of Torture and Inhuman or Degrading Treatment or Punishment, 26 Nov 1987, ETS No 126.

69 European Charter for Regional or Minority Languages, 5 Nov 1992, ETS No 148.

70 Framework Convention on the Protection of National Minorities, 1 Feb 1995, ETS No 157.

71 Convention on Human Rights and Biomedicine, 4 Apr 1997, ETS No 164; Additional Protocol on the Prohibition of Cloning Human Rights, 12 Jan, 1988, ETS No 168; Additional Protocol concerning Genetic Testing for Health Purposes, 17 Nov 2008, ETS No 203.

72 Treaty of Lisbon, amending the Treaty on the European Union, entry into force 13 Dec 2007, OJ C 306/01.

states in its preamble that the rights it affirms result, in particular, from the constitutional traditions and international obligations common to the Member States, the ECHR, the Social Charters of the Union and the Council of Europe, and the case law of the Court of Justice and of the Eur. Ct. HR. Article 52 § 4 of the Charter provides that, in so far as the Charter recognizes fundamental rights as they result from the constitutional traditions common to the Member States, such rights are to be interpreted in harmony with those traditions. The Charter essentially codified the various fundamental rights the Court of Justice had developed in its extensive case law. The Charter is regularly invoked before and by the Court of Justice in cases that raise human rights issues. In a process of cross fertilisation, the Court of Justice today interprets the Charter with regard to case law developed by the Eur. Ct. HR – indeed it is mandated to do so by Article 52 § 3 of the Charter – and the broader wording of provisions of the Charter and their interpretation by the Court of Justice in turn influence the Strasbourg Court.

Finally, within Europe, the OSCE has engaged in constant standard-setting by utilizing the follow-up process foreseen in Basket IV of the Helsinki Final Act. These follow-up conferences provide a forum to review compliance with human rights commitments and to expand the human rights catalogue through amendment and revision of the HFA. The meetings also have been used to focus public attention on the failure of certain States to live up to their human rights commitments. The normative evolution has been accomplished by the consensus adoption at each conference of a "concluding document" in which the participants proclaim new OSCE commitments or expand, modify or interpret the scope and meaning of existing ones. These documents include discussion of the rights of minorities, the rule of law, and democratic governance, as well as the traditional list of individual rights. In this respect, the OSCE pioneered a holistic approach to human rights. The Eur. Ct. HR has relied on OSCE documents and findings in several cases.[73]

---

73 See *Russian Conservative Party of Entrepreneurs & Others v Russia*, in which the Eur. Ct. HR quoted from the OSCE Final Report on parliamentary elections in the Russian Federation, using it in part to hold that the elections "acclaimed as competitive and pluralistic by international observers" did not unduly restrict the individual applicant's right to take part in free elections. *Ibid.*, 80. The Court also referred to OSCE findings in *Chapman v United Kingdom*, 2001-I EurCtHR 41 (concerning the situation of Roma and Sinti minorities in Europe generally and the United Kingdom specifically) and in *Sukhovetskyy v Ukraine*, 2006-VI EurCtHR 193 (holding that there was no violation in requiring electoral candidates to pay a financial deposit).

The Inter-American system has also expanded its protections over time. The major instruments are: the Inter-American Convention for the Prevention and Punishment of Torture; the Additional Protocol to the American Convention on Human Rights in the Area of Economic, Social and Cultural Rights;[74] the Second Additional Protocol to the American Convention on Human Rights to Abolish the Death Penalty; the Inter-American Convention on the Prevention, Punishment, and Eradication of Violence against Women;[75] and the Inter-American Convention on Forced Disappearance of Persons.[76] On 5 June 2013 the OAS adopted two conventions on the topic of equality and non-discrimination: the Inter-American Convention against Racism, Racial Discrimination, and Related Forms of Intolerance[77] and the Inter-American Convention against All Forms of Discrimination and Intolerance.[78] The reason for adopting two agreements lies in the opposition of some States to including sexual orientation and sexual minorities among the prohibited grounds of discrimination. Important non-binding texts are the Inter-American Democratic Charter and the IACHR's Declaration of Principles on Freedom of Expression and the Principles and Best Practices on the Protection of Persons Deprived of Liberty in the Americas.

Following Europe and the Americas, African States developed their regional approach to human rights protections with additional instruments supplementing the African Charter on Human and Peoples' Rights. The OAU/African Union has adopted a protocol on the rights of women[79] and a treaty on the rights of the child. The African Commission on Human and Peoples' Rights has also adopted declarations and guidelines on freedom of expression, freedom from torture, and rights of access to justice and fair trial. Most of the provisions of the African Convention on the Rights of the Child, adopted in 1999, are modelled after the articles of the UN Convention on the Rights

---

74 Additional Protocol to the American Convention on Human Rights in the Area of Economic, Social and Cultural Rights, 17 Nov 1988, OAS TS No 69, OAS doc OEA/Ser A/42 (SEPF).

75 Inter-American Convention on the Prevention, Punishment, and Eradication of Violence against Women, 9 Jun 1994, No A-61.

76 Inter-American Convention on Forced Disappearance of Persons, 9 Jun 1994, No A-60.

77 Inter-American Convention against Racism, Racial Discrimination, and Related Forms of Intolerance, 5 Jun 2013, AG/RES/2805 (XLIII-O/13).

78 Inter-American Convention against All Forms of Discrimination and Intolerance, 5 Jun 2013, AG/RES/2805 (XLIII-O/13).

79 African Charter Protocol on the Rights of Women in Africa, 13 Sep 2000, OAU Doc No CAB/LEG/66/6.

of the Child. The main distinction between the two documents lies in the African treaty's provisions concerning children's duties, provisions that align with the African Human Rights Charter. An OAU Convention Governing the Specific Aspects of Refugee Problems in Africa protects those who flee a well-founded fear of persecution. The OAU Convention expands the definition of refugee to include "every person who, owing to external aggression, occupation, foreign domination or events seriously disturbing public order in either part or the whole of his country of origin or nationality, is compelled to leave his place of habitual residence in order to seek refuge in another place outside his country of origin or nationality" (Art. 1(2)).

Additionally, the New Partnership for Africa's Development (NEPAD) began in response to the need for an economic programme developed by African leaders to pursue the political and socio-economic development of Africa, especially sustainable growth and the eradication of poverty. The mandate of NEPAD includes human development, which addresses the rights to education and health. NEPAD also includes a component on democracy and political governance, which is based on the premise that democracy and respect for human rights, as well as good governance, are prerequisites for economic development.[80]

The League of Arab States approved the Arab Charter on Human Rights on 15 September 1994, building on earlier texts adopted by regional non-governmental and intergovernmental organizations. Many Arab and international NGOs criticized the 1994 Charter for falling below international standards for human rights, and the treaty never entered into force. The Council of the Arab League subsequently adopted resolutions in 2002 calling for the revision of the Arab Charter. On 24 March 2003 the Council of the Arab League, through Resolution 6032-129, encouraged the Permanent Arab Commission on Human Rights to "modernize" the Arab Charter on Human Rights. Amr Musa, Secretary General of the League, explained that the term "modernization" should be understood as the process to bring Charter provisions into compliance with international standards for human rights. In May 2004 the League adopted a revised version of the Arab Charter on Human Rights, which entered into force on 15 March 2008, after its

---

80 For further information and critiques of NEPAD, see Evarist Baimu, *Human Rights in NEPAD and Its Implications for the African Human Rights System* (2002) 2 AFR HUM RTS LJ 301; Bronwen Manby, *The African Union, NEPAD and Human Rights: The Missing Agenda* (2004) 26 HUM RTS Q 983; Sabelo Gumedze, *The NEPAD and Human Rights* (2006) 22 S AFR J HUM RTS 144.

acceptance by seven States: Algeria, Bahrain, United Arab Emirates, Jordan, Libya, Palestine and Syria. Yemen and Qatar subsequently ratified the Charter.

Within ASEAN, the AICHR, an intergovernmental body, was responsible for drafting the 2012 ASEAN Declaration of Human Rights, but the actual drafting was done by a group of human rights experts appointed by the AICHR. The Working Group's terms of reference were not made public and drafts of the Declaration remained confidential, although some versions were leaked. AICHR held two regional consultations with civil society organizations late in the drafting and some individual members of AICHR organized national consultations. Overall, the UN High Commissioner for Human Rights criticized the process as "not the hallmark of the democratic global governance to which ASEAN aspires" and opined that the process would undermine respect for the declaration.[81]

In sum, standard-setting in international human rights law is a political process in which each organization's member States determine the content of the rights and obligations they are willing to accept. The degree to which experts or civil society may be involved varies considerably from one organization to another.

4.5   Universality and regional diversity

Adoption of the many regional human rights treaties reinforced questions about universality and diversity in human rights law. While regional systems might have raised the risk of fragmentation and undermining of universal norms, each regional system has in fact grounded its guarantees on the UDHR, resulting in a common core of norms on which each system has built. The normative guarantees set forth in the regional instruments often explicitly state the source of their original inspiration in the human rights provisions of the UN Charter and the UDHR. The 1950 ECHR, for example, states in its preamble that it was drafted in order "to take the first steps for the collective enforcement of certain of the rights stated in the Universal Declaration".

Yet, it is undeniable that the systems differ in how certain rights are treated, reflecting regional concerns, priorities and legal traditions.

---

81 OHCHR, Press Release, 8 Nov 2012.

Economic, social and cultural rights were largely excluded from the European Convention, but a decade later were enshrined in the 1961 ESC, which has its own monitoring mechanism and a subsequently added collective complaints procedure. In contrast, the 1948 American Declaration, like the UDHR, proclaims not only civil and political, but also economic, social and cultural rights. Nonetheless, following the European precedent, the 1969 American Convention included only a single article referring to the progressive implementation of economic and social rights. Thereafter, the American States adopted a treaty on economic, social and cultural rights as a protocol to the American Convention rather than enacting a free-standing agreement and made at least some of the rights justiciable before the Inter-American Commission and Court, thus maintaining a unified institutional framework.

The 1981 African Charter on Human and Peoples' Rights included several progressive elements in law and procedure, yet, like the subsequent 2004 Arab Charter, it adopted the model of the earlier regional systems in basing its normative guarantees on the UDHR. It added a requirement, moreover, that the African Commission draw upon universal and other regional standards in interpreting and applying the African Charter. During the drafting process of the African Charter, experts and State representatives relied upon the UDHR and UN Covenants, as well as the European and Inter-American Conventions. Many of the provisions in the African Charter restate universal norms, but there are also divergences that speak to regional specificities. Given the economic situation on the African continent, it is unsurprising that the 1981 African Charter of Human and Peoples' Rights contains civil, political, economic, social and cultural rights in a single instrument. The African Commission emphasized in the case of *SERAC v Nigeria*[82] that all of these rights are binding and justiciable.

The Arab Charter and ASEAN Declaration, like the African Charter, incorporate economic, social and cultural rights. These include core labour rights, social security, the right to an adequate standard of living, the right to health, the right to education, cultural rights and the right to development. The right to self-determination is also guaranteed in the African and Arab Charters, but notably absent from the ASEAN Declaration.

---

82 Comm 155/96, *Social and Economic Rights Center (SERAC) v Nigeria* [2001] AHRLR 60 (AfCHPR, 27 Oct 2001), paras 44, 63.

The 2012 ASEAN Declaration revived the question of regional diversity in part because of the methodology used for its drafting and in part because critics claim some of its provisions fall below global standards. Despite defects in its drafting process, the content of the ASEAN Declaration is rooted in universal norms. The Preamble reaffirms adherence to the ASEAN Charter, in particular respect for and promotion and protection of human rights and fundamental freedoms, "as well as the principles of democracy, the rule of law and good governance", and a "commitment to the Universal Declaration of Human Rights, the Charter of the United Nations, the Vienna Declaration and Programme of Action,[83] and other international human rights instruments to which ASEAN Member States are parties".

ASEAN Articles 10 and 26 affirm all of the civil and political rights and all of the economic, social and cultural rights in the UDHR, as well as the specific rights contained in the ASEAN Declaration itself. Several provisions are quoted verbatim from the UDHR, including Articles 3, 5 and 14, which mirror UDHR Articles 5, 6 and 8, concerning the right to recognition before the law, the right to an enforceable remedy and the prohibition of torture and cruel, inhuman and degrading treatment. Other provisions are expressed in slightly different terms, but with no change in the scope or meaning, while a few add new dimensions to UDHR rights, including the reference to human trafficking in the Article 13 provision banning slavery and servitude with specific mention of the problem of child labour in Article 27, which concerns the right to work.[84] More generally, Article 7 echoes the language of the 1993 Vienna Declaration in proclaiming all human rights to be universal, indivisible, interdependent and interrelated, to be treated in a fair and equal manner, on the same footing and with the same emphasis. At the same time, the Declaration notes that the regional and national context must be considered in the realization of human rights, also reflecting the outcome of the Vienna Conference. It cannot be asserted that the ASEAN Declaration exactly conforms to the UDHR and the Covenants, and the formulation of certain rights may have a significant

---

83 Vienna Declaration and Programme of Action, 12 Jul 1993, A/CONF.157/23, endorsed by GA Res 48/121 (20 Dec 1993).

84 Art. 27(3) provides: "No child or any young person shall be subjected to economic and social exploitation. Those who employ children and young people in work harmful to their morals or health, dangerous to life, or likely to hamper their normal development, including their education should be punished by law. ASEAN Member States should also set age limits below which the paid employment of child labour should be prohibited and punished by law".

impact in the future on their scope and implementation by the ASEAN member States.

Each system has exercised leadership on specific issues, reflecting regional priorities. Europe led the way in calling for abolition of the death penalty, Africa on the right to a safe and healthy environment, the Arab system on rights of the elderly, and the Inter-American system on combating forced disappearances and violence against women. In nearly all instances, global action on these issues followed the regional initiatives, which were led by key States acting in concert with civil society to promote their fundamental values.

4.6   The interpretation of human rights instruments

Human rights standard-setting occurs not only through the adoption of new agreements but also through the dynamic interpretation given to the guaranteed rights and corresponding obligations contained in international instruments. International human rights texts, like many bills of rights within domestic legal systems, are commonly expressed in general terms, leaving ample scope for international bodies to interpret their provisions and for national authorities to differ about the meaning of the rights and obligations stated therein. The dynamic reading given human rights guarantees by global and regional monitoring bodies has prevented a rigid formalism from reducing the relevance of human rights texts as circumstances change and new problems arise. To a certain extent in both the drafting process and interpretation of norms, a leap-frogging phenomenon appears, with a practice originating in one system bounding over the others on a certain issue and other systems subsequently adopting the innovation as a starting point to move further ahead in their own jurisprudence or drafting.

4.6.1   Treaty provisions on interpretation

Choice of law rules or principles of interpretation are implied from or contained in specific provisions of many human rights treaties. The general approach calls for application of the rule most favourable to the individual, making it important to compare the texts of all applicable instruments. Most of the explicit instructions are found in regional treaties, although ICESCR Article 24 and ICCPR Article 46 safeguard the UN Charter as well as the law of various specialized agencies and organs of the UN.

The European Convention Article 60 provides that nothing in the convention "shall be construed as limiting or derogating from any of the human rights and fundamental freedoms which may be ensured under the laws of any High Contracting Party or under any other agreement to which it is a Party". The American Convention's Article 29 more broadly provides that no provision of the Convention can be interpreted to restrict a right recognized in the national or international law applicable to a State Party, allowing reference to customary international law as well as treaties and domestic law. Article 29 further allows reference to or application of the American Declaration and "other international acts of the same nature" as well as "other rights or guarantees that are inherent in the human personality or derived from representative democracy as a form of government".

The African Charter confers the broadest interpretive mandate among the regional instruments. Its Article 60 is comprehensive in calling on the African Commission to "draw inspiration from international law on human and peoples' rights", explicitly mentioning the UN Charter, the UDHR and other instruments adopted by the UN, including those of the UN specialized agencies. Article 61 adds a list of subsidiary means to determine principles of law; these include other general or special international conventions, African practices "consistent with international norms on human and peoples' rights", customs generally accepted as law, and general principles of law recognized by African States as well as legal precedents and doctrine. The African court is similarly directed in Protocol Article 7 to apply the provisions of the African Charter and "other human rights instruments". The African Commission uses Articles 60 and 61 to refer to international agreements and declarations, as well as the pronouncements of UN treaty bodies and the jurisprudence of other regional bodies. Using Articles 60 and 61 the Commission has implied rights into the Charter, including the rights to food and housing, and identified and applied the law most favourable to the rights of individuals and groups in Africa.

4.6.2   The Vienna Convention on the Law of Treaties

In addition to applying specific treaty provisions regarding interpretation, human rights tribunals have recourse to the general rules of treaty interpretation contained in VCLT Article 31. Its first paragraph provides that: "A treaty shall be interpreted in good faith in accordance with the ordinary meaning to be given to the terms of the treaty in their context and in the light of its object and purpose". Article 31(2) defines the "context" to include any preamble and annexes to the treaty as well as any other related agreements. Article 31(3) further broadens the interpretive methodology in requiring decision makers to take into account, together with the context:

(a) any subsequent agreement between the parties regarding the interpretation of the treaty or the application of its provisions;

(b) any subsequent practice in the application of the treaty which establishes the agreement of the parties regarding its interpretation;

(c) any relevant rules of international law applicable in the relations between the parties.

By beginning the search for meaning with the text, the VCLT seems to suggest following the traditional approach of international law whereby restrictions on State sovereignty are not presumed, and treaty obligations are thus to be read narrowly to preserve State freedom of action.[85] Yet, context is also cited and is important: the ICJ,[86] which refers to the VCLT rules as a codification of customary international law,[87] determines the meaning of a treaty text by taking into account "all the consequences which normally and reasonably flow from the text".[88] With respect to human rights instruments, tribunals generally give primary place to the object and purpose of such treaties. The Eur. Ct. HR, for example, has held that it is necessary "to seek the interpretation that is most appropriate to realise the aim and objective of

---

85 As first enunciated in the *Lotus* case: "International law governs relations between independent States. The rules of law binding upon States therefore emanate from their own free will as expressed in conventions or by usages generally accepted as expressing principles of law and established in order to regulate the relations between these co-existing independent communities or with a view to the achievement of common aims. Restrictions upon the independence of States cannot therefore be presumed". *The Case of The SS Lotus (France v Turkey)* 1927 PCIJ (Ser A) no 9 (1927).

86 See *Avena and Other Mexican Nationals (Mexico v United States of America)* 2004 ICJ 37–48 at para. 83 (31 Mar).

87 In the *Fisheries Jurisdiction* case, the ICJ included as custom other provisions of the VCLT, stating in para. 36 that "Article 62 of the Vienna Convention on the Law of Treaties, ... may in many respects be considered as a codification of existing customary law on the subject of the termination of a treaty relationship on account of change of circumstances" *Fisheries Jurisdiction Case* 1973 ICJ 63 at para. 36 (2 Feb).

88 Ibid., 121.

the treaty, not which would restrict to the greatest possible degree the obligation undertaken by the Parties".[89]

VCLT Article 31 has played a critical role in the development of a dynamic, evolutionary approach to treaty interpretation that is widely applied by human rights bodies. The VCLT relegates the drafting history of a treaty to a subsidiary role in Article 32: recourse to such history is called a "supplementary means of interpretation". The VCLT provisions omit any reference to the agreed intention of the drafters of a treaty, perhaps viewing that such intent is implicitly expressed in those provisions that indicate the object and purpose of the agreement. The subsidiary role of drafting history (*travaux préparatoires*) may also reflect an understanding of the compromises and sometimes deliberate obfuscation necessary to reach agreement on multilateral treaties. When numerous States engage in drafting an agreement in multiple languages,[90] the search for a common intention as to the meaning of a specific provision or word may be futile.

Most governments, courts and human rights bodies regard the VCLT rules as a codification of customary international law. As discussed further below, the Eur. Ct. HR, in *Golder v UK*,[91] established that the VCLT rules concerning interpretation apply to the ECHR because they enunciate "generally accepted principles of international law".[92] Other regional bodies also apply the VCLT principles of interpretation, but at the same time, all such bodies have enunciated specific additional principles because of the unique character and object and purpose of human rights treaties.[93]

---

89 *Wemhoff v Germany* (1969) ECHR (Ser A) no 7 at para. 8. See also *Lozidiou v Turkey* (Preliminary Objections) (1995) 38 YEARBOOK OF ECHR 245. ". . . the object and purpose of the Convention as an instrument for the protection of individual human beings requires that its provisions be interpreted an applied so as to make its safeguards practical and effective".

90 On the problem of interpreting treaties drafted in several languages, see D Shelton, *Reconcilable Differences? The Interpretation of Multilingual Treaties* (1997) 20 HASTINGS INT'L & COMP L REV 611.

91 *Golder v UK* (n. 14) at para. 29.

92 See also *Luedicke, Belkacem and Koç v Germany* (1978) 2 EHRR 149 at para. 46.

93 Judge R Bernhardt, *Thoughts on the Interpretation of Human Rights Treaties*, in F MATSCHER AND H PETZOLD, PROTECTING HUMAN RIGHTS: THE EUROPEAN DIMENSION (Carl Heymanns Verlag 1988) 70–71.

4.6.3   Jurisprudence and doctrines of human rights bodies

Using the VCLT rules and the interpretive mandates given to them under their respective treaties, human rights bodies have developed several overarching principles of interpretation. Human rights bodies acknowledge the primacy of the texts of human rights treaties, but also focus intently on their basic purpose, which is the protection of the rights of the individual. Tribunals thus tend to interpret the rights guaranteed in an expansive and dynamic manner, avoiding a static or "originalist" interpretation of the texts.

The concept of "object and purpose" has been of great importance in the jurisprudence of human rights tribunals, which have emphasized the general purpose of such treaties to further human rights. Such reliance on the object and purpose of a treaty is deemed to be justified by VCLT Article 31(1) and particularly appropriate to the field of human rights. From this the most prevalent doctrines that have emerged are the *pro homine* principle, the notion of the *effet utile*, and the evolutionary approach or rule of dynamic interpretation. Applying these doctrines and their broad interpretive mandates, global and regional bodies often seek to identify and apply the most favourable rule to petitioners appearing before them.[94]

In the *Golder* case,[95] the European Court interpreted the scope of the right to a fair trial contained in Convention Article 6 to determine whether that right included the right of access to a court, something not expressly mentioned in the treaty. The Court held it was already implicitly included in Article 6 and therefore did not create any new obligations for the Contracting Parties, despite arguments by the UK government that the Court could not and should not imply any right not written explicitly into the Convention.

The European Court's approach has relied decisively on what it perceives as the uniqueness of human rights treaties, in particular the special non-contractual character of human rights norms. In *Golder*, the Court rejected searching for the original meaning of terms or the

---

94 See, for example, *Compulsory Membership in an Association Prescribed by Law for the Practice of Journalism*, Advisory Opinion OC-5/85 of 13 Nov 1985, 5 Inter-Am Ct HR (Ser A) at para. 52 (1985) finding that if the American Convention and another international treaty are applicable, the rule most favourable to the individual must prevail.

95 *Golder v UK* (n. 14), at 524.

intent of the drafters,[96] instead relying on the object and purpose of the Convention, pursuant to VCLT Article 31(1), and secondly on other provisions of international law, in compliance with Article 31(3)(c).[97] The Court's elaboration of and reliance on the object and purpose of the Convention became the fundamental principle for future interpretation of its provisions.[98]

Two other concepts have emerged from the emphasis on the object and purpose of the European Convention: the concept of a living instrument; and the principle of commonly accepted standards. The two concepts were enunciated together in the *Tyrer* judgment:

> [t]he Court must also recall that the Convention is a living instrument which, as the Commission rightly stressed, must be interpreted in the light of the present-day conditions. In the case now before it the Court cannot but be influenced by the developments and commonly accepted standards in the penal policy of the member States of the Council of Europe in this field.[99]

The European Court maintains this dynamic and evolutionary approach because it finds it is "of critical importance that the Convention is interpreted and applied in a manner which renders its rights practical and effective, not theoretical and illusory".[100] Such an approach helps the Court to address new issues, such as the impact of environmental degradation on human rights.

The search for "commonly accepted standards" greatly extends the examination the European Court can undertake in interpreting the scope of the guaranteed rights. It allows the Court to seek common European values in other national and international legal instruments, binding and non-binding.[101] In an early application of this approach in the *Marckx* case, the Court relied on two conventions not ratified by the majority of the parties to the European Convention at the time, because "[t]he existence of these two treaties denotes that there

---

96 Ibid. 513–14.

97 Ibid. 514.

98 See, for example, *Young, James and Weber v United Kingdom* (1989) 11 EHRR 439.

99 *Tyrer v United Kingdom* (1978) 2 EHRR 1, at para. 30.

100 *Christine Goodwin v The United Kingdom* [GC] 2002-VI; 35 EHRR 18 (2002) at para. 74.

101 See *The use of Article 31 (3) (c) of the VCLT in the Case-Law of the ECTHR: An Effective Anti-Fragmentation Tool or A Selective Loophole for the Enforcement of Human Rights Teleology?* (2010) 31 MICHIGAN JOURNAL OF INTERNATIONAL LAW 621–90.

is a clear measure of common ground in the area among modern societies".[102] Some decisions cross-reference specific articles of other instruments. The Eur. Ct. HR has utilized Article 19(2) of the CCPR to extend the application of Article 10 of the European Convention to cover freedom of artistic expression.[103] It has referred to the UN Convention on the Rights of the Child in regard to education[104] and both the ICCPR and American Convention in regard to the right to a name as part of European Convention Article 8.[105] Most well known is the *Soering* case, where the Court found implicit in Article 3 of the European Convention the obligation in the UN Torture Convention not to extradite someone who might face torture in the destination country.[106]

In 2008 a Grand Chamber of the European Court discussed at length its interpretive methodology in *Demir and Baykara v Turkey*, a case on trade union freedoms. Using the VCLT as a starting point, the Court elucidated that it "is required to ascertain the ordinary meaning to be given to the words in their context and in the light of the object and purpose of the provision from which they are drawn". At issue in the case was the Turkish government's argument that the Court could not rely on international instruments other than the Convention, on the ground that such reliance would risk wrongly creating, by way of interpretation, new obligations not contained in the Convention. In particular, the government contended that an international treaty to which the party concerned had not acceded could not be relied upon against it by reference to VCLT Article 31(3)(c).[107] The Court disagreed.

The Court cited to its earlier jurisprudence on the Convention as a "living instrument", which "must be interpreted in the light of present-day conditions", taking into account "evolving norms of national and international law in its interpretation of Convention provisions".[108] The

---

102 *Marckx v Belgium* (1979) App no 6833/74, 31 ECHR (Ser A), 2 EHRR 330. See generally GEORGE LETSAS, A THEORY OF INTERPRETATION OF THE EUROPEAN CONVENTION ON HUMAN RIGHTS (2nd edn, OUP 2009).

103 *Muller et al v Switzerland* (1988) 133 ECHR (Ser A) at para. 227.

104 *Costello-Roberts v UK* (1993) App no 13134/87, 247C ECHR (Ser A) at para. 27.

105 *Burghartz v Switzerland* (1994) 280B ECHR (Ser A) at para. 24.

106 *Soering v UK* (1989), § 102, 161 ECHR (Ser A) no 161 at para. 88; see also *Gestra v Italy* (1995) Case no 210/92, 80A ECHR Dec & Rep 93.

107 *Demir and Bayakara* (n. 21), para. 55.

108 Ibid., at para. 68, citing *Soering v the United Kingdom* (n. 106), at § 102; *Vo v France* [GC] (2004)

Court pointed to the variety of sources it deemed relevant to this general approach, first looking to other international human rights treaties that are applicable in the particular sphere;[109] and then to "general principles of law recognized by civilized nations" as mentioned in Article 38 § 1 (c) of the Statute of the International Court of Justice. According to the European Court, general principles of law may be identified in texts of universal and regional scope (not only human rights treaties), and in the jurisprudence of international and domestic courts that apply these instruments. In addition, the Court may use "intrinsically non-binding instruments of Council of Europe organs, in particular recommendations and resolutions of the Committee of Ministers and the Parliamentary Assembly".[110] The Court may further support its reasoning by reference to norms emanating from other Council of Europe organs, whether supervisory mechanisms or expert bodies.

When common ground among the norms is found, the Court will not distinguish between sources of law according to whether or not they have been signed or ratified by the respondent State. It is sufficient for the Court that the relevant international instruments denote a continuous evolution in the norms and principles applied in international law or in the domestic law of the majority of Member States of the Council of Europe and show, in a precise area, that there is common ground in modern societies.[111] The result of the approach serves to blur the distinction between binding treaty law and non-binding norms and to further reduce the role of consent in human rights law.

App no 53924/00, § 82, ECHR 2004-VIII; and *Mamatkulov and Askarov v Turkey* [GC] (2005) App nos 46827/99 and 46951/99, §121, ECHR 2005-I.

109 *Ibid.*, at para. 69.

110 *Ibid.*, at para. 77.

111 In the cases of *Christine Goodwin v the United Kingdom*, *Vilho Eskelinen and Others v Finland* and *Sørensen and Rasmussen v Denmark*, the Court was guided by the EU's Charter of Fundamental Rights, even though this instrument was not binding. In the cases of *McElhinney v Ireland*, *Al-Adsani v the United Kingdom* and *Fogarty v the United Kingdom*, the Court took note of the European Convention on State Immunity, which had only been ratified at the time by eight Member States. In the *Öneryıldız v Turkey* judgment, it referred among other texts to the Convention on Civil Liability for Damage resulting from Activities Dangerous to the Environment and the Convention on the Protection of the Environment through Criminal Law. The majority of Member States, including Turkey, had neither signed nor ratified these two Conventions. Finally, in the *Taşkın and Others v Turkey* case, the Court built on its case law concerning Art. 8 of the Convention in matters of environmental protection largely on the basis of principles enshrined in the Aarhus Convention on Access to Information, Public Participation in Decision-making and Access to Justice in Environmental Matters. Turkey had not signed the Aarhus Convention.

Other human rights bodies have similarly emphasized the non-reciprocal and "public order" nature of human rights treaties in seeking to give effect to the object and purpose of the treaties. Thus, the IACHR has said that "the American Convention enshrines a system that constitutes a genuine regional public order the preservation of which is in the interests of each and every State Party".[112] The Inter-American Court in its first decision declared that "the object of international human rights protection is to guarantee the individual's basic human dignity by means of a system established in the Convention".[113] The Inter-American Court thus relies heavily on the *pro homine* and *effet utile* principles,[114] its aim being the effective application of the applicable human rights treaty or treaties.[115]

The Inter-American Court's well-established jurisprudence on interpretation of the American Convention on Human Rights[116] is derived in large part from the express mandate it is given by Article 29. While the Court has deferred to the VCLT norms, it has also departed from them on occasion by arguing that human rights law is *lex specialis*. The Inter-American institutions agree that human rights law has to be interpreted according to present-day standards; in other words, agreements are living instruments that are differentiated to a certain degree from classical international law.

Relevant developments in the corpus of international human rights law may be drawn from the provisions of other international and regional human rights instruments.[117] According to the Commission, this allows the American Declaration to be interpreted with reference to the American Convention, "which, in many instances, may be considered to represent an authoritative expression of the funda-

---

112 IACHR, *Nicaragua v Costa Rica*, Report no 11/07, InterState Case 01/06 at para. 197 (2008).

113 *In the Matter of Viviana Gallardo et al v Government of Costa Rica*, Decision of 13 Nov 1981 I-A Court HR 12, OEA/Ser.L/V/III.7 doc 13, Ser A and B No G/101/81 at para. 15 (1982).

114 Lucas Lixinski, *Treaty Interpretation by the Inter-American Court of Human Rights Expansion at the Service of Unity of International Law* (2010) 21 EJIL 588.

115 Antonio Cancado Trindade, *Towards a New* Jus Gentium *(II): General Course on Public International Law*, 317 RCADI (1) 2006, 60.

116 See Lixinski (n. 114) 585–604.

117 See Advisory Opinion OC-10/89, para. 37; Advisory Opinion OC-16/99, para. 115; IACHR, *Juan Raul Garza (United States)*, Report No 52/01, Case 12.243, I/A Comm, Annual Report of the IACHR 2000 at para. 89 (2000).

mental principles set forth in the American Declaration".[118] The Inter-American Court or Commission has also referred to the European Convention,[119] the ICCPR,[120] the Geneva Conventions of 1949,[121] the United Nations Convention on the Rights of the Child,[122] the Vienna Convention on Consular Relations[123] and various binding and non-binding instruments concerning indigenous peoples, including ILO Convention No 169 concerning Indigenous and Tribal Peoples in Independent Countries and the United Nations Declaration on the Rights of Indigenous Peoples (UNDRIP),[124] as well as decisions of the European Human Rights Commission and the Court.[125] The I-A Court has explicitly stated, however, that it will use cases decided by the European Court and the Human Rights Committee when their value is to augment rights protection[126] and not when it would serve to import restrictions from other systems.[127]

---

118 See IACHR, *Report of the Situation of Human Rights of Asylum Seekers within the Canadian Refugee Determination System*, Doc. OEA/Ser.L/V/II.106, Doc. 40 rev. (28 Feb 2000), para. 38; *Garza Case* (n. 117), at paras 88, 89.

119 See, for example, *Compulsory Membership in an Association Prescribed by Law for the Practice of Journalism* (n. 94), at paras 43–6; and *Enforceability of the Right to Reply or Correction* Advisory Opinion OC-07 I-A Court HR, Ser A, No. 7 at para. 25 (1986).

120 Ibid.; *Proposed Amendments to the Naturalization Provisions of the Political Constitution of Costa Rica*, Advisory Opinion OC-04, I-A Court HR, Ser A No 4 at paras 50–51 reprinted in 5 HRLJ 161 (1984).

121 See, for example, IACHR *Juan Carlos Abella (Argentina)* Report No 55/97, Case 11.137, Annual Report of the IACHR 1998 at paras 157–71 (1998).

122 See, for example, *Villagrán Morales Case*, I-A Court HR, Ser C, No. 63 (19 Nov. 1999) at para. 188; IACHR *Michael Domingues (United States)* Report No 62/02, Case 12.285, Annual Report of the IACHR 2002 at para. 56 (2002).

123 See, for example, Advisory Opinion OC-16/99 (n. 116), para. 137; IACHR, *Ramón Martinez Villareal (United States)* Report No 52/02, Case No 11.753, Annual Report of the IACHR 2002 at para. 77 (2002).

124 See, for example, IACHR *Mary and Carrie Dann (United States)* Report No 75/02, Case 11.140, Annual Report of the IACHR 2002 at para. 127 (2002).

125 *The Effect of Reservations on the Entry into Force of the American Convention*, Advisory Opinion OC-2/83, I-A Court HR, Ser A, No. 2 (1983) at para. 29; *Proposed Amendments*, para. 56; *The Word Laws in Article 30 of the American Convention on Human Rights*, Advisory Opinion OC-6/86, I-A Court HR at para. 20 (1986); *Compulsory Membership* (n. 94), paras 43–6, 69; *In the Matter of Viviana Gallardo et al v Government of Costa Rica* (n. 113), paras. 26–27; *Gangaram Panday Case*, I-A Court HR, Ser C No 16 (1994) at para. 39; *Caballero Delgado and Santana Case* (Preliminary Objections) I-A Court HR, Ser C No 22 (1994).

126 *Compulsory Membership* (n. 94), at para. 52 ("if in the same situation both the American Convention and another international treaty are applicable, the rule most favourable to the individual must prevail").

127 Ibid. at para. 51 (the comparison of the American Convention with the provisions of other international instruments should never be used to read into the Convention restrictions that are not grounded in its text).

The African Commission has adopted these same approaches to treaty interpretation. In *Kevin Mgwanga Gunme v Cameroon*, the Commission had to interpret and clarify its understanding of "peoples' rights" within the African Charter.[128] The Commission looked to the drafting history, noting that the drafters of the Charter refrained deliberately from defining this concept. Nor had the concept been defined under international law, although the Commission found recognition that certain objective features attributable to a collective of individuals may warrant considering them to be a "people".[129] Apart from an inconclusive look at the Charter's drafting history, the Commission relied on reports done by UNESCO, but also reflected on the term "people" in the overall context and structure of the African Charter and its own jurisprudence and reports. It concluded that peoples' rights are as important as individual rights and they must be given protection. The minimum that can be said of peoples' rights is that "each member of the group carries with him/her the individual rights into the group, on top of what the group enjoys in its collectivity, in other words, common rights which benefit the community such as the right to development, peace, security, a healthy environment, self-determination, and the right to equitable share of their resources".[130] The African Commission has also adopted the *pro homine* principle and stated that the Charter should be interpreted as a living document.

The decisions of the African Commission have adopted several doctrines established in European and Inter-American case law: presumption of the truth of the allegations from the silence of government,[131] the notion of continuing violations,[132] continuity of obligations in

---

128 *Kevin Mgwanga Gunme v Cameroon*, Afr. Comm'n HPR Comm no 266/2003, EX.CL/529 (XV), 45th Ordinary Session, Annex 4 (2009).

129 Case of the Mayagna Community (SUMO) *Awas Tingni Community v Nicaragua* (Merits, Reparations and Costs) I-A Court HR, Ser C No 79 (31 Aug 2001), para. 169.

130 Ibid., para. 176.

131 See for example, the African Commission's decisions in communications 59/91, 60/91, 87/93, 101/93 and 74/92. *Free Legal Assistance Group, Lawyers' Committee for Human Rights, Union Interafricaine des Droits de l'Homme* Afr Comm'n HPR Comm no 98/93, 13th Ann Activity Rep (2000), *Les Temoins de Jehovah v Zaire* Afr Comm'n HPR Comms nos 25/89/47/90, 56/91, 100/93, Afr Comm HPR Annex VIII at 7 (1995). Art. 42 of the Regulations of the Inter-American Commission allows it to presume the facts in the petition are true if the government fails to respond to the complaint.

132 See for example, *Muthuthurin Njoka v Kenya* Afr Comm'n HPR Comm 142/94 at 13 reprinted in (1997) 18 HRLJ 29; *Annette Pagnoulle on behalf of Abdoulaye Mazou v Cameroon* Afr Comm'n HPR Case 39/90, Comm 64/92 reprinted in (1997) 18 HRLJ 29.

spite of a change of government,[133] State responsibility for failure to act,[134] and the presumption that the State is responsible for custodial injuries.[135] In regard to admissibility of communications, the African Commission, like other regional bodies, has found that some so-called remedies are "not of a nature that requires exhaustion" because they are discretionary and non-judicial.[136]

Finally, human rights tribunals have insisted that terms in the treaties have their own meaning regardless of national legislation, applying the principle of autonomous interpretation.[137] The difference in outcome resulting from prioritizing the object and purpose over a strictly textual approach can be seen in the specific example of the right to property as interpreted in the Inter-American and African jurisprudence. The right is guaranteed by Article 21 of the American Convention, a provision whose interpretation was presented to the Inter-American Court for the first time in the case of the *Mayagna Community (SUMO) Awas Tingni v Nicaragua*.[138] The Court explained that the terms of an international human rights treaty have an autonomous meaning. Faced with a textual interpretation based on the intent of the drafters, which would have denied protection to indigenous communal land rights or a more expansive reading of the term property, the I-A Court concluded that "Article 21 of the Convention protects the right to property in a sense which includes, among others, the rights of members of the indigenous communities within the framework of communal property, which is also recognized by the Constitution of Nicaragua".[139] The Court ordered Nicaragua, inter alia, to delimit, demarcate and title the Mayagna territory and in the meantime take no state action that would affect the territory in any way and abstain from acquiescing in any action by third parties that would have such impact.[140]

---

133 *Jean Yaovi Degli, Union Interafricaine des Droits de l'Homme, Commission International de Juristes v Togo* Afr Comm'n HPR Joined Cases 83/92, 88/93 and 91/93 (2000).

134 *Commission Nationale des Droits de l'homme et des Libertés v Chad* Afr Comm'n HPR Comm 74/92 (1995).

135 In the European system, see *Tomasi v France* (1992) 241 ECHR (Ser A) no 19 at paras 40, 41.

136 See Comm 104/94, 141/94, 145/95 (joined) *Constitutional Rights Project and Others v Nigeria* [2000] AHRLR 227 (AfCHPR 1999), p. 3.

137 See for example, *Engel and Others v The Netherlands* App nos 5100/71, 5101/71, 5102/71, 5354/72 and 5370/72 (ECtHR, 8 Jun 1976).

138 *Case of the Mayagna (Sumo) Awas Tingni Community* Judgment of 31 Aug 2001 Inter-Am Ct HR (Ser C) no 79 (2001).

139 Ibid., at para. 148.

140 Ibid., at para. 153.

The fact that the various regional bodies find each other's interpretations to be persuasive in supporting their own views helps to strengthen the decisions and develop a common approach to interpretation that results in greater uniformity and universality in favour of the effective application of human rights guarantees. In general, the judges and the commissioners have been willing to substantiate or give greater authority to their interpretations of the rights guaranteed by referencing not only their own prior case law but the decisions of other global and regional bodies. To the extent that this results in progressive convergence of human rights norms, it is in large part stimulated by victims and their lawyers. They submit memorials that draw attention to the relevant case law of other systems and help to expand human rights protections by obtaining a progressive ruling in one system, then invoking it in another. This tendency is enhanced by the liberal standing rules of the Inter-American and African systems. The resulting progressive development of regional human rights law indicates that no human rights lawyer should rely solely on the jurisprudence of a single system in pleading a case.

4.7   Regime conflict and normative hierarchy

Systems of law usually establish a hierarchy of norms based on the particular source from which the norms derive. In national legal systems, it is commonplace for the fundamental values of society to be given constitutional status and afforded precedence in the event of a conflict with norms enacted by legislation or adopted by administrative regulation; administrative rules themselves must conform to legislative mandates, while written law usually takes precedence over unwritten law and legal norms prevail over non-legal (political or moral) rules. Norms of equal status must be balanced and reconciled to the extent possible. The mode of legal reasoning applied in practice is thus naturally hierarchical, establishing relationships and order among normative statements and levels of authority.[141] In the international legal system, the question of hierarchy of norms involves issues of the nature and structure of international law.

The problem of potential conflict has grown with the "fragmentation of international law", a phrase used by the International Law Commission,

---

141 See Martti Koskenniemi, *Hierarchy in International Law: A Sketch* (1997) 8 EUR J INT'L L 566.

which took up the topic, based on a feasibility study in 2000.[142] As international law has expanded into new subject areas in recent decades, with a corresponding proliferation of international treaties and institutions, conflicts increasingly have arisen between substantive norms or procedures within a given subject area or across subject areas, necessitating means to reconcile or prioritize the competing rules. Conceptual problems abound because almost every purported principle of precedence (for example, *lex specialis derogate lex generali*) has exceptions and no rule establishes when to apply the principle and when to apply the exception. Claims of primacy may be made by those involved in promoting or ensure respect for a particular body of international law. Some human rights institutions, for example, have asserted the priority of human rights guarantees in general over other international law, without necessarily claiming that the entire body of law constitutes *jus cogens*. The UN Committee on Economic, Social and Cultural Rights, for example, in a 1998 statement on globalization and economic, social, and cultural rights, declared that the realms of trade, finance and investment are in no way exempt from human rights obligations.[143] The Committee's concerns were raised a second time in a statement urging WTO members to adopt a human rights approach to trade matters, asserting that the "promotion and protection of human rights is the first responsibility of Governments". The claimed primacy of all human rights law has not been reflected in State practice thus far, although some human rights tribunals appear to be moving towards this view.

The VCLT provides that all treaties should be interpreted according to the rules of international law in force between the parties (Art. 31(3) (c)). It also states that generally, subject to the primacy of the UN Charter, the treaty later in time should prevail when the two instruments concluded by the same parties relate to the "same subject-matter". Determining whether or not two or more instruments relate to the same subject matter can be problematic if no express provision addresses the issue, although rules of interpretation may help to reconcile the conflicts that emerge.

---

142 The Commission subsequently established a Study Group to work on the issue between 2003 and 2006. See Report of the International Law Commission, GAOR 60th Sess, Supp No 10 (A/60/10), chapter XI.

143 See Sabine Schlemmer-Shulte, *Fragmentation of International Law: The Case of International Finance & Investment Law versus Human Rights Law* (2012) PACIFIC MCGEORGE GLOBAL BUSINESS & DEVELOPMENT LJ 409–24; Linos-Alexander Sicilianos, *The Human Face of International Law – Interactions between General International Law and Human Rights: An Overview* (2012) HUMAN RIGHTS LAW JOURNAL 1–11.

Human rights as a distinct field of international law can encounter resistance or problems of coordination with other areas of international regulation. This problem has arisen in particular in considering the human rights implications of international trade or investment law and international environmental law. If a conflict is found to exist, the legal system may establish a hierarchy requiring that priority be given to one body of law over another, allowing it to "trump". This is most likely to occur when a specialized court has been established to enforce a particular body of law. Not surprisingly, human rights courts enforce human rights law and the WTO dispute settlement bodies apply trade law, without evident effort to accommodate the other body of law implicated in the dispute.

5 The rights guaranteed

This chapter summarizes the rights guaranteed and jurisprudence of human rights bodies interpreting some of the rights. As it is not possible to fully analyse all the rights mentioned in international instruments, the chapter examines several rights as examples of the development of human rights jurisprudence.

The human rights catalogue today includes civil, political, economic, social and cultural rights. All these rights are understood as interdependent and indivisible.[1] The early decision to draft separate Covenants for civil and political rights, on the one hand, and economic, social and cultural rights, on the other hand, both reflected and reinforced perceptions common at the time that these constituted separate categories of rights with clear distinctions between them. In part, the division reflected Cold War ideological views about the role of the State. The two categories of rights were also believed to require different measures of implementation, whereby civil and political rights would require that States abstain from interfering with their exercise (negative obligations) while economic, social and cultural rights would demand positive State policies and programmes to ensure the provision of medical care, education, social security and similar rights within this category. In part as a consequence of the negative/positive distinction, civil and political rights were perceived to be capable of domestic enforcement through litigation, while economic and social rights were restricted to the purview of political organs of government.

The stated differences are not as clear in practice as they are in theory. Civil rights like the right to a fair trial or free and fair elections require positive action, including the expenditure of State funds for their effective exercise. Discrimination in education is as justiciable as

---

1 First proclaimed at the 1968 UN Conference on Human Rights in Teheran, this recognition was reaffirmed by a significantly larger UN membership in the Vienna Declaration, which concluded the 1993 UN Conference on Human Rights.

discrimination in voting rights. The right to property does not fit exclusively into either category, but has elements of a civil right and other elements more appropriately considered in the category of economic rights. Both the right to education and the right to property are contained in the first protocol to the ECHR, although other human rights instruments place them with economic and social rights. Even the distinction in international monitoring between the Covenants has blurred with the adoption in 2008 of a petition procedure for the ICESCR.

5.1   The rights in the UDHR and other general instruments

The UDHR begins with an affirmation of the foundation of human rights in human dignity and equality (Art. 1). This statement is supplemented by provisions setting forth basic principles, including equality and non-discrimination (Art. 2) and the obligation of States to create societies and an international order in which human rights can be fully realized (Art. 28), as well as the duty of everyone to respect the rights of others and the need to balance individual rights with the needs of society (Art. 29). The principle of abuse of rights is contained in Article 30, which prohibits activities by any State, group or person aimed at destruction of the rights and freedoms set forth in the Declaration.

UDHR Articles 3–27 contain civil, political, economic, social and cultural rights. Fundamental civil and political rights appear in Articles 3 to 21, including the rights to life, liberty and security; freedom from slavery and servitude; freedom from torture and inhuman treatment or punishment; the right to recognition as a person before the law; freedom from arbitrary arrest, detention or exile; the right to equal protection of the law; the right to an effective remedy; the right to a fair trial; the right to privacy; freedom of movement and residence; the right to a nationality; freedom of thought, conscience and religion; freedom of opinion and expression; freedom of assembly and association; the right to property; and the right to participate in government. All of these rights are stated in general terms without definitions of key terms like torture, fair trial, or servitude. The UDHR list of economic, social and cultural rights includes the right to social security; the right to work; the right to rest and leisure; the right to an adequate standard of living; the right to education; and the right to participate in cultural life, as well as to have legal protection for inventions, authorship and other creative works.

The rights set forth in the UDHR have exerted a profound influence on the content and scope of other human rights instruments at the global and regional levels, as well as on constitutional law since 1948. The 1993 Vienna Declaration reaffirms the commitment of UN member States to the UDHR, a significant statement given the growth in UN membership from 53 to 193 States since adoption of the Declaration.

The ICCPR Articles 1–27 contain substantive rights and general principles on equality and non-discrimination. Unlike the UDHR and some regional instruments, the two Covenants include a common Article 1 that guarantees the right of peoples to self-determination. Jurisprudence of the Human Rights Committee[2] considers that such a collective right is excluded from the procedure of complaints under the Optional Protocol to the ICCPR, which only extends to *individuals* who claim their rights have been violated (although one might also consider the right to protection of the family as such a collective right). All the other rights in the ICCPR are individual and include the right to life; the prohibition on torture, inhuman and degrading treatment or punishment; the prohibition of slavery and forced labour; the right to personal liberty and security; freedom of movement; protection of aliens against arbitrary expulsion; due process guarantees in civil and criminal trials; recognition of legal personality, privacy, freedom of thought, conscience, religion and belief; freedom of opinion, expression and information; freedom of assembly, association and trade unions; right to marry; rights of the child; political rights; equality; and rights of persons belonging to minorities. The ICCPR does not include UDHR rights to property, nationality and asylum, but adds freedom from imprisonment for debt, the right of all persons deprived of liberty to be treated with humanity and with respect for the inherent dignity of the human person, and children's rights to acquire a nationality and to be accorded measures of protection.

The European Convention originally contained a shorter list of civil and political rights but through protocols has added the right to education (found in the ICESCR), the right to property, free and secret elections, freedom of movement, due process rights for aliens and freedom from collective expulsions, the right to criminal appeals, and prohibition of double jeopardy. The American Convention adds a right of reply and correction, right to a name, and a prohibition of prior

---

2 *Bernard Ominayak Chief of the Lubicon Lake Band v Canada* CCPR Comm no 167/1984, Report of the HRC, Vol II, GAOR 46th Sess UN Doc Supp no 40, A/45/40, 1–30 (26 Mar 1990).

censorship. Other regional conventions and declarations generally follow the ICCPR in respect to civil and political rights, although the ASEAN Declaration is notable in not mentioning freedom of association and the African Charter does not include the right to privacy.

The ICESCR guarantees, broadly, the right to work, including fair and non-discriminatory conditions of employment; trade union freedoms; the right to social security; the right to protection of the family; the right to an adequate standard of living, including the right to food, clothing and housing; the right to health; the right to education; and the right to culture. Most of the rights are stated in general terms, lacking the detail found, for example, in comparable ILO Conventions, but they have benefitted from subsequent CESCR general comments and the work of UN rapporteurs on topics like the right to housing and the right to food. Many of the ICESCR rights are reaffirmed in other instruments, including the Convention on the Rights of the Child, the CERD, and the CEDAW, as well as certain ILO and UNESCO Conventions. At the regional level, the European Social Charter, the Protocol of San Salvador to the American Convention, the African Charter on Human and Peoples' Rights, the 2004 Arab Charter of Human Rights, and the 2012 ASEAN Declaration also contain economic, social and cultural rights.

The more recently adopted African, Arab and ASEAN instruments include rights not mentioned in the earlier global and regional texts. The newer instruments have provisions on the right to development, environmental rights, freedom from human trafficking, the rights of the elderly and, in the case of the Arab and ASEAN instruments, the rights of persons with disabilities. The ASEAN Declaration adds mention of migrant workers as well. The African Charter is unique in its inclusion of a section on peoples' rights: self-determination, permanent sovereignty over natural resources, the right to development, the right to peace and security, and the right to "a general satisfactory environment favourable to their development". The Arab Charter prohibits trafficking in human organs and the exploitation of children in armed conflict. Article 25 also guarantees cultural rights, including those of language and religion, to persons belonging to minorities.

In addition to the general human rights instruments that have been adopted, other treaties and declarations address particular rights or particular groups. The rights to be free from torture and cruel, inhuman and degrading treatment or punishment, as well as to be free from forced disappearance, have both been elaborated in specific global and regional treaties that define the terms and provide more detailed obligations to prevent, prosecute and punish violations of these rights. The UN Convention against Torture (CAT) applies to acts of torture committed "by or at the instigation of or with the consent or acquiescence of a public official or other person acting in an official capacity". Torture is "any act by which severe pain or suffering, whether physical or mental, is intentionally inflicted on a person" for one of the purposes stated in the agreement. The States Parties must ensure that all acts of torture are criminal offences under their law and treat torture as an extraditable offence. Expulsion or return of a person to a country where there is a danger that the person would be subjected to torture is prohibited. There are no exceptions to the obligations in this treaty. Parallel regional treaties against torture have been adopted in Europe and the Americas, although the former does not define torture. In practice the Eur. Ct. HR utilizes the CAT definition.

The core UN agreements adopted in addition to the Covenants mostly concern identifiable groups that are deemed to benefit from further legal protection: racial and ethnic groups, women, children, migrant workers, and persons with disabilities. The CERD includes a long list of civil, political, economic, social and cultural rights to which the obligation to eliminate racial discrimination applies. The CERD definition of discrimination and its provisions on the duty to prevent and redress discrimination and secure equality have been highly influential in the drafting of later treaties addressing other types of discrimination, such as that against women and persons with disabilities. The Migrant Workers Convention is an exception, as it distinguishes between the rights to be afforded all migrant workers irrespective of their legal status (Arts 8–24), the rights of lawfully resident migrants (Part IV) and the rights of those in particular categories of employment (Part V). A key provision establishes that in respect of terms and conditions of work, migrants shall enjoy treatment not less favourable than that which applies to the employment of nationals of the State (Art. 25(1)).

The Convention on the Rights of the Child, the most widely ratified among UN human rights treaties, recognizes a full catalogue of civil, political, economic, social and cultural rights for those below the age of 18. The guiding principle of the Convention is that "in all actions concerning children, whether undertaken by public or private social welfare institutions, courts of law, administrative authorities or legislative bodies, the best interests of the child shall be a primary consideration".

Two optional protocols to the Convention, adopted by the General Assembly on 25 May 2000, are designed to strengthen the protections afforded children. The first optional protocol, concerning the involvement of children in armed conflicts, aims to raise the minimum age of persons participating in armed conflicts to 18. States Parties are to take all feasible measures to ensure that members of their armed forces under the age of 18 years do not take a direct part in hostilities; they shall also ensure that persons below the age of 18 years are not forced to serve in their armed forces. The laws on voluntary recruitment are to include special measures to protect those under 18. In one of the rare provisions addressing the conduct of non-State actors, Article 4 provides that armed groups that are distinct from the armed forces of a State should not, under any circumstances, recruit or use in hostilities persons under the age of 18 years. The second Optional Protocol deals with the sale of children, child prostitution and child pornography. Each State Party must ensure that, as a minimum, the acts and activities specified in the Protocol are made criminal, whether such offences are committed within their territory or outside, on an individual or organized basis.

Global and regional human rights law contains a set of special norms concerning indigenous and tribal peoples. While no general international human rights treaty mentions indigenous peoples, the ICCPR has two relevant provisions (Arts 1 and 26) and the broad definition of racial discrimination in the CERD extends to indigenous and tribal peoples.[3] In addition ILO Convention No 169 and the 2007 UN Declaration on the Rights of Indigenous Peoples provide specific guarantees for indigenous peoples and communities, including the right of self-determination, "the heart and soul of the declaration".[4] Articles 3 and 4 of the Declaration specify a right of (internal) self-determination, while other provisions guarantee rights of prior consultation and participation, and, in particular, rights to ancestral lands, territories and resources. The I-A system has developed considerable jurisprudence

---

3 See Committee on the Elimination of Racial Discrimination, General Recommendation No 23, para. 4 (calling on States to take certain measures to recognize and ensure the rights of indigenous peoples); see also Committee on the Elimination of Racial Discrimination, General Recommendation No 21, Right of Self-Determination, Report of the Committee on the Elimination of Racial Discrimination, UN GAOR, 51st Sess, Supp No 18, Annex V, UN Doc A/51/18 (8 Mar 1996), paras 1, 4.

4 Quoted in INDIGENOUS PEOPLE, THE UNITED NATIONS AND HUMAN RIGHTS 46 (Pritchard ed., Federation Press 1998).

on the rights of indigenous and tribal peoples[5] and other standard-setting has been done by the UN Rapporteur on the rights of indigenous peoples.

5.2   An overarching norm: equality and non-discrimination

Although the UN Charter frequently mentions human rights, it specifies only the principle of equal rights and self-determination of peoples and the right to equality and non-discrimination in the enjoyment of rights. The UN Charter states as one of its objectives "to develop friendly relations among nations based on respect for the principle of equal rights and self-determination of peoples". Some of the original UN member States had a strong interest in the issue of decolonization and pressed to include the topic of self-determination in the Charter. In addition, member States recognized and reacted to the pervasive racism that inspired the Holocaust. Thus, with one exception in Article 62, each time the phrase "human rights and fundamental freedoms" appears in the UN Charter, the phrase is followed by the words "without discrimination on the basis of race, sex, language or religion". The combined focus on equality and self-determination has directed much of the work of the UN political bodies on human rights issues.[6] A delegate to the UN General Assembly's Third Committee once claimed that "the United Nations Organization had been founded principally to combat discrimination in the world".[7] Commentators agree that equality and non-discrimination "are central to the human rights movement".[8]

In sessions of the General Assembly, racial discrimination has been the topic most often on the agenda, taking up almost as much time as discussion of all civil and political rights combined. In 1962 the

---

5 See IACHR, *Indigenous And Tribal Peoples' Rights Over Their Ancestral Lands and Natural Resources: Norms and Jurisprudence of the Inter-American Human Rights System*, OEA/Ser.L/V/II, Doc 56/09, 30 Dec 2009.

6 See ANTONIO CASSESE, SELF-DETERMINATION OF PEOPLES: A LEGAL REAPPRAISAL (CUP 1995), 36–7.

7 UN Doc A/C.3/SR.l 00, p. 7.

8 Jerome Shestack, *The Jurisprudence of Human Rights* in HUMAN RIGHTS IN INTERNATIONAL LAW: LEGAL AND POLICY ISSUES, Vol. 2 (Th. Meron ed., Clarendon 1984), 101. See also John P Humphrey, *Preventing Discrimination and Positive Protection for Minorities: Aspects of International Law* (1986) 27 LES CAHIERS DE DROIT 23, 27.

General Assembly established the Special Committee on the policies of apartheid of the Government of South Africa. Several years later, in Resolution 2145 (XXI) of 27 October 1966, the General Assembly terminated South Africa's mandate over South-West Africa (now Namibia). In a 1971 advisory opinion, the ICJ agreed that South Africa's denial of human rights and fundamental freedoms on the basis of race constituted "a flagrant violation of the purposes and principles of the Charter". The ICJ thus emphasized the importance of non-discrimination in the language of the Charter and the practice of the UN organs.

Although human rights texts expressly recognize the rights of "all persons", in practice probably few if any of the rights are absolutely guaranteed in full equality to all humans at all times. Even when a law is neutral on its face it may have a disparate impact on particular groups or individuals, leading those affected to claim that the measure is discriminatory. In addition, consistency of treatment may fail to ensure the broader aims of equality, if applied without taking into account differences as well as similarities within society. In principle, non-discrimination calls for treating equally those who are in an equal position and treating unequally those who are in unequal positions insofar as relevant criteria are concerned. The difficulty lies in determining what differences constitute relevant criteria among individuals and groups. The problem is two-fold: determining what attributes have relevance and deciding what reasons are sufficient to make distinctions based on those attributes. Although international human rights instruments have core equality provisions in common, variation in language of the different texts, the interpretations given their provisions, and the nature of the cases considered, produce different results.

5.2.1 Textual references

The UDHR begins its Preamble by reaffirming human solidarity, recognizing the inherent dignity and "equal and inalienable rights of all members of the human family". In Article 1 it proclaims that "[a]ll human beings are born free and equal in dignity and rights". Article 2 adds that everyone is entitled to all the rights in the UDHR "without distinction of any kind, such as race, colour, sex, language, religion, political or other opinion, national or social origin, property, birth or other status". The use of the words "such as" and inclusion of "other status" make clear that this list is not exhaustive. Article 7 provides for equality before the law and equal protection of law, as well as equal protection against discrimination and incitement to discrimination. This provision is reinforced by Article 10, which guarantees everyone "in full equality" a fair and public hearing before an independent and impartial tribunal. The right to marry, in Article 16, is guaranteed "without any limitation due to race, nationality or religion". Men and women are provided equal rights to marriage, during marriage and at its dissolution. Article 23 assures everyone the right to equal pay for equal work. Express distinctions are nonetheless made in some provisions: prohibiting imposition of the death penalty on those under the age of 18 at the time of the offence and on pregnant women (ICCPR Art. 6(5)); requiring the separation of juvenile and adult offenders and accused persons from those convicted (ICCPR Art. 10); and limiting some political rights to citizens of a State (ICCPR Art. 25).

Among the early human rights treaties, only CERD, ILO Convention No 111 (Employment and Occupation), and the 1960 UNESCO Convention on Discrimination in Education defined the word discrimination. According to Article 1 of the UNESCO Convention, discrimination means "any distinction, exclusion, limitation or preference which, being based on race, colour, sex, language, religion, political or other opinion, national or social origin, economic condition or birth, has the purpose or effect of nullifying or impairing equality of treatment in education".[9] Article 2(1) permits States to establish separate educational systems for boys and girls and is problematic because it requires only "equivalent" access to education and "equivalent" courses of study. CEDAW's Article 10 strengthened the educational guarantees for girls and women by requiring that States provide the "same" rather than "equivalent" educational opportunities.[10] States Parties are required to change laws and practices that involve discrimination in education.[11] They are also required to take positive measures to guarantee non-discrimination in education by private actors.[12]

The ICCPR restates many of the provisions of the UDHR, but also imposes corresponding obligations on each State Party to respect and ensure the rights recognized by the Covenant to all individuals within its territory and subject to its jurisdiction "without distinction of any kind, such as race, colour, sex, language, religion, political or other

---

9 UNESCO Convention against Discrimination in Education, 14 Dec 1960, 429 UNTS 93.
10 Ibid.
11 Ibid.
12 Ibid.

opinion, national or social origin, property, birth or other status". The General Assembly added Article 3, which specifies the equal rights of men and women, to emphasize and reinforce the obligation of non-discrimination. Article 26 calls for effective protection against discrimination with regard to all rights and benefits recognized by law and Article 20 imposes a duty to prohibit any advocacy of national, racial or religious hatred that constitutes incitement to discrimination, hostility or violence. Taken together, the provisions make non-discrimination the dominant single theme in the Covenant.

Like the ICCPR, the ICESCR prohibits discrimination of any kind in respect to the enjoyment of rights within the scope of the Covenant, with one notable and controversial exception. Article 2(3) provides that "developing countries, with due regard to human rights and their national economy, may determine to what extent they would guarantee the economic rights recognized in the present Covenant to non-nationals". Many Western countries argued that this provision had destroyed the basic principle of non-discrimination,[13] but defenders said it was necessary to eliminate economic inequality between nationals of developing and developed countries; that is, the distinction allowed for a proportionate response to a relevant distinction.

The definitions subsequently included in CEDAW and the Migrant Workers Convention provide that for the purpose of each treaty, discrimination means any distinction, exclusion or restriction (CERD adds "or preference") which has the effect or purpose of impairing or nullifying the recognition, enjoyment or exercise on an equal footing of human rights (CERD adds "and fundamental freedoms") in the political, economic, social, cultural (CEDAW adds civil) or any other field (CERD adds "of public life"). Unlike Article 2(1) of the ICCPR and Article 14 of the ECHR, which only address distinctions in the enjoyment of rights recognized by the respective treaties, CERD and CEDAW prohibit discrimination in respect to all rights and freedoms guaranteed by national and international law. Special temporary measures of preferential treatment for women or disadvantaged racial or ethnic groups or individuals are not considered discrimination if their sole purpose is to secure their advancement towards equality (CERD, Art. 1(4) and CEDAW Art. 4).

---

13 UN Doc A/C3/SR.1207, p. 362. The paragraph was narrowly adopted 41–38, with 12 abstentions. UN Docs A/5365, pp. 22–3; A/C3/L.1027/revs pp. 1–4; A/5365, pp. 15–16.

On the regional level, Article 14 of the ECHR proscribes discrimination in the enjoyment of Convention rights. Article 14 has been called "an almost parasitic provision, which has no independent existence as it is linked exclusively to the enjoyment of the rights and freedoms laid down in the other substantive provisions".[14] Out of concern with the limitations of Convention Article 14, the Council of Europe concluded Protocol No 12, which entered into force in April 2005. The Protocol prohibits discrimination in the enjoyment of any right set forth by law, in recognition of the need for an independent or free-standing right to strengthen the Convention's protection of equality. The preamble to Protocol 12 reaffirms, however, that the principle of non-discrimination does not prevent States from taking positive action, provided that it is objectively and reasonably justified.

Within the EU, Article 13 of the EC Treaty gives the EU specific powers to combat discrimination on grounds of sex, racial or ethnic origin, religion or belief, age, disability or sexual orientation. Based on this mandate, the Council has passed Directives prohibiting direct and indirect discrimination, including harassment, on grounds of race, religion and belief, disability, age, and sexual orientation related to employment and occupations, including education and vocational training, membership in professional or related bodies; social protection; access to and supply of goods and services; and "social advantages" (for example, concessionary travel on public transport, reduced prices for access to cultural or other events and subsidized meals in schools for children from low-income families).[15]

Article 1(1) of the ACHR and Article 2 of the African Charter affirm the right of all persons to enjoy all guaranteed rights without discrimination. The American Convention's provision broadly prohibits discrimination on grounds that include "any other social condition" suggesting that it is an open-ended prohibition of discrimination, like some UN treaties that prohibit discrimination on the basis of "other status". Article 24 adds a guarantee of equality before the law and equal protection of the law like Article 26 of the ICCPR. In Advisory

---

14 Luzius Wildhaber, *Protection against Discrimination under the European Convention on Human Rights – A Second-Class Guarantee?* (2002) 2 BALTIC YEARBOOK OF INTERNATIONAL LAW 71–2.

15 Council Directive 2000/43/EC, 29 June 2000, implementing the principle of equal treatment between persons irrespective of racial or ethnic origin (the "Race Directive") and Council Directive 2000/78/EC, establishing a general framework for equal treatment in employment and occupation (the "General Framework Directive").

Opinion OC-4/84, the I-A Ct. HR held that Article 1(1) is dependent on linkage to a right guaranteed by the Convention while Article 24 guarantees equality not only in the enjoyment of the rights set forth in the Convention but also in the application of any domestic legal norm.

The General Assembly of the OAS on 5 June 2013 adopted two separate treaties on discrimination: the Inter-American Convention against Racism, Racial Discrimination, and Related Intolerance and the Inter-American Convention against All Forms of Discrimination and Intolerance, concluding a dozen years of drafting work. Both treaties are sweeping in their coverage, with the second one including within its scope any distinction, exclusion, restriction or preference, in any area of public or private life, which affects rights and is based on age; sex; sexual orientation; gender identity and expression; language; religion; cultural identity; political opinions or opinions of any kind; social origin; socio-economic status; educational level; migrant, refugee, repatriate, stateless or internally displaced status; disability; genetic trait; mental or physical health condition, including infectious-contagious condition and debilitating psychological condition; or any other condition. The obligations of States Parties include limiting not only hate speech, but expressions of intolerance, defined as an "action or set of actions or expressions that denote disrespect, rejection, or contempt for the dignity, characteristics, convictions, or opinions of persons for being different or contrary". The provisions could be read to prohibit expressions critical of government policies; in Latin American "contempt" or *desacato* laws have often been used to suppress political dissent, as have criminal defamation laws. Both types of measures seem to be allowed by the new treaties. Article 4 expressly requires States Parties to prevent, eliminate, prohibit and punish the publication, circulation or dissemination, by any form and/or means of communication, including the Internet, of any materials that promote intolerance as broadly defined, as well as teaching materials that include stereotypes and preconceptions.

The African Charter, in addition to its Article 2 general prohibition on discrimination, adds that every individual shall be equal before the law and entitled to equal protection of the law (Art. 3), thus adding a free-standing guarantee of non-discrimination similar to Article 26 of the ICCPR and Article 24 of the American Convention on Human Rights. Article 12(5) addresses the considerable problem of mass and discriminatory expulsion of non-nationals. Unlike other international and regional instruments that focus only on the individual, the African Charter also expressly prohibits domination or discrimination of one group of people by another group, including with respect to economic, social and cultural development. Article 18(3) further provides that each State Party shall ensure the elimination of discrimination against women, as well as protection for the rights of women. On 11 July 2003 the African Union supplemented the Charter with a separate detailed Protocol on the Rights of Women in Africa, which entered into force on 25 November 2005, concentrating on the principle of equality with regard to sex and gender. It prohibits direct and indirect discrimination "in all spheres of life" and promotes positive action.

The 2004 Arab Charter refers to equality in its preamble and in Article 3(a) guarantees all rights and freedoms in the Charter "without distinction on grounds of race, colour, sex, language, religious belief, opinion, thought, national or social origin, wealth, birth or physical or mental disability". This guarantee is supplemented in the following paragraph by an obligation imposed on States Parties to "take the requisite measures to guarantee effective equality in the enjoyment of all the rights and freedoms", so as to ensure protection against all forms of discrimination on any of the grounds mentioned. Two other provisions in the Charter address aspects of this topic in a more controversial manner. First, Article 2 condemns all forms of racism and Zionism as "impediment[s] to human dignity" and calls for efforts to eliminate them. Second, the third paragraph of Article 3 affirms equality between men and women "in the framework of the positive discrimination established in favour of women by the Islamic Shariah and other divine laws and by applicable laws and international instruments". The paragraph does not indicate how to reconcile potential conflicts between these various sources of norms, but obliges States Parties to "take all the requisite measures to guarantee equal opportunities and effective equality between men and women in the enjoyment of all the rights set out" in the Charter.

The ASEAN Declaration Article 2 contains the essential principle of non-discrimination, entitling everyone to all the rights and freedoms set forth in the Declaration without distinction of any kind, such as race, gender, age, language, religion, political or other opinion, national or social origin, economic status, birth, disability, or other status. Efforts to include express mention of "sexual orientation and gender identity" proved contentious and ultimately did not garner the unanimity necessary to be included.

Finally, human rights treaties that permit States to suspend rights by derogation during periods of national emergency generally include a nondiscrimination requirement in the relevant provision. Article 4 of the ICCPR, for example, provides that any measures taken by a State following a notified derogation may "not involve discrimination solely on the ground of race, colour, sex, language, religion or social origin". The language of Article 27 of the American Convention and Article 4 of the Arab Charter is comparable.

The pervasiveness of the treaty obligations of nondiscrimination, equal rights and equality before the law, taken with domestic laws and practices, provide evidence that a norm of non-discrimination in the respect and observance of human rights and fundamental freedoms is now viewed as part of the corpus of customary international law.[16] Indeed, the Inter-American Court termed the prohibition of discrimination part of *jus cogens* in its advisory opinion on the *Juridical Condition of the Undocumented Migrants*. For its part, the former European Commission on Human Rights held that some forms of discrimination may amount to prohibited degrading treatment.[17]

5.2.2   Jurisprudence

Human rights treaty bodies have issued decisions, comments on State reports and general comments applying or articulating definitions of discrimination, determining which groups of individuals are protected, the nature of the prohibited acts or omissions, the purpose or effect of the actions taken, and what distinctions may be permissible. The UN Human Rights Committee, in paragraph 7 of its General Comment 18, defined "discrimination" for purposes of ICCPR Article 2 and Article 26 in language very similar to that contained in several human rights agreements:

> The Committee believes that the term "discrimination" as used in the Covenant should be understood to imply any distinction, exclusion, restriction or preference which is based on any ground such as race, colour, sex,

---

16 See Theodor Meron, *The Meaning and Reach of the International Convention on the Elimination of All Forms of Racial Discrimination* (1985) 79:2 AJIL 283, citing RESTATEMENT OF THE FOREIGN RELATIONS LAW OF THE UNITED STATES (REVISED) sec 702 (referring to the prohibition of racial discrimination as a norm of customary international law).

17 *East African Asians v the United Kingdom*, Apps 14116/88 and 14117/88, 76A ECtHR (1993); 3 EHRR 76 Com Rep.

language, religion, political or other opinion, national or social origin, property, birth or other status, and which has the purpose or effect of nullifying or impairing the recognition, enjoyment or exercise by all persons, on an equal footing, of all rights and freedoms.[18]

Positive action in favour of individuals or groups who have been subject to discrimination is a way to recognize the resulting inequality or even to provide reparations. ICCPR General Comment 4 provides that "Article 3, as Articles 2(1) and 26 . . . requires not only measures of protection but also affirmative action to ensure the positive enjoyment of those rights". General Comment 18 similarly recognized the need for positive action "in order to diminish or eliminate conditions which cause or help to perpetuate discrimination prohibited by the Covenant". The HRC has approved the use of quotas in several of its country reports. For example, in its concluding observations on India, it approved a constitutional amendment in India that reserves one-third of seats in elected local bodies for women. It also approved the practice of reserving elected positions for members of certain tribes and castes.[19]

International tribunals may approve positive action, but they insist that all such action be reasonable, objective and proportionate to its goals. Taking this into account, positive action is often limited in time and scope to respond to the specific disadvantage suffered by a person or group. In General Comment 23 on ICCPR Article 27, the Human Rights Committee stressed that "positive measures by States may also be necessary to protect the identity of a minority and the rights of its members to enjoy and develop their culture and language and to practice their religion, in community with other members of the group" (para. 6.2).

Regionally, European case law has defined discrimination as inequality of an arbitrary nature, or distinctions lacking an objective and reasonable justification or disproportionate in nature.[20] In *Thlimmenos v Greece* the Court held that discrimination also arises if States "without objective and reasonable justification fail to treat differently persons

---

18 CCPR, General Comment 18: Non-discrimination (1989), in *Compilation of General Comments and General Recommendations adopted by Human Rights Treaty Bodies* (HRI/GEN/1/Rev.8), 8 May 2006, p. 185.

19 UN Doc CCPR/C/79/Add.81, para. 10.

20 *Belgian Linguistic Case* App no 1474/62 at sec 1B, para. 10 (1968) 11 Yearbook of the ECHR 832.

whose situations are significantly different".[21] If the applicant proves that a distinction has been made, it is up to the State to prove that the difference in treatment is reasonably and objectively justifiable. "Objective and reasonable justification" is established if the measure in question has a legitimate aim and there is "a reasonable relationship of proportionality between the means employed and the aim sought to be realized".[22] Reasonable distinctions and those that are designed to promote rather than to undermine equality are not discriminatory, as long as they are not disproportionate to their aim. Certain grounds for distinctive treatment may require "particularly serious" reasons in order to be justified.[23]

In the Inter-American system, the IACHR has similarly defined "unequal treatment" for the purpose of American Convention Article 24 as: (i) the denial of a right to someone which is accorded to others; (ii) diminishing a right of someone while fully granting it to others; (iii) the imposition of a duty on some that is not imposed on others; or (iv) the imposition of a duty on some which is imposed less strenuously on others.[24] The Commission has employed a "heightened scrutiny" similar to the "strict scrutiny" employed by some domestic courts or the European Court's demand for "weighty reasons" regarding the justification for different treatment based on race or sex.[25]

In Advisory Opinion OC-18/03, the I-A Court expressed its view that the American Convention obliges States to take positive measures to promote equality, advising that:

> States are obliged to take affirmative action to reverse or change discriminatory situations that exist in their societies to the detriment of a specific group of persons. This implies the special obligation to protect that the State

---

21 *Thlimmenos v Greece* App no 34369/97 at para. 44 (ECtHr, 6 Apr 2000).

22 Ibid. para. 10.

23 *Belgian Linguistic Case* App no 1474/62 Yearbook of the ECHR 832 (1968); *National Union of Police Case* (1975) 18 Yearbook of the ECHR 294; *Sunday Times case* (*The Sunday Times v United Kingdom*) (1979) 2 EHRR 245.

24 *Carlos Garcia Saccone v Argentina* Inter-Am Comm'n HR Case 3/98, OEA/SerL/V/II98 (1998). See also *Marcelino Hanriquez et al v Argentina* Inter-Am Ct HR Case 73/00 (2000), in which the Commission stated that under Art. 24 a distinction involves discrimination when "(a) the treatment in analogous or similar situations is different, (b) the difference has no objective and reasonable justification and (c) the means employed are not reasonably proportional to the aim being sought" (para. 37).

25 *Maria Eugenia Morales de Sierra v Guatemala* Inter-Am Comm'n HR Report no 4/01, Case 11.625, OAE/Ser.L/V/II.111 Doc 20 rev (2000).

must exercise with regard to acts and practices of third parties who, with its tolerance or acquiescence, create, maintain or promote discriminatory situations.[26]

Human rights bodies have addressed the issue of disparate impact as well as *de jure* discrimination, concluding that, in general, it is not necessary to demonstrate intent to discriminate in order to prove a violation. In *Singh Binder v Canada*, for example, the Human Rights Committee found a Canadian law to be indirectly discriminatory because it required all persons to wear hard hats in certain jobs, which had a negative impact on Sikhs whose religion requires them to wear turbans. The Canadian government ultimately prevailed in the matter, however, when it demonstrated that the disparate treatment was justified as "reasonable and directed towards objective purposes that are compatible with the Covenant".[27] The European Court reached a similar conclusion in *Hugh Jordan v the United Kingdom*.[28] In Advisory Opinion OC-18/03, the Inter-American Court also suggested that disparate impact may give rise to a violation, opining that "States must abstain from carrying out any action that, in any way, directly or indirectly, is aimed at creating situations of de jure or de facto discrimination" (para. 103). Finally, the jurisprudence of the African Commission also suggests that indirect or de facto discrimination is prohibited.[29]

The non-discrimination clauses single out certain distinctions as unacceptable: race, colour, sex, language, religion, political or other opinion, national or social origin, property, birth or other status. In *Gueye v France*, the Human Rights Committee held that although the ICCPR did not explicitly mention nationality, discrimination on grounds of nationality was prohibited by the words "other status" because the ICCPR applies to "all persons" unless otherwise specified.[30] The Human Rights Committee has examined cases of discrimination on the grounds of nationality or "national origin" in the context of

---

26 OC-18, para. 104.

27 See also *Althammer et al v Austria* CCPR Comm no 998/2001, UN Doc CCPR/C/78/D/998/2001 (8 Aug 2003); *Simunek et al v Czech Republic* CCPR Comm no 516/1992, UN Doc CCPR/C/54/D/516/1992 (19 Jul 1995).

28 *Hugh Jordan v United Kingdom* App no 24746/94 at para. 154 (ECtHR, 4 May 2001).

29 See *Association Mauritanienne des Droits de l'Homme v Mauritania* Afr Comm'n HPR Comm no 210/98 at para. 131 (2000).

30 *Gueye et al v France* App no 196/1983 (ECtHR, 3 Apr 1989).

employment,[31] property,[32] voting rights, tax and social security, pensions[33] and immigration. In these cases, "mere administrative inconvenience" cannot be invoked to justify unequal treatment, nor can differences in economic, social or financial conditions. Deportation of migrant workers who have lived and worked in the State for a long period has been criticized.[34] In its concluding observations on periodic State reports, the Human Rights Committee has expressed concern about some State distinctions between citizens by birth and those who are naturalized,[35] requirements for non–nationals that do not apply to nationals,[36] and stringent criteria for citizenship that discriminate against minority or foreign groups who are permanent residents.[37]

Other disapproved measures include the failure to confer nationality on stateless persons born in the State, stripping persons of citizenship who are critical of the government, mass expulsions of non-nationals and discriminatory rules that prejudice women in the transmission of nationality to children.[38] Tribunals generally agree that naturalization, although it is the prerogative of the State, should be granted on the basis of objective criteria and within a reasonable time frame, especially for persons who have lived in the State for many years. CERD

---

31 *Karakurt v Austria* CCPR Comm no 965/2000, UN Doc CCPR/C/74/D/965/2000 (4 Apr 2002); *Sprenger v the Netherlands* CCPR Comm no 395/1990, UN Doc CCPR/C/44/D/395/1990 (22 Mar 1991).

32 *Adam v Czech Republic* CCPR Comm no 586/1994, UN Doc CCPR/C/57/D/586/1994 (23 Jul 1996), *Simunek et al v Czech Republic* (n. 27), *Blazek et al v Czech Republic* CCPR Comm no 857/1999, UN Doc CCPR/C/72/D/857/1999 (12 Jul 2001), *Des Fours v Czech Republic* CCPR Comm no 747/1997, UN Doc CCPR/C/73/D/747/1997 (30 Oct 2001), *Drobek v Slovakia* CCPR Comm no 643/1995, UN Doc CCPR/C/60/D/643/1995 (14 Jul 1997), *Malik v Czech Republic* CCPR Comm no 669/1995, UN Doc CCPR/C/64/D/669/1995 (21 Oct 1998), and *Schlosser v Czech Republic* CCPR Comm no 670/1995, UN Doc CCPR/C/64/D/670/1995 (21 Oct 1998).

33 *Gueye et al v France* (n. 30).

34 See, for example, CESCR, Concluding Observations: Dominican Republic (E/1991/23), p. 55, para. 249; and CESCR, Concluding Observations: Nigeria (E/1999/22), p. 27, para. 105.

35 Human Rights Committee, Concluding Observations: Ireland (A/48/40) (1993), paras 551 et seq.

36 Human Rights Committee, Concluding Observations: Japan (A/49/40) (1994), paras 98 et seq.

37 Human Rights Committee, Concluding Observations: Latvia (A/50/40) (1995), paras 334 et seq. Examples of discriminatory criteria include a language requirement that no foreigner can meet (for example, Human Rights Committee, Concluding Observations: Estonia (A/51/40) (1996), paras 99 et seq).

38 In its concluding observations on State reports, the CESCR has criticized laws preventing a woman from vesting nationality in her child or depriving women of their original nationality when they marry foreign men. See, for example CESCR, Concluding Observations: Egypt (E/2001122), p. 38, paras 159 and 175; and CESCR, Concluding Observations: Jordan (E/2001/22), p. 49, para. 234.

suggested in the case of *B.M.S. v Australia*,[39] that a distinction aimed at or adversely affecting a particular group of non-citizens would violate the Convention.

The Eur. Ct. HR has similarly condemned discrimination on the basis of nationality,[40] concluding that "very weighty reasons" would have to be put forward before it would regard differential treatment on the basis of nationality as being in compliance with the European Convention.[41] The African Commission has been sceptical of changes in nationality laws or application of such laws to deprive individuals of their nationality. In Comm No 97/93, the African Commission held that the deprivation of the applicant's citizenship by Botswana denied him the right of equal access to the public services of the country guaranteed under Article 13(2) of the Charter.[42] In *UIDH, FIDH and Others v Angola*, the African Commission held that mass expulsions of any category of persons, whether on the basis of nationality, religion, ethnic, racial or other considerations "constitute a special violation of human rights".[43] The Commission also stated that "a government action specially directed at a specific national, racial, ethnic or religious group is generally qualified as discriminatory in the sense that none of its characteristics has any legal basis" (para. 15).

The area of religious discrimination has also raised difficult issues, because the desire to practise or manifest religious belief often leads individuals to claim exemptions from laws neutral on their face. It is often difficult to distinguish between the permissible enforcement of laws that have a legitimate need for uniform application and those whose enforcement amounts to unwarranted discrimination against a particular religion because its different beliefs entitle it to different treatment. Neutral government regulations – ones that do not demand

---

39   *B.M.S. v Australia*, 12 Mar 1999 (Comm No 8/1996), UN Doc CERD/C/54/D/8/1996 (1999).

40   See, for example, *Gaygusuz v Austria* App no 17371/90 (ECtHR, 16 Sep 1996).

41   See *Koua Poirrez v France* App no 40892/9830 (ECtHR 30 Sep 2003); *Murray v United Kingdom* App no 18731/91 (ECtHR, 8 Feb 1996), and *Moustaquim v Belgium* App no 12313/86 (ECtHR, 18 Feb 1991).

42   *Legal Resources Foundation v Zambia* Afr Comm'n HPR Comm no 211/98 (2001) similarly resulted in the Commission finding a violation, this time of Art. 2, due to a proposed new constitutional provision that required anyone seeking the office of the President to prove that both parents were Zambians by birth or descent.

43   See also *OMCT and others v Rwanda* Afr Comm'n HPR Comm nos 27/89, 46/91, 49/91 and 99/93 (1996). In *RADDHO v Zambia* Afr Comm'n HPR Comm no 71/92 (1996), the manner of the expulsions violated the Charter.

adherence to religion in general or a specific religion in particular – generally are upheld and applied to all persons in society. However, certain exemptions or accommodations may be required, where the governmental interest can be served by other means and where the demands of the law are particularly onerous on religious objectors.[44] In *Thlimmenos v Greece*,[45] the European Court held that Greek legislation discriminated on the basis of religion. Greek authorities had refused to appoint the applicant, a Jehovah's Witness, as a chartered accountant, because he had a previous criminal conviction for disobeying an order to wear a Greek military uniform. The applicant proved that he refused to wear military uniform as a conscientious objector, because Jehovah's Witnesses are committed to pacifism. The Court found that Greek law wrongly treated him like any other criminal, whereas his criminal conviction arose from the exercise of his freedom of religious belief; the law's failure to make the distinction was discriminatory.

Other problems stem from laws regulating religions and their relationship with the State. Some national constitutions establish the primacy of a particular religion and grant it privileges that are not afforded other religions or non-believers, raising issues of equality and non-discrimination. Conversely, governments sometimes repress religious activities, providing that no one may invoke religious liberty contrary to secular law. International jurisprudence has recognized that the existence of established or official State religion can result in discrimination against other religious groups. In *Waldman v Canada*, the Human Rights Committee held that where a State Party chooses to provide public funding to religious schools, the funding must be made available without discrimination.[46] In *Canea Catholic Church v Greece*, the Eur. Ct. HR similarly found a violation of Article 14 (non-discrimination) in conjunction with Article 6(1) (right to a fair hearing) because both the Greek Orthodox Church and the Jewish community had legal personality to protect their property rights under Greek law, but the Roman Catholic Church did not and there was no objective and reasonable justification for it to be treated any differently.[47]

The views of society invariably impact the jurisprudence on discrimination. *Hoffman v Austria*, a 5–4 decision of the Eur. Ct. HR, consid-

---

44 See *Cha'are Shalom Ve Tsedek v France* App no 27417/95 (ECtHR, 27 Jun 2000).

45 *Thlimmenos v Greece* 2000-IV [GC]; (2001) 31 EHRR 411.

46 *Waldman v Canada* CCPR Comm no 694/1996 (3 Nov 1999).

47 See *Canea Catholic Church v Greece* App no 25528/94 (ECtHR, 16 Dec 1997).

ered whether denying custody to an applicant because of her religion (Jehovah's Witness) constituted impermissible discrimination on the basis of religion or was a legitimate distinction based on the independent test of the best interest of the children.[48] The Court held that there was both a distinction and a legitimate aim, but the measure was disproportionate and therefore impermissible. Both the European Court and the HRC have made clear that traditional notions of gender roles in employment and the home do not justify discrimination,[49] nor are distinctions between legitimate and illegitimate children acceptable.[50] Differential treatment based on sexual orientation is increasingly held to be discriminatory.[51]

Comparing recent case law on homosexuality with European Court judgments concerning the Roma indicates the need for further evaluation of what constitutes discrimination and what distinctions are permissible.[52] Discrimination often results from deeply embedded social norms and common understandings held by the majority. It seems that the determination of what is a reasonable and relevant distinction cannot be decided without reference to evolving values in society,[53] but

---

48 *Hoffman v Austria* (1993) App no 129875/87, 255-C ECHR (Ser A), 17 EHRR 293.

49 In *SWM Broeks v Netherlands* CCPR Comm no 172/1984 at para. 12.4, UN Doc CCPR/C/OP/2 at 196 (9 Apr 1987) the HRC found that the denial of social security benefits to a married woman on an equal footing with a married man constituted discrimination under Art. 26 of the ICCPR.

50 *Marckx v Belgium* (1979) App no 6833/74, 31 ECHR (Ser A), 2 EHRR 330; *Inze v Austria* (1987) App no 8695/79, 126 ECHR (Ser A), 19 EHRR 394; *Sahin v Germany* [GC] (2003) 36 EHRR 43; *Sommerfeld v Germany* (2003) 38 EHRR 35.

51 In *Young v Australia* CCPR Comm no 941/2000, UN Doc CCPR/C/78/D/941/2000 (6 Aug 2003), the HRC held that sexual orientation was covered by the "other status" ground of Art. 26 of the ICCPR. See also *Joslin v New Zealand* CCPR Comm no 902/1999, UN Doc CCPR/C/75/D/9021999 (17 Jul 2002). For European Court cases, see, for example, *L and V v Austria* App nos 39392/98 and 39829/98 (ECtHR, 9 Jan 2003); *Karner v Austria* (2004) App no 40016/98, 38 EHRR 24; *B.B. v the United Kingdom; Smith and Grady v the United Kingdom* (1999) 29 EHRR 493; and *Lustig-Prean and Beckett v United Kingdom* App nos 31417/96 and 32377/96 (ECtHR, 27 Sep 1999); *Beck, Copp and Bazeley v United Kingdom* App nos 48535/99, 48536/99 and 48537/99 (ECtHR, 22 Jan 2003) and *Perkins and R v United Kingdom* App nos 43208/98 and 44875/98 (ECtHR, 22 Oct 2002).

52 See *Beard v United Kingdom* App no 24882/94 (ECtHR, 18 Jan 2001); *Chapman v United Kingdom* 2001-I EurCtHR 41; *Coster v UK* App no 24876/94 (ECtHR, 18 Jan 2001); *Jane Frette v France* (2002) App no 36515/97, 38 EHRR 21. But see *Salgueiro Da Silva Mouta v Portugal* App no 33290/96 (ECtHR, 21 Dec 1999); *Smith v United Kingdom* App no 25154/92 (ECtHR, 18 Jan 2001); and *Lee v United Kingdom* App no 25289/94 (ECtHR, 18 Jan 2001).

53 Despite the obvious negative impact of the planning laws, interference with the applicants' rights was held to be permissible as a proportionate measure to serve the legitimate aim of preservation of the environment. The Court gave little weight to allegations of systematic discrimination against the Roma.

prevailing social views cannot always be the test of what is a reasonable and proportionate distinction in human rights law. In practice, the outcome of discrimination cases is often closely linked to and dependent on the issue of who decides.

The results of a recent study on gaps in international human rights law on the issue of discrimination, produced by a working group appointed by the UN Human Rights Council, identified certain groups as continuing to be under-protected: religious groups, refugees, asylum seekers, stateless persons, migrant workers, internally displaced persons, descent-based communities, indigenous peoples, minorities and people under foreign occupation.[54]

5.3 The jurisprudence of selected rights

5.3.1 Self-determination

As noted earlier, the UN Charter enshrines the principle of self-determination; it also appears as common Article 1 to the two Covenants. The right of self-determination has long been celebrated for bringing independence and self-government to oppressed groups, yet it remains a highly controversial norm of international law. From the breakup of the Austro-Hungarian and Ottoman Empires after the First World War to the struggle of colonial territories for independence following the Second World War and the later dissolution of the former Yugoslavia and secession of Southern Sudan from Sudan, there has been an unavoidable conflict between the efforts of peoples to achieve independence and the demands of existing States to preserve their territorial integrity.[55] The UN Declaration on Principles of International Law (DPIL) reflects this tension. It gives the principle of self-determination universal scope as a right belonging to undefined "peoples" but rejects any secession from independent States "conducting themselves in compliance with the principle of equal rights and self-determination of peoples . . . and thus possessed of a government representing the whole people belonging to the territory without distinction as to race, creed or colour". The 1993 Vienna Declaration

---

54 See Complementary International Standards: Report on the study by the five experts on the content and scope of substantive gaps in the existing international instruments to combat racism, racial discrimination, xenophobia and related intolerance (A/HRC/4/WG.3/6), 27 Aug 2007, para. 20.

55 See Cassese (n. 6).

adopted by the World Conference on Human Rights similarly affirmed the universal application of the right of self-determination to peoples under colonial or other forms of alien domination or foreign occupation, but also specified, in conformity with the DPIL, that the right shall not be construed as authorizing or encouraging any action which would dismember or impair, totally or in part, the territorial integrity or political unity of sovereign and independent States conducting themselves in compliance with the principle of equal rights and self-determination of peoples and thus possessed of a government representing the whole people.

In its advisory opinion on the *Kosovo Declaration of Independence*, the ICJ noted that "during the second half of the twentieth century, the international law of self-determination developed in such a way as to create a right to independence for the peoples of non-self-governing territories and peoples subject to alien subjugation, domination and exploitation".[56] Moreover, the Court observed, a great many new States have come into existence as a result of the exercise of this right and also have issued declarations of independence outside the colonial context. Nonetheless, the Court noted sharp disagreements about "[w]hether, outside the context of non-self-governing territories and peoples subject to alien subjugation, domination and exploitation, the international law of self-determination confers upon part of the population of an existing State a right to separate from that State".[57] Similar differences were found to exist regarding whether international law provides for a right of "remedial secession" and, if so, in what circumstances. The Court declined to resolve these debates, finding it was unnecessary to do so in order to respond to the question posed by the General Assembly, which concerned only whether or not the declaration of independence was in accordance with international law.

The issues that the Court did not address have been sources of conflict in State practice and jurisprudence. Africa continues to confront the aftermath of colonialism, during which arbitrary boundaries were drawn, dividing some peoples and forcing others together, even those with a tradition of mutual hostility or enmity. To resolve one such problem, the residents of South Sudan voted to secede from the largest

---

56 Accordance with International Law of the Unilateral Declaration of Independence in Respect of Kosovo, Advisory Opinion 2010 ICJ 403 (22 July).

57 Ibid. para. 82.

country on the continent.[58] The African Union was caught between its Constitutive Act, which enshrines as a founding principle "respect of borders existing on achievement of independence",[59] and its significant role as a signatory and guarantor of the Sudan peace agreement.

Self-determination does not necessarily imply secession. Indigenous and tribal peoples in Africa and the Americas often seek to obtain internal self-determination or autonomy and, in particular, control over their ancestral lands and resources. The right to such internal self-determination is recognized by the two international instruments devoted to the rights of indigenous and tribal peoples: ILO Convention (No 169) Concerning Indigenous and Tribal Peoples in Independent Countries and UNDRIP, whose Article 3 explicitly recognizes indigenous peoples' right to self-determination. For its part, ILO Convention No 169 contributes to defining "peoples" by regarding self-identification as the fundamental criterion, but specifies that the use of the term "shall not be construed as having any implications as regards the rights which may attach to the term under international law". The Convention nonetheless recognizes the aspirations of indigenous peoples to control their own institutions, ways of life, and economic development "within the framework of the State in which they live".[60] In fact, the major part of ILO Convention No 169 can be characterized as setting forth elements of internal self-determination for indigenous and tribal peoples, as groups entitled to special treatment. The World Bank Operational Manual, OP 4.10 (July 2005) also recognizes the customary rights of indigenous peoples over lands and resources, and affirms the principle of their "free, prior, and informed consultation" in relation to Bank-funded projects affecting them.[61]

---

58 The referendum was stipulated under the Comprehensive Peace Agreement of 2005, which formally ended a 20-year civil war between the government in Khartoum and the south Sudan People's Liberation Movement Army. See Comprehensive Peace Agreement Between the Government of the Republic of Sudan and the Sudan People's Liberation Movement/Sudan People's Liberation Army (9 Jan 2005) at www.aec-sudan.org/docs/cpa/cpa-en.pdf.

59 Constitutive Act of the African Union, 11 July 1981, 1520 UNTS I-37733, Art. 4(b).

60 ILO No 169, pmbl., para. 5.

61 See also Committee on the Elimination of Racial Discrimination, General Recommendation No 23, Indigenous Peoples, para. 5 (18 Aug 1997), Report of the Committee on the Elimination of Racial Discrimination, UN GAOR, 52d Sess, Supp No 18, Annex V, UN Doc A/52/18 (1997), calling upon States, inter alia, to "recognize and protect the rights of indigenous peoples to own, develop, control and use their communal lands, territories and resources".

In contrast to the silence of the American and European human rights instruments about the principle or right of self-determination, the African Charter on Human and Peoples' Rights contains detailed provisions on this point. Given the context of decolonization in Africa and the struggle against apartheid in Southern Africa, both of which are referred to in the preamble to the African Charter, this is not surprising. African Charter Article 20, on the right to self-determination, stipulates:

1. All peoples shall have the right to existence. They shall have the unquestionable and inalienable right to self-determination. They shall freely determine their political status and shall pursue their economic and social development according to the policy they have freely chosen.

2. Colonized or oppressed peoples shall have the right to free themselves from the bonds of domination by resorting to any means recognized by the international community.

3. All peoples shall have the right to the assistance of the States parties to the present Charter in their liberation struggle against foreign domination, be it political, economic or cultural.

The article appears to recognize two distinct groups of peoples: those living under colonialism and oppression, and those that are not. The first group is entitled to independence and foreign assistance in the struggle for liberation (external self-determination). Other peoples are entitled to maintain their existence and exercise their self-determination, but within existing States.

Article 20 must be read in the context of the entire African Charter, whose very title indicates that it is concerned with collective peoples' rights as well as individual rights. The Charter contains six separate articles on peoples' rights (Arts 19–24), beginning with the right of all peoples to be equal and to enjoy the same respect and the same rights. Although such rights were included, the drafters of the Charter made a deliberate choice not to define peoples.[62] In keeping with this drafting history, the African Commission initially avoided defining the concept, also in part due to the dearth of international jurisprudence and textual definition.[63]

---

62 See Willem van Genugten, *Protection of Indigenous Peoples on the African Continent: Concepts, Position Seeking, and the Interaction of Legal Systems* (2010) 104 AJIL 29, 38–43.

63 REPORT OF THE AFRICAN COMMISSION'S WORKING GROUP OF EXPERTS ON INDIGENOUS

Most of the African Charter's articles on peoples' rights seem to apply broadly to indigenous and tribal groups within Africa that are not in a colonial or oppressive State. The African Commission has so found in several cases. Although the applicants in these cases were unable to prove the alleged violations, the African Commission had no doubt that peoples' rights apply to identifiable groups by reason of their common ancestry, ethnic origin, language or cultural habits.[64] The right of peoples to freely dispose of their wealth and natural resources, guaranteed in Article 21, has similarly been applied to identifiable groups within African States.[65]

The right of self-determination is nonetheless constrained in African texts and jurisprudence, reflecting the tension between "the total emancipation of the African territories which are still dependent"[66] and commitment to the principle of territorial integrity through respecting colonial frontiers of those States that had achieved independence.[67] The 1999 Algiers Declaration adopted by the OAU Assembly of Heads of State and Government reaffirmed that respect for borders inherited at independence retains its "validity and permanence as a fundamental norm".[68]

The African Commission has considered several claims of external self-determination brought under the African Charter. In the first case, decided in 1995, the Katangese Peoples' Congress asked the African Commission to recognize the right of the Katangese people to independence from Zaire. The African Commission declined to do so, with terse legal analysis. It noted that the applicants had complained only of a violation of Charter Article 20 (the right of self-determination),

---

POPULATIONS/COMMUNITIES 72–73 (2005), at www.achpr.org/english/Special%20Mechanisms/Indegenous/ACHPR%20Report%20ENG.pdf.

64 See, for example, *Legal Resources Foundation v Zambia* (n. 42) and the series of cases against Mauritania: *Malawi African Association v Mauritania, Amnesty International v Mauritania,* and *Union Interafricaine des droits de l'homme v Mauritania,* Consolidated Comms 54/91, 61/91, 98/93, 164/97, 196/97, 210/98 (AfCHPR 2000), in which the African Commission found some discriminatory practices against certain sectors of the Mauritanian population, but insufficient evidence to show domination of one section of the population against another).

65 *Soc. & Econ. Rts. Action Centre v Nigeria* Afr Comm'n HPR Comm no 155/96, 15th Ann Activity Rep (2001).

66 OAU Charter, Art. 3(6).

67 Ibid., Art. 3(3); See also *Border Disputes Among African States,* OAU Doc AHG/Res 16(I) (17–21 Jul 1964), at www.africa-union.org/root/au/Documents/Decisions/hog/bHoGAssembly1964.pdf. See also *Frontier Dispute (Burkina Faso v Mali)* 1986 ICJ 554 (22 Dec).

68 Algiers Declaration, 12–14 Jul 1999, OAU Doc AHG/Decl 1 (XXXV).

without indicating that other Charter rights were being violated. Considering that self-determination could be exercised not only by independence, but also by self-government, local government, federalism, confederalism, unitarism "or any form of relations that accords with the wishes of the people",[69] the African Commission held that it is only when the will of the people is denied, through a lack of ability to participate in government or due to massive human rights violations, that the principles of sovereignty and territorial integrity give way to self-determination through secession and independence. The decision thus seems to support the notion of "remedial secession" or in the words of the UDHR preamble the need "to have recourse, as a last resort, to rebellion against tyranny and oppression".

The African Commission returned to the issue of secession and independence in the landmark case of *Kevin Mgwanga Gunme v Cameroon* concerning the people of southern Cameroon.[70] Applicants complained that they had been deprived of the right of self-determination as a separate and distinct people, but instead they had been marginalized, deprived of equal rights of representation in government, and denied the right to development. They also claimed, inter alia, that the government denied their right to education and discriminated against them in the legal system and in language rights.

To arrive at a definition of people and determine whether the term applies to the applicants, the African Commission relied on, but did not consider itself bound by, the findings of a UNESCO group of experts convened to consider the concept of peoples' rights.[71] The UNESCO group concluded that a group could be considered a people if it shared some of the following characteristics: a common historical tradition, a racial or ethnic identity, cultural homogeneity, linguistic unity, religious and ideological affinities, territorial connection and a common economic life.[72] Moreover, a people can be self-identified by their common consciousness of constituting a people. Thus, for the African Commission, the collective rights in the Charter can be

---

69 *Katangese Peoples' Congress v Zaire*, Afr Comm'n HPR Comm no 75/92, 8 Ann Activity Rep at para. 4 (1994–1995).

70 The African Charter allows the filing of an *actio popularis*. Ibid., para. 67; see *Malawi African Ass'n v Mauritania*, Consolidated Comms 54/91, 61/91, 98/93, 164/97–196/97 and 210/98, ACHPR, 13 Ann Activity Rep, Appendix V (1999–2000).

71 See *Final Report and Recommendations, International Meeting of Experts on Further Study of the Concept of the Rights of Peoples*, UNESCO Doc SHS-89/CONF.602/7 (1990).

72 Ibid., para. 22.

exercised by a people bound together by their history and traditions, as well as by their racial, ethnic, cultural, linguistic, religious, ideological, geographical, economic or other bonds. Applying these criteria, the African Commission concluded that the southern Cameroonians can legitimately claim to be a people with a distinct identity that attracts certain collective rights. "More importantly, they identify themselves as a people with a separate and distinct identity".[73]

The African Commission nonetheless reaffirmed its obligation to uphold the territorial integrity of States in the African system, stating that it could not therefore envisage, condone or encourage secession, except in cases of massive violations of human rights or the denial of participation in public affairs. Although the African Commission found violations of Charter Articles 2, 4, 5, 6, 7, 11 and 19, it held that these violations were not so serious as to call into question the territorial integrity of the State. Most important in this regard was the finding that the State had not violated Article 13, the right to participate in government, because the evidence demonstrated a representation of the people of southern Cameroon in the National Assembly. Thus, the conditions of domination and oppression required by Charter Article 20(2) had not been met to the extent warranting invocation of the right to self-determination through secession and independence.

None of the cases of indigenous peoples brought to the Inter-American human rights system has included a claimed right to secede. Instead, indigenous peoples have demanded recognition and titling of their ancestral lands and the right to decide on the scope and nature of development projects that affect their lands and resources – in particular, infrastructure projects and extractive industries. The IACHR and I-A Court have primarily assessed indigenous cases under the right to property (Convention Art. 21), but they have begun to refer to the right of self-determination in the context of land and resource claims. In the first case on indigenous land and resource rights to reach the I-A Court, *Awas Tingni v Nicaragua*, the court insisted that the right to property encompasses the rights of members of indigenous communities to their communal property.[74] In *Saramaka People v Suriname* the I-A Court referred for the first time to the right of self-determination

73 *Kevin Mgwanga Gunme v Cameroon*, Afr. Comm'n HPR Comm no 266/2003, EX.CL/529 (XV), 45th Ordinary Session, Annex 4 (2009), at para. 179.

74 *Case of the Mayagna (Sumo) Awas Tingni Community* Judgment of 31 Aug 2001 Inter-Am Ct HR (Ser C) no 79 (2001), para. 148.

in interpreting indigenous land and resource rights under Convention Article 21.[75] The I-A Court concluded that Convention Article 21 calls for the right of members of indigenous and tribal communities to freely determine and enjoy their own social, cultural and economic development, which includes the right to enjoy their particular spiritual relationship with the territory that they have traditionally used and occupied. As a corollary, the State has an obligation to adopt special measures to recognize, respect, protect and guarantee the communal property right of the members of indigenous and tribal communities to such territory.

The Court also inferred that natural resources found in and within indigenous and tribal peoples' territories are protected under Article 21, if those natural resources are traditionally used and are necessary for the survival, development and continuation of such peoples' way of life. In order to guarantee that concessions issued within the territory of an indigenous people are consistent with the people's rights, the State must abide by three safeguards: first, it must ensure the effective participation of the group, in conformity with their customs and traditions, regarding any development, investment, exploration or extraction plan within the ancestral territory; second, the State must guarantee that they will receive a reasonable benefit from any such plan within their territory; and third, the State must ensure that no concession will be issued within the territory unless and until independent and technically capable entities, with the State's supervision, perform a prior environmental and social impact assessment. The Court added that large-scale development or investment projects that would have a major impact within indigenous ancestral lands give rise to a duty for the State not only to consult with members of the indigenous people, but also to obtain their free, prior and informed consent, according to their customs and traditions.

5.3.2   Right to life

The right to life provisions in global and regional human rights instruments prohibit arbitrary deprivations of life and generally require that States protect life by law. The 1950 ECHR set the pattern for provisions that followed in other regional and global treaties. ECHR Article 2 indicates that "[n]o one shall be deprived of his life intentionally save in the

---

75 *Saramaka People v Suriname*, Preliminary Objections, Merits, Reparations, and Costs 2007 Inter-Am Ct HR (Ser C) no 172 (2007).

execution of a sentence of a court following his conviction of a crime for which this penalty is provided by law". The American Convention is unique in adding to its Article 4 guarantee that life shall be protected by law "beginning, in general, from the moment of conception".[76] The IACHR has interpreted this clause to mean that the regulation of abortion is to be determined with broad discretion by each State. Apart from abortion, the issues that arise in connection with the right to life include use of force by police and military personnel, State responsibility for failing to prevent non-State actors from causing loss of life, and the death penalty.

Most human rights instruments adopted in the early days of modern human rights law explicitly permit imposition of the death penalty, with restrictions. Neither of the two earliest instruments, the ADRDM and UDHR, both adopted in 1948, mentions the topic, as each contains only a short and general Article 1 guaranteeing all human beings the right to life.[77] The 1966 ICCPR establishes strict limits on imposition of the death penalty in its Article 6. The American Convention on Human Rights and the Arab Charter, Article 6, are similar. The I-A Court noted almost 30 years ago that the American Convention "imposes restrictions designed to delimit strictly its application and scope, in order to reduce the application of the penalty to bring about its gradual disappearance".[78] In contrast, Article 4 of the African Charter recognizes the right to life and does not refer to the death penalty.

Among the most common restrictions on the application of the death penalty found in international and regional treaties are those that prohibit imposing the death penalty on individuals below the age of 18 and on those with specific physical or mental conditions. The American Convention on Human Rights, Article 4(5) also prohibits imposition of capital punishment on persons who, at the time the crime was committed, were over 70 years of age. Pregnant women and new mothers

---

76 See IACHR, *Res. 23/81, Cases 2141* ("Baby Boy") (United States). Compare the European Court judgments in *R.R. v Poland*, 26 May 2011, and *A, B and C v Ireland* [GC] 16 Dec 2010.

77 The first draft of the UDHR prepared by the Secretariat made explicit reference to the permissibility of the death penalty. UN Doc E/CN.4/AC.1/3/Add.1. The Chairman of the Committee, Eleanor Roosevelt, suggested that it might be better not to use the phrase "death penalty" and it was removed. UN Doc E/CN.4/AC.1/SR.2, at 10. After the Commission referred the completed draft to the Third Committee of the General Assembly, the debate on the death penalty resumed. Several countries proposed an amendment calling for the abolition of the death penalty in times of peace, but after much debate the proposal was rejected.

78 IA Ct HR, *Restrictions to the Death Penalty*, para. 57.

are similarly protected by ICCPR Article 6(5); the ECOSOC Safeguards of 1984 paragraph 3; Protocol I, Article 76(3)[79] and Protocol II, Article 6(4) of the Geneva Conventions.[80] Article 4(2)(g) of the Protocol to the African Charter on Human and Peoples' Rights on the Rights of Women in Africa establishes that the penalty shall not be applied to pregnant or nursing women. Given the widespread treaty provisions and State practice, the UN HRC has referred to the prohibition of executing children or pregnant women under Article 6 of the ICCPR as a rule of customary international law, which may not be the subject of a reservation made by a State which becomes a party to that Covenant.[81] The UN Special Rapporteur on Extrajudicial, Summary or Arbitrary Executions has simply noted that "international law prohibits the capital punishment of mentally retarded or insane persons, pregnant women and mothers of young children".[82]

Global and regional bodies have strengthened their guarantees through the adoption of instruments devoted explicitly to abolition of the death penalty. In 1983 the Council of Europe adopted Protocol 6 to the ECHR abolishing the death penalty, except in times of war or imminent threat of war.[83] Two decades later, in 2002, the Council of Europe adopted Protocol No 13 concerning the abolition of the death penalty in all circumstances.[84] The Council of Europe has made abolition of the death penalty a prerequisite for membership in the organization and made clear that it expects those States granted observer status to adopt this position as well.[85] In sum, the Member States of the Council of Europe have established a zone free of capital punishment and no execution has taken place on the territory of any Member State since 1997.

---

79 Protocol Additional to the Geneva Conventions of 1949 and Relative to the Protection of Victims of International Armed Conflicts (Protocol I), 8 Jun 1977, 1125 UNTS 17512.

80 Protocol Additional to the Geneva Conventions of 1949 and Relative to the Protection of Victims of Non-International Armed Conflicts (Protocol II), 8 Jun 1977, 1125 UNTS 17513.

81 General Comment 24 on issues relating to reservations made upon ratification or accession to the Covenant or the Optional Protocols thereto, or in relation to declarations under article 41 of the Covenant, adopted on 4 Nov 1994.

82 Extrajudicial, summary or arbitrary executions: Report by the Special Rapporteur, UN Doc E/CN.4/1994/7.

83 Protocol No 6 to the Convention for the Protection of Human Rights and Fundamental Freedoms, concerning the abolition of the death penalty, 28 Apr 1983, ETS No 114.

84 Protocol No 13 to the Convention for the Protection of Human Rights and Fundamental Freedoms, concerning the abolition of the death penalty in all circumstances, 3 May 2002, ETS No 187.

85 See Eur Parl Assembly, *Abolition of the Death Penalty in Council of Europe Observer States*, Res 1349 (1 Oct 2003).

In 1989 the General Assembly adopted the Second Optional Protocol to the ICCPR aimed at the abolition of capital punishment. More recently, the UN General Assembly adopted resolutions in 2007, 2008 and 2010, calling upon States that maintain the death penalty to establish a moratorium on executions with a view to abolition.[86] In addition to these General Assembly resolutions, the UN Secretary-General has reported on the status of capital punishment every five years since 1975, reports that demonstrate the trend towards abolition around the world.

One year after adoption of the ICCPR Protocol, the General Assembly of the Organization of American States adopted its own Protocol to the American Convention to Abolish the Death Penalty.[87] Parties to this Protocol undertake that they will not apply the death penalty, although a reservation is possible to allow for its application in times of war. In the African system the African Commission on Human and Peoples' Rights established a Working Group on the Death Penalty that recommended in November 2010 that the African Commission draft a protocol to the African Charter concerning the abolition of the death penalty in Africa.[88] The African Commission issued resolutions in 1999 and 2008 calling on States to observe a moratorium on the execution of death sentences with a view to abolishing the death penalty.[89]

The gradual evolution towards abolition of the death penalty is also reflected in the penalties that international criminal tribunals may impose. The International Criminal Court established by the Rome Statute which entered into force in 2002, excludes capital punishment as a possible penalty.[90] Life imprisonment is the maximum penalty

---

86 See GA Res 62/149, *Moratorium on the Use of the Death Penalty*, 18 Dec 2007; GA Res 63/168, *Moratorium on the Use of the Death Penalty*, 21 Dec 2010.

87 Protocol to the American Convention on Human Rights to Abolish the Death Penalty, 8 Jun 1990, OAS TS No 73.

88 Progress Report of the African Commission on Human and Peoples' Rights Working Group on the Death Penalty in Africa, presented by the Chairperson of the Working Group on the Death Penalty, Commissioner Zainabo Sylvie Kayitesi, 48th Ordinary Session of the African Commission, 10–25 Nov 2010, Banjul, The Gambia.

89 ACHPR/Res 42 (XXVI) calling on States to consider observing a moratorium on the death penalty, adopted at the 26th Ordinary Session of the African Commission on Human and Peoples' Rights held from 1st to 15th November 1999 in Kigali, Rwanda; ACHPR/Res 136(XXXXIIII).08: Resolution calling on State Parties to observe the moratorium on the death penalty, 44th Ordinary Session held from 10th to 24th November 2008 in Abuja, Federal Republic of Nigeria, 24 Nov 2008.

90 Art. 77 "Applicable Penalties", ICC Statute, entry into force 1 Jul 2002 (2187 UNTS 3).

provided. The Statutes of the International Criminal Tribunal for the Former Yugoslavia (ICTY, 1993), the International Criminal Tribunal for Rwanda (ICTR, 1994), the Special Court of Sierra Leone (SCSL, 2002) and the Extraordinary Chambers in the Courts of Cambodia (ECCC, 2004) all exclude the application of capital punishment.[91]

Jurisprudence has further restricted the circumstances under which the penalty may be imposed.[92] HRC General Comment 6/16 makes clear that the death penalty can be imposed only by a competent, independent and impartial tribunal provided for by law and after a fair, public hearing that is non-discriminatory and guarantees the presumption of innocence and the minimum rights of the accused, including the right to appeal to a higher tribunal, as provided by ICCPR Article 14.[93] The State is prohibited from *ex post facto* imposition of criminal law and double jeopardy (*ne bis in idem*). The conclusion from HRC cases is that conviction in violation of the fair trial proceedings of ICCPR Article 14, if it results in imposition of the death penalty, *ipso facto* violates Article 6 as well.

The IACHR has interpreted and applied both the American Convention and the American Declaration on the basis that any deprivation of the right to life must be subject to the highest possible level of scrutiny ("strict scrutiny"),[94] consistent with the restrictive approach taken by other international human rights authorities,[95] and based on the "death

---

91 Art. 24 of the ICTY Statute, Art. 23 of the ICTR Statute, Art. 19 of the SCSL Statute, and Art. 3 of the ECCC Law, as amended in 2004.

92 See IACHR, *McKenzie and others*, paras 186–7; *Edwards*, para. 109; IACHR; *Ramón Martinez Villareal (United States)* Report No 52/02, Case No 11.753, at para. 52, and IACHR Rep 38/00, Case 11.743, *Rudolph Baptiste v Grenada*, 31 Apr 2000, paras 74 and 75. See also HRC, *Anthony McLeood v Jamaica* and I-A Court, *Restrictions on the Death Penalty (Arts 4(2) and 4(4) of the American Convention on Human Rights)*.

93 For application of these rules, see *Mansaraj et al v Sierra Leone* CCPR Comm nos 839, 840, 841/1998, UN Doc CCPR/C/72/D/839-841/1998 (16 Jul 2001), *Thomas v Jamaica* CCPR Comm no 272/1988 (31 Mar 1992), *Robinson v Jamaica* CCPR Comm no 223/1987, UN Doc CCPR/C/35/D/223/1987 (30 Mar 1989).

94 For a detailed examination of the jurisprudence of the Inter-American system, see IACHR, *The Death Penalty in the Inter-American Human Rights System: From Restrictions to Abolition*, OEA/Ser.L/V/II.Doc 68, 31 Dec 2011.

95 *Medellín, Ramírez Cardenas and Leal García v United States*, para. 122; *The Right to Information on Consular Assistance in the Framework of the Guarantees of the Due Process of Law*, Advisory Opinion OC-16/99, I-A Court HR, Ser A No. 16 (1999) at para. 136. See also IACHR *Baboheram–Adhin et al v Suriname* Comm no 148-154/1983 at para. 14.3 (1985); Report by the UN Special Rapporteur on Extra-judicial Executions, Mr Bacre Waly Ndiaye, submitted pursuant to Commission on Human Rights Resolution 1994/82, *Question of the Violation of Human Rights*

is different" rationale previously articulated by the US Supreme Court: "due in part to its irrevocable and irreversible nature, the death penalty is a form of punishment that differs in substance as well as in degree in comparison with other means of punishment, and therefore warrants a particularly stringent need for reliability in determining whether a person is responsible for a crime that carries a penalty of death".[96]

To avoid being deemed arbitrary deprivation of life, imposition of the death penalty must be limited to the most serious common crimes (excluding political offences). In its General Comment on Article 6 of the ICCPR the HRC called for a narrow reading of "most serious crimes".[97] According to it and other human rights bodies, the phrase "most serious crimes" excludes: economic offences, political offences, robbery, abduction not resulting in death, apostasy, non-violent acts, religious and political activities, expression of conscience, sexual relations between consenting adults, drug-related offences, "victimless offences" and offences primarily related to "prevailing moral values". In its General Comment on the Right to Life, the HRC concluded that "crimes that do not result in loss of life" may not be punished by the death penalty. Thus, in *Lubato v Zambia*, the HRC held that a mandatory death sentence for armed robbery in a case where no one was wounded or killed violated the "most serious crime" requirement of the ICCPR Article 6(2).[98]

The death penalty is also restricted due to the requirement of individualized sentencing. A majority in the UN HRC has found the implementation of a death sentence based upon a mandatory sentencing law violates the right not to be arbitrarily deprived of one's life under ICCPR Article 6(1).[99] Similarly, for more than a decade, the Inter-American Commission and the Court have rejected the mandatory imposition of the death penalty upon conviction for murder, as is the law in a number of countries in the Commonwealth Caribbean,

---

and Fundamental Freedoms in any part of the World, with particular reference to Colonial and Other Dependent Countries and Territories, UN Doc E/CN.4/1995/61 (14 Dec 1994), para. 378.

96 IACHR, *Chad Roger Goodman v The Bahamas* (Merits) Report no 78/07, Case 12265 (15 Oct 2007) at para. 34.

97 General Comment 6 on Art. 6 of the ICCPR, July 1982, para. 7.

98 CCPR No 390/1990, sec 7.2. See also *Piandong et al v the Philippines* CCPR Comm no 869/1999, UN Doc CCPR/C/70/D/869/1999 at sec 7.4 (19 Oct 2000).

99 *Eversley Thompson v St. Vincent and the Grenadines*, Comm No 806/1998, UN Doc CCPR/C/70/D/806/1998 (2000); *Rawle Kennedy v Trinidad and Tobago*, Comm No 845/1998, UN Doc CCPR/C/74/D/845/1998 (2002) sec 7.3.

whereby judges have had no discretion to consider aggravating or miti-
gating circumstances with respect to the crime or the offender.[100]

ICCPR Article 6(4) grants all persons sentenced to death the right to
seek pardon or commutation of the sentence. The execution of the
sentence must therefore be postponed at least until the conclusion of
any such procedure. Article 4(6) of the American Convention similarly
stipulates that any person sentenced to death has the right to apply
for amnesty, pardon or commutation of sentence, and may not be
executed while such a petition is pending. The I-A Court established in
the case of *Fermín Ramírez* that the right to seek pardon or commutation "forms part of the international corpus juris, specifically of the
American Convention and the International Pact of Civil and Political
Rights".[101] The failure of domestic law to attribute to a State body
the power to analyse and decide upon measures of grace meant that
the State failed to comply with the obligations derived from Article
4(6).[102]

5.3.3   Prohibition of torture and cruel, inhuman or degrading punishment

The relevant provisions distinguish torture from cruel, inhuman or
degrading treatment or punishment and impose differential obligations for the two categories. The definition of torture in UN CAT
Article 1 extends to all severe pain or suffering, whether physical or
mental, but limits it to that inflicted intentionally for one of several
specific reasons, such as obtaining information. The definition is further limited to pain or suffering inflicted by or at the instigation of, or
with the consent or acquiescence of, the State authorities. Normal pain
or suffering arising from lawful sanctions is not included. The main
obligations under the CAT include prohibiting and punishing any act

---

100 *Dacosta Cadogan v Barbados*, Case 1460-01, Report No. 7/08, Inter-Am. C.H.R., OEA/Ser.L/V/
II.130 Doc. 22, rev. 1 (2008); I-A Court HR Ser. C No. 204 (24 Sept. 2009) paras 63–4; IACHR,
McKenzie et al Jamaica, Report 41/00 Case 12.043, para. 197; *Case of Boyce et al v Barbados*,
I-A Court HR, Ser. C, No. 169 (20 Nov 2007), paras 57, 58; Cf. *Case of Hilaire, Constantine and
Benjamin et al v Trinidad and Tobago* (Merits, reparations and costs), I-A Court HR, Ser C No 9
(21 Jun 2002), para. 105, citing *Woodson v North Carolina*, 428 US 280, 304 (1976).

101 *Fermín Ramírez v Guatemala*, I-A Court HR, Ser. C No. 126 (20 Jan 2005) para. 109, citing in
the same sense Inter-American Commission on Human Rights, *Fifth Report on the Situation
of Human Rights in Guatemala*, 6 Apr 2001, Chapter V; and MINUGUA, *Eleventh Report on
Human Rights*, Sep 2000, para. 26.

102 *Fermín Ramírez* (n. 101), para. 110.

of torture or complicity in it. States are also to refrain from *refoulement* of any person to a country where there are substantial grounds for believing that the person would be subjected to torture, but they are to consider torture an extraditable offence under current and future extradition treaties. Victims of torture are entitled to redress and no statement obtained through torture can be admitted or used as evidence in any proceedings.

Torture is defined in Article 2(1) of the Inter-American Convention to Prevent and Punish Torture (I-A CPPT) in the following terms:

> Any act intentionally performed whereby physical or mental pain or suffering is inflicted on a person for purposes of criminal investigation, as a means of intimidation, as personal punishment, as a preventive measure, as a penalty, or for any other purpose. Torture shall also be understood to be the use of methods upon a person intended to obliterate the personality of the victim or to diminish his physical or mental capacities, even if they do not cause physical pain or mental anguish.[103]

In comparing definitions of torture, it should be noted that the UN CAT requires that the suffering of an individual be severe, which the I-A CPPT does not. Both international instruments include the material element of the intentional infliction of pain and suffering, as well as the purposive element. As regards intentionality, violations of the American Convention do not require taking into account psychological factors to establish individual responsibility; in fact, it is not even necessary to determine the identity of the perpetrator, but only whether the violation took place with the acquiescence or support of the government, or if the State allowed the act to take place by failing to take measures to prevent it, or to punish those responsible after the fact.[104] The I-A Court has concluded that

> subjecting a person to official repressive bodies that practice torture and assassination with impunity is itself a breach of the duty to prevent violations of the rights to life and physical integrity of the person, even if that particular person is not tortured or assassinated, or if those facts cannot be proven in a concrete case.[105]

---

103 Inter-American Convention to Prevent and Punish Torture, 9 Dec 1985, OAS TS No 67.
104 *Velásquez-Rodríguez v Honduras* (Merits) I-A Court HR, Ser C, No 4 (29 Jul 1988), para. 173.
105 Ibid., para. 175.

Human rights bodies have made clear that the treatment of detainees must not constitute torture or constitute cruel, inhuman or degrading punishment. In *Ng v Canada*, the HRC held in 1993 that extradition to a place where the applicant faced a real risk that he would be executed by gas asphyxiation would violate ICCPR Article 7, because "execution by gas asphyxiation may cause prolonged suffering and agony and does not result in death as swiftly as possible . . ."[106] In contrast, the HRC concluded a year later in *Cox v Canada* that execution by lethal injection did not amount to a violation of Article 7.[107] The European Court has established that the personal circumstances of the convicted perpetrator, the conditions of detention and the duration of detention are examples of factors capable of requiring examination under Article 3 of the European Convention.[108] Similarly, the Inter-American Commission has observed that the conditions afforded to prisoners are often inhumane.[109] The Court found that "[k]eeping a person imprisoned in overcrowded conditions, without ventilation and natural light, without a bed to rest on or adequate conditions of hygiene, in isolation or incommunicado, or with undue restrictions in the visiting regime, is a violation of his personal integrity". The IACHR and I-A Court have held that the State is obliged to ensure that the rights of persons in custody are only restricted to the extent this corresponds to the criminal conviction and no further.[110] In their decisions on cases of torture, the IACHR has considered objective elements, such as the duration of the acts that caused the pain or suffering, the methods used, the social and political context, whether the victim was deprived of liberty, along with other elements such as the victim's age, sex or vulnerability. The IACHR was the first human rights body to define rape as torture in the context of a particular case.[111]

The jurisprudence is clear on the State's obligation to investigate any complaints of torture or other mistreatment. In such instances, the burden of proof cannot rest on the complainant.[112] The State is

---

106 CCPR, No 469/1991, §§ 16.1–16.5 (four committee members dissented).

107 CCPR, No 539/1993. This controversial case led to 13 separate or concurring opinions among the 18 members of the Committee.

108 See *GB v Bulgaria* App no 42346/98 at para. 73 (ECtHR, 11 Mar 2004).

109 *Boyce Case* (n. 100); *Hilaire, Constantine and Benjamin* (n. 100).

110 See generally, IACHR, *Report on the Human Rights of Persons Deprived of Liberty in the Americas*, OEA/Ser.L/V/II. Doc 64, 31 Dec 2011.

111 *Raquel Martin de Mejia v Peru*, IACHR, Rep 5/96, Case 10.970, 1 Mar 1996.

112 *Cabrera García and Montiel Flores v Mexico* and *Maritza Urrutia v Guatemala* (Merits, Reparations and Costs) I-A Court HR Ser C No 103 (2003), para. 136.

responsible for the observance of the right to humane treatment of every person under its custody and accordingly "the State must provide a satisfactory and convincing explanation of what happened and disprove the allegations regarding its responsibility, using adequate supporting evidence".[113] Human rights bodies may apply presumptions from the silence of the State or its ambiguous response; either may be interpreted as an acceptance of the allegations of the claimant, as long as the contrary does not arise from the evidence or result from judicial conviction.[114] The State cannot rest on the fact that the petitioner has failed to present evidence when such evidence can only be obtained with cooperation from the same State. This is because the State controls the means to verify the acts that take place within its territorial jurisdiction, and even though human rights bodies have the power to investigate human rights violations, they cannot do so without an express authorization from the State in question.[115]

In addition to examining the specific conditions of confinement, human rights bodies have considered the "death row phenomenon", which is characterized by a prolonged period of detention while awaiting execution. In assessing this phenomenon, human rights bodies have hesitated to convey any message to States Parties that they should carry out capital punishment as expeditiously as possible.[116] Thus, the HRC concluded that prolonged periods of detention on death row do not per se constitute cruel, inhuman or degrading treatment. In the leading case of *Errol Johnson v Jamaica*, concerning a prisoner who had spent more than 11 years on death row the HRC expressed the view that although life on death row is harsh, it "is preferable to death". In contrast, in *Soering v United Kingdom*, the Eur. Ct. HR found that the "death row phenomenon" in the United States amounts to cruel, inhuman and degrading treatment, taking into account numerous aspects of the conditions of confinement.

5.3.4   Freedom of thought, conscience and religion

In reaction to both the positive demands of religion and the negative experiences of religious conflict, freedom of conscience and belief

---

113   Ibid.
114   *Velásquez-Rodriguez v Honduras* (n. 104), para. 138.
115   Ibid., paras 135–6.
116   CCPR No 588/1994, sec 8.1–8.5. See also *LaVende v Trinidad and Tobago* CCPR Comm no 554/1993, UN Doc CCPR/C/61/D/554/1993 (17 Nov 1997) (18 years on death row).

has long been pursued.[117] Yet, despite this and the non-discrimination clauses in the UN Charter, religious freedom proved to be one of the most contentious issues to arise in drafting the UDHR. What became Article 18 underwent considerable revision during the drafting process, ultimately ensuring freedom of thought conscience and belief, as well as the right to manifest or practise religion. Article 18 of the ICCPR expands on the UDHR provision and is supplemented by Article 19 on freedom of opinion and expression. ICCPR Article 18(2) is particularly significant in adding to the guarantees of the UDHR that "[n]o one shall be subject to coercion which would impair his freedom to have or to adopt a religion or belief of his choice".[118] Significantly, no State has filed a reservation to Article 18, either at the time of signing or at ratification.

The 1981 UN Declaration on the Elimination of All Forms of Intolerance and of Discrimination Based on Religion or Belief (A/RES/36/55), which took nearly two decades to draft, gives content to the right to freedom of thought, conscience and religion. A decade later, the 1993 Concluding Document of the Vienna Conference on Human Rights expanded the guarantees of the 1981 Declaration, specifying the rights of religious groups to govern their own polity, property and personnel, to establish charities, schools and seminaries, and to have access to literature, media and religious worship items. The 2007 UN Declaration on the Rights of Indigenous Peoples extends these rights of religious self determination even further for indigenous, aboriginal or first peoples and their distinctive religious sites and rites.

The UN Human Rights Council has expressed its concern about "continuing acts of intolerance and violence based on religion or belief against individuals, including persons belonging to religious

---

117 Guarantees of religious liberty are far older and more diverse than is generally credited. In Persia some 2,500 years ago, the emperor Cyrus (580–29 BCE) established a broad regime of religious tolerance, restoring sanctuaries that had been destroyed and providing guarantees against religious discrimination. The text of the Cyrus cylinder is available at: www.britishmuseum.org/explore/highlights/articles/c/cyrus_cylinder_-_translation.aspx. The Edicts of Asoka in India (400 BCE) also guaranteed religious liberty. An English version of the Edicts is available at www.cs.coloState.edu/~malaiya/ashoka.html.

118 Such coercion can be direct or indirect, including not only the threat or use of force or sanctions, but also policies and practices conditioning access to education, medical care, employment or other rights, as well as State-imposed obligations to disclose one's religion or belief. See General Comment No. 22, UN Doc. CCPR/C/21/Rev.1/Add.4 (1993), Annex 5.

communities and religious minorities around the world".[119] The Council has emphasized the importance of freedom of thought, conscience, and religion or belief, reiterating the fundamental guarantees of prior texts. It has specifically called on States to ensure nondiscriminatory constitutional and legislative guarantees of freedom of thought, conscience and religion.

Regional instruments also guarantee freedom of conscience and belief. Article 9 of the European Convention drew its inspiration and its text from UDHR Article 18. The EU Charter of Fundamental Rights adds to the religious guarantees a specific mention of the right of conscientious objection to military service. The countries participating in the OSCE affirmed in the Copenhagen Concluding Document of 1990 that "everyone will have the right to freedom of thought, conscience and religion. This right includes freedom to change one's religion or belief".[120] The American Convention (Art. 12), African Charter on Human and Peoples' Rights (Art. 8), the African Charter on the Rights and Welfare of the Child (Art. 9),[121] the Revised Arab Charter of Human Rights (Art. 30), and the ASEAN Declaration of Human Rights (Art. 22) all contain similar guarantees.

These instruments generally distinguish between the right to freedom of conscience, religion or belief (often referred to as the *forum internum*) and the freedom to manifest one's religion or belief. The internal dimension encompasses the freedom to have, to alter or to adopt a religion of one's choice and is an absolute right from which there can be no derogation and which may not be restricted. In contrast, freedom to *manifest* or exercise one's religion (individually or collectively, publicly or privately) may be limited, but only when prescribed by law and when necessary to protect public safety, order, health or morals or the fundamental rights and freedoms of others.[122] The requirement

---

119 Res 22/20, *Freedom of Religion or Belief*, Human Rights Council, 12 Apr 2013. Res 22/31, adopted 15 Apr 2013, reinforces the first resolution by calling for action to combat intolerance, negative stereotyping and stigmatization of, and discrimination, incitement to violence and violence against, persons based on religion or belief.

120 Para. 9.4, Section II of the Document of the Copenhagen Meeting of the Conference on the Human Dimension of the OSCE 1990 (1990) 29 ILM 1311, also reprinted in OSCE/ODIHR, *Guidelines for Review of Legislation Pertaining to Religion or Belief* (Jun 2004), p. 45.

121 African Charter on the Rights and Welfare of the Child, 11 Jul 1990, entered into force 29 Nov 1999, OAU Doc CAB/LEG/24.9/49.

122 See *Raihon Hudoyberganova v Uzbekistan*, HRC, Comm No 931/2000, UN Doc CCPR/C/82/D/931/2000 5 Nov 2004; contrast *Leyla Sahin v Turkey*, ECtHR (2007), 44 EHRR 5.

of necessity implies that any such limitation on the manifestation of religion must be proportionate to its aim to protect one of the listed State interests.[123] Notably, the ICCPR adds a prohibition of religious hate speech: "any advocacy of national, racial, or *religious* hatred that constitutes incitement to discrimination, hostility, or violence".

In practice, defining religion has been problematic. Governments often deny religious status to new or controversial groups they label "sects" or "cults". Human rights bodies have not denied the permissibility of States having an official registration process that allows the government to define what is and is not a religion, or to recognize only certain (theistic) religions. In Resolution 22/20 of 12 April 2013, the Human Rights Council recommended only that States review registration practices "in order to ensure that such practices do not limit the right of all individuals to manifest their religion or belief, either alone or in community with others and in public or private".

Beyond defining religion, perhaps the most common problem is determining the limits of a State's proscriptions or prescriptions that run directly counter to core claims of conscience or faith-based commandments. Questions arise about the limits of religious exercises and expressions, including teaching and soliciting converts, carrying out practices that may offend others or elicit charges of blasphemy, defamation or sacrilege.

Criminalization of expression is increasingly supported under the guise of promoting tolerance. The European Court appears to accept as appropriate State enforcement of "tolerance", finding within the Article 9 guarantee of peaceful enjoyment of religion a right to be free from gratuitously offensive and profane expression in regard to objects of veneration, imposing a corresponding duty on others. The result has been to defer to State enactments of criminal blasphemy statutes, even when their application is limited to one or more specific, preferred religions. The decisions give religious beliefs a zone of protection not extended to political opinions or other deeply held beliefs.[124] In fact, numerous States have enacted vaguely worded laws

---

123 See Symposium, *The Permissible Scope of Legal Limitations on the Freedom of Religion and Belief* (2005) 19 EMORY INTERNATIONAL LAW REVIEW 465–1320.

124 The European Court expressly allows States a wider margin of appreciation to regulate freedom of expression when it touches on matters "liable to offend" religious convictions. *Wingrove v United Kingdom*, 1996-V; 24 EHRR 1, para. 58.

against "religious vilification", "religiously aggravated harassment" or maintained and reinforced laws against blasphemy or insulting religion, or for teaching doctrines contrary to the established religion. [125]

The core of the international test for government limitations on religion lies in assessing whether the particular limitation is "necessary in a democratic society", that is, whether it serves a "pressing social need" and is "proportionate to the legitimate aim pursued". In assessing which limitations are proportionate, international tribunals have recalled that freedom of thought, conscience and religion is one of the foundations of a democratic society. Moreover, State conduct must remain neutral and impartial, not imposing arbitrary or discriminatory constraints on the right to manifest religion. Even neutral State regulations cannot impose excessive and arbitrary burdens on the right to associate and worship in community with others. Restrictive laws may be found to violate religious liberty if they are not narrowly tailored to further one of the permissible legitimating grounds for limitation, or if alternative and less burdensome ways exist to achieve the State objective. Restrictions on religious freedom "must not impair the very essence of the right in question".

International and domestic jurisprudence on these matters varies widely. On the one hand, conscientious objection has rarely served to justify exemption from the payment of income taxes, service on civil or criminal juries, education of children, their immunization against disease, the requirement that parents provide them financial support, or service in the defence of the country. Increasingly, however, exemptions are provided for conscientious objection to armed military service or to oath taking that violates religious beliefs. Decisions on dress codes and acts motivated or influenced by a religion or belief, such as war protests or withholding a portion of taxes dedicated to mili-

---

125 Section 194 of the Penal Code of Yemen, for example, provides as follows: "Every person who publicly broadcasts opinions that deride or disparage religion or religious beliefs, practices or teachings, publicly incites contempt for a confessional group, or promotes the idea of the superiority of a confessional group, in such a way as to undermine public order, shall be liable to a term of imprisonment of not more than three years or a fine". The penality is extended by section 195 to five years "[w]here the religion or creed that is the subject of the disparagement, derision or contempt is the Islamic religion . . ." For a critique of limits on artistic expression, see Sharnon Shah, *Freedom of Expression and Religious Harassment: An Artist's Perspective* (2008) 2 THE EQUAL RIGHTS REVIEW 28.

tary purposes, are inconsistent.[126] Prejudice as much as principle may sometimes influence decision makers.

5.3.5   Freedom of expression

At its first session in 1946, the UN General Assembly affirmed that "[f]reedom of information is a fundamental human right and is the touchstone of all the freedoms to which the United Nations is consecrated. Freedom of information implies the right to gather, transmit and publish news anywhere and everywhere without fetters".[127] This ringing affirmation was countered the following year by resolution 110 (II) of 3 November 1947, which condemned all forms of propaganda involving a threat to the peace. During the same session, resolution 127 (II) invited member States to study what national measures might be taken, within constitutional limits, to combat "the diffusion of false or distorted reports likely to injure friendly relations between States". The tension revealed by these resolutions between upholding the right to freedom of expression and allowing appropriate limitations to serve other societal interests has occupied global and regional human rights bodies for more than 60 years. The controversy has not precluded guarantees of freedom of opinion and expression from being included in all the major human rights instruments, balanced by limitations clauses. Human rights instruments usually contain a single, often detailed article on freedom of expression. Article 19 of the UDHR affirms: "Everyone has the right to freedom of opinion and expression; this right includes freedom to hold opinions without interference and to seek, receive and impart information and ideas through any media and regardless of frontiers". Article 19 of the ICCPR[128] provides greater detail, but ICCPR Article 20 suggests that certain speech is not protected by Article 19: States are expected to prohibit by law propaganda for war and advocacy of national, racial or religious hatred that constitutes incitement to discrimination, hostility or violence.[129] The inclusion of Article 20 in the ICCPR proved controversial, because many States felt that the limitations clause of Article 19(3) would be

---

126   See the cases discussed by PAUL M TAYLOR, FREEDOM OF RELIGION: UN AND EUROPEAN HUMAN RIGHTS LAW AND PRACTICE (CUP 2005), ch. 3.

127   Res 59(I) of 14 Dec 1946.

128   See also Art. 13 of the CRC (guaranteeing freedom of expression to each child in terms similar to that of the ICCPR).

129   Art. 4 of CERD similarly calls for measures to combat propaganda and incitement to discrimination. Arts 5 and 10(c) of CEDAW less ambitiously refer to education and other promotional measures to combat stereotypes.

sufficient to restrict the speech referred to in Article 20; others felt that the former measure was inadequate to reach prohibited advocacy and propaganda. The provision was adopted, but 16 Western European and other industrialized States have filed reservations to Article 20.

Regional provisions on freedom of expression and information vary in content. The ECHR[130] Article 10, is similar to the later-drafted ICCPR, but adds that its guarantees "shall not prevent States from requiring the licensing of broadcasting, television or cinema enterprises". The American Convention contains a much longer and more detailed Article 13, which expressly prohibits prior censorship and "indirect means of restriction on expression". The African Charter of Human and Peoples Rights Article 9 grants every individual the right to receive information and the right to express and disseminate opinions "within the law". The 2004 Revised Arab Charter on Human Rights Article 32 "guarantees the right to information and to freedom of opinion and expression, as well as the right to seek, receive and impart information and ideas through any media, regardless of frontiers", but like other treaties provides that "such rights and freedoms shall be exercised in conformity with the fundamental values of society and shall be subject only to such limitations as are required to ensure respect for the rights or reputation of others or the protection of national security, public order and public health or morals". Both the American Convention and Arab Charter contain specific guarantees for individuals to be protected by law against attacks on their honour and reputation[131] with the American Convention uniquely adding a right of reply in Article 14. The ASEAN Declaration couples the right to protection by law against attacks on honour and reputation with the right to privacy in Article 21. Article 23 on freedom of opinion and expression guarantees "the freedom to hold opinions without interference and to seek, receive and impart information, whether orally, in writing or through any other medium of that person's choice". Incitement to hatred based on religion and beliefs "shall be eliminated" according to ASEAN Declaration Article 22. The ASEAN text also contains a general limitation clause in Article 8 and a linking of rights and duties in Article 6, provisions that potentially limit the exercise of freedom of expression.

---

130 See generally MALCOLM SHAW, INTERNATIONAL LAW (5th edn, CUP 2002), 321; Jean-François Flauss, *The European Court of Human Rights and the Freedom of Expression* (2009) 84 INDIANA LJ 809.

131 American Convention, Art. 11; Arab Charter, Art. 21.

In sum, more variation exists in the formulation of the right to freedom of expression than exists with respect to most other rights common to global and regional human rights instruments. All of them guarantee freedom of opinion and expression, but all of them also permit or even require some content-based restrictions or sanctions for abusive expression. A growing jurisprudence has applied these provisions without necessarily clarifying the exact scope of the right or assuring its enjoyment in a non-discriminatory manner.

Human rights tribunals recognize that freedom of expression has several interdependent components, including an individual dimension and "a collective right to receive any information whatsoever and to have access to the thoughts expressed by others".[132] The individual dimension of freedom of expression is broader than the theoretical right to write and speak. The individual dimension "includes and cannot be separated from the right to use whatever medium is deemed appropriate to impart ideas and to have them reach as wide an audience as possible".[133]

In its collective or societal dimension, freedom of expression is guaranteed because it is "indispensable for the formation of public opinion. It is also a condition sine qua non for the development of political parties, trade unions, scientific and cultural societies and, in general, those who wish to influence the public. It represents the means that enable a community to be sufficiently informed".[134] Thus, freedom of speech is not only an individual right essential for each person's self-fulfilment, but it is fundamental to the establishment and maintenance of a democratic society[135] based on pluralism, tolerance and open-mindedness.[136] Public confidence in government institutions and authorities requires transparency;[137] in addition States have an affirmative obligation to

---

132 *Canese v Paraguay* Inter-Am Ct HR (Ser C) no 111 at 77 (2004).

133 Advisory Opinion OC-5/85, para. 31; *"The Last Temptation of Christ"* 2001 Inter-Am Ct HR (Ser C) no 73 at para. 65 (2001); *Herrera Ulloa v Costa Rica* 2004 Inter-Am Ct HR (Ser C) no 107 at para. 109 (2004).

134 Advisory Opinion OC-5/85, para. 70; *Herrera Ulloa* (n. 133), para. 112; *Canese* (n. 132), para. 82.

135 See *Handyside v United Kingdom* (1976) 24 ECHR (Ser A); *Lingens v Austria* (1986) 103 ECHR (Ser A) para. 41; *Oberschlick v Austria (no 2)* (1997) 1997-IV ECHR 1266, 1270 para. 57; *Castells v Spain* (1994) App no 15890/89 (Ser A) No 298, 19 EHRR 445 para. 42; *Jersild v Denmark* (1995) 298 ECHR (Ser A) para. 31; *Goodwin v United Kingdom* [GC] (2002) 35 EHRR 18, para. 38; *Karhuvaara & Italehti v Finland* App no 53678/00 para. 37 (ECtHR, 21 Dec 2004); *Busuioc v Moldova*, App No 61513/00), 21 Dec 2004, para. 58.

136 See *Handyside* (n. 135) at 23.

137 See *De Haes v Belgium* (1997) 25 EHRR 1.

ensure that freedom of expression is protected against attacks coming from private individuals.[138]

The I-A Court and the Eur. Ct. HR agree in principle that freedom of expression goes beyond the dissemination of the information and ideas that are favourably received or considered inoffensive or indifferent.[139] The European Court has consistently stated, if not consistently upheld, that freedom of expression extends to information, ideas and opinions "that offend, shock or disturb", or those that counter conventional wisdom.[140] In political discourse, polemic and sarcastic language is acceptable.[141] Indeed, the Court views fierce attacks as part of the nature of politics: "in the domain of political discourse, the invective often touches upon a personal note; these are the occupational hazards of the game of politics and part and parcel of the open debate of ideas, the guarantors of a democratic society".[142] The same broad acceptance of militant speech may apply to some other areas of public policy, such as environmental protection.[143] The court has been uneven, however, in the protection afforded shocking artistic expression.[144] Sensationalism for its own sake is not legitimate, according to the Court,[145] nor is the gratuitous insult of another, but language such as "beasts in uniform", "wild beasts in uniform" and "sadistic brutes" uttered against police officers is not considered unacceptably insulting.[146] International tribunals are generally sceptical of criminal defamation laws.

---

138 See *Fuentes Bobo v Spain* (2001) 31 EHRR 1115, and *KL v The Netherlands*, CERD case No 4/1991, CERD 1994 Report, A/48/18, Annex IV; *VgT Verein Gegen Tierfabriken v Switzerland* App no 24699/94 (ECtHR, 28 June 2001); *Ozgur Gundem v Turkey* (2000) 2000-III ECHR 1, 21.

139 *Herrera Ulloa* (n. 133), para. 113; *Canese* (n. 132), para. 83 quoting *Scharsach and News Verlagsgesellschaft v Austria* (2003) 2003-XI ECHR 125, 2003 EHHR 596 at para. 29; *Sunday Times v United Kingdom* (n. 23), para. 65.

140 *Hertel v Switzerland* (1998) 1998-VI ECHR 2298, 2330. See, for example, *Giniewski v France* App no 64016/00 (ECtHR, 31 Jan 2006).

141 See *Lopes Gomes da Silva v Portugal* (2000) 2000-X ECHR 101, *Oberschlick v Austria* (n. 135), *Walb v Austria* App no 24773/94 (ECtHR, 21 Mar 2000) *Katrami v Greece* App no 19331/05 (ECtHR, 6 Dec 2007).

142 *Sanocki v Poland* App no 28949/03 (ECtHR, 17 Jul 2007).

143 See *Steel v United Kingdom* (2005) 2005-II ECHR 3.

144 See *Vereinigung Bildender Kunstler v Austria* App no 68354/01 (ECtHR, 25 Jan 2007), but see *Muller et al v Switzerland* (1988) 133 ECHR (Ser A).

145 See *Stoll v Switzerland* App no 69698/01 (ECtHR, 10 Dec 2007).

146 *Thorgeirson v Iceland* (1992) 239 ECHR (Ser A) at 17. Contrast *Klein v Slovakia* App no 72208/01 (ECtHR, 31 Dec 2006), where the court considered insulting the use of vulgar double entendres and sexual references against an archbishop, who had proposed banning a film he considered profane and blasphemous.

The European Court has determined that some speech is completely excluded from the guarantees of Article 10, while the HRC deems the protection afforded by ICCPR Article 19 to extend to "information and ideas of all kinds", including artistic, commercial, political, sexual, religious and even hate speech.[147] The prohibition of hate speech demanded by Article 20 must therefore be compatible with Article 19 and meet the tests set forth in Article 19(2).[148] Nonetheless, the HRC declared two early communications inadmissible, suggesting that the expressions in question did not fall within the guarantees of Article 19.[149] More recently, the Committee has chosen to address such petitions on the merits and explicitly linked Articles 19 and 20. The European Court has explained its contrasting view: that "remarks aimed at inciting racial hatred in society or propagating the idea of a superior race can not claim any protection under Article 10 of the Convention";[150] that "expressions that seek to spread, incite or justify hatred based on intolerance, including religious intolerance, do not enjoy the protection afforded by Article 10";[151] and again that the protection granted by Article 10 does not apply to "concrete words constituting hate speech that might be offensive to individuals or groups".[152]

Article 4(a) of CERD expressly includes a requirement to prohibit hate speech based on "ethnic origin", which is deemed to extend to immigrants and aliens. When Denmark presented its periodic report to the CERD[153] after the publication of notorious cartoons deemed insulting by Muslims, the CERD Committee called for broader measures

---

147 *Ballantyne, Davidson and McIntyre v Canada* CCPR Comm nos 359 and 385/1989, UN Doc CCPR/C/47/D/359/1989 and 385/1989/Rev 1 (10 Apr and 21 Nov 1989 (finding commercial advertising to be protected by Art. 19).

148 In the HRC, see *Malcolm Ross v Canada* CCPR Comm no 736/1997, UN Doc CCPR/C/70/D/736/1997 (2000) and *Faurisson v France* CCPR Comm no 550/1993, UN Doc CCPR/C/58/D/550/1993 at paras 9–10 (1995).

149 *Western Guard Party v Canada* CCPR Comm no 104/1981 (1990) was brought by a radical, right-wing political party that had been prevented from using telephone services to disseminate anti-Semitic messages. ICCPR, App No 104/1981. The Committee found that the messages fell within Art. 20(2) and therefore banning them could not be a violation of Art. 19. *MA v Italy* was brought by an individual convicted of participating in the re-establishment of the dissolved fascist party. The Committee rejected it as an abusive petition but added that it could also have been reviewed on the merits under the limitation clause in Art. 19(3). *MA v Italy* CCPR Comm no 1117/1981, UN Doc Supp no 40 (A/39/40) (10 Apr 1984).

150 *Aksoy v Turkey* (1996) ECHR 1996-VI, 23 EHRR 53.

151 *G and Z v Turkey* (2003) 2003-XI ECHR 257.

152 *Erbakan v Turkey* App no 59405/00 (ECtHR, 6 Jul 2006).

153 Report of Denmark, CERD/C/496/Add.1 2 September 2005.

in respect of refugees, asylum seekers and other immigrants.[154] The CERD Committee noted the government's efforts to combat hate crimes, but expressed concern about the increase in the number of racially motivated offences and complaints of hate speech and asked the government to remind public prosecutors of the importance of prosecuting racist acts and racially motivated offences.[155]

In general, restrictions on the right to freedom of protected speech are only permissible when they are prescribed by law, satisfy a legitimate purpose, and are necessary in a democratic society.[156] A restriction has been prescribed by law when there is a domestic statute in effect that limits freedom of expression. The State must identify the domestic law that authorizes the restriction and show that the law has a legitimate purpose. The legitimate purposes permitted by the American Convention include ensuring "respect for the rights or reputations of others or the protection of national security, public order, or public health or morals".[157] Even though a domestic law has a legitimate purpose, it may not limit freedom of expression more than is strictly necessary in a democratic society.[158] The State must choose the least restrictive option available to limit a protected right.[159] The I-A Court stated in this regard that the necessity and thus the legality of restrictions "depend[s] upon showing that the restrictions are required by a compelling public interest".[160] To demonstrate a compelling public interest the State has the burden of specifically showing that there is a pressing social need for the restriction.[161] In addition, the restriction must be proportionate to the interest that justifies it and closely tailored to accomplishing this legitimate objective, interfering as little as possible with the effective exercise of the right to freedom of expression.

---

154 Concluding Observations of the Committee on the Elimination of Racial Discrimination, CERD/C/DEN/CO/17, 25 Oct 2006.

155 Ibid., para. 11.

156 *Herrera Ulloa* (n. 133).

157 American Convention, Art. 13(2).

158 *Canese* (n. 132), para. 95.

159 Ibid., para. 96; *Herrera Ulloa* (n. 133), para. 121; Advisory Opinion OC-5/85, paras 46, 59; see also *Sunday Times v United Kingdom* (n. 23), para. 59.

160 *Canese* (n. 132), para. 96.

161 The I-A Court espoused the Eur. Ct. HR's interpretation of "necessary" to require the existence of a "pressing social need". *Herrera Ulloa* (n. 133), para. 122 (citing *Sunday Times v United Kingdom* (n. 23), para. 9; Advisory Opinion OC-5/85, para. 46; *Canese* (n. 132), para. 96.

The European Court often upholds limits on speech for the "protection of rights of others" when speech concerns a matter of religion or belief.[162] This has sometimes led to preventing minority groups from openly expressing their beliefs and exercising their right to freedom of expression. The importance given to the defence of religious convictions at time tends to confuse the moral views of the majority with the "protection of the rights of others" and to lead to coerced politeness. The Court deems that each speaker has "an obligation to avoid as far as possible expressions that are gratuitously offensive to others and thus an infringement on their rights, and which therefore do not contribute to any form of public debate capable of furthering progress in human affairs".[163] While the Court holds that expressions of doctrines antagonistic to the faith of believers must be tolerated, an important exception is made for injurious attacks against sacred symbols or objects of religious veneration.[164] The criteria seem at times to be selectively applied,[165] but in general, European jurisprudence appears to privilege religious belief over freedom of expression.[166] Remarks aimed at discrediting non-believers do not fall within the category of hate speech based on religious intolerance.[167]

Many of the complaints presented to the UN HRC have concerned censorship of particular media, such as films, broadcasts or art. All of the interferences are examined under the limitations clause of Article 19(3), although the *travaux préparatoires* indicate an intention to prohibit prior censorship completely,[168] similar to the prohibition contained in the American Convention. Eleven Latin American States proposed expressly excluding every form of prior censorship[169] and only withdrew their motion on the understanding that it was already precluded by the text. The European Court does not prohibit prior restraints on expression, but it does subject any such measure to

---

162 *Otto-Preminger-Institut v Austria* (1994) 295 ECHR (Ser A) at 6, 12, 19.

163 See, for example, *Giniewski v France* (n. 140).

164 See *Tatlav v Turkey* App no 50692/99 (ECtHR, 2 May 2006); *IA v Turkey* (2005) 2005-VIII ECHR 249, 257–8.

165 *Paturel v France* App no 54968/00 (ECtHR, 22 Dec 2005).

166 See *IA v Turkey* (n. 164), at 260–61 (Costa, Cabral Barreto and Jungwiert, JJ, dissenting).

167 See *Nur Radyo Ve Televizyon Yayinciligi A v Turkey* App no 6587/03 (ECtHR, 27 Nov 2007) (commenting that the court is to measure remarks by whether they encourage violence or hatred against non-believers); *G and Z v Turkey* (n. 151) 275 (finding that defending a religious view without calling for violence to establish it is not hate speech).

168 See Marc Bossuyt, Guide to the Travaux Preparatoires of the International Covenant on Civil and Political Rights (Nijhoff 1987), 398 ff.

169 A/C.3/L.926.

rigorous control.[170] As for post-publication sanctions, the Court tends to consider that any penal sanction must be disallowed, whether in the form of a monetary fine or a prison sentence.[171] Nonetheless, the Court has held that criminal law fines do not necessarily conflict with the demands of Article 10 of the Convention.[172] The Court has also been reluctant to allow excessive civil fines or other remedies that are likely to have a dissuasive effect on open discourse in light of the limited financial resources of the defendant.[173]

In sum, international tribunals recognize that the public dissemination of opinions and information carries with it risks and consequences. As the International Criminal Tribunal for Rwanda observed, "[t]he power of the media to create and destroy fundamental human values comes with great responsibility. Those who control such media are accountable for the consequences".[174] Thus, it is permitted to restrict the exercise of the right to freedom of expression, but only under strict simultaneous conditions that the restrictions are provided by law; they pursue an aim recognized as lawful, and they are proportionate to the accomplishment of that aim.[175]

5.3.6   Economic, social and cultural rights

The long and detailed list of economic, social and cultural rights contained in the ICESCR includes the right to work; the right to the enjoyment of just and favourable conditions of work; the right to form and join trade unions; the right to social security, including social insurance; the right to the protection of the family; the right to an adequate standard of living; the right to the enjoyment of the highest attainable standard of physical and mental health; the right of everyone to education; and the right to take part in cultural life. The ICESCR outlines the

---

170 The *Observer and Guardian*, 216A ECtHR (1992) 14 EHRR 153, para. 53 and *The Sunday Times* (n. 23), para. 51.

171 See *Falakaoglu v Turkey* App no 11461/03 (ECtHR, 19 Dec 2006); *Selisto v Finland* App no 56767/00 (ECtHR, 16 Nov 2004); *Erdal Tas v Turkey* App no 77650/01 (ECtHR, 19 Dec 2006).

172 *Stoll v Switzerland*, (n. 145).

173 See *Steel v United Kingdom* (n. 143); *Brasilier v France* App no 71343/01 (ECtHR, 4 Nov 2006); *Giniewski v France* (n. 140).

174 *Prosecutor v Nahimana, Barayagwiza and Ngeza*, Judgment and Sentence ICTR Case ICTR-99-52, 945 (2003).

175 Ibid., para. 46. The CCPR has insisted that all restrictions on the exercise of Art. 19 rights "must meet a strict test of justification". *Park v Republic of Korea*, App No 628/1995, para. 10.3; *Kim v Republic of Korea* CCPR Comm no 574/1994, UN Doc CCPR/C/64/D/574/1994, 64th Sess at paras 12.4–12.5 (4 Jan 1999).

content of the rights and some of them have been further elaborated in ILO and UNESCO conventions and by the work of other specialized agencies like the WHO and FAO. For some of the rights, including housing, food and education, the HRC has approved and maintained mandates for special rapporteurs. The CRC and CEDAW Committees may also be considered herein, as the rights in these treaties include both civil and political and economic and social rights.[176] The CERD Committee and the HRC have taken up economic, social and cultural rights at times as well.

In its General Comments and its observations on the periodic reports of States Parties, the CESCR has often provided a programme for States to achieve the rights in the Covenant, in some cases implying further rights. This active role is in part necessitated by the broad formulation of many of the rights, which are not defined or detailed, leaving States without guidance on the precise contents of the rights and their corresponding obligations. The generic obligations in the ICESCR, discussed in Chapter 6, are generally programmatic and to be achieved progressively, but there are some duties of immediate application. The two most often emphasized are to take steps towards realizing the rights and to ensure that the rights are exercised without discrimination. In General Comment No 3, the CESCR also insists that a minimum core obligation exists to ensure the satisfaction of at least certain minimum essential levels of each of the rights. These minimum levels are indicated in other General Comments addressing specific rights, but generally mean availability of essential foodstuffs, essential primary medical care, and basic shelter and housing.

In correlation with the obligation of progressive realization, human rights bodies have articulated a conditional duty of not adopting retrogressive steps. The CESCR Committee concluded that "any deliberately retrogressive measures in that regard would require the most careful

---

176 The CRC contains rights to health and welfare, education and culture. The CRC Committee has indicated that it views all the rights in the CRC as justiciable. See General Comment No 5 (2003), para. 25. In General Comment No 3 (2002) the CRC Committee discussed the rights of children with HIV. CEDAW similarly refers to education, health care, family life, employment and other areas of public life. The first CEDAW recommendation on economic and social rights, adopted in 1989, concerns equal pay for equal work. General Recommendation No 13 (1989). The CEDAW Committee has also adopted, among other recommendations giving content to the economic and social rights, a General Recommendation on the right to health. CEDAW Committee, General Recommendation No 24 (1999).

consideration and would need to be fully justified by reference to the totality of the rights of the [International] Covenant [on Economic, Social and Cultural Right] and in the context of the full use of the maximum available resources [of the State]".[177] The Inter-American Commission similarly has considered that in order to evaluate whether a regressive measure is compatible with the American Convention, it is necessary to "determine if it was justified by strong reasons".[178] Based on these analyses, the I-A Court has concluded that regression in respect to economic, social and cultural rights is actionable through the complaint mechanism.

Some of the ICESCR General Comments spell out in great detail the contents of the rights in the Covenant. These include General Comment No 4 (1991) on the right to adequate housing and General Comment No 15 (2002), which provides a comprehensive programmatic water policy, spelling out a right to water implied from the right to an adequate standard of living guaranteed in Article 11 and the right to health in Article 12.

The regional systems began with quite different approaches to economic, social, and cultural rights. The European system enshrined them in a separate treaty, the 1961 European Social Charter. In contrast, the African Charter, like the American and Universal Declarations, fully incorporates economic, social and cultural rights, as well as civil and political rights. In contrast to the American Declaration, the American Convention only contains a single article on the topic, Article 26, entitled "Economic, Social and Cultural Rights". In 1988 the OAS adopted the Protocol of San Salvador, adding economic and social rights but specifying that only the trade union rights of Article 8 and the right to education in Article 13 may be subject to the Convention's individual petition process. For the remaining rights, the Commission is given a mandate to formulate observations and recommendations to States, taking into account the progressive nature of the obligations, in line with Article 19 of the Protocol of San Salvador. The meaning and

---

177 Ibid.; United Nations, Committee on Economic, Social and Cultural Rights, Declaration on the "Evaluation of the obligation to take steps to the "Maximum of available resources" under an Optional Protocol to the Covenant", E/C.12/2007/1, 38° Period of Sessions, 21 Sep 2007, para. 10.

178 Report on Admissibility and Merits No 38/09, Case 12.670; *National Association of Ex-E mployees of the Peruvian Social Security Institute et al v Perú*, adopted by the Inter-American Commission on Human Rights, 27 Mar 2009, paras 140–47.

interaction of the three Inter-American instruments is the subject of considerable debate.[179]

The Eur. Ct. HR has no jurisdiction to apply the European Social Charter, which has its own complaints mechanism. Moreover, the ECHR is almost exclusively devoted to civil and political rights. Yet, the European Court inevitably monitors economic and social rights, in part because the rights to a fair hearing and redress extend to rights guaranteed under domestic law as well as rights contained in the ECHR. Thus, if economic and social rights are included in domestic constitutional provisions or laws, the rights of access to justice and a fair hearing will apply to them.[180]

More generally, rights in the ECHR often have an economic and social dimension. As early as the case of *Airey*, the European Court noted that:

> Whilst the Convention sets forth what are essentially civil and political rights, many of them have implications of a social or economic nature. The Court therefore considers, like the Commission, that the mere fact that an interpretation of the Convention may extend into the sphere of social and economic rights should not be a decisive factor against such an interpretation; there is no water-tight division separating that sphere from the field covered by the Convention.

This approach has led the European Court to interpret the right to privacy and home life in ECHR Article 8 to apply, for example, to severe environmental pollution which may affect individuals' well-being and adversely affect their private and family life, without necessarily endangering their health.[181] The jurisprudence also applies Article 8 where an

---

179   See James L Cavallaro and Emily J Schaffer, *Less as More: Rethinking Supranational Litigation of Economic and Social Rights in the Americas* (2005) 56 HASTINGS LJ 217; Tara Melish, *Rethinking the "Less as More" Thesis: Supranational Litigation of Economic, Social and Cultural Rights in the Americas* (2006) 39 NYU J INT'L. & POL 171; James L Cavallaro and Emily Schaffer, Rejoinder: *Justice before Justiciability: Inter-American Litigation and Social Change* (2006) 39 NYU J INT'L L & POL 345; Tara Melish, Counter-Rejoinder: *Justiced vs. Justiciability? Normative Neutrality and Technical Precision, the Role of the Lawyer in Supranational Social Rights Litigation* (2006) 39 NYU J INT'L L & POL 385.

180   See *Taskin v Turkey*, 2004-X; 42 EHRR 1127 (domestic right to a safe and healthy environment).

181   See *Lopez-Ostra v Spain*, 303-C ECtHR (1994); *Anna Maria Guerra and 39 others against Italy*, 1998-1 ECHR, Judgment of 19 Feb 1998; *Arrondelle v United Kingdom*, (1980) 19 DR 186; (1982) 26 DR 5; *Powell & Raynor v United Kingdom*, 172 ECtHR (1990); *Hatton and Others v The United*

environmental impact assessment has established a sufficiently close link between the dangerous effects of an activity to which the individuals concerned are likely to be exposed and the private and family life of the individuals. The Court will scrutinize both the decision-making process leading to the activity and the substantive merits of the decision, granting a wide margin of appreciation to authorities in respect to the merits. The decision-making process must involve appropriate investigations and studies in order to allow the authorities to predict and evaluate in advance the effects of those activities that might damage the environment and infringe individuals' rights, to enable the authorities to strike a fair balance between the various conflicting interests at stake. Public information, participation and redress are among the obligations of the State.

The European Social Charter establishes a regional European system for the protection of economic and social rights. The original Charter was opened for signature on 18 October 1961, and entered into force on 26 February 1965. An Additional Protocol to the Charter, expanding its catalogue of rights, was concluded on 5 May 1988. On 21 October 1991 the Turin Protocol Amending the European Social Charter was signed. This instrument reformed the supervisory mechanism of the Charter, and most of its provisions were implemented quickly through actions taken by the supervisory organs pending its entry into force. Two further instruments continued the evolution of the Social Charter. On 9 November 1995 an Additional Protocol provided for a system of collective complaints. Finally, in 1996 a revised Social Charter, bringing up to date the earlier documents and adding some new rights, was opened for signature. It entered into force on 1 July 1999, and it will progressively replace the original Charter.

The Revised Charter proclaims a list of 31 categories of "rights and principles", including the right to work, to just conditions of work, to safe working conditions, to fair remuneration, to organize, and to bargain collectively. Also included are the right of workers to equal treatment and to non-discrimination on the grounds of sex, the right to be informed and consulted, and the right to take part in the determination and improvement of the working conditions and environment in places of employment. Under the Revised Charter, disabled persons have the right to training and rehabilitation, and all workers have the

---

Kingdom (GC, 2003, 37 EHRR 28); *Okyay and Others v Turkey* (App no 36220/97, Judgment of 12 Jul 2005). In the case of *Fadeyeva v Russia*, App No 55723/00, Judgment of 9 Jun 2005.

right to engage in gainful occupations in the territory of another contracting party on an equal footing with nationals of that State.

The Revised Charter proclaims the right of protection for children, young people and women. Also recognized are the right of the family to social, legal and economic protection; the right of mothers and children to social and economic protection; and the right of migrant workers and their families to protection and assistance. The Charter also addresses vocational guidance and training, health protection, social security, social and medical assistance, and social welfare services benefits. The Charter provides that "every elderly person has the right to social protection" and contains guarantees in case of termination of employment or employer insolvency. Protections also are afforded for dignity at work, against discrimination due to family responsibilities, and against poverty. Finally, the Charter contains a provision on the right of everyone to housing.

These rights are proclaimed in general terms in Part I of the Revised Charter, where the contracting parties declare that they "accept as the aim of their policy, to be pursued by all appropriate means both national and international in character, the attainment of conditions in which ... [these] rights and principles may be effectively realized". These "rights and principles", or policy objectives, are to be transformed into enforceable rights. Part II of the Revised Charter defines the meaning of and elaborates on the "rights and principles" proclaimed in general terms in Part I.

Article A (Part III) of the Revised Charter specifies the obligations the States Parties assume by ratifying the Charter. The instrument gives the States a number of options. First, by becoming a party to the Charter, a State undertakes "to consider Part I of this Charter as a declaration of the aims which it will pursue by all appropriate means". Second, the State must accept as binding the undertakings contained in at least six out of nine articles found in Part II. The nine provisions are Article 1 (right to work), Article 5 (right to organize), Article 6 (right to bargain collectively), Article 7 (the right of children and young persons to protection), Article 12 (right to social security), Article 13 (right to social and medical assistance), Article 16 (right of the family to social, legal and economic protection), Article 19 (right of migrant workers and their families to protection and assistance) and Article 20 (right to equal opportunities and equal treatment in matters of employment and occupation without discrimination on the grounds of sex). Third, each State Party must select another specified number of rights or subcategories of rights with which it agrees to comply. See Revised Charter, Article A(1)(c).

This flexible system encourages States to ratify the Charter without forcing them either to accept all the rights it proclaims or to make complex reservations. It is also drafted so as to ensure that all States Parties will at the very least be bound to guarantee some of the most basic rights. Very few States have accepted all the rights the Charter proclaims.

The ESC complaint procedure is being increasingly utilized and has made the European Committee on Social Rights an increasingly judicialized body. The adversarial process received more than 65 complaints in the first decade after the entry into force of the Additional Protocol of the ESC in 1998, and the ECSR has addressed many of the rights in the ESC, including the right to housing,[182] freedom from child[183] and forced labour,[184] access to medical treatment,[185] and the right to education,[186] often in connection with allegations of discrimination.[187] Like the ILO complaints procedures, many of the collective complaints have concerned trade union freedoms, including collective bargaining rights.[188]

The ECSR looks to the object and purpose of each right in determining the scope of the guarantee. The right to housing, for example, is

---

182 *European Roma Rights Centre v Italy* (Merits), App 51/2008, Eur Ctte of Social Rights, 19 Oct 2009.

183 Complaint 1/1998, *International Commission of Jurists v Portugal*, Merits (1999).

184 Complaint 7/2000, *International Federation of Human Rights v Greece*, Merits (2000).

185 Complaint No 14/2003, International Federation of Human Rights Leagues *(FIDH) v France*.

186 See *Association internationale Autisme-Europe (AIAE) v France*, Complaint No 13/2002, Merits, ECSR, 4 Nov 2003.

187 Many of the discrimination cases concern the Roma. See, for example, *European Roma Rights Centre (ERRC) v Greece*, Complaint No 15/2003, Merits, ECSR, 8 Dec 2004; *European Roma Rights Centre (ERRC) v Italy*, Complaint No 27/2004, Merits, ECSR, 21 Dec 2005; *European Roma Rights Centre (ERRC) v Bulgaria*, Complaint No 31/2005, Merits, ECSR, 18 Oct 2006; *International Helsinki Federation for Human Rights (IHF) v Bulgaria*, Complaint No 44/2007, Merits, ECSR, 14 Sep 2007; *European Roma Rights Centre (ERRC) v Bulgaria*, Complaint No 46/2007, Merits, ECSR, 3 Dec 2008; *European Roma Rights Centre (ERRC) v Bulgaria*, Complaint No 48/2008, Decision on admissibility, ECSR, 2 Jun 2008; *European Roma Rights Centre (ERRC) v France*, Complaint No 51/2008, Merits, ECSR, 19 Oct 2009; *Centre on Housing Rights and Evictions (COHRE) v Italy*, Complaint No 58/2009, Merits, ECSR, 25 Jun 2009.

188 For a summary of all the complaints, see ECSR, *Collective Complaints Procedures: Summaries of Decisions on the Merits 1998–2012* (30 May 2013).

seen as "directed to the prevention of homelessness with its adverse consequences on individuals' personal security and well being. The right to housing secures social inclusion and integration of individuals into society and contributes to the abolishment of socio-economic inequalities". Given this, adequate housing

> means a dwelling which is structurally secure; safe from a sanitary and health point, i.e. it possesses all basic amenities, such as water, heating, waste disposal, sanitation facilities, electricity; not overcrowded and with secure tenure supported by law. The temporary supply of shelter cannot be considered as adequate and individuals should be provided with adequate housing within a reasonable period.[189]

More generally, the Committee has insisted that one of the underlying purposes of the social rights protected by the Social Charter "is to express solidarity and promote social inclusion. It follows that States must respect difference and ensure that social arrangements are not such as would effectively lead to or reinforce social exclusion".[190] This means the Committee strictly scrutinizes complaints alleging discrimination.

For the Americas, the Inter-American Commission first addressed the issue of economic and social rights in its 1979–80 annual report, positing a relationship between neglect of such rights and the suppression of political participation. Describing the relationship as one of cause and effect, the Commission stated that "the neglect of economic and social rights, especially when political participation has been suppressed, produces the kind of social polarization that then leads to acts of terrorism by and against the government". The Commission urged OAS member States to provide information concerning health, nutrition and literacy levels and the measures they were adopting to improve those levels so that the Commission could expand its efforts to make economic and social rights effective. Thereafter, beginning with country reports on El Salvador (1978), Nicaragua (1981) and Guatemala (1981), the Commission has examined economic, social and cultural rights, as well as civil and political rights in the hemisphere.

Like the European Court, the Inter-American bodies have used Convention rights traditionally regarded as civil and political rights to

---

189 *European Roma Rights Centre v Italy* (n. 187) para. 35.
190 *European Roma Rights Centre v Greece* (n. 187).

address problems often falling broadly within the scope of economic and social rights, like health care, food and shelter. A broad interpretation and application of the right to life, in particular, has been a key to this development within the Inter-American system.[191] Human rights advocates have filed petitions with the IACHR alleging violations of economic and social rights using a combination of the American Declaration and Convention Article 26.

In *Acevedo Buendía v Perú* the I-A Court for the first time considered allegations of a violation of the right to social security based on Article 26 of the Convention. The applicants' legal representative argued that the general obligations in the Convention to respect and guarantee rights, as well as adapt domestic law to the Convention, apply not only with regard to civil and political rights but also to economic, social and cultural rights. In response, the I-A Court insisted that it is competent to monitor compliance with all the rights in the Convention. The Court nonetheless examined the drafting history of Article 26, noting that it underwent an intense debate during the Convention's drafting. The Court's review proved to it that States sought to give economic, social and cultural rights "the maximum protection compatible with the peculiar conditions to most of the American States" (para. 99). The Court noted that Article 26 is positioned in Part I of the Convention, entitled "State Obligations and Rights Protected" and, therefore, is subject to the general obligations contained in Articles 1(1) and 2, to the same extent as civil and political rights. The Court concluded that all of the rights should be fully understood as human rights, without any rank and enforceable in all the cases before competent authorities. The State is obliged to adopt provisions and provide the means and elements necessary to give effect to the rights in question, within the scope of its economic and finance resources.[192] The obligations may be subjected to accountability before human rights tribunals.

In the African Commission's landmark case of *SERAC v Nigeria*, complainants alleged that the Nigerian government violated the right to

---

191 See for example *Xákmok Kásek Indigenous Community v Paraguay* I-A Court HR Ser. C No. 214 (24 Aug 2010) (interpreting the right to life to mean a dignified existence, incorporating inter alia rights to water, food, health and education).

192 United Nations, Committee on Economic, Social and Cultural Rights, Declaration on the "Evaluation of the obligation to take steps to the 'Maximum of available resources' under an Optional Protocol to the Covenant", E/C.12/2007/1, 38° Period of Sessions, 21 Sep 2007, para. 8.

health and the right to clean environment guaranteed by Articles 16 and 24 of the African Charter by failing to fulfil the minimum duties required by these rights. The Commission commented that "these rights recognize the importance of a clean and safe environment that is closely linked to economic and social rights in so far as the environment affects the quality of life and safety of the individual" (para. 9) and insisted that it "requires the State to take reasonable and other measures to prevent pollution and ecological degradation, to promote conservation, and to secure an ecologically sustainable development and use of natural resources" (para. 10). The Commission cited the ICESCR in adding that the right to enjoy the best attainable state of physical and mental health enunciated in Article 16(1) of the African Charter and the right to a general satisfactory environment favourable to development (Art. 16(3)) obligate governments to desist from directly threatening the health and environment of their citizens. The African Commission took the opportunity to reflect on the significance of the regional system and to make clear that there is no right in the African Charter that cannot be made effective (para. 26). Subsequent cases have further elaborated the content of various economic, social and cultural rights in the African Charter.[193]

In the application of economic, social and cultural rights the various human rights bodies influence each other. The Eur. Ct. HR has referred to the ESCR's work and the latter committee, in turn, has referred to the case law of the Eur. Ct. HR, the Court of Justice of the EU, as well as the judgments of the I-A Court, the General Comments of the UN Committee of Economic, Social and Cultural Rights and the work of the ILO.

5.3.7   Right of access to justice and remedies

Reparation is the "indispensable complement" of a failure to comply with the law; it is a duty of the wrong-doing State as well as a right of the injured party; the duty arises automatically upon the commission

---

193 See *Centre for Minority Rights Development (Kenya) and Minority Rights Group International on behalf of Endorois Welfare Council v Kenya* Afr Comm'n HPR Case 276/2003 (2010) (right to culture, indigenous land rights); *Free Legal Assistance Group et al v Zaire* [2000] AHRLR 74 (AfCHPR 1995) (right to water and sanitation); *Socio Economic Rights Project v Nigeria*, Comm 300/05 (right to education). Chidi Odinkalu, *Analysis of Paralysis or Paralysis of Analysis? Implementing Economic, Social, and Cultural Rights Under the African Charter on Human and Peoples' Rights* (2001) 23 HUMAN RTS Q 327.

of a wrongful act.[194] Reparation should, insofar as possible, wipe out the consequences of the illegal act and re-establish the situation which would, in all probability, have existed if that act had not been committed.[195] The right to a remedy in human rights law comprises two aspects – on the one hand, the procedural right of access to justice and, on the other hand, the substantive right to redress or reparation for injury suffered because of an act or acts committed in violation of rights contained in national or international law.

On the procedural side, the attributes of an effective remedy include the institutional independence of the remedial body from the authority responsible for the violation, the ability to invoke the guaranteed right, procedural fairness, capability of the remedial body to afford redress, and effectiveness in fact. Some international agreements explicitly call for the development of judicial remedies for the rights they guarantee, although others accept that effective remedies also may be supplied by non-judicial bodies. These elements have been developed in the case law of human rights bodies. Although no definition of the term "remedy" is found, the Eur. Ct. HR has been clear in finding that it does not cover discretionary actions or matters of grace, such as a "petition to the Queen".[196]

In general, the reparation provided through an effective remedy should be proportional to the gravity of the violations and damages suffered. The measures taken include restitution, whenever possible, to restore the victim to the situation existing before the violation occurred. Restitution can involve return of property or money, release of detainees, reinstatement of an individual wrongfully or arbitrarily discharged, or other measures to eliminate the wrong. Rehabilitation may include medical and psychological care as well as legal and social services.

Satisfaction, as a form of reparation, has been important in the human rights field. Satisfaction may require cessation; disclosure of the truth; measures to restore the dignity, the reputation and the rights of the victim and of persons closely connected with the victim; public apology, including acknowledgement of the facts and acceptance of responsibility; judicial and administrative sanctions against persons liable

---

194 *Factory at Chorzow (Germany v Poland)* (Jurisdiction), Judgment No 8, 1927 Permanent Court of International Justice (PCIJ) Series A, No 9, p. 21.

195 Ibid., p. 47.

196 *Greece v The United Kingdom*, Apps 176/56 and 299/5, 2 YB 176 (1958).

for the violations; and commemorations and tributes to the victims. Satisfaction thus includes truth telling, recovery and reburial of victims' remains, actions to restore victims' reputation, apology and commemorations. It also may include judicial and administrative sanctions against those responsible. Guarantees of non-repetition are important in human rights cases and may include strengthening of national institutions under the rule of law, including independence of the judiciary and civilian control of the military and security forces.

Compensation is required for pecuniary and moral damages in most cases. Compensation is deemed "adequate" if it is "proportionate to the gravity of the human rights violation (eg the period of disappearance, the conditions of detention, etc) and to the suffering of the victim and the family". Amounts shall be provided for any damage, including physical or mental harm, lost opportunities, material damages and loss of earnings, harm to reputation, and costs required for legal or expert assistance.

The UDHR provides that "[e]veryone has the right to an effective remedy by the competent national tribunals for acts violating the fundamental rights granted him by the constitution or laws". The ICCPR contains three separate articles on remedies. The first, Article 2(3), obliges the States Parties to the Covenant to afford an effective remedy to a victim notwithstanding that the violation has been committed by persons acting in an official capacity; to ensure that claims are heard by competent judicial, administrative or legislative authorities; and to ensure that the competent authorities shall enforce such remedies when granted. Articles 9(5) and 14(6) add that anyone unlawfully arrested, detained or convicted shall have an enforceable right to compensation or be compensated according to law.

On the procedural side, ICCPR Article 2(3)(b) defines the general obligation to provide an effective remedy by specifying that all persons have a right to a decision by a competent domestic authority, if possible a judicial body. HRC General Comment 32 (2007) provides further detail on the right to a fair and public hearing by a competent independent and impartial tribunal. The right to equality before courts and tribunals and the right to a fair trial are called key elements of human rights protection and procedural means to safeguard the rule of law. As such, the guarantees of fair trial may never be made subject to measures of derogation that would circumvent the protection of non-derogable rights. General Comment No 3 issued by the CESCR, concerning the nature of state obligations pursuant to Covenant Article 2(1), proclaimed that appropriate measures to implement the ESC Covenant might include judicial remedies with respect to rights that may be considered justiciable. It specifically pointed to the non-discrimination requirement of the treaty and cross-referenced to the right to a remedy in the ICCPR. A number of other rights also were cited as "capable of immediate application by judicial and other organs".

Access to justice may also require affording individuals recourse to tribunals to obtain preventive measures when a violation is threatened. CERD Article 6 requires that States Parties assure to everyone within their jurisdiction effective protection and remedies, through the competent national tribunals and other State institutions, against any acts of racial discrimination in violation of the Convention, as well as the right to seek from such tribunals just and adequate reparation or satisfaction for any damage suffered as a result of such discrimination. The language of this provision anticipates the use of injunctive or other preventive measures against discrimination, as well as compensation or other remedies for consequential damages. A similar provision requiring effective protection of women from discrimination is found in Article 2(c) of CEDAW. The UDHR and several global and regional treaties similarly refer to the right to legal protection for attacks on privacy, family, home or correspondence, or attacks on honour and reputation.

The HRC has identified the kinds of remedies required, depending on the type of violation and the victim's condition. The Committee has indicated that a State that has engaged in human rights violations, in addition to treating and compensating the victim financially, must undertake to investigate the facts, take appropriate action, and bring to justice those found responsible for the violations. The Committee's recommended actions have included: public investigation to establish the facts; bringing to justice the perpetrators; paying compensation; ensuring non-repetition of the violation; amending the offending law; providing restitution; and providing medical care and treatment. In the case of *Hugo Rodriguez v Uruguay*, the Committee affirmed that amnesties for gross violations of human rights are incompatible with the duty to provide effective remedies to the victims of those abuses. Nor are purely disciplinary and administrative remedies adequate and effective within the meaning of Article 2(3) for particularly serious violations. The CESCR also has indicated the types of remedy it would consider appropriate under its quasi-judicial optional protocol.[197]

The United Nations Convention against Torture, (adopted 10 December 1984, in force 26 June 1987) 1465 UNTS 85, Article 14, specifies as follows:

> Each State Party shall ensure in its legal system that the victim of an act of torture obtains redress and has an enforceable right to fair and adequate compensation, including the means for as full rehabilitation as possible. In the event of the death of the victim as a result of an act of torture, his dependents shall be entitled to compensation.

Among treaties adopted by the specialized agencies, the ILO Convention No 169 Concerning Indigenous and Tribal Peoples in Independent Countries refers to "fair compensation for damages" (Art. 15(2)), "compensation in money" (Art. 16(4)) and full compensation for "any loss or injury" (Art. 16(5)).

Non-monetary remedies may be specified. In General Recommendation No 5[198] the Committee on the Elimination of Discrimination against Women announced that States Parties should make more use of temporary special remedial measures such as positive action, preferential treatment or quota systems to advance women's integration into education, the economy, politics and employment. The Working Group on Involuntary or Enforced Disappearances also made reference to non-monetary remedies in a commentary to Article 19 of the 1992 UN Declaration on the Protection of All Persons from Enforced Disappearance. The Working Group noted that the Declaration imposes a primary duty to establish the fate and whereabouts of disappeared persons as an important remedy for victims.

Various UN declarations further specify the remedies and redress to which those injured are entitled. The UN Declaration of Basic Principles of Justice for Victims of Crime and Abuse of Power also contains broad guarantees for those who suffer pecuniary losses, physical or mental harm and "substantial impairment of their fundamental

---

197 CESCR Statement, "An Evaluation of the Obligation to Take Steps to the 'Maximum of Available Resources' under an Optional Protocol to the Covenant", 10 May 2007, E/C.12/2007/1, para. 13.
198 7th Sess 1988, UN Doc A/43/38.

rights" through acts or omissions, including abuse of power.[199] In 1992 the UN Human Rights Sub-Commission took up the question of the impunity of perpetrators of human rights violations.[200] The final report submitted in 1997 speaks of three fundamental rights of victims: the right to know, the right to justice, and the right to reparation. The report refers to "the right of victims or their families to receive fair and adequate compensation within a reasonable period of time" and annexes a set of principles on this topic, including issues directly relating to the right to restitution, compensation and rehabilitation of victims.[201] An independent expert subsequently appointed to study best practices and make recommendations to assist States in strengthening their domestic capacity to combat impunity, making use of the principles on the topic, submitted a study in 2004 that contains a chapter on the right to reparation,[202] referred to as a fundamental tenet of international human rights law.

Finally, the UN General Assembly in Resolution 60/147 adopted and proclaimed Basic Principles and Guidelines on the Right to a Remedy and Reparation for Victims of Gross Violations of International Human Rights Law and Serious Violations of International Humanitarian Law.[203] The GA recommended that States

> take the Basic Principles and Guidelines into account, promote respect thereof and bring them to the attention of members of the executive bodies of government, in particular law enforcement officials and military and security forces, legislative bodies, the judiciary, victims and their representatives, human rights defenders and lawyers, the media and the public in general.[204]

In the preamble, the GA emphasized its view that the Basic Principles and Guidelines do not entail new international or domestic legal obligations but only "identify mechanisms, modalities, procedures

---

199 GA Res 40/34 (adopted 29 Nov 1985), Annex, "Declaration of Basic Principles of Justice for Victims of Crime and Abuse of Power", para. 1.

200 Sub-Commission Res 1992/23 of Aug 1992, approved by the Commission on Human Rights in Res 1993/43 of 5 Mar 1993.

201 E/CN.4/Sub.2/1997/20 of 26 Jun 1997 and E/CN.4/Sub.2/1997/20/Rev.1 of 2 Oct 1997.

202 *Independent Study on Best Practices, including Recommendations, to Assist States in Strengthening their Domestic Capacity to Combat all Aspects of Impunity, by Professor Diane Orentlicher*, E/CN.4/2004/88, 24 Feb 2004.

203 GA Res 60/147 (adopted 16 Dec 2005).

204 Ibid. para. 2.

and methods for the implementation of existing legal obligations under international human rights law and international humanitarian law which are complementary though different as to their norms".

Summarizing the principles, victims of gross violations of international human rights law and serious violations of international humanitarian law are entitled to:

(a) equal and effective access to an effective judicial remedy as provided for under international law; access to administrative and other bodies, as well as mechanisms, modalities, and proceedings conducted in accordance with domestic law;

(b) adequate, effective and prompt reparation for harm suffered proportional to the gravity of the violations and the harm suffered, and including: restitution, compensation, rehabilitation, satisfaction, and guarantees of non-repetition; States should provide effective mechanisms for enforcing reparation judgments under their domestic laws; and

(c) access to relevant information concerning violations and reparation mechanisms.

On the regional level, the ECHR Article 13 is modelled after Article 8 of the UDHR. The Eur. Ct. HR has interpreted Article 13 as guaranteeing an effective remedy "to everyone who claims that his rights and freedoms under the Convention have been violated".[205] The notion of an effective remedy may require, in addition to the payment of compensation where appropriate, a thorough and effective investigation capable of leading to the identification and punishment of those responsible, including effective access by the complainant to the investigative procedure.[206] In other instances, the possibility of obtaining compensation may constitute an adequate remedy. In addition to Article 13, European Convention Article 5(5) requires compensation for breach of the right to be free from arrest in violation of the provisions of Article 5. Article 3 of Protocol 7 provides for compensation in cases of a reversed criminal conviction. Article 4 of Protocol 7 provides for the possibility of reopening the case following a fundamental defect during the criminal proceeding.

---

205 *Klass v Germany*, 28A ECtHR (1978); 2 EHRR 214, paras 34–8.
206 *Dogan and Others v Turkey*, 2004-VI; 41 EHRR 231.

While the principle of full redress applies in domestic proceedings, the Eur. Ct. HR has held that it is not a regional tribunal's role "to function akin to a domestic tort mechanism court in apportioning fault and compensatory damages between civil parties". Rather, it held that "its guiding principle is equity, which above all involves flexibility and an objective consideration of what is just, fair and reasonable in all the circumstances".[207] In contrast to the European Court's practice to limit redress to a declaratory judgment, some compensation, costs and fees, the I-A Court has an extensive jurisprudence affording a wide range of reparations to victims.

Given the widespread recognition of the right to a remedy in law and practice, many consider it to be a norm of customary international law.

5.4   New rights and linkages

Through adopting new instruments and interpreting existing rights in new ways, States and human rights institutions have explicitly set forth guarantees not mentioned in the UDHR and other early instruments. In some instances, the recognition can be seen as simply giving greater specificity to existing rights, such as expressly recognizing a right to safe drinking water – a substance essential to the enjoyment of the rights to life and health. In other instances, however, broad new claims seem to be adding to the catalogue of human rights.

The ASEAN Declaration, for example, includes a number of new formulations and incorporation of standards from UN specialized agencies, including in its Article 27(3) prohibitions on child labour "harmful to their morals or health, dangerous to life, or likely to hamper their normal development, including their education". Other new elements include explicit mention of the rights of those suffering from communicable diseases, including HIV/Aids, and the right to reproductive health within the provision on the right to health (Art. 29). The right to an adequate standard of living includes the right to safe drinking water and sanitation (Art. 28). The rights to development, peace and a healthy environment also appear.

---

207 *Case of Varnava and others v Turkey* [GC] (merits and just satisfaction), App Nos 16064/90, 16065/90, 16066/90, 16068/90, 16069/90, 16070/90, 16071/90, 16072/90 and 16073/90, ECtHR, 18 Sep 2009 (GC).

Environmental rights have been proclaimed in two regional human rights treaties,[208] various environmental instruments,[209] and international declarations.[210] Apart from the African Commission on Human and Peoples' Rights, however, no international human rights tribunal monitors compliance with an explicit treaty-based "right to environment" provision, because no such right was written into UN human rights treaties or the European and American Conventions. Instead UN treaty bodies and the Inter-American and European tribunals hear complaints about failures to enforce national environmental rights[211] or about environmental degradation that violates one or more of the guaranteed rights in the agreements over which they have jurisdiction.[212]

The incorporation of some measures of environmental protection through interpretation has expanded the scope of several human rights, especially the rights to life, health, privacy and home life. The ICESCR, for example, provides that each person has a right to the "highest attainable standard of physical and mental health". In 2000 the Committee on Economic, Social and Cultural Rights adopted General Comment No 14,[213] which extended the right to health to

---

208 The African Charter of Human and Peoples' Rights provides that "[a]ll peoples shall have the right to a general satisfactory environment favorable to their development". African Charter of Human and People's Rights, 27 Jun 1981, Art. 24, (1982) 21 ILM 58 [hereinafter African Charter]. The Additional Protocol to the American Convention on Human Rights provides that "everyone shall have the right to live in a healthy environment and to have access to basic public services". Additional Protocol to the American Convention on Human Rights in the Area of Economic, Social and Cultural Rights, 17 Nov 1988, OAS TS No 69, OAS doc OEA/Ser A/42 (SEPF).

209 See, for example, Convention on Access to Information, Public Participation in Decision-Making and Access to Justice in Environmental Matters, 25 Jun 1998. Doc ECE/CEP/43 [hereinafter Aarhus Convention].

210 Declaration of the UN Conference on the Human Environment, princ. 1 (16 Jun 1972) UN Doc A/.CONF.48/14/Rev.1 (1973); UN Conference on Environment and Development: Rio Declaration on Environment and Development, UN Doc A/CONF.151/5/Rev.1 (1992), *reprinted in* 31 ILM 874; Draft Declaration of Principles on Human Rights and the Environment, UN Hum Rts Comm (16 May 1994). See also, *Need to Ensure a Healthy Environment for the Well-Being of Individuals*, GA Res 45/94, UN GAOR, 45th Sess, UN Doc A/RES/45/94 (1990).

211 In many of the cases the applicants cite constitutional provisions guaranteeing the right to a safe and healthy or other quality environment. See, for example, *Okyay v Turkey* (n. 181) and *Kyrtatos v Greece*, 2003-IV; 40 EHRR 390.

212 Most commonly invoked are the rights to life, health, property, culture, information, privacy and home life. See D Shelton, *Human Rights And The Environment: What Specific Environmental Rights Have Been Recognized?* (2006) 35 Denv J Int'l L & Pol'y 129.

213 UN Econ & Soc Council [ECOSOC], Committee on Economic Social and Cultural Rights, General Comment No 14: The Right to the Highest Attainable Standard of Health, 11, UN

"the determinants of health, such as access to safe and potable water and adequate sanitation, an adequate supply of safe food, nutrition and housing, [and] healthy occupational and environmental conditions".[214]

In addition to formulating new rights or new approaches to long-recognized rights, human rights bodies are increasingly considering overarching links between human rights, democracy and the rule of law. An earlier concentration on free and fair elections has evolved into concern with a variety of democratic institutions and guarantees, including an independent judiciary and a free press. The former Commission on Human Rights in 2000 recommended legislative, institutional and practical measures to consolidate democracy (resolution 2000/47). In 2002 the Commission defined the essential elements of democracy in resolution 2002/46. The UN OHCHR considers democracy one of the universal core values and principles of the UN, essential elements of which include respect for human rights and fundamental freedoms and the principle of holding periodic and genuine elections by universal suffrage as embodied in the UDHR and further developed in the ICCPR. The OHCHR Rule of Law and Democracy Unit works to develop concepts and operational strategies to enhance democracy and assists the UN Democracy Fund, the Department of Political Affairs and the UN Working Group on Democracy.

The European Court has called democracy "without doubt a fundamental feature of the European public order"[215] and underlined the importance of democratic principles underlying the interpretation and application of the Convention[216] and the critical importance of political rights to establishing and maintaining the foundations of an effective and meaningful democracy governed by the rule of law. Thus, it considers the right to vote is not a privilege, but a right that can only be infringed for legitimate reasons and by proportional measures.[217] In the Inter-American system the relationship between human rights, representative democracy and political rights, in particular, is

---

Doc E/C.12/2000/4 (11 Aug 2000), available at www.unhchr.ch/tbs/doc.nsf/(symbol)/E.C.12.2000.4.En?OpenDocument [hereinafter General Comment No 14].

214 General Comment No 14, 11.

215 *Refah Partisi (The Welfare Party) v Turkey* [GC] App nos 41340/98, 41342/98, 41343/98 and 41344/98 at para. 86 (ECtHR, 13 Feb 2003).

216 See, among other authorities, *United Communist Party of Turkey and Others v Turkey* (1998) ECHR1998-I, § 45.

217 *Mathieu-Mohin Mohin and Clerfayt v Belgium*, 113A ECtHR (1987); 10 EHRR 1, para. 51, citing *X v Germany; Hirst v United Kingdom* [GC] Judgment [2005] ECHR 681.

established in the Inter-American Democratic Charter, adopted on 11 September 2001. This instrument indicates that:

> Essential elements of representative democracy include, *inter alia*, respect for human rights and fundamental freedoms, access to and the exercise of power in accordance with the rule of law, the holding of periodic, free, and fair elections based on secret balloting and universal suffrage as an expression of the sovereignty of the people, the pluralistic system of political parties and organizations, and the separation of powers and independence of the branches of government.

The Inter-American Court considers that the effective exercise of political rights constitutes an end in itself and also a fundamental means that democratic societies possess to guarantee the other human rights established in the Convention.[218]

In general, democracy, the rule of law and respect for human rights are now seen as interlinked and mutually reinforcing. The main constitutive elements include free and fair elections, democratic institutions with separation of powers, responsible political parties, independent electoral commissions, and a strong and free civil society. These should lead to inclusive and participatory governance and decision making in which all may exercise freedom of expression and self-determination. Also emphasized are accountability and transparency, checks and balances, free and independent media, and access to information. The challenges identified, in addition to traditional abuses of power, are poverty, corruption and exclusions.[219]

---

218 *Castaneta Gutman v Mexico*, I-A Court HR, Ser C No 184 (6 Aug 2008).
219 A/HRC/24/54 of 6 Aug 2013: Outcome of the panel discussion on common challenges facing States in their efforts to secure democracy and the rule of law from a human rights perspective. See also the UNHCHR study A/HRC/22/29 from 2012.

6   Obligations

Human rights law imposes a complex set of binding obligations on States. Global and regional instruments variously call for States Parties to "respect", "ensure", "secure", "prevent and punish", "adopt measures", "guarantee", and, often, "cooperate with each other" to achieve the full enjoyment by everyone of the rights set forth. The language adopted in the texts makes clear that in many instances it is not enough for the State to abstain from directly infringing rights; authorities must also take positive action to secure the exercise of the rights. In addition, certain human rights obligations demand results, for example, to end torture or abolish the death penalty without exception. In contrast, other rules impose obligations of conduct, such as to exercise due diligence over the actions of non-State actors. Both types of obligation are legally binding.

A nuanced set of obligations, developed by scholar Asjborn Eide[1] and taken up by various human rights bodies,[2] distinguishes the duties of States to respect, protect, promote and fulfil guaranteed rights. The duty of respect means that States Parties must refrain from restricting the exercise of rights when not expressly permitted to do so. The obligations to protect, promote and fulfil indicate the positive character of some rights, requiring States Parties to take positive steps to give effect to or realize the rights guaranteed, through adopting necessary legislative and other measures, including providing effective remedies and redress. Numerous cases have explored the scope of positive State obligations to prevent, investigate, prosecute and punish violations committed by non-State actors. In particular, the activities of extractive industries and other transnational enterprises have generated claims that States are failing to regulate them adequately to prevent human rights violations.

---

1 ASBJORN EIDE, CATARINA KRAUSE AND ALLAN ROSAS (eds), ECONOMIC, SOCIAL AND CULTURAL RIGHTS: A TEXTBOOK (Martinus Nijhoff Publishers, 1995), 35–40.

2 See *Social and Economic Rights Centre (SERAC) v Nigeria* [2001] AHRLR 60 (AfCHPR, 27 Oct 2001).

Human rights obligations fall on all State actors, irrespective of the level or branch of government in which they serve. Any impairment of guaranteed rights which can be attributed under the rules of international law to the action or omission of any public authority constitutes an act imputable to the State and thereby the State becomes responsible for the conduct. The duty of the State "is to organize the governmental apparatus and, in general, all the structures through which public power is exercised, so that they are capable of juridically ensuring the free and full enjoyment of human rights".[3] In other words, the government must conduct itself so as effectively to ensure the free and full exercise of human rights. Whenever a State organ, official, or public entity violates a guaranteed right, this constitutes a failure of the State's obligation, even if the organ or official has contravened provisions of internal law or exceeded its scope of authority. That violation may be cured, however, by the provision of timely and effective remedies and redress.

Although all State actions are attributable to the State, human rights agreements sometimes contain express provisions to address the specific situation of federal States. The ICCPR makes clear in Article 50 that "the provisions of the present Covenant shall extend to all parts of the federal States without any limitations or exceptions". The United States has filed understandings to four of the treaties it has ratified, including the ICCPR, to indicate that the powers of the federal government are not expanded through acceptance of the treaty. Many other federal States, including Canada and Germany, have adhered to these instruments without federal-State reservations or understandings. The ECHR, the Genocide Convention, and the UN Racial Convention do not speak to the federalism issue. The Inter-American Convention contains a federal clause that is opposite in tenor to the ICCPR, which aims to limit the obligations of federal governments to matters over which they exercise constitutional authority.

6.1   State obligations in human rights instruments

The obligations of States Parties to the ICCPR are set forth in Article 2, which requires that each State Party respect and ensure to all individuals within the State's territory and subject to its jurisdiction the rights recognized in the Covenant, without discrimination of any kind. This

---

3 *Velasquez-Rodriguez v Honduras* (Merits) I-A Court HR, Ser C No 4 (29 Jul 1988).

obligation is supplemented by other paragraphs in Article 2 that require implementation and enforcement of rights in domestic law. First, the State must enact legislative or other measures as may be necessary to give effect to the rights, and second, the State has a duty to provide access to justice and measures of redress and enforcement when rights are violated. These obligations take effect immediately from the date of entry into force of the Covenant for each State. Jurisprudence on the rule of law also makes clear that States are required to enforce their own domestic rights and other treaties to which they are party when these afford additional guarantees.

The HRC has further detailed the ICCPR obligations in several General Comments, most recently in General Comment No 31.[4] In addition to reaffirming the positive and negative obligations of States Parties, the HRC addressed the issue of domestic incorporation of the Covenant rights, making clear its view that the Covenant need not be considered self-executing in the courts of a State Party. The General Comment instead indicates that unless Covenant rights are already protected by domestic laws or practices, States Parties are required on ratification to make such changes to their laws and practices as are necessary to ensure their conformity with the Covenant; how this is to be done is a matter of domestic law. Any inconsistencies between domestic law and the Covenant require that the domestic law or practice be changed in accordance with the State's constitutional structure "and accordingly does not require that the ICCPR be directly applicable in the courts, by incorporation of the Covenant into national law".[5] Nonetheless, the HRC expressed its view that Covenant guarantees "may receive enhanced protection in those States where the Covenant is automatically or through specific incorporation part of the domestic legal order".

The ICESCR also addresses State obligations in its Article 2. It establishes that each State Party is to "take steps", individually and "through international assistance and cooperation", "to the maximum of its available resources, with a view to achieving progressively" all the rights in the Covenant. This formula requires that steps be taken immediately from the moment the Covenant enters into force, although the actual realization of the rights is to be achieved progres-

---

4 General Comment No 31 [80] Nature of the General Legal Obligation Imposed on States Parties to the Covenant, 26 May 2004, CCPR/C/21/Rev.1/Add.13.

5 Ibid. para. 13.

sively. Lack of resources may impede the full realization of rights, but it is not considered a barrier to the implementation of some obligations. The right to equal pay for equal work, trade union freedoms, and the right of parents to choose their children's educational institutions, freedom of scientific research and similar intellectual pursuits, are all seen as capable of immediate realization. The same is true of the overarching obligation of non-discrimination. In fact, nearly all of the rights have at least some aspect of negative obligation requiring respect for the exercise of the right. The right to housing, for example, requires that States respect existing home ownership; thus, arbitrary forced evictions are a violation of the right to housing, prima facie incompatible with the requirements of the Covenant.[6] Indeed, the CESCRR has determined that it is possible to identify a "minimum core" of each right that must be applied irrespective of a State's economic position. Notably, there is no derogation provision in the ESC Covenant.

In jurisprudence, the duty to ensure rights has raised difficult issues of the standard of care, attribution of conduct to the State, and evidence. In the case of *Oneryildiz v Turkey*, the Eur. Ct. HR explained that ECHR Article 2 (right to life) "must be construed as applying in the context of any activity, whether public or not, in which the right to life may be at stake, and *a fortiori* in the case of industrial activities, which by their very nature are dangerous, such as the operation of waste-collection sites". Article 2 thus imposes obligations on the State whether the activity is conducted by the State or by a private company. The resulting duty of care depends on several factors: the harmfulness of the phenomena inherent in the activity; the contingency of the risk of death to the applicant; the status of those involved in creating the risk, and whether or not the conduct was deliberate. In *Oneryildiz*, the Court found that the authorities must have known of the risk and of the need to take preventive measures "particularly as there were specific regulations on the matter".[7] They therefore breached their obligation under Convention Article 2, to take such preventive measures as were necessary and sufficient to protect the lives of those individuals.

---

6 General Comment No 4, para. 18. CESCR, Report on the Sixth Session. ECOSOC OR 1992, Supp No 3, E/1992/23, pp. 11320. See also General Comment No 7 (Forced Evictions), CESCR, Report on the 16th and 17th Sess ECOSOC OR 11998, Supp No 2, E/1998/22, pp. 113–18.

7 *Oneryildiz v Turkey*, 2004-XII; (2005) 41 EHRR 324 [GC], para. 101.

The I-A Court, in its first contentious cases, discussed the positive obligation of States to guarantee rights not only by refraining from violating them, but also by protecting individuals from violations perpetrated by non-State actors. In the context of forced disappearances, the I-A Court insisted that the State has the duty "to prevent human rights violations and to use the means at its disposal to carry out a serious investigation of violations committed within its jurisdiction, to identify those responsible, to impose the appropriate punishments on them, and to ensure the victim adequate compensation". The obligation is one of due diligence[8] and exists even if neither the State nor its agents were the direct perpetrators of the violation.[9] The obligation of prevention encompasses all those measures of a legal, political administrative and cultural nature that ensure the safeguarding of human rights. A critical question of fact is whether a violation has occurred with the support or the acquiescence of the government or whether the State has allowed the act to take place without taking measures to prevent it or to punish those responsible.[10] The obligation to punish does not necessarily mean criminal prosecution; other sanctions are appropriate for violations that do not constitute crimes under national or international law.

6.2   The territorial and temporal scope of human rights obligations

International agreements concerned with civil and political rights commonly impose State obligations in favour of those individuals "within the territory and subject to the jurisdiction" of the acting State. Even when the text refers only to jurisdiction and not to territory, tribunals like the Eur. Ct. HR have viewed jurisdiction as "primarily territorial". The European Court applies an "effective control" test to determine the applicable *espace juridique* in which the Convention applies.[11]

---

8 *Velasquez Rodriguez* (n. 3), para. 237. See, further: A CLAPHAM, HUMAN RIGHTS IN THE PRIVATE SPHERE (Clarendon Press 1993); J McBride, *Protecting Life: A Positive Obligation to Help* (1999) 24 EUROPEAN LAW REVIEW HUMAN RIGHTS SURVEY 54; K Starmer, *Positive Obligations Under the Convention*, in UNDERSTANDING HUMAN RIGHTS PRINCIPLES (J Jowell and J Cooper eds, Hart Publishing 2001), 159.

9 *Mouvement Burkinabé des Droits de L'Homme v Burkina Faso*, Comm No 204/97, AfCHPR (2001).

10 *Velasquez-Rodriguez* (n. 3). Concerning this case, see Dinah Shelton, *Judicial Review of State Action by International Courts* (1989) 12 FORDHAM INT'L LJ 361; *Private Violence, Public Wrongs, and the Responsibility of States* (1989–1990) 13 FORDHAM INT'L LJ 1.

11 See *Issa and Others v Turkey* (2004) 41 EHRR 567; *Loizidou v Turkey* (Preliminary Objections)

The IACHR more expansively evaluates whether or not a State has exercised extraterritorial power and authority over the persons whose rights were violated, wherever they are located.[12]

The limiting language of "jurisdiction and control" contained in instruments concerned primarily with civil and political rights is undoubtedly deliberate, reflecting the fact that in most instances States do not and cannot legally assert power over the exercise of civil and political rights in another State's territory. Economic interdependence and global wealth disparity create a different set of circumstances for the exercise of economic and social rights; the corresponding treaty language is therefore different.

The UN Charter includes a specific pledge by member States to "take joint and separate action in cooperation with the Organization" for the achievement of, inter alia, higher standards of living, economic and social progress and development, and respect for and observance of human rights and fundamental freedoms. The ICESCR's statement of obligation in Article 2(1) also explicitly encompasses transnational action: "Each State Party . . . undertakes to take steps, individually and through international assistance and co-operation, especially economic and technical, to the maximum of its available resources, . . ." to realize the rights contained in the Covenant. Article 11(2) reiterates the obligation to take measures individually and through international cooperation, in this instance to combat hunger, adding specific reference to the need for States, "[t]aking into account the problems of both food-importing and food-exporting countries, to ensure an equitable distribution of world food supplies in relation to need". Article 15(4) recognizes the benefits to be derived from the encouragement and development of international contacts and cooperation in the scientific and cultural fields.

As for the temporal obligations of States, the general principle that treaties are not retroactive means that in general human rights

---

310A ECtHR (1005); 20 EHRR 99 (1996); *Ilascu and Others v Moldova and Russia* 2004-VII; 40 EHRR 1030 [GC]. Compare: *Behrami and Behrami v France* and *Saramati v France, Germany and Norway*, Apps Nos 71412/01 and 78166/01 (2007) 45 EHRR SE10 [GC].

12 *Coard and Others (United States)* Case 10.951, Report No 109/99, 29 Sep 1999, para. 37; *Salas and Others v United States*, Case 10.573, Report No 31/93, I-A Court HR, OEA/Ser.L/V/II.85 Doc 9 rev at 312 (1994) para. 6; *Frankind Gujillermo Aisalla Molina (Ecuador-Colombia)*, Case IP-02, Report No 112/10, I-A Court HR, OEA/Ser.L/V/II.140 Doc 10 (2010), paras 90–91; *Armando Alejandre Jr., Carlos Costa, Mario de La Pena and Pablo Morales (Cuba)*, Rep No 86/99, Case 11.589, 29 Sep 1999. For the European system, see *Ocelan v Turkey*, 2005-IV; 41 EHRR 985 [GC].

instruments do not apply to State acts or omissions occurring before the treaty enters into force for the State. Certain acts, however, such as forced disappearances, are deemed to continue until the State clarifies the circumstances and location of the disappeared person. The notion of "continuing violations" allows those representing victims of such violations to invoke international jurisdiction even when the original wrongful act preceded acceptance of the treaty in question. The duty to investigate and, where appropriate, prosecute and punish violations is a continuing obligation.

The duty to investigate is an obligation of means and not of results. It must be assumed by the State as an inherent legal obligation and not as a mere formality preordained to be ineffective. The State's obligation to investigate must be complied with diligently in order to avoid impunity and the repetition of the human rights violation. Regional bodies have specified that as soon as State authorities are aware of the violating act, they should initiate, *ex officio* and without delay, a serious, impartial and effective investigation using all available legal means, aimed at determining the truth and the pursuit, capture, prosecution and eventual punishment of all the perpetrators of the violations.

The requirements of investigation, prosecution and punishment are held to be incompatible with amnesty laws. In the late 1970s, a number of Latin American governments granted amnesty to the military, police, and security forces for crimes such as kidnapping, assassination and torture. Military dictatorships were responsible for some of these laws. Others were promulgated by civilian governments in direct or indirect response to pressure from the military or security forces that benefitted from the amnesty and succeeded in escaping responsibility for their actions. When confronted with this issue, the HRC held that Uruguay's Amnesty Law of December 1986 could not be upheld because it "contributed to an atmosphere of impunity which may undermine the democratic order and give rise to further grave human rights violations".[13] The regional human rights commissions and courts have also considered whether or in what circumstances an amnesty for human rights violators should be respected following a change of government. In the landmark *Barrios Altos* case, the I-A Court held firmly that amnesty laws passed in relation to gross human rights violations do not comply with the dictates of the American

---

13 *Hugo Rodriguez v Uruguay*, Comm No 322/1988, UN Doc CCPR/C/51/D/322/1988 (1994).

Convention or international human rights law generally.[14] Such actions are incompatible with the American Convention because "they are intended to prevent the investigation and punishment of those responsible for serious human rights violations such as torture, extrajudicial, summary or arbitrary execution and forced disappearance, all of them prohibited because they violate non-derogable rights recognized by international human rights law".[15] In sum, States may not "resort to measures such as amnesty, extinguishment and [others] designed to eliminate responsibility".[16]

At the other end of the temporal spectrum, some human rights treaties permit withdrawal or denunciation upon notice or after a period of time. The HRC adopted a general comment in October 1997 on issues relating to the continuity of obligations of States Parties to the Covenant. The Committee noted that the Covenant omits any provision allowing denunciation or withdrawal. Taking this fact together with the object and purpose of the Covenant, the Committee concluded that international law does not permit a State that has ratified or acceded to the Covenant to denounce it or withdraw from it.[17]

6.3   Limitations and derogations

Few human rights apart from freedom from torture and slavery are stated in absolute terms, guaranteed for all times and all places without the possibility of reservation, limitation or derogation. Most rights may be restricted through a State's exercise of one of these mechanisms. In addition, some rights like the right to privacy are qualified by prohibiting only "arbitrary" interference with their enjoyment. Other rights contain definitions that limit their scope. Forced labour, for example, is defined to exclude civic duties and certain other responsibilities from its scope,[18] while most treaties guarantee political rights only for citizens of a State.[19]

---

14 See *Barrios Altos v Peru* (Merits) I-A Court HR Ser C, No 75 (14 Mar 2001), paras 41–4.

15 Ibid. para. 41.

16 *Case of the Caracazo v Venezuela* (Merits), I-A Court HR Ser C, No 58 (11 Nov 1999); Ser C, No 95 (29 Aug 2002), (Reparations and Costs) para. 119.

17 General Comment No 26 of 29 Oct 1997, UN Doc CCPR/C/21/Rev.1/Add.8.

18 ICCPR Art. 8(3).

19 ICCPR Art. 28; Arab Charter, Art. 24; American Convention, Art. 23; African Charter, Art. 13.

Limitation clauses are general provisions in human rights treaties, primarily attached to rights that have a public dimension, such as assembly, speech, association and manifestations of religion or belief. The clauses authorize the State to enact by law[20] restrictions on the exercise of the rights, provided the restrictions are consistent with other rights and are necessary in a democratic society for achieving a stated permissible purpose (often national security, public safety, protection of the rights of others or public welfare). The overarching principles of proportionality and non-discrimination apply as well. ICCPR Article 22 is typical of this type of provision in setting forth the right in the first paragraph followed by a limitations clause in the second paragraph.

1.   Everyone shall have the right to freedom of association with others, including the right to form and join trade unions for the protection of his interests.

2.   No restrictions may be placed on the exercise of this right other than those which are prescribed by law and which are necessary in a democratic society in the interests of national security or public safety, public order (*ordre public*), the protection of public health or morals or the protection of the rights and freedoms of others. This article shall not prevent the imposition of lawful restrictions on members of the armed forces and of the police in their exercise of this right.

Being stated in the negative in paragraph 2 implies, according to the interpretation of human rights bodies, that the limitations clause is to be interpreted restrictively against the State. In practice, once an applicant makes a prima facie case of interference with the right stated in paragraph 1, the burden shifts to the State to demonstrate that the requirements of paragraph 2 for a valid limitation on the exercise of the right have been met.

In contrast to this type of provision, Article 8 of the ASEAN Declaration, like the UDHR, contains a general limitations clause. It provides as follows:

The human rights and fundamental freedoms of every person shall be exercised with due regard to the rights and duties of others. The exercise of human rights and fundamental freedoms shall be subject only to such limitations as are determined by law solely for the purpose of securing due rec-

---

20 See *The Word "Laws" in Article 30 of the American Convention on Human Rights*, I-A Court HR, Advisory Opinion OC-6/86, Ser A No 6 (9 May 1986).

ognition for the human rights and fundamental freedoms of others and to meet the just requirements of national security, public order, public health and public morality and the general welfare of the peoples in a democratic society.

During the drafting of the ASEAN Declaration, civil society organizations raised objections to the placement of the article, although not to its content, which is similar to that of the UDHR. The critics argued that placing the limitations clause in the General Principles section of the Declaration suggested that the States intended the provision to apply to all rights, including those considered absolute and non-derogable under international law.

Other restrictions on the exercise of rights may be enacted pursuant to so-called "clawback" clauses. These clauses specify that the rights to which they are attached must be exercised in accordance with national law, seemingly subordinating the scope of the guarantee to the limits imposed by each State in its discretion. Clawback clauses exist in all human rights treaties, but are most prevalent in the African and Arab Charters and in the ASEAN Declaration. The African Charter attaches clawback clauses to the rights to freedom of conscience and religion; freedom of expression; freedom of association; freedom of movement and residence; and political rights. The ASEAN Declaration refers to national law in relation to the rights of asylum and nationality as well as the more commonly circumscribed right to marry and found a family. The European Convention (Art. 12), American Convention (Art. 17) and Arab Charter (Art. 33) attach clawback clauses to marriage and family rights. The American Convention (Art. 22) also provides for freedom of movement and residence "subject to the provisions of the law".

The provisions in the African Charter that refer to the exercise of the guaranteed rights "according to" or "under" domestic law have been narrowly interpreted by the African Commission. In the eyes of the Commission, the principle of *effet utile* demands this interpretation. In *Amnesty International v Zambia*, which concerned an illegal deportation, the Commission added that

such clauses must not be interpreted against the principles of the Charter. Recourse to these should not be used as a means of giving credence to violations of the express provisions of the Charter. Secondly, the rules of natural justice must apply. Among these are in the *audi alterm partem* rule, the right to be heard, the right of access to the Court ... The onus is on the State to prove that it is justified to resort to the limitation clause. The Commission should act bearing in mind the provisions of Articles 61 and 62 of the Charter.[21]

The African Commission has followed the approach of the other regional bodies in undertaking a two-step analysis of the permissibility of limitations on the exercise of guaranteed rights. The Commission first tests whether the complaining party has made out a prima facie violation of the Charter and then imposes on the responding State a requirement to demonstrate that any limitation or restriction on the right is acceptable and proportional to achieve a permissible end: "limitations must be strictly proportionate with and absolutely necessary for the advantages that are to be obtained"; in no case may such limitations render the right illusory.[22] Moreover, the African Charter does not permit the suspension of rights,[23] in contrast to other regional instruments and the ICCPR. The African Commission has concluded that even a civil war cannot be used as an excuse by a State violating or permitting violations of rights in the African Charter.[24]

The derogation clauses of the European Convention, the ICCPR and the American Convention are similar. All demand a serious threat to the nation as a condition precedent to derogation and limit the measures that may be taken to those strictly required by the exigencies of the situation, with the proviso that such measures not be inconsistent with other international obligations of the State concerned. There are, nonetheless, differences between the provisions. The European Convention, Article 15, limits the permissible reasons for suspending rights to "time of war or other public emergency threatening the life of the nation". ICCPR Article 4 refers to a "time of public emergency which threatens the life of the nation and the existence of which is officially proclaimed", while the American Convention, Article 27, more broadly allows States to derogate in "time of war, public danger, or other emergency that

---

21 *Amnesty International v Zambia* Afr Comm'n HPR Comm 212/98, Afr Comm HPR 1998–1999 at para. 50 (1999). Arts 60 and 61 of the African Charter call for broad interpretation of the Charter's guarantees.

22 *Media Rights Agenda et al v Nigeria* Afr Comm'n HPR Comms 105/91, 128/94, 130/94 and 152/96 at paras 69–70 (1998).

23 *Amnesty International and Others v Sudan*, African Commission on Human and Peoples' Rights, Comm Nos 48/90, 50/91, 52/91, 89/93 (1999).

24 *Commission Nationale des Droits de l'homme et des Libertes v Chad* Afr Comm'n HPR Comm 74/92 (1995).

threatens the independence or security of a State Party". Although States in the Inter-American system apparently have more latitude to declare an emergency, this discretion is balanced by including a much longer list of non-derogable rights than is found in the other treaties. The 2004 Arab Charter, Article 4, is identical to the ICCPR.

Only four rights are consistently mentioned by all the instruments as exempt from suspension: the right to life, freedom from torture, freedom from slavery, and freedom from *ex post facto* application of criminal law. To these core rights, others are added in one treaty or another.

International tribunals have reviewed with some deference the necessity and scope of derogations proclaimed by States. The Eur. Ct. HR, for example, expressed concern about exercising too much scrutiny over State decisions in an early inter-State case:

> It falls in the first place to each Contracting State, with its responsibility for "the life of [its] nation", to determine whether that life is threatened by a "public emergency" and, if so, how far it is necessary to go in attempting to overcome the emergency. By reason of their direct and continuous contact with the pressing needs of the moment, the national authorities are in principle in a better position than the international judge to decide both on the presence of such an emergency and on the nature and scope of derogations necessary to avert it. In this matter Article 15 para. 1 leaves those authorities a wide margin of appreciation.
>
> Nevertheless, the States do not enjoy an unlimited power in this respect. The Court, which, with the Commission, is responsible for ensuring the observance of the States' engagements (Article 19), is empowered to rule on whether the States have gone beyond the "extent strictly required by the exigencies" of the crisis. The domestic margin of appreciation is thus accompanied by a European supervision . . . [25]

The Inter-American institutions have been more assertive in reviewing State action during periods of emergency, perhaps because abusive declarations of emergency have been much more common in the Americas than in Europe. The I-A Court has insisted, for example, that the suspension of guarantees cannot be disassociated from the "effective exercise of representative democracy" referred to in Article 3 of the OAS Charter and has also determined that the writ of habeas

---

25 See, for example, *Ireland v United Kingdom* (1979–80) 2 EHRR 25, para. 207.

corpus is one of the judicial guarantees that cannot be suspended in an emergency.[26] Indeed, all rights are to be guaranteed and enforced unless very special circumstances justify the suspension of some of those that are susceptible of being suspended; some rights may never be suspended, however serious the emergency.

The HRC issued a General Comment on ICCPR Article 4 in 2001,[27] replacing an earlier comment on the topic. The HRC emphasized that the predominant objective of a State Party derogating from the Covenant must be restoration of a state of normalcy where full respect for the Covenant can be secured. States must act within their constitutional powers and other provisions of law that govern such proclamation and the exercise of emergency powers. The Committee monitors the laws in question with respect to whether they comply with Article 4. The General Comment notes that during armed conflict, whether international or non-international, rules of international humanitarian law become applicable and also serve to prevent the abuse of a State's emergency powers. Even during an armed conflict, though, measures derogating from the Covenant are allowed only if and to the extent that the situation constitutes a threat to the life of the nation. Moreover, the principle of proportionality means that even when there is a justified derogation from a provision, the State must show that the specific measures taken pursuant to the derogation are required by the exigencies of the situation. When considering States Parties' reports the Committee has expressed its concern over insufficient attention being paid to the principle of proportionality.[28] In particular, the fact that some of the provisions of the Covenant have been listed in Article 4 as not being subject to derogation does not mean that other articles in the Covenant may be subjected to derogations at will, even when a threat to the life of the nation exists.

6.4   Non-State actors

International society, at least since the seventeenth century, has been largely organized on a territorial basis; UN membership, open to inde-

---

26 *Habeas Corpus in Emergency Situations* 8 Inter-Am Ct HR (Ser A) (1987) *(Arts 27(2), 25(1) and 7(6) American Convention on Human Rights)* (1987); *Judicial Guarantees in States of Emergency* 9 Inter-Am Ct HR (Ser A) (1987) *(Arts 27(2), 25 and 8 American Convention on Human Rights)* (1987). See also para. 16 of General Comment No. 29, States of Emergency (Art. 4)(2001).

27 Human Rights Committee, General Comment 29, States of Emergency (Art. 4), UN Doc CCPR/C/21/Rev.1/Add.11 (2001).

28 See, for example, concluding observations on Israel (1998), CCPR/C/79/Add.93, para. 11.

pendent States, has reached 193 States. The UN Charter and human rights treaties hold States Parties responsible for ensuring the enjoyment of the rights and freedoms the treaties guarantee. Yet, there are also many transnational bodies and societies with their own governing structures and claims of loyalty on those who belong to them, from corporations and intergovernmental organizations, to religious bodies, non-governmental organizations, terrorist networks and organized crime syndicates. As the non-State sector has grown in size and power, international law has begun to address private conduct as well.

In general, human rights instruments are devoted to recognizing the rights of individuals and the corresponding obligations of States, but several texts also contain one or more provisions that speak to the duties of persons in society. UDHR Article 29(1) provides that "[e]veryone has duties to the community in which alone the free and full development of his personality is possible". The Preamble to the 1948 American Declaration of the Rights and Duties of Man provides that "the fulfilment of duty by each individual is a prerequisite to the rights of all. Rights and duties are interrelated in every social and political activity of man. While rights exalt liberty, duties express the dignity of that liberty". Similarly, the ICCPR in its Preamble refers to duties, while the American Convention considers that "[e]very person has responsibilities to his family, his community, and mankind". The African Charter mentions duties in the Preamble and lists them in Articles 27–29. The Arab Charter uniquely implies human duties in the statement of its aims, contained in Article 1, as follows:

2. To teach the human person in the Arab States pride in his identity, loyalty to his country, attachment to his land, history and common interests and to instill in him a culture of human brotherhood, tolerance and openness towards others, in accordance with universal principles and values and with those proclaimed in international human rights instruments.

3. To prepare the new generations in Arab States for a free and responsible life in a civil society that is characterized by solidarity, founded on a balance between awareness of rights and respect for obligations, and governed by the values of equality, tolerance and moderation.

The most recently adopted instrument, the ASEAN Declaration, provides that the enjoyment of human rights and fundamental freedoms "must be balanced" with the performance of corresponding duties. The notion of conditioning respect for human rights on fulfilment of duties troubled civil society organizations and led the UN High Commissioner for Human Rights to state that "the balancing of human rights with individual duties was not a part of international human rights law, misrepresents the positive dynamic between rights and duties and should not be included in a human rights instrument".[29] Yet, as the survey of existing instruments reveals, the idea of linking rights and duties is common in human rights law, the only major exception being the European Convention, but even it implicitly acknowledges duties in the related concept of abuse of rights, contained in Article 17:

> Nothing in this Convention may be interpreted as implying for any State, group or person any right to engage in any activity or perform any act aimed at the destruction of any of the rights and freedoms set forth herein or at their limitation to a greater extent than is provided for in the Convention.

Some human rights treaties directly regulate or call for regulation of private individual and company conduct: the Optional Protocol on the Sale of Children, Child Prostitution and Child Pornography to the Convention on the Rights of the Child, Article 3, specifically encourages States to provide for the liability of legal persons. Private actor liability exists for acts of genocide,[30] slavery and war crimes,[31] without distinguishing between natural and juridical individuals.

6.4.1   Individuals

Historically, individuals were considered objects of international law but were not subjects of that law, that is, they had no international personality in and of themselves. International law could and did impose criminal responsibility on individuals but this is distinct from the question of what duties individuals may have to promote, respect or ensure the human rights of others. The former UN Sub-Commission undertook a study on the issue of individuals' duties and their relation-

---

29 UNHCHR, Statement by the High Commissioner for Human Rights at the Bali Democracy Forum, 7 Nov 2012.

30 Under Art. 4 of the Genocide Convention, a private corporation can commit or aid and abet in genocide. Convention on the Prevention and Punishment of the Crime of Genocide, 78 UNTS 277.

31 Common Art. 3 of the Geneva Convention binds all parties to an armed conflict, including non-State actors. Geneva Convention (IV) Relative to the Protection of Civilian Persons in Time of War (1949), Art. 3; Geneva Convention (III) Relative to the Treatment of Prisoners of War (1949), Art. 3.

ship to human rights, identifying a rather lengthy list of duties.[32] Some States made an effort at the UN to draft a universal declaration of the duties of man, to parallel the UDHR, but this was successfully opposed by those who saw the proposal as an effort to undermine respect for human rights.

The development of international criminal law can be seen as the extension of some of human rights law to the realm of individual conduct.[33] Most human rights norms are not part of criminal law, but a relatively small number of acts may be considered to be both violations of international human rights law (when committed under colour of governmental authority) and international crimes. Such international crimes may be punished by international and/or domestic tribunals. There are sporadic examples of international trials even prior to the emergence of human rights law. In 1474 Peter von Hagenbach was tried by an ad hoc tribunal for atrocities committed during the occupation of Breisach, in Alsace. As with many later war crimes trials, von Hagenbach asserted that he was only following orders, but he was convicted and executed. The German Kaiser was indicted following the First World War and various domestic war crimes trials took place.

At the end of the Second World War, an ad hoc international tribunal sitting at Nuremberg tried Nazi war criminals for crimes against peace, war crimes and crimes against humanity. After Nuremberg, efforts were made to codify certain large-scale or particularly grave human rights violations as international crimes, the commission of which would render the offender subject to trial in domestic or international courts. As a result of such developments, individuals have become responsible for certain gross violations of human rights during peace and war, in particular for genocide, crimes against humanity, war crimes, slavery and forced labour, torture, apartheid, forced disappearances and certain terrorist acts.

---

32 Erica-Irene A Daes, *Freedom of the Individual under Law: an Analysis of Article 29 of the Universal Declaration of Human Rights*, UN Sales No E.89.XIV.5, at 53–60 (1990) (originally issued as UN Docs E/CN.4/Sub.2/432/Rev.1 and E/CN.4/Sub.2/432/Adds.1-7 (1980)).

33 For further reading on international criminal law, see Antonio Cassese, International Criminal Law (2nd edn, OUP 2008); Steven R Ratner and Jason S Abrams, Accountability for Human Rights Atrocities in International Law (3rd edn, OUP 2009); David Stewart, International Criminal Law in a Nutshell (West Publishing 2013).

In addition to codifying a list of international crimes in various treaties, the international community has moved to establish international
tribunals to try those accused of international crimes. On 25 May 1993
the Security Council, acting under Chapter VII, unanimously adopted
Resolution 827 in order "to establish an international tribunal for
the sole purpose of prosecuting persons responsible for serious violations of international humanitarian law committed in the territory
of the former Yugoslavia between 1 January 1991 and a date to be
determined by the Security Council upon the restoration of peace".[34]
Three years later, as a consequence of the genocide in Rwanda, the
Security Council created a second ad hoc tribunal, based in Arusha,
Tanzania, the International Criminal Tribunal for the Prosecution
of Persons Responsible for Genocide and Other Serious Violations
of International Humanitarian Law Committed in the Territory of
Rwanda and Rwandan Citizens Responsible for Genocide and Other
Such Violations Committed in the Territory of Neighbouring States
Between 1 January and 31 December 1994 (ICTR)[35] (SC Res 955 (8
November 1994)). Many of the provisions in the statute of the ICTR
were repeated from the statute of the Yugoslav War Crimes Tribunal.
Criminal tribunals with at least some formal element of interna-
tional involvement also have been created in East Timor, Bosnia and
Herzegovina, Kosovo, Cambodia and Sierra Leone.[36]

The growing number of ad hoc efforts eventually made evident the
need for a permanent criminal tribunal and on 17 July 1998, 120 states
signed the Statute of the International Criminal Court (ICC) at the
conclusion of the UN Diplomatic Conference of Plenipotentiaries convened in Rome to create the court. Ratifications of the Statute followed
relatively quickly, and the Rome Statute entered into force on 1 July

---

34 Guenael Mettraux, *Crimes Against Humanity in the Jurisprudence of the International Criminal
Tribunals for the Former Yugoslavia and for Rwanda* (2002) 43 HARV INT'L LJ 237; VIRGINIA
MORRIS AND MICHAEL P SCHARF, INSIDER'S GUIDE TO THE INTERNATIONAL CRIMINAL
TRIBUNAL FOR THE FORMER YUGOSLAVIA: A DOCUMENTARY HISTORY AND ANALYSIS
(Transnational Publishers 1995).

35 See Christina M Carroll, *An Assessment of the Role and Effectiveness of the International Criminal
Tribunal for Rwanda and the Rwandan National Justice System in Dealing with the Mass
Atrocities of 1994* (2000) 18 BU INT'L LJ 163; Mark A Drumbl, *Law and Atrocity: Settling Accounts
in Rwanda* (2005) 31 OHIO NUL REV 41; Alex Obote Odora, *Prosecution of War Crimes by the
International Criminal Tribunal for Rwand* (2001) 10 U MIAMI INT'L & COMP L REV 43; William
A Schabas, *Hate Speech in Rwanda: The Road to Genocide* (2000) 46 MCGILL LJ 141.

36 See generally INTERNATIONALIZED CRIMINAL COURTS AND TRIBUNALS: SIERRA LEONE, EAST
TIMOR, KOSOVO, AND CAMBODIA (Cesare PR Romano, Andre Nollkaemper, and Jann K Kleffner,
eds, OUP 2004).

2002. As of January 2014, 122 States are parties to the treaty. The Rome Statute includes and defines the international crimes of genocide, crimes against humanity, and war crimes, referred to as "core crimes" throughout the negotiations. Aggression is also listed, but must be defined by the States Parties before it becomes a matter for prosecution. The Statute makes some important innovations, including recognizing rape, sexual slavery and other forms of sexual violence as war crimes and crimes against humanity, and including enlisting or using children under 15 in any conflict as a war crime.

The ICC's jurisdiction is limited in several ways, including by the Statute's careful definition of crimes, as well as by a number of other provisions. First, the ICC may only exercise jurisdiction if the alleged crime was either committed in the territory of a State that is a party to the Statute or committed by a national of a State Party (Art. 12). Second, the ICC may undertake an investigation or prosecution only upon the referral of a situation by a State Party (Arts 13 and 14); a referral from the UN Security Council (Art. 13); or on the prosecutor's own initiative, subject to the authorization of a Pre-Trial Chamber of the court (Arts 13 and 15). The Security Council may delay the court's investigation or prosecution of a case for a renewable period of one year, if it so requests in a resolution adopted under Chapter VII of the Charter (Art. 16). Finally, the ICC has complementary rather than primary jurisdiction over crimes that fall within its mandate, thus ensuring that a State concerned has the first opportunity to investigate and prosecute alleged crimes. Pursuant to Article 17, the ICC will defer to national investigation and/or prosecution, unless the State concerned is unable or unwilling to carry out a genuine investigation or prosecution or is acting in bad faith. Many countries may consider themselves capable of prosecuting international crimes on the basis that they have "universal" jurisdiction over such offences.[37]

To the end of 2013, the ICC had opened investigations into eight situations: the Democratic Republic of the Congo (1); Uganda (2); the Central African Republic (3); Darfur, Sudan (4); the Republic of

---

37 On universal jurisdiction generally, see Anthony J Colangelo, *The Legal Limits Of Universal Jurisdiction* (2006) 47 Va J Int'l L 149; Mitsue Inazumi, Universal Jurisdiction in Modern International Law: Expansion of National Jurisdiction for Prosecuting Serious Crimes Under International Law (Intersentia 2005) Stephen Macedo, Universal Jurisdiction: National Courts and the Prosecution of Serious Crimes Under International Law (University of Pennsylvania Press 2006); Luc Reydams, Universal Jurisdiction: International and Municipal Legal Perspectives (OUP 2004).

Kenya (5); Libya (6); the Republic of Côte d'Ivoire (7); and the Republic of Mali (8), indicted 36 people and has issued arrest warrants for 27 individuals. The Prosecutor's office in 2013 was also conducting preliminary examinations of situations in Afghanistan, Georgia, Guinea, Colombia, Honduras, Korea and Nigeria. The fact that all of the eight situations under investigation concern Africa has led many African States to criticize the prosecutor's office, accusing it of bias. It should be noted, however, that Uganda, the Democratic Republic of the Congo, the Central African Republic and Mali themselves referred the situations occurring on their territories to the Court. In addition, the Security Council referred the situation in Darfur, Sudan, and the situation in Libya. Only the cases of Kenya and Côte d'Ivoire resulted from prosecutorial decisions. Nonetheless, many in Africa have proposed creating the world's first permanent regional criminal court, in order to remove jurisdiction from the ICC and emphasize crimes of concern to the continent.

6.4.2   Business entities

In general, international law has encouraged the formation of multinational companies. In the proliferating bilateral investment treaties (BITs),[38] signatory States pledge to recognize each other's respective legal business forms and permit their companies to establish subsidiaries, financial investments, joint ventures and franchises. BITs provide basic rights to foreign businesses, including protection against expropriation and guarantees of most-favoured-nation status, and identify the accepted dispute resolution mechanisms. Corporations are also recognized in some human rights instruments as having internationally guaranteed rights.[39] In addition to the network of BITs and limited human rights protections, the WTO has adopted Trade-Related Investment Measures (TRIMs) that limit the ability to regulate foreign-owned or foreign-controlled firms or joint ventures. The overall picture is one of relative freedom of economic movement and activity.

---

38 David Shea Bettwy, *The Human Rights and Wrongs of Foreign Direct Investment: Addressing the Need for an Analytical Framework* (2012) RICHMOND JOURNAL OF GLOBAL LAW AND BUSINESS 239–72.

39 The ECHR has applied in some instances to protect the rights of corporations, for example, in respect to property and freedom of expression. See, for example, *VgT Verein Gegen Tierfabriken v Switzerland* App no 24699/94 (ECtHR, 28 June 2001); *Case of Pine Valley Developments Ltd and Others v Ireland* 222A ECtHR (1992); 14 EHRR 319; *Matos e Silva, Lda and Others v Portugal*, 1996-IV; 24 EHRR 573.

One explanation for why few positive norms of corporate accountability have emerged is because corporate conduct is often deemed
controlled predominately by market forces in the private sector. Yet,
regulations to limit monopolies and fraudulent activities are long
standing; notably, too, the early campaign against slave trading was
directed at private commercial conduct. Human rights law is considered to be located in the public realm, imposing obligations of protection and promotion predominately, if not exclusively, on the State. The
public–private division has become increasingly blurred over the past
three decades as traditional public functions have been transferred
to corporate actors, including during periods of armed conflict. Even
within domestic legal systems, however, holding multinational corporations accountable for human rights violations has proved difficult.[40]

The power of large multinational businesses, bringing with it the potential for abuse of workers and others, has led many human rights activists
and developing countries to mount renewed efforts to establish international legal obligations of corporations and other business entities,
especially since the era of governmental deregulation and privatiza-
tion began in the 1980s.[41] To date only non-binding declarations have
been adopted, such as the Organisation for Economic Co-operation
and Development (OECD) Guidelines for Multinational Enterprises,[42]
the UN Draft Code on Transnational Corporations, the UN Global
Compact,[43] and the World Bank's Guidelines on the Treatment of
Foreign Direct Investment. The OECD Guidelines are typical in specifying that they are "voluntary and not legally enforceable".[44] There are

---

40 See Stephen Bottomley, *Corporations and Human Rights*, in COMMERCIAL LAW AND HUMAN
   RIGHTS (Stephen Bottomley and David Kinley, eds, Ashgate 2002), 51–5.

41 For a discussion of earlier attempts to develop norms on corporate behaviour, see Steven R
   Ratner, *Corporations and Human Rights: A Theory of Legal Responsibility* (2001) 111 YALE L
   J 443, 452–4. See also: Bottomley and Kinley, eds, (n. 40); Larry Catá Backer, *Multinational
   Corporations, Transnational Law: The United Nations' Norms on the Responsibilities of
   Transnational Corporations as a Harbinger of Corporate Social Responsibility in International
   Law* (2006) 37 COLUM HUM RTS L REV 287; Emeka Duruigbo, *Corporate Accountability and
   Liability for International Human Rights Abuses: Recent Changes and Recurring Challenges* (2008)
   6 NW J INT'L HUM RTS 222.

42 "Guidelines for Multinational Enterprises", DAFFE/IME/WPG (2000) 15/FINAL (31 Oct 2001),
   were first adopted by the OECD in 1976, reprinted in (1976) 15 ILM 969 and revised in 2000,
   reprinted in (2001) 40 ILM 237.

43 The Global Compact is the voluntary corporate citizenship initiative of the UN Secretary-General,
   which brings together companies, labour, UN agencies and civil society to support ten principles
   derived from key international instruments including the UDHR.

44 OECD Guidelines, para. 1.

also numerous voluntary codes of conduct and similar initiatives[45] and some effective consumer action through boycotts, labelling campaigns and procurement policies like anti-sweatshop initiatives.[46]

In 2003 the former Sub-Commission on the Promotion and Protection of Human Rights adopted *Norms on the Responsibilities of Transnational Corporations and Other Business Enterprises with Regard to Human Rights*, a set of human rights, environmental and consumer protection responsibilities of business.[47] The accompanying report indicated that the Norms were more than aspirational statements of desired conduct; instead the report ambitiously claimed that they constituted a restatement of international legal principles applicable to companies. The Sub-Commission transmitted the Norms to the Commission on Human Rights, which did not endorse them, perhaps because they purported to be obligatory.[48]

In 2005 the UN Office of the High Commissioner on Human Rights prepared a report for the former Commission on Human Rights about the responsibilities of multinational companies with regard to human rights.[49] The report reiterated that States are the primary duty bearers of human rights, but agreed that business can affect significantly the

---

45 Such initiatives include: Voluntary Principles on Security and Human Rights for the Extractive and Energy Sectors; Worldwide Responsible Apparel Production (WRAP), SA8000 (Social Accountability International); Kimberley Process Certification Scheme (2002); the Global Sullivan Principles; Global Reporting Initiative (GRI); the Extractive Industry Transparency Initiative; Caux Round Table Principles for Business; International Peace Operations Code of Conduct. See, generally, Sean D Murphy, *Taking Multinational Corporate Codes to the Next Level* (2005) 43 COLUM J TRANSNAT'L L 389; AA Fatouros, *On the Implementation of International Codes of Conduct* (1981) 30 AM UL REV 941; Hans Baade, *The Legal Effects of Codes of Conduct for Multinational Enterprises* (1979) 22 GER YB INT'L L 11; Steven K Chance, *Codes of Conduct for Multinational Corporations* (1978) 33 BUS LAW 1799.

46 See the studies reported in COMMITMENT AND COMPLIANCE: THE ROLE OF NON-BINDING NORMS IN THE INTERNATIONAL LEGAL SYSTEM (D Shelton, ed., OUP 2000).

47 Resolution 2003/16. See David Weissbrodt and Muria Kruger, *Norms on the Responsibilities of Transnational Corporations and Other Business Enterprises with Regard to Human Rights* (2003) 97 AM J INT'L L 201.

48 The Commission resolution adopted in 2004 stated that the Norms had "not been requested", that the document "has no legal standing", and that the Sub-Commission "should not perform any monitoring function in this regard". UN Commission on Human Rights Res No 2004/116, UN Doc E/CN.4/2004/L.11/Add.7 (2004). See also Giovanni Mantilla, *Emerging International Human Rights Norms for Transnational Corporations* (2009) 15 GLOBAL GOVERNANCE 279, 286–7.

49 *Report of the United Nations High Commissioner on Human Rights and Responsibilities of Transnational Corporations and Related Business Enterprises with Regard to Human Rights*, UN Doc E/CN.4/2005/91 (15 Feb 2005).

enjoyment of human rights. The report turned to the UN's Global Compact as a starting point and proposed three forms of responsibility. The first two responsibilities – to respect and to support human rights – relate to the acts and omissions of the business entity itself. The third responsibility of business entities – to "make sure they are not complicit" in human rights abuses – concerns the relationship between business entities and third parties, in particular State agents.

The report noted that corporations often act with other partners in joint ventures or with national and local governments, leading to allegations of complicity if the partner abuses human rights. The legal standard of complicity is one of the major controversies in respect to corporate accountability. One definition of complicity would label a company complicit in human rights abuses if it authorizes, tolerates or knowingly ignores human rights abuses committed by an entity associated with it, or if the company knowingly provides practical assistance or encouragement that has a substantial effect on the perpetration of human rights abuse. There is also a question of how to ensure respect for human rights in situations where effective governance and accountability are absent because the State is unwilling or unable to protect human rights – for example due to a lack of control over its territory, a weak judiciary, lack of political will or corruption.

The OHCHR report prompted the UN Secretary-General to appoint a Special Representative on Human Rights and Transnational Corporations and Other Business Enterprises. In 2008 the Special Representative suggested a framework for regulating multinational corporations built around a State duty to protect human rights, a corporate responsibility to respect human rights, and adequate access to remedies for those whose rights have been violated.[50] The Representative insisted that in addition to compliance with national laws, the baseline responsibility of companies is to respect human rights. Failure to meet this responsibility can subject companies to the public opinion of employees, communities, consumers, civil society, as well as investors, and occasionally to judicial action. To discharge its responsibility to respect requires companies to exercise due

---

50 *Protect, Respect and Remedy: a Framework for Business and Human Rights, Report of the Special Representative of the Secretary-General on the Issue of Human Rights and Transnational Corporations and other Business Enterprises*, UN Doc A/HRC/8/5 (7 Apr 2008); *Business and Human Rights: Towards Operationalizing the "Protect, Respect and Remedy" Framework*, UN Doc A/HRC/11/13 (22 Apr 2009).

diligence to become aware of, prevent and address adverse human rights impacts.

Increasing attention is also being given to whether and to what extent companies should be subject to the law and jurisdiction of their home countries in relation to their operations abroad. On the legislative front, over the last several decades, States around the world have responded to the activities of multinational corporations and have passed legislation designed to pressure both governments and corporations in situations in which respect for human rights is lacking.[51] First, the domestic law may prohibit all corporate presence in a country or trade associated with that country when human rights are being grossly violated.[52] Second, a State may restrict access to governmental contracts or market access unless a corporation is in compliance with human rights norms.[53] Third, a law or regulation can operate directly and compel the observance of certain standards such as those related to occupational safety and health.[54] Finally, statues or regulations, especially as they relate to investment securities, can require full disclosure of offshore activities that have potential impact on human rights.[55]

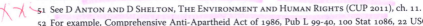

Some domestic legal systems allow individuals alleging harm to bring lawsuits to establish the civil liability of multinational companies for their activities abroad.[56] The United States Alien Tort Statute (ATS)[57] gives federal courts the power to hear civil claims by foreign citizens for injuries caused by actions in violation of the law of nations or a treaty of the United States. The ATS remained little noticed or used

---

51 See D Anton and D Shelton, The Environment and Human Rights (CUP 2011), ch. 11.

52 For example, Comprehensive Anti-Apartheid Act of 1986, Pub L 99-40, 100 Stat 1086, 22 USC §§5000–116 et seq. (Supp IV 1986) (now repealed).

53 See, for example, Los Angeles, Cal, Admin Code div 10, ch 1, Art. V (1986) (requiring city to refuse contracts to companies doing business with apartheid-era South Africa).

54 See, for example, Exec Order 13,126 Prohibition of Acquisition of Products Produced by Forced or Indentured Child Labour, 64 Fed Reg 32383 (1999).

55 Section 1504 of the Dodd-Frank Wall Street Reform and Consumer Protection Act, HR 4173 requires disclosure by companies of amounts paid to foreign governments for extractive licences.

56 Common law courts may hear corporate liability cases under the common law theory of transitory tort. See, for example, *Mostyn v Fabrigas*, 1 Cowp 161 (1774), quoted in *McKenna v Fisk*, 42 US (1 How.) 241, 248, 11 L Ed 117 (1843); *McKenna v Fisk*, 42 US (1 How) 241, 11 L Ed 117; *Dennick v Railroad Co.*, 103 US 11, 26 L Ed 439 (1880).

57 The United States Alien Tort Statute (ATS) provides: "the district courts shall have original jurisdiction of any civil action for a tort only, committed in violation of the law of nations or a treaty of the United States" 28 USC §1350. The Act was adopted as part of the first Judiciary Act in 1789, ch. 20, § 9, 1 Stat 73–93.

until Paraguayan nationals successfully invoked the law in a 1978 suit,[58] accusing a former Paraguayan official of torturing a family member to death. Thereafter, plaintiffs filed hundreds of suits under the ATS to seek redress for various alleged human rights violations committed around the world, including many cases brought against corporate defendants.[59] Some cases have been dismissed on jurisdictional, political or factual grounds, or under the *forum non conveniens* doctrine. Other doctrines of judicial abstention, such as the act of State doctrine,[60] have proven less of a litigation barrier.[61] Several important cases settled, including *Doe v Unocal Corp.*[62] in which a Burmese subsidiary of the Union Oil Company of California was alleged to have directly or in complicity with the Burmese military subjected Burmese nationals to forced labour, murder, rape and torture, in order to complete an oil pipeline.[63]

The US Court of Appeals for the Second Circuit rejected any corporate civil liability for complicity in human rights violations in the case of *Esther Kiobel et al. v Royal Dutch Petroleum Co.*[64] In doing so, the court concluded that international law sources "lead inescapably to the conclusion that the customary international law of human rights has not to date recognized liability for corporations that violate its norms".[65] The Supreme Court upheld the judgment, if not the reasoning, in *Kiobel v Royal Dutch* Shell,[66] casting doubt on the scope of corporate

---

58 In 1980 the Second Circuit issued its landmark decision in *Filartiga v Peña-Irala* 630 F 2d 876 (2d Cir 1980). *Filartiga* held that the Alien Tort Statute conferred federal jurisdiction over a suit by Paraguayan torture victims against the responsible Paraguayan official, who acted under colour of governmental authority.

59 Among the more significant cases seeking to hold corporations accountable for alleged human rights violations, see *In re South African Apartheid Litigation*, 346 FSupp. 2d 538 (SDNY 2004); *Khulumani v Barclay Nat Bank Ltd.*, 504 F3d 254 (CA 2, 2007); *Aguinda v Texaco, Inc.* 303 F3d 470 (2d Cir 2002); *Sarai v Rio Tinto*, 550 F3d 822 (9th Cir. 2008); *Joo v Japan*, 332 F3d 679 (DC Cir 2003), vacated and remanded 124 SCt. 2835 (2004); and *Presbyterian Church of Sudan v Talisman Energy, Inc.*, 582 F3d 244 (CA 2, 2009), petition for cert denied.

60 The act of State doctrine precludes courts from evaluating the validity of actions that a foreign government has taken within its own borders. See *W.S. Kirkpatrick & Co. v Environmental Tectonics Corp* 493 US 400, 409, 110 SCt. 701, 107 L Ed 2d 816 (1990); *Sabbatino*, 376 US at 401, 84 SCt. 923; *Underhill v Hernandez*, 168 US 250, 252, 18 SCt. 83, 42 L Ed 456 (1897); see also *Timberlane Lumber Co. v Bank of America*, 549 F2d 597, 605-07 (9th Cir 1976).

61 *Provincial Gov't Of Marinduque v Placer Dome, Inc., Barrick Gold Corp.*, 582 F3d 1083 (9th Cir. 2009).

62 395 F3d 932 (9th Cir 2002).

63 *Doe I v Unocal*, 395 F3d 978 (9th Cir 2003).

64 621 F3d 111 (2d Cir 2010), cert granted 17 Oct 2011.

65 *Sosa v Alvarez-Machain* 542 US 692, 732 (2004).

66 *Kiobel v Royal Dutch Shell*, 133 US 1659 (2013). See Ziad Haider, *Corporate Liability for Human*

accountability in US courts for human rights abuses committed outside the United States. The Justices held that the ATS does not apply
to human rights violations committed in other countries, unless there
is a strong connection to the United States. The Justices unanimously
agreed that the mere presence in the United States of a multinational
corporation was not a sufficient connection.

In contrast to the judgments of domestic courts, the work of the UN
Special Representative suggests that States are required to take appropriate steps to provide access to justice for corporate-related abuse of
the rights of individuals within their territory and/or jurisdiction.[67]
Without sanctions and redress, the State duty to protect rights could
 be rendered weak or even meaningless. Remedies may be provided
through judicial, administrative, legislative or other appropriate
means.

Current guidance suggests that States are not required to regulate
or adjudicate the extraterritorial activities of businesses incorporated in their jurisdiction, but they are not prohibited from doing
so either, as long as there is a recognized jurisdictional basis and
an overall reasonableness test is met,[68] that is, where the actor or
victim is a national, where the acts have substantial adverse effects
on the State, or where specific international crimes are involved.[69]
Within those parameters, the Committee on Economic, Social and
Cultural Rights and the CERD Committee have encouraged States
to take steps to prevent abuse abroad by corporations within their
jurisdiction.

Rights Abuses: Analyzing Kiobel and Alternatives to the Alien Tort Statute (2012) GEORGETOWN
JOURNAL OF INTERNATIONAL LAW 1361.

67 Report of the Special Representative of the Secretary-General on the issue of human rights and
transnational corporations and other business enterprises, A/HRC/11/13, 22 Apr 2009.

68 Report of the Special Representative of the Secretary-General on the issue of human rights and
transnational corporations and other business enterprises, John Ruggie. *State obligations to provide access to remedy for human rights abuses by third parties, including business: an overview of
international and regional provisions, commentary and decisions*, A/HRC/11/13/Add.1, 15 May
2009.

69 The HRC has indicated that States must redress the harm caused by acts violating human rights
committed by private persons or entities. UN Human Rights Comm, Gen Cmt No 31, UN Doc
CCPR/C/21/Rev.1/Add.13 ¶ 8 (29 Mar 2004). Similarly, CERD obliges States to remedy "any acts
of racial discrimination", and the CERD Committee has consistently stated that this provision
includes the acts of corporations. Concluding Observations for the United States, 2008, CERD/C/
USA/CO/6, at 30.

Finally, some bilateral or multilateral treaties may provide a basis for recognizing corporate obligations in the field of human rights. Notably, the OAS Charter, Article 36, provides as follows: "Transnational enterprises and foreign private investment shall be subject to the legislation of the host countries and to the jurisdiction of their competent courts and to the international treaties and agreements to which said countries are parties, and should conform to the development policies of the recipient countries". This provision appears to have been largely ignored, but on its face opens the door to arguing that OAS member States have extended the obligations contained in human rights treaties to which they are party to the business sector.

6.4.3   International organizations

Like business entities, international organizations have taken on a multitude of new roles, from election observing to establishment of international criminal tribunals to de facto governance of States emerging from violent conflict. With these new roles, they are being pushed to accept accountability for their own conduct measured by international human rights and humanitarian law. Particularly prevalent are discussions about the role of international financial institutions and the WTO, and the responsibility of the UN for its peacekeepers. Like States, international organizations are generally immune from the jurisdiction of domestic courts.

The World Bank Group (WBG) has not directly assumed any human rights obligations.[70] During most of its history, the WBG's legal department considered human rights to be "political" matters outside the institution's mandate. This has changed to some extent as the WBG has engaged in activities, such as governance reform, seen as essential to successful development outcomes. In 2006 the WBG's general counsel issued an internal legal opinion stating that the Bank was able and, in some cases legally obligated, to address human rights concerns. The subsequent WBG's general counsel interpreted the opinion as allowing, but not mandating, activities on the part of the Bank in relation to human rights.

Despite the Bank's reticence on the issue, the former UN Commission on Human Rights suggested that multilateral financial and trade

---

70 Mary Dowell-Jones, *Financial Institutions and Human Rights* (2013) HUMAN RIGHTS LAW REVIEW 423–68.

institutions must conform their policies and practices to international human rights norms. In practice this may be accomplished by action taken by the member States. In Resolution 2005/17 (14 April 2001), paragraph 2, the Commission recognized that "in addition to States' separate responsibilities to their individual societies, they have a collective responsibility to uphold the principles of human dignity, equality and equity at the global level as an essential element in the construction and shaping of an ethnical foundation for globalization". The UN Sub-Commission affirmed "the importance and relevance of human rights obligations in all areas of development, including international and regional trade, investment and financial policies and practices, while confirming that this in no way implies the imposition of conditionalities upon aid to development".[71] The Sub-Commission urged all governments and international economic policy forums to take international human rights obligations fully into account in international economic policy formulation.[72]

The World Bank established an Inspection Panel in 1993 because of growing concerns about the accountability of it and other international development agencies that had supported projects and programmes having a negative impact on the enjoyment of human rights, such as forced evictions resulting from the construction of large dams. The Panel is an independent investigatory body that receives and investigates complaints from those in the territory of a borrower whose rights or interests have been adversely affect by the Bank's failure to comply with its policies and procedures in the design, appraisal and implementation of a Bank-financed project. The Panel may investigate complaints upon authorization by the Bank's Board of Executive Directors and assess to what extent the Bank has complied with its own standards. At the first stage, the Panel registers the request and asks Management to respond to the concerns expressed in it. The Panel then assesses whether or not the request meets the eligibility requirements, in particular, whether prima facie the Bank has engaged in a serious violation of its operational policies and procedures resulting or likely to result in material and adverse harm to those making the request and to which Management has failed to respond adequately. On the basis of this assessment, the Panel recommends to the Executive Directors whether or not to authorize an investigation. If authorized, the Panel investigates the merits and reaches findings. The

---

71 Sub-Comm'n Res 2001/5 (15 Aug 2001), para. 2.
72 Ibid. para. 3.

process can result in a remedial action plan requiring management to take action. Two outside reviews, completed in 1996 and 1999, led to some improvements in the operation of the Inspection Panel. The 1999 review paid particular attention to the relatively small number of full reviews that had been undertaken. The Clarifications made clear that the Board will authorize an investigation recommended by the Panel without making any judgment on the merits or without discussion, except in relation to technical eligibility criteria or admissibility requirements.

As with the WBG, the increasing role of the WTO in facilitating international economic activities has brought with it concerns about the possible impact that liberalized economic policies might have on human rights. Issues of particular concern include protecting labour rights, upholding economic and social rights (such as the right to health, which may conflict with intellectual property protection for pharmaceutical companies), and permitting the use of economic sanctions or boycotts for human rights purposes, for example, to ban the sale of "conflict diamonds" or implements of torture.

The preamble of the WTO Agreement recites the objectives of the organization and seems clearly to view trade as a means to the fulfilment of basic human values, including the improvement of living standards for all people and sustainable development, rather than as an end in itself. These objectives require respect for human rights and thus allow the WTO to take human rights into consideration in its work. In addition, the balance of rights and obligations in the underlying General Agreement on Tariffs and Trade includes GATT Article XX,[73] a provision that is an essential part of the international trade regime. Moreover, in the conflicts that have arisen between human rights obligations and those arising from a trade or investment agreement, human rights bodies have contended that States may not rely on a trade or investment agreement as a defence when human rights

---

73 GATT Art. XX provides in relevant part as follows: "Subject to the requirement that such measures are not applied in a manner which would constitute a means of arbitrary or unjustifiable discrimination between countries where the same conditions prevail, or a disguised restriction on international trade, nothing in this Agreement shall be construed to prevent the adoption or enforcement by any contracting parties of measures: (a) necessary to protect public morals; (b) necessary to protect human, animal or plant life or health; . . . (e) relating to the products of prison labor; (f) imposed for the protection of national treasures of artistic, historic or archaeological value".

violations occur.[74] WTO dispute settlement panels might conceivably find that the reverse is also true.

Finally, the expansion of UN peacekeeping operations has brought with it allegations of human rights abuse and concern about accountability for the conduct of peacekeepers. The peacekeepers usually remain under the control of their State's military command, but operate under the authority of the UN. The result may be an inability to hold anyone accountable when violations of rights occur.[75] In 2000 the UN's International Law Commission (ILC) decided to include the topic "responsibility of international organizations" in its long-term programme of work, a decision approved by the General Assembly.[76] In May 2002 the ILC appointed a Special Rapporteur and established a Working Group on the topic. By 2009 the Commission had adopted the text of the draft articles on first reading, and they were finally approved and sent to the General Assembly in 2011.[77] The basic principles contained in Articles 3 and 4 establish that an international organization is responsible for the breach of an international obligation of the organization resulting from an act or omission attributable to it. In this way, the rules parallel those in the domain of State responsibility. The fact that the object and purpose of the UN includes the promotion of human rights may open the door to arguing that it has an obligation not to violate those rights.

The responsibility of international organizations for human rights violations also has an internal dimension. International civil service law largely governs the rights and obligations of staff members within international organizations. Several international organizations have administrative tribunals, including the UN, the ILO and the World Bank. The International Labour Organization's Administrative Tribunal (ILOAT) has jurisdiction over more than three dozen specialized agencies, including UNESCO, WHO and FAO. Although their competence varies, international administrative tribunals deal with appeals by international civil servants against measures taken by an

---

74 See, for example, *Sawhoyamaxa v Paraguay* (Merits, Reparations and Costs) I-A Court HR, Ser C No 146 (29 Mar 2006).

75 *Agim Behrami and Bekir Behrami v France*, Apps 71412/01 and 78166/01 (2007) 45 EHRR SE10[GC]; *Ruzhdi Saramati v France, Germany and Norway*.

76 GA Res 55/152, para. 8 (12 Dec 2000).

77 Adopted by the International Law Commission at its sixty-third session, in 2011, and submitted to the General Assembly as a part of the Commission's report covering the work of that session (A/66/10, para. 87).

organization in breach of conditions of appointment and benefits, including workers' rights, discrimination and sexual harassment. The tribunals may overturn the decisions of employers in some cases and may grant financial compensation. The ILOAT has stated that "the law that the Tribunal applies in entertaining claims that are put to it includes not just the written Rules of the defendant organization but the general principles of law and basic human rights".[78]

---

78 *Franks and Vollering v EPO*, ILOAT Judgment No 13333 of 31 Jan 1994, Consideration 5. See Karel Wellens, Remedies against International Organizations (OUP 2002); CF Amerasinghe, Law of the International Civil Service (2 vols, Clarendon 1994); id., Case Law of the World Bank Administrative Tribunal (2 vols, Clarendon 1989, 1993).

7 Compliance and monitoring mechanisms

Human rights governance started with a revolutionary concept – that a government's treatment of those within its power is a matter of international concern – but it began modestly, declaring and defining a set of fundamental rights in the UDHR and ADRDM, leaving to States the choice of means and policies to implement the norms. Human rights compliance mechanisms and enforcement procedures have evolved over time, however, and become gradually stronger with the adoption of global and regional treaties and protocols.

In both national and international legal systems, law making is undoubtedly and deliberately a political process. Various interests press their agendas to obtain favourable decisions on norms they advocate or support. The process may be distorted by powerful groups who intervene by offering financial incentives or disincentives, threatening to withhold support or block other goals of legislators, but legislative decision making is the legitimate and accepted procedure for enacting laws in democratic societies. Once laws are adopted, however, politics supposedly disappear from compliance monitoring and enforcement; the fundamental principle of equality before the law demands fair and principled enforcement.

Numerous international procedures today monitor State compliance with human rights obligations, calling for remedies to individuals and groups whose rights have been violated. Independent monitoring bodies increasingly have investigatory functions and jurisdiction to hear complaints brought by non-State actors. At the global level, acceptance of such jurisdiction is usually made optional for the States Parties and supplements other international procedures to promote compliance, such as discussion and debates, review of periodic State reports, studies, and on-site visits and hearings. Most of these procedures, developed by various committees and commissions, involve some degree of fact finding and result in recommendations to improve

compliance. Three regional systems in addition have courts with jurisdiction to issue binding judgments and afford remedies to victims.

Human rights bodies interpret the rights guaranteed, the obligations imposed and their own express, inherent and implied powers in
a manner intended to make human rights fully effective. All human
rights monitoring bodies lack true powers of enforcement and depend
upon the political will of the States Parties for their funding, personnel and cooperation to support compliance with the decisions they
take. In evaluating monitoring procedures, it is important to recall that
they have been established by treaties to which States must consent.
These States also retain the power to amend the treaties and "reform"
the institutions they have created. Civil society organizations and the
media may help generate the political will to support compliance and
resist weakening the international institutions.

Commentators generally agree with State assertions that human rights
treaties typically confer neither binding interpretive authority nor
direct enforcement power on treaty bodies.[1] A contrasting view supports the authority of treaty bodies to define and interpret the obligations contained in human rights treaties and elaborate the scope
and protection of human rights consistent with the treaty provisions.
As a matter of legitimacy, States have conferred on treaty bodies a
monitoring role, one of gathering information, developing a body of
jurisprudence, and engaging in constructive dialogue to move States
Parties effectively to implement the treaty's guaranteed rights and its
object and purpose.

7.1   Debates and recommendations

The mechanisms for supervising the UN Charter obligations of
member States were initially very limited, because the UN legal office
insisted that the UN human rights bodies could not take action with
respect to petitions alleging human rights violations.[2] Nonetheless, as

---

1 See Robert Harris, Assistant Legal Advisor, Dep't of State, US Delegation Response to
   Oral/Questions from the Members of the Committee (18 Jul 2006) ("As a general matter, only
   the parties to a treaty are empowered to give a binding interpretation of its provisions unless the
   treaty provides otherwise or the parties have otherwise so agreed").
2 ECOSOC, Report of the Sub-Committee on the Handling of Communications, UN Doc
   E/CN.4/14.Rev 2 (6 Feb 1947).

Egon Schwelb noted in looking back over the first 25 years of the UN practice, "neither the vagueness and generality of the human rights clauses of the Charter nor the domestic jurisdiction clause have prevented the UN from considering, investigating, and judging concrete human rights situations, provided there was a majority strong enough and wishing strongly enough to attempt to influence the particular development".[3]

Procedures to advance compliance with the UN Charter's human rights obligations now range from debates in the General Assembly to investigations of particular countries or issues to binding decisions on enforcement actions by the Security Council.[4] Most of these techniques have to be initiated by a member State or group of States and require the cooperation of other members.

Initially, the only procedure available at the UN to promote and protect human rights was political debate, which could potentially conclude with a resolution of criticism or condemnation. From the first session of the General Assembly, member States invoked the human rights clauses of the UN Charter, especially those concerning self-determination and non-discrimination. Delegations have referred to the human rights obligations of members at each subsequent General Assembly session. The introduction of human rights issues for discussion and debate almost invariably confronted objections from target States that any mention of their human rights situation violated the principle of State sovereignty as reflected in Article 2(7) of the UN Charter, which prohibits the organization from intervening in matters exclusively within the domestic jurisdiction of member States. Such objections have become less frequent with general recognition that respect for human rights is a legitimate matter of international concern, but they have not entirely disappeared.[5] In quite a few instances, the debates have led to investigations or denunciations of human rights violations in member States, but States sometimes assert lobbying and political pressure to avoid condemnation, leading to concerns about uneven application of the law.

---

3 Egon Schwelb, *The International Court of Justice and the Human Rights Clauses of the Charter*, (1972) 66 Am J Int'l L 337, 341.

4 See Antonio Cassese, *The General Assembly: Historical Perspective 1945–1989*, in The United Nations and Human Rights (Philip Alston, ed., OUP 1992), 25; Sydney D Bailey, *The Security Council*, in ibid. 304.

5 Russia's veto on 5 Feb 2012 of a proposed UN Security Council resolution on Syria was justified in part on the claim that it interfered in Syria's internal affairs.

In the former UN Human Rights Commission as well as in the General Assembly, diplomatic protocol and widespread resistance to discussing human rights in any but the most general terms made it difficult in the early decades to adopt resolutions condemning human rights violations. Although individual countries were occasionally criticized, the situation did not change until the mid-1960s. In 1966 the General Assembly, in Resolution 2144(XXI), invited ECOSOC and the Commission to give urgent consideration to the ways and means of improving the capacity of the UN to put a stop to violations of human rights wherever they might occur. The Council responded by adopting ECOSOC Resolution 1235,[6] approving the Commission's decision to give annual public consideration to a new agenda item entitled: "Question of the violation of human rights and fundamental freedoms, including policies of racial discrimination and segregation and of apartheid, in all countries, with particular reference to colonial and other dependent countries and territories".

Resolution 1235 left no doubt about its focus, given its references to discrimination and colonialism. In its operation, the resolution authorized the Commission and Sub-Commission to examine information relevant to gross violations of human rights.[7] The Commission could then "in appropriate cases, and after careful consideration . . . make a thorough study of situations which reveal a consistent pattern of violations of human rights, as exemplified by . . . apartheid . . . and racial discrimination" and report and make recommendations to ECOSOC.[8]

Pursuant to Resolution 1235, the Commission began to examine southern Africa and the territories occupied by Israel during and after the 1967 war.[9] Chile, after the 11 September 1973 military coup, became the first situation on the agenda that was not part of what the majority of the Commission considered to be situations of occupation or colonialism.[10] Each case was taken up on the understanding that it would not create a precedent for broader human rights investigations.[11] By the end of the decade, however, pressure from NGOs and the human rights initiatives of the Carter administration caused an expansion of

---

6 ECOSOC Res 1235, UN Doc E/4393 (6 Jun 1967).
7 Ibid.
8 Ibid. 3.
9 Alston (n. 4) at 157.
10 Ibid. at 158.
11 Ibid.

the procedure[12] and, as of the creation of the Human Rights Council in 2006, the Commission had under study 13 countries: Belarus, Burundi, Cambodia, Cuba, Democratic Republic of Korea, Democratic Republic of Congo, Haiti, Liberia, Myanmar, the Israeli-occupied territories, Somalia, Sudan and Uzbekistan.[13] Three of these States, Belarus, Korea and Iran, were condemned by the General Assembly in December 2006 for human rights violations.[14] Although resolutions rarely express strongly critical language, States sought vigorously to avoid being the subject of a resolution.

The political bodies of regional systems may also take up human rights issues and specific situations. As discussed in Chapter 9, most of them now condition participation or membership in the organization on compliance with human rights norms. The Organization of American States and the African Union have both suspended governments from participation because of anti-democratic actions and human rights violations.

7.2   Thematic and country studies

Over several decades, the former UN HRC developed its system of UN "special procedures": independent experts appointed to work individually or in working groups to examine human rights situations in particular countries or in connection with certain issues or themes. The first such mandate was the working group on disappearances, created in 1980 at the initiative of NGOs and the UN secretariat, who believed that this was the only politically feasible way to address gross violations of human rights then taking place in Argentina and Chile. When the Human Rights Council replaced the Commission, it reviewed the special procedures, confirming all of the thematic procedures and creating new ones. Some country-specific mandates were discontinued without formal debate.[15]

---

12 Ibid. at 159.

13 UN Comm'n on Hum Rts, *Report on the Sixty-Second Session*, at 1–2, UN Doc E/CN.4/2006/122 (13–27 Mar 2006).

14 Press Release, *General Assembly Adopts 46 Third Committee Texts on Human Rights Issues, Refugees, Self-Determination, Racism, Social Development*, UN Doc GA/10562 (19 Dec 2006) (summarizing General Assembly Resolutions 61/174, 61/175 and 61/176).

15 As of mid-2012, there were country rapporteurs for Myanmar (mandate established 1992), Palestinian Occupied Territories (1993), Somalia (1993), Haiti (1995), Burundi (2004), Democratic People's Republic of Korea (2004) and Sudan (2005). Additionally, there were 32 thematic experts

The mandates of the special procedures vary in accordance with the specific resolutions of the Council establishing or re-authorizing them. Nonetheless, there are some common features in the mandates and the corresponding work methods, especially since the Human Rights Council adopted a Code of Conduct in 2006, containing rules that govern all procedures; the Council also adopted a uniform method and set of criteria for selection of mandate holders.

Thematic Special Procedures investigate the situation of human rights in all parts of the world, irrespective of whether a particular government is a party to human rights treaties. Indeed, most of the Human Rights Council resolutions establishing or re-authorizing thematic mandates do not specify the human rights instruments, whether declarations or treaties, that the mandate holder is to utilize.

Mandate holders are expected to monitor and respond quickly to allegations of human rights violations, either globally or in a specific country or territory, and to report on their activities. Despite voting to create the mandates, governments have a low rate of response to communications from the special procedures on specific cases of alleged human rights abuse. In 2009, mandate holders sent a total of 689 communications (excluding cases dealt with by the Working Group on Enforced or Involuntary Disappearances), and less than one-third of them (32 per cent) received responses from governments.[16]

The Inter-American and African Commissions also designate thematic rapporteurs. In the Inter-American system, all but one of the rapporteurships concern vulnerable groups (women, children, afro-descendants, indigenous peoples, human rights defenders, migrant

---

or working groups established to examine disappearances (established 1980); extrajudicial, summary or arbitrary executions (1982); torture (1985); freedom of religion (1986); the sale of children and child prostitution and pornography (1990); arbitrary detention (1991); racism and xenophobia (1993); freedom of opinion and expression (1993); the independence of the judiciary (1994); violence against women (1994); toxic and dangerous products and wastes (1995); children and armed conflict (1997); poverty (1998); right to education (1998); migrants (1999); human rights defenders (2000); economic reform policies and foreign debt (2000); right to housing (2000); right to food (2000); indigenous peoples (2001); physical and mental health (2002); people of African descent (2002); internally displaced persons (2004); human trafficking (2004); mercenaries (2005); minorities (2005); international solidarity (2005); protection of human rights while countering terrorism (2005); transnational corporations (2005); contemporary forms of slavery (2007); the right to water (2008); cultural rights (2009); and discrimination against women (2010).

16 Office of the High Commissioner for Human Rights. OHCHR, *United Nations Special Procedures: Facts and Figures* 7 (2009).

workers and detainees). The exception is the special rapporteur on freedom of expression, a full-time independent position. The African system focuses more on specific rights or areas of concern, having mandates on extra-judicial, summary or arbitrary execution; freedom of expression and access to information; human rights defenders; prisons and conditions of detention; refugees, asylum seekers, migrants and internally displaced persons; and the rights of women. The Commission also has working groups of the Commissioners on indigenous populations/communities in Africa; economic, social and cultural rights; the rights of older persons and people with disabilities; the death penalty; extractive industries, environment and human rights violations; fair trial; and communications.

7.3   Hearings and on-site visits

The regional courts as well as the Inter-American and African Commissions hold public hearings. The courts do so in regard to specific cases or advisory opinions; the commissions also schedule hearings on thematic issues or the situation in a particular country. Individuals, groups or a State may request a hearing, or the Commissions may schedule hearings on their own initiative. UN treaty bodies normally do not hold hearings on matters they are considering but may provide for written submissions, for example on draft general comments or general recommendations. A few UN bodies allow for oral presentations on communications, but rarely grant hearings in practice.

The mandate holders for UN special procedures and some treaty bodies, as well as the regional courts and commissions, may schedule fact-finding or consultations in any State, with the permission of that State's government. In some instances, the visits lead to special reports on the situation generally in the country or concerning a specific issue.

Some human rights treaties that focus on prevention contain the possibility of an inquiry procedure, initiated by the treaty body if it receives reliable information which appears to contain well-founded indications that gross or systematic violations are occurring. This is the case with the Convention against Torture, in which the Commission may respond by visiting the country in question if the government agrees. The Committee transmits the findings of such an inquiry to the State Party concerned, together with any comments or suggestions. These proceedings are confidential in nature, but the Committee may, after consultation with the State Party, decide to include a summary account of the proceedings in its annual report. The Convention includes an "opt out" provision allowing States to avoid the procedure by filing a declaration to that effect at the time of ratification; 11 States have done so. The Committee's competence to receive individual and inter-State complaints is also far from universally accepted.

Under the OPCAT, the SPT has unrestricted access to all places of detention, their installations and facilities and all relevant information. The SPT visits police stations, prisons (military and civilian), detention centres (for example, pre-trial detention centres, immigration detention centres, juvenile justice establishments, and so on), mental health and social care institutions and any other places where people are or may be deprived of their liberty. The SPT must also be granted access to have private interviews with the persons deprived of their liberty, without witnesses, and to any other person who in the SPT's view may supply relevant information including government officials, representatives of national human rights institutions, NGOs, custodial staff, lawyers, doctors, and so on. People who provide information to the SPT shall not be subject to sanctions or reprisals for having provided information to the SPT. At least two members of the SPT conduct the visits. These members may be accompanied, if needed, by experts of demonstrated professional experience and knowledge in the field.

7.4   Periodic State reporting

The only mandatory compliance procedure for all UN member States and parties to the core UN human rights treaties is an obligation to file periodic State reports. States undoubtedly view reporting as the least intrusive and most non-confrontational device to promote compliance. Well before the adoption of UN and regional human rights treaties, the ILO had established a procedure of State reporting to monitor compliance with its treaties and recommendations, a system still in effect.[17] Such reporting is less common at the regional level, being

---

17 The organization still requires that member States report not only on ratified but also on unratified conventions and indicate the obstacles to ratification. The ILO Independent Committee of Experts meets annually to examine reports and may follow up with "Direct Requests" to governments and to organizations of workers and employers in the State concerned. If the Committee discovers serious or persistent problems, it may make "Observations" to the government, which are published in the Committee's annual report to the Conference. In addition, the ILO has individual complaints procedures. See Lee Swepston, *The International Labour Organization*, in

required only by the African Charter on Human and Peoples' Rights, the Arab Charter and the European Social Charter. The reporting required by the core UN human rights treaties is now supplemented by the initiation of Universal Periodic Review, in which each UN member State must report to the Human Rights Council and be subject to peer review on a regular basis.

UN human rights treaties require periodic reports on steps States Parties have taken to implement the provisions of the relevant treaty. The treaties are particularly terse on how each respective treaty body is to handle the State reports. Nearly all call for "consideration", "study" or "examination" of reports and allow for the adoption of "general comments" or "suggestions and general recommendations". Nearly all of the treaties expressly allow the relevant committee to request additional information from States Parties and the States Parties to make observations on a treaty body's comments, recommendations or suggestions. Beyond these few indications, the treaties are silent as to reporting procedures. The fact that treaty bodies are generally given authority to draft their own rules of procedure has facilitated the development of relatively robust reporting systems, although all of them are burdened by the sheer number of reports they receive and the limited time and resources available to consider them.[18]

Many instruments require an initial report one year after a State becomes a party to the treaty and thereafter with a frequency set by the monitoring body, usually four to five years, but provide little other detail about the procedure. The treaties empower committees to formulate their own rules of procedure, which has enabled them to draft provisions about State participation in the reporting mechanism, follow-up procedures and other details not made explicit in the treaties.[19] All human rights treaty bodies have adopted the practice introduced by CERD in 1972 of considering States Parties' reports in public in the presence of representatives from the reporting State.[20] Treaty bodies also now follow the practice established by CESCR in 1990 of formulat-

---

GUIDE TO INTERNATIONAL HUMAN RIGHTS PRACTICE (4th edn, Hurst Hannum, ed., University of Pennsylvania Press 2004).

18 See *Report of the Secretary General on measures taken to implement resolution 9/8 and obstacles to its implementation, including recommendations for further improving the effectiveness of, harmonizing and reforming the treaty body system,* UN Doc A/HRC/19/28, 14 Dec 2011, para. 20).

19 All operative committees have adopted rules of procedure, compiled in the document HRI/GEN/3, which is revised regularly.

20 Treaty bodies nonetheless may consider reports in the absence of a State delegation.

ing concluding observations following the consideration of the reports of States Parties. These observations indicate the positive aspects and principal subjects of concern, including difficulties that have hampered the implementation of the treaty, making suggestions and recommendations to the State Party. Several treaty bodies have also adopted formal procedures to monitor implementation of concluding observations and usually request States Parties to provide information on compliance with the recommendations that have been made.

The principle of "constructive dialogue" governs the process, and the review of reports involves critical examination and assessment of State compliance. Although the role of civil society and human rights NGOs was initially controversial, international and local NGOs now provide "shadow reports" expressing their views on the situation of human rights in the respective countries. Most UN human rights committees have established working groups or rapporteurs to examine thoroughly all information received in order to make comments and pose questions during the public hearing.

There has been considerable scepticism about the effectiveness of the reporting mechanism. First, States may be tempted to file self-serving statements that underplay or deny existing human rights problems. Reporting systems are also confronted with the problem of absent or delayed reports. The High Commissioner for Human Rights reported at the end of 2011 that only one-third of States Parties comply in a timely manner with their reporting obligations. Treaty bodies have initiated various practices designed to encourage timely reporting, including listing the States Parties whose reports are overdue and sending them reminders about their reporting obligation. Perhaps most effectively, nearly all committees have adopted the practice, pioneered by CERD in 1991, of proceeding with examining the State Party's implementation of the relevant treaty if it fails to submit a report.

Equally problematic, the system is not capable of coping with all of the reports, should States fully comply with their reporting duties. Treaty bodies simply lack the time and resources to make an in-depth analysis of all the issues and reports. During 2011, for example, some 250 reports were pending consideration by the treaty bodies.[21]

---

21 The situation is no better at the regional level, which has added to the reporting burden on States. The reporting obligation appears in the European Social Charter (Arts 21, 22), European Charter for Regional or Minority Languages (Art. 15), the European Convention on Human

Despite the problems, there is some empirical evidence of the value of State reporting. It obliges States to undertake a self-examination that might not otherwise take place. A growing number of governments take seriously their obligation to submit comprehensive reports and respond to committee questions and comments on both the de jure and de facto human rights situations within their borders. Additionally, to make the reporting duty less onerous for States, the various committees have adopted guidelines regarding the form and contents of initial and periodic reports, as well as lists of issues and questions. Advisory services are also provided and a single initial report may be submitted for distribution to all relevant treaty bodies.

Given the generally positive experience of reporting, the General Assembly decided to adopt the reporting procedure when it created the Human Rights Council in 2006, asking the Council to "[u]ndertake a universal periodic review, based on objective and reliable information, of the fulfilment of each State of its human rights obligations and commitments in a manner which ensures universality of coverage and equal treatment with respect to all States".[22] The universal periodic review (UPR) is essentially a process of peer review based on the standards of the UN Charter, the UDHR and the treaties to which the State under review is a party. The Council also considers information from relevant sources within the UN system and from other stakeholders, including NGOs and national human rights institutions. It then engages in an "interactive dialogue" with representatives of the State under review. Based on all of the information gathered, the Council adopts a report after discussion and makes recommendations to the reporting State.[23]

Rights and Biomedicine (Art. 30), the Protocol to the American Convention on Economic, Social and Cultural Rights (Art. 19), the American Convention on Persons with Disabilities (Art. VI), the Arab Charter on Human Rights (Art. 48), and the African Charter on Human and Peoples Rights (Art. 62). The African Commission on Human and Peoples' Rights reported that as of the end of 2010, only nine of 53 States Parties had filed all their reports. Almost one-quarter of the States had never submitted a report.

22 GA Res 60/251 (2006), para. 5(e). See Felice D Gaer, *A Voice Not an Echo: Universal Periodic Review and the UN Treaty Body System*, (2007) 7 HUM RTS L REV 109.

23 See generally Purna Sen, UNIVERSAL PERIODIC REVIEW OF HUMAN RIGHTS: TOWARD BEST PRACTICES (Commonwealth Secretariat, 2009).

7.5   Complaints

International law envisages the possibility that one State may initiate proceedings against another State to settle a legal dispute, assuming that both States accept the jurisdiction of an appropriate judicial or arbitral tribunal. Many human rights treaties provide for inter-State complaints whenever one State alleges that another is in breach of its obligations under the relevant treaty. Among the major UN treaties, only CERD makes this procedure mandatory. All of the other treaties require States to file a declaration separately accepting the inter-State complaints procedure when or after ratifying the treaty. The regional systems are split on the mandatory nature of inter-State complaints. Inter-State complaints may be filed of right in the European and African systems but are optional in the American system.

To date, no inter-State complaint has been filed before any of the UN bodies. The European system has received about two dozen complaints, usually involving politically charged cases such as divided Cyprus,[24] Northern Ireland,[25] the military coup in Greece in 1967[26] and the 2009 conflict between Georgia and Russia.[27] Two inter-State cases have been filed in the Inter-American system; the first one was declared inadmissible and the second one the parties settled.[28] The Democratic Republic of the Congo submitted the first inter-State complaints to the African Commission on Human and Peoples Rights (as well as to the ICJ) over incursions into its territory by Rwanda, Burundi and Uganda.[29] More cases involving human rights issues are also being submitted to the ICJ.[30] Such cases often originate

---

24 *Cyprus v Turkey* (2001) App no 25781/94, ECHR 2001-IV.

25 *Ireland v The United Kingdom* (1979–80) 2 EHRR 25.

26 *Denmark, Norway, Sweden, Netherlands v Greece*, Eur Comm'n HR, 12 YB (1969).

27 *Georgia v Russia*, App 13255/07 (Admissibility) 30 Jun (2009) (alleged harassment of Georgian migrants in Russia).

28 *Nicaragua v Costa Rica* Inter-Am Comm'n HR Report no 11/07, InterState Case 01/06; *Frankind Gujillermo Aisalla Molina (Ecuador-Colombia)*, Case IP-02, Report No 112/10, I-A Court HR, OEA/Ser.L/V/II.140 Doc 10 (2010), paras 90–91.

29 *Democratic Republic of Congo v Burundi, Rwanda, and Uganda*, AfCHPR, Comm 227/99 (2003).

30 See, for example, *Case Concerning Application of the Convention on the Prevention and Punishment of the Crime of Genocide (Bosnia and Herzegovina v Serbia and Montenegro)* ICJ, 26 Feb 2007; *Application of the Convention on the Elimination of All Forms of Racial Discrimination (Georgia v Russian Federation)* (2008); *Jurisdictional Immunities of the State (Germany v Italy)* (23 Dec) available at www.icj-cij.org/docket/files/143/14923.pdf; *Questions Relating to the Obligation to Prosecute or Extradite (Belgium v Senegal)* ICJ (Merits) 20 Jul 2012; see generally Ludovic Hennebel, *La Cour internationale de Justice face au droit internaitonal des droits de l'homme*, in

in larger disputes between the States Parties, and the respondent State may deem the complaint an unfriendly act or file responsive accusations against the initiating State. These concerns, plus the cost and time involved in litigation, explain why States rarely bring such cases.

More than inter-State complaints, the right of individual petition has long been considered the key to effective enforcement of international human rights law, but petition procedures at the global level are almost entirely optional for the States Parties. All such procedures are considered subsidiary to domestic enforcement through adequate and effective local remedies, which must be provided by the State and utilized by victims. The Inter-American Court has explained the rationale for the exhaustion requirement:[31] the rule of prior exhaustion of domestic remedies allows the State to resolve the problem under its internal law before being confronted with an international proceeding.

The right of petition was slow in coming to the UN. Despite the fact that the UN received thousands of complaints from individuals alleging human rights violations for over a decade after 1945, no UN organ would consider such petitions except as foreseen by the UN Charter in the context of trust and non-self-governing territories. The HR Commission requested advice from the UN legal counsel about the petitions, and the legal counsel responded that the Commission had no power to take any action with regard to any complaints concerning human rights. The Commission accepted this opinion, which was approved by ECOSOC in 1947 in Resolution 75(V) and reaffirmed in 1959 in Resolution 728(F).[32] The influx of newly independent States in the 1960s led to a re-examination of the question and the Commission eventually approved a procedure whereby it would examine "communications, together with replies of governments, if any, which appear to reveal a consistent pattern of gross violations of human rights". In Resolution 1503 (XLVIII) of 1970, ECOSOC approved the Commission's decision. The Sub-Commission and Commission of the UN thereafter examined communications to identify situations of gross and systematic violations.

LIBERAE COGITATIONES: LIBER AMICORUM MARC BOSSUYT (Andre Alen et al eds, Intersentia 2013).

31 *Velásquez-Rodríguez v Honduras*, (Merits) I-A Court HR, Ser. C, No 4 (29 Jul 1988), paras 61–2.

32 See ESC Res 728F (XXVIII) (1959).

Numerous restrictions were placed on the limited 1503 petition procedure: the examination had to take place in closed session;[33] the consideration was limited to situations that appeared to reveal a consistent pattern of gross and reliably attested violations of human rights;[34] no hearings or redress were afforded the petitioner; and the outcome was limited to a thorough study or an investigation "with the express consent of the State concerned".[35] Moreover, considering the petitions required a lot of time because each body met only once a year for a limited session, petitions had to go from Sub-Commission Working Group to the Sub-Commission to a Commission Working Group and the Commission, before action could be taken; at any stage the petition could be returned to the beginning for further consideration. When the Human Rights Council replaced the Commission in 2006, Resolution 1503 provided the foundation for the Council to continue having a confidential complaint procedure, but improvements were made to the procedure, including suggested time limits for consideration, and communication with the author of the complaint.

Despite the secrecy enjoined by ECOSOC, the names of the targeted countries usually became public.[36] In 1972 Greece, Iran and Portugal were referred by the Working Group to the Sub-Commission, which very cautiously referred them back to the Working Group because their governments had not replied.[37] The following year, the Sub-Commission referred eight countries to the Commission: Brazil, Britain, Burundi, Guyana, Indonesia, Iran, Portugal and Tanzania.[38] By 2005 the 1503 procedure had resulted in the examination of 84 countries in all regions of the world.[39] Nonetheless, political considerations kept several major cases off the Commission's agenda, despite referrals from the Sub-Commission.[40] The procedure remains hampered by the

---

33 Ibid.

34 Ibid. 1.

35 Ibid. 7(a). The procedure was revised in 2000 to reduce the role of the independent Sub-Commission and enhance the role of the political Commission. ECOSOC Res 2000/3, UN Doc E/2000/99 (16 Jun 2000).

36 See Alston (n. 4), at 148.

37 Ibid. at 148–9.

38 HOWARD TOLLEY, THE UN COMMISSION ON HUMAN RIGHTS (Westview Press 1987) 77, 128.

39 A list of the States examined under the 1503 procedure since 2006 is available on the website of the OHCHR.

40 The most notorious case is probably that of Uganda under President Idi Amin. Between 1974 and 1978 the Sub-Commission placed the case on the Commission's agenda, but no action was taken. See Alston (n. 4), at 149. By the time the Commission decided to act and send a confidential envoy, Amin had been overthrown. Ibid.

fact that it ends up before a political body, by the length of time it takes to obtain results, and by the limited options for responding when there is a finding of gross and systematic violations of internationally guaranteed human rights. Nonetheless, States exert significant effort to avoid being considered under this procedure, particularly because the threshold of gross and systematic violations reflects a decision by the UN member States that such violations constitute a material breach of the UN Charter.

The first UN human rights treaty containing a petition process, CERD, required a separate declaration by States Parties to accept the procedure set forth in Article 14. The ICCPR, adopted one year later, was even less accepting of petitions: the possibility of individual "communications" was included in an Optional Protocol requiring separate ratification or accession. The Protocol gives the HRC the jurisdiction to receive communications from victims against a State that has accepted both the treaty and the Protocol. In addition to limiting access to "victims", the Protocol indicates that the HRC must decide the issues raised by communications exclusively on the written record, following which it may issue its "views". Many UN treaties were initially adopted without even this limited petition procedure, but some of them have been supplemented by later instruments allowing complaints.

Today in addition to the 1503 legacy, seven of the UN treaty bodies (CAT, CEDAW, CERD, CMW, CRPD, CESCR and the HRC[41]) are entitled to consider individual communications when States Parties have accepted this procedure. A few of the specialized agencies also have petition or complaint procedures. UNESCO established a non-judicial procedure in 1978, which allows a victim or anyone with reliable knowledge about a human rights violation concerned with education, science or culture to submit a petition to UNESCO.[42] The ILO has several different procedures, discussed in Chapter 8.

Among regional systems, Europe was the first, in 1950, to create a commission and court that could hear complaints, followed by the Americas and Africa. A decade later, the IACHR interpreted its power "to make general recommendations to each individual State as well as

---

41 The Committee on Enforced Disappearances, once operational, will also be empowered to consider individual complaints.

42 See Stephen P Marks, *The UN Educational, Scientific, and Cultural Organization* in Hannum, ed. (n. 17).

to all of them"[43] to include the power to take cognizance of individual petitions and use them to assess the human rights situation in a particular country. The inter-American system was thus the first to make the complaints procedure mandatory against all member States. The African system also has a mandatory system of communications.

The regional commissions and courts have gradually strengthened their procedures for handling complaints. In the European system, a slow evolution towards individual standing first allowed individuals to appear before the European Court in the guise of assistants to the Commission. A protocol later permitted them to appear by right. Under Protocol 11 to the ECHR, individual complainants have had standing since 1998. The European Social Charter with the 1995 Additional Protocol provides for a system of collective complaints from trade unions and employers' organizations and from NGOs.

The strengthening of procedural access and increased State membership has its own dangers. In Europe, more than 800 million individuals have the right to bring complaints to the Eur. Ct. HR. At the end of 2012 more than 150,000 applications were pending. The interplay between complaints and compliance is evident in the system, where repetitious complaints are a large problem due to non-compliance with prior judgments. Other regional systems are similarly burdened with a rising caseload linked to non-compliance exacerbated by a shortage of staff and other resources. The part-time African and Inter-American Commissions similarly have rising caseloads and increased mandates, creating backlogs and a need to prioritize among cases and issues.

7.6   Precautionary measures and urgent actions

Nearly all human rights bodies have developed a system of precautionary or provisional measures to request States to take action to avoid an imminent threat of serious and irreparable injury to individuals or groups. The ability to issue precautionary measures has been implied by treaty bodies as necessary to ensure the effectiveness of complaints procedures, although some more recent treaties, like the

---

43 Inter-American Commission on Human Rights, First Report 1960, OAS Doc OEA/Ser.L/V/II.1, Doc 32 (1961).

I-A Convention on Forced Disappearance of Persons, expressly confer the power to issue requests for interim or precautionary measures.[44]

Precautionary or interim measures have proven controversial in some instances because the power to request them is implied rather than expressly mentioned by the treaties. Their scope is therefore developed by the treaty bodies in practice, and the procedures for expanding, limiting or revoking them are often not clear. Such measures have sometimes extended to large groups of people, especially in the context of internal armed conflict, raising difficult issues of compliance. In other instances, the beneficiaries of the measures may object to actions taken by the State from whom such protection is sought.

Despite the controversies, most treaty bodies assert that these measures are legally binding, at least when linked to the substance of an alleged violation, such as imposition of a death penalty following an unfair trial. The HRC has called the failure to comply with its interim measures "a grave breach" of a State's obligations under the Covenant:

> Apart from any violation of the Covenant found against a State Party in a communication, a State Party commits grave breaches of its obligations under the Optional Protocol if it acts to prevent or to frustrate consideration by the Committee of a communication alleging a violation of the Covenant, or to render examination by the Committee moot and the expression of its Views nugatory and futile.[45]

In one instance, the HRC declared that Canada violated the ICCPR by refusing, pursuant to an HRC interim measure, to stay the deportation of a man seeking review before the HRC.[46] The IACHR has taken a similar view of its power to call for precautionary measures and the duty of a State to respond to such requests in good faith.[47]

---

44 Inter-American Convention on Forced Disappearance of Persons, 9 Jun 1994, No A-60.

45 CCPR, Communication No 1150/2002, *Uteev v Uzbekistan* (Views adopted on 26 Oct 2007) para. 5.2, Report of the Human Rights Committee, A/63/40 (Vol II), p. 14.

46 *Ahani v Canada*, UN Human Rights Comm, Communication No 1051/2002, 1.2, 5.3, UN Doc CCPR/C/80/D/1051/2002 (2004), available at www.worldlii.org/int/cases/UNHRC/2004/20.html.

47 On 25 Feb 2002 the Center for Constitutional Rights, a US-based NGO, filed a request for precautionary measures under Art. 25 of the Commission's regulations, in respect to detainees held by the United States in Guantanamo Bay, Cuba. The Commission accepted the petition and, on 12 Mar 2002, requested the United States "to take the urgent measures necessary to have the legal status of the detainees at Guantanamo Bay determined by a competent tribunal". In its letter to the government, the Commission stated that decisions on precautionary measures, when consid-

In addition to issuing interim measures, some treaty bodies have the mandate to develop urgent action procedures. CERD began its procedures relating to early warning measures and urgent action starting in 1993. Early warning is directed at preventing existing problems in States Parties from escalating into new conflict or preventing a resumption of conflict. Urgent action responds to problems requiring immediate attention to prevent or limit the scale or number of serious violations of the Convention. Following CERD, other treaty bodies have adopted similar initiatives.

---

ered "essential to preserving the Commission's mandate", are legally binding. Inter-Am Comm'n HR, 1 Annual Report 2002, OAS Doc OEA/Ser.L/V/II.117 Doc 1 rev 1, para. 80 (7 Mar 2003).

8   Complaint procedures

As previous chapters have indicated, a growing number of procedures exist globally and regionally whereby those affected by or concerned about human rights violations may file communications or complaints. At the global level, with the exception of the procedure for gross and systematic violations pursuant to Resolution 1503, access remains optional with States Parties to the various treaties. In contrast, the three regional systems that provide such a mechanism automatically make their States Parties subject to the right of petition. In addition, beginning with Europe, some regional systems have created judicial bodies to supervise State implementation and provide redress. Access to the international procedures depends on the exhaustion of available and effective local remedies within the State alleged to have committed the violation.

Most procedures focus on individuals whose rights have been violated, but several are concerned with broader situations of widespread violations within a country. Both types of procedure aim to secure compliance with international human rights law by the State in question. Different mechanisms address the two types of case, however.

Four of the UN human rights treaty bodies (HRC, CERD, CEDAW and CAT) may consider individual complaints or communications. The ICESCR also has initiated a collective complaints procedure discussed herein. The Convention on Migrant Workers contains provisions allowing individual communications that will become operative when ten States Parties have made the necessary declaration under CPMW Article 77.

A few of the UN specialized agencies, most importantly the ILO and UNESCO, also have procedures created under their constituent instruments. The ILO has three separate complaint mechanisms. First, "representations" may be made under the ILO Constitution (Arts 24, 25 and 26(4)) against any State that has "failed to secure in any respect the effective observance within its jurisdiction of any Convention to which it is a Party"; second "complaints" may be filed concerning ratified Conventions under Constitution Articles 26–29 and 31–34. Freedom of association is guaranteed by the ILO's basic principles and is subject to a third, widely used complaints procedure that applies to all ILO member States, whether or not they have ratified the ILO conventions on this topic. UNESCO created a non-adversarial procedure by resolution of the Executive Board in 1978, according to which anyone with reliable knowledge about violations of rights within the mandate of UNESCO may submit individualized cases or general situations to the organization.[1]

At the regional level, the European system has an individual complaint process that allows cases to be brought to the Eur. Ct. HR once domestic remedies have been exhausted. The rights protected are primarily civil and political rights. A separate collective complaint procedure exists under the European Social Charter allowing submissions about non-compliance with the Charter.

The I-A procedures governing complaints are set forth in the IACHR's Statute and Regulations, as well as in the American Convention. The procedures are identical for all petitions, including criteria for admissibility, procedural stages, fact finding and decision making, but only petitions arising under the American Convention, Disappearances Convention, and Article 7 of the Convention on Violence against Women may be submitted to the Court and only if the State in question has accepted the Court's jurisdiction. Petitions against other States conclude with a report of the Commission.

The African system uniquely allows the possibility of filing at the African Commission or bypassing the Commission and filing a case directly with the African Court. The latter is optional with State Parties however, while the Commission procedure is mandatory for all States Parties to the African Charter.

8.1 Personal jurisdiction

Most human rights treaties limit procedural standing to those persons who were the subject of violations of their rights, or to their

---

1 Decision 104 EX/3.3.

personal representatives if they are unable to file themselves. The Inter-American and African systems, however, allow broad standing to anyone to file on behalf of victims of violations. In the IACHR NGOs must be registered in one of the OAS member States in order to bring a complaint. In contrast, the European system only allows victims of violations to file cases with the court. The European system is one of the few that extends its complaints procedure to protect the rights of legal persons as well as human beings, including companies, trade unions and religious institutions.[2] In addition, only the European Court requires that a petitioner be represented by a lawyer once the complaint has been declared admissible. Legal aid is available in this system and is slowly becoming available in other regional systems.

The European Social Charter procedure allows complaints to be filed by international organizations of employers and trade unions that participate in the work of the Governmental Committee; other international NGOs that have consultative status with the Council of Europe and have been listed for this purpose by the Governmental Committee; and national trade union and employers' organizations within the jurisdiction of the State against which they are lodging the complaint. States may by declaration authorize national NGOs to file complaints as well.

The term "victim" has been interpreted to include anyone personally affected by a violation, including those subject to a law that violates their rights, even if the law has not been enforced.[3] Most global and regional systems recognize that there may be direct and indirect victims. The latter are those with a close connection to the direct victim. The individual must be "subject to the jurisdiction" of the State in question. Normally that means present within the territory, but treaty bodies have given a broad interpretation that includes those under the authority of the State or its effective control, even if outside the State's territory.[4] The UN treaty bodies may only receive communications against a State Party accepting the procedure, either by ratifying the Optional Protocol creating petition jurisdiction (ICCPR, ICESCR,

---

2 *The Sunday Times Case* (*The Sunday Times v United Kingdom*) (1979) 2 EHRR 245; *Stran Greek Refineries and Stratis Andreadis v Greece* ECtHR, Ser A, No 301-B (1994); 19 EHRR 293.

3 *Toonen v Australia* CPPR Comm no 488/1992, UN Doc CCPR/C/50/D/488/1992 (30 Mar 1994); *Dudgeon v UK* (1982) 4 EHRR 149.

4 *Lopez Burgos v Uruguay*, HRC, Comm No R.12/52, UN Doc Supp No 40 (A/36/40) at 176 (1981); *Cyprus v Turkey* (2001) App no 25781/94, ECHR 2001-IV; *Bankovic and Others v Belgium and Others*, 2001-XII; 44 EHRR SE5 [GC].

CEDAW), or by filing a separate declaration pursuant to the relevant article in the treaty (CERD, CAT). As of late 2013, 115 States Parties to the ICCPR had accepted the right of individual petition under the Optional Protocol, but far fewer had acknowledged this procedure under CERD, CEDAW and CAT. Only 11 States had become party to the Optional Protocol to the ICESCR providing for a collective petition procedure. The CESCR adopted provisional rules of procedure for the new mechanism in January 2013.

Under CERD, CEDAW and the ICESCR, communications may be submitted by or on behalf of individuals or groups of individuals under the jurisdiction of a State Party, claiming to be victims of a violation of any of the rights set forth in the treaty by that State Party. The ICESCR Optional Protocol rules and CEDAW provide that where a communication is submitted on behalf of individuals or groups of individuals, it must be with their consent unless the complainant can justify acting on their behalf without such consent.

Standing to file representations or complaints at the ILO varies with the procedure being invoked. Representations may be submitted by a national, regional or international industrial association of employers or workers. The ILO determines what constitutes an industrial association and may insist that the submitting body have some link to the events denounced. In contrast, a complaint under ILO Constitution Article 26 may be filed by any State that has ratified the same convention whose violation is the subject of the complaint; any delegate to the ILO Labour Conference; or the ILO Governing Body. The special procedure on freedom of association is open to any workers' or employers' organization, ILO bodies, States and the UN ECOSOC.

The 1503 procedure, UNESCO and the African regional system allow a communication to originate not only from victims, but from any person, group of persons or NGO having reliable knowledge of the violations. There need not be any connection between the person or organization submitting the complaint and the alleged victim.

Any person, group of persons, or NGO legally recognized in one or more of the member States of the OAS may submit a petition to the IACHR. The petition need not be filed directly by a victim but may be submitted by third parties, with or without the victim's knowledge or authorization. The petition may involve an individual or may indicate numerous victims of a specific incident or practice (a collective petition). Where the petitioners allege the existence of widespread human rights violations not limited to a specific group or event the Commission may use the information in studying human rights practices within the State in question (a country report) or as part of a thematic studies, rather than as a specific case. Collective petitions can refer to specific victims, although none of the victims need personally submit or approve the petition. The concept of victim includes those who are within the scope of legislation that violates human rights guarantees, even if the legislation has not yet been enforced. The petition must include the name, nationality and signature of the person or persons making the submission or, if the petitioner is an NGO, the name and signature of its legal representative. The petition must also indicate if the petitioner wishes to have his or her identity withheld from the State concerned. Each petition must include an address for receiving correspondence from the Commission and, if available, a telephone or fax number and email address.

8.2   Subject matter jurisdiction

Any complaint filed must compatible with the provisions of the treaty invoked and relate to a right guaranteed by the treaty, a right that has not been restricted by a State Party's reservation or subject to a lawful suspension due to public emergency (CERD contains no provision for derogation in an emergency so the latter would not apply to its procedure). All human rights bodies apply the doctrine of "fourth instance", meaning they will not examine the proceedings and evidence presented in domestic courts or the judgments reached, unless the allegations involve violations of due process, or lack of an independent judiciary or a fair hearing. Mere disagreement with the outcome of domestic remedies does not provide a basis for an international complaint.

The ICCPR sets out the rights that may be invoked through a complaint in Articles 6 to 27 inclusive, comprising Part III of the Covenant. This excludes Article 1, the right of self-determination. The HRC has consistently held that the right to self-determination is not an individual right and thus no individual can claim to be the victim of its violation.[5] CERD and CEDAW set out a series of obligations for States Parties to ensure legal and practical enjoyment of the right to be free

---

5 *Ominayak v Canada; Marie-Helene Gillot et al v France*, HRC, Comm No 167/1984 (26 Mar 1990) UN Doc Supp No 40 (A/45/40) at 1 (1990).

from discrimination. The substantive obligations are contained in CERD Articles 1 to 7 and in CEDAW Articles 1 to 6. The Convention against Torture and Other Cruel, Inhuman or Degrading Treatment or Punishment sets forth its complaint mechanism for invoking breaches of rights under the Convention in Article 22. States Parties may lodge a declaration under that article recognizing the competence of the Committee against Torture to consider complaints against that State from an individual or group of individuals alleging violations of their rights under the Convention.

UNESCO's procedure is based in its constitution rather than a specific human rights treaty and therefore allows communications to be filed concerning any human right falling within UNESCO's competence in the fields of education, science, culture and information. UNESCO has included within these domains the specific rights to education, scientific advancement, participation in cultural life, freedom of information, conscience and expression, intellectual property rights, freedom of assembly and association, and freedom of movement.

The European Convention initially contained a short list of a dozen civil and political rights to which additional guarantees have been appended by a series of protocols. The European Court does not exercise jurisdiction over the rights contained in the European Social Charter or other human rights treaties concluded by the Council of Europe.[6]

In the Inter-American system, provided that the formal and substantive requirements are met, a petition may be filed with the IACHR against any OAS member State that allegedly has violated its human rights obligations. For States that are not party to the Convention, the recognized rights are those contained in the American Declaration. For parties to the American Convention, the rights contained in the Convention are protected in relation to all events which occur after the date of ratification, including continuing violations that may have begun prior to that date. Petitions also may be filed against a State Party that violates its obligations under the Disappearances Convention or Article 7 of the Convention on Violence against Women. The Convention's petition procedures also extend to two rights in the Protocol on Economic, Social and Cultural Rights: the right to form trade unions (Art. 8a) and the right to education (Art. 13).

---

6 *Zehnalova & Zehnal v The Czech Republic*, App 38621/97 (2002) (inadmissible).

The African system contains individual and peoples' rights of a civil, political, economic, social and cultural nature. The African Commission has emphasized that all rights in the Charter are justiciable and may be the subject of complaints.[7] Although Articles 60 and 61 of the Charter call on the Commission to have regard to UN and other regional treaties in the interpretation of the Charter, this does not extend jurisdiction of the Commission to hear complaints directly asserting violations of these other agreements.

Human rights tribunals do not require or consider themselves bound by the applicant's legal characterization of the facts presented in the case, instead applying the ancient principle *jura novit curia* (the court knows the law). In modern practice, particularly in continental Europe, it signifies in general the judicial power to address a case based on a law or legal theory not presented by the parties.[8] To some, its application represents the legal aspect of justice because it ensures that a party will not lose a case simply because of a failure to invoke the correct legal ground.[9] Other authors link the concept to notions of equity whereby the court can recognize rights that an applicant or petitioner may not have invoked and may not even be aware pertain to the issues before the court.[10] The decision maker may not modify the claim, but, based on the submissions and being presumed to know the law, applies the relevant norms to the proven facts to decide the claim. This litigation structure may avoid difficulties when the parties themselves disagree over the applicable norms – as is often the case with customary international law – or fail to state the legal basis of the case clearly and completely.

In practice, there is a wide disparity in the willingness of human rights tribunals to reformulate the rights invoked by the applicants. The more a human rights tribunal emphasizes its compliance-monitoring func-

---

7 Comm 155/96, *Social and Economic Rights Center (SERAC) v Nigeria* [2001] AHRLR 60 (AfCHPR, 27 Oct 2001).

8 M Damaška, The Faces of Justice and State Authority (Yale University Press 1986), 116; JR Fox, Dictionary of International and Comparative Law (Oceana Publishing Inc 1992).

9 Sophie Geeroms, Foreign Law in Civil Litigation: A Comparative and Functional Analysis (OUP 2004).

10 Black's Law Dictionary (6th edn, West Publishing 1991), 852 translates the principle as "the court knows the law; the court recognizes rights". See Douglas Brooker, *Va Savoir! – The Adage Jura Novit Curia in Contemporary France*, 845 bepress Legal Series at 9 (17 Nov 2005), available at http://law.bepress.com/expresso/eps/845.

tion, the more likely it may be to apply *jura novit curia* and to insist on including all possible rights linked to the alleged acts or omissions, in order to advise the respondent State on the full range of potential deficiencies in its comportment. The Human Rights Committee appears never to have referred to *jura novit curia* in its decisions under the Optional Protocol but seems clearly to have applied it in fact in rare instances,[11] generally to address communications that would be inadmissible without recharacterization.[12]

The European Court, too, is reticent to reformulate cases,[13] although it accepts that it may do so.[14] A handful of references to *jura novit curia* can be found in Grand Chamber judgments analysing a case differently from the Chamber that first heard the matter. Notably, the Grand Chamber usually exercises jurisdiction when the matter is one of first impression or when the Chamber has declined to follow prior case law. Grand Chamber decisions have consistently held that the scope of Grand Chamber jurisdiction in a case is limited by the Chamber's decision on admissibility,[15] but within that limit it can examine all the issues raised by the record. The Grand Chamber has expressed concern when applying *jura novit curia*, despite its rare use, for the right of the parties to be heard.[16]

The IACHR and the I-A Court have made the most extensive use of *jura novit curia* to reframe petitions and include rights not invoked by the petitioners, even at times adding victims to the case. In *Hilaire*,

---

11 See, for example, *BdB et al v The Netherlands*, Comm No 273/1989, UN Doc Supp No 40 (A/44/40) at 286 (1989).

12 In the *Ominayak Case*, for example, the applicant invoked the right of self-determination (ICCPR, Art. 1) in respect to the rights of his indigenous community in Canada. The Committee determined that its jurisdiction did not extend to alleged violations of Art. 1, because it does guarantee individual rights. Rather than declare the communication inadmissible, the Committee considered it as falling within the provision concerning minority rights, ICCPR Art. 27.

13 In only 15 cases has the European Court recharacterized the legal issues before it and assessed the complaint for violation of a right not cited by the applicant. See *Guerra and Others v Italy* (1998) 26 EHRR 357; *Philis v Greece (no. 1)* App 16598/90; 66 DR 260 (1990); *Berktay v Turkey*, App 22493/93, Judgment of 1 Mar 2001; and *Eugenia Lazăr v Romania*, App 32146/05 (Merits and Just Satisfaction) Judgment of 16 Feb 2010.

14 *Scoppola v Italy (No. 2)*, *Powell & Raynor v UK* (2010) 51 EHRR 561.

15 See *Perna v Italy*, 2003-V; 39 EHRR 563 [GC]; *Azinas v Cyprus*, 2004-III; 40 EHRR 166; *Case of Contrada v Italy*, Judgment of 24 Aug 1998, 1998-V.

16 *Scoppola v Italy (No. 2)* (n. 14), *Castravet v Moldova*, App 23393/05, Judgment of 13 Mar 2007, para. 23; *Marchenko v Ukraine*, App 4063/04, Judgment of 19 Feb 2009, para. 34; *Berhani v Albania*, App 847/05, Judgment of 27 May 2010, para. 46; and *Anusca v Moldova*, App 24034/07, Judgment of 18 May 2010, para. 26.

the Inter-American Court invoked the ICJ precedents in stating that it had not only the right but also the obligation to find a violation of any provision of the American Convention on Human Rights found to be applicable.[17] One scholar has noted that "[t]he Court also exercises the authority to find different violations from those the Commission has alleged on the same facts, formulating its own legal theories on the principle of *jura novit curia*".[18] The IACHR also applies *jura novit curia* to acts that could violate a combination of rights, rather than following the European Court's practice of focusing on the central issues and claims pleaded.[19]

8.3   Temporal jurisdiction

Human rights treaties do not apply retroactively. As a rule, therefore, complaints must concern events that took place after the relevant treaty entered into force for the State in question. In the case of the ICCPR, this means both the Covenant itself and the Optional Protocol must be in force when the violation takes place. There are, however, exceptions in cases where the effects of the event in question have extended into the period covered by the complaint mechanism and are considered continuing violations.[20]

Most UN procedures have no specific time limitation to file a complaint after local remedies have been exhausted, but CERD requires a filing within six months of the final decision. The regional systems also have short and strictly applied periods, usually six months from the date of the final decision or a reasonable time after the violation if local remedies do not exist. What constitutes a reasonable time varies considerably, particularly when continuing violations like forced disappearances are concerned; some cases have been admitted more than two decades after the disappearance.

---

17 *Case of Hilaire, Constantine and Benjamin et al v Trinidad and Tobago* (Merits, reparations and costs), I-A Court HR Series C no 9, 21 June 2002, paras 107, 187.

18 Gerald L Neuman, *Import, Export, and Regional Consent in the Inter-American Court of Human Rights* (2008) 19 Eur J Int'l L 101.

19 This practice can sometimes reach the point of including nearly every provision of the Convention. See Report No 144/10 petition 1579-07 (Adm) *Residents of the Village of Chichupac and the Hamlet of Xeabaj, Municipality Of Rabinal v Guatemala*.

20 *Machado v Uruguay*, Comm No 83/1981 (15 Oct 1982) UN Doc Supp No 40 (A/39/40) at 148 (1984).

8.4   Processing and admissibility

All petitions or communications are screened to ensure they meet the formal requirements of admissibility. For procedures that can only be accessed by victims of violations, the petition must show that the applicant is personally and directly affected by the law, policy, practice, act or omission of the State Party which is the basis of the claim. Only UNESCO[21] and the African system permit an *actio popularis*. If the victim cannot personally submit a claim, in general the treaties require that the submitter have the written authorization to represent the victim, unless that cannot be obtained.

Unlike cases in most domestic systems, the initial complaint is often the complete case file, containing witness statements, domestic judgments, national laws and supporting documentation. It is especially required to submit information about domestic remedies. Generally, it is not required to file in one of the official languages of the organization, but doing so may speed up the process. Most procedures now have model complaint forms that can be completed and submitted via the organization's website.

The complaint must contain sufficient information on the facts and the arguments concerning the violation to make a prima facie case. Otherwise, the complaint may be rejected as insufficiently substantiated or "manifestly ill-founded" for the purposes of admissibility.

The UN treaty bodies follow very similar procedures in processing complaints; that applied by the Human Rights Committee is an example. Complaints under the ICCPR Optional Protocol that contain the necessary elements are referred to the Committee's Special Rapporteur on New Communications. If a complaint contains the essential elements set forth in the treaty and rules, the case is registered and transmitted to the State Party concerned to give it an opportunity to comment. The State is requested to submit its observations within a set time frame. Once the State replies to the submission, the petitioner is offered an opportunity to comment within a specified time.

---

21 UNESCO is unique in having no formal rules governing initial communications, which usually originate in letters addressed to the headquarters. In practice, if the letter has an identifiable author and an allegation of a human rights violation, the author is sent a form to complete seeking further information, including about the link between the alleged violation and UNESCO's mandate.

If the State Party fails to respond to a complaint, the ICCPR will take a decision based on the information supplied by the petitioner. Given the large number of complaints received under the ICCPR Optional Protocol, the HRC generally considers admissibility and the merits of a case simultaneously. Occasionally, the Committee adopts a different procedure, for example, if a State Party presents timely submissions on admissibility that raise serious doubts on that score, it may invite the petitioner to respond and then take a preliminary decision on admissibility alone, thereafter proceeding to the merits stage if the case is declared admissible. Notably, in some systems up to 90 per cent of communications fail to survive the admissibility examination, usually for failure to exhaust local remedies.

The requirement that the complainant exhaust available and effective domestic remedies before filing an international complaint gives the State an opportunity to correct any wrong done and redress the resulting harm. Theoretical, illusory, inadequate and ineffective remedies need not be accessed, as recourse to these processes would be futile. Uncertainty about the effectiveness of such actions, however, does not generally dispense with this requirement. Many human rights treaties set forth certain examples of ineffective remedies, such as undue delay in proceedings. Lack of an independent judiciary or absence of jurisdiction to hear human rights complaints would also suffice to excuse recourse to local remedies. The applicant is required initially to give detailed reasons why the rule should not apply; the burden will then shift to the State to indicate what available and effective remedies exist within the State. The I-A Court has indicated in an advisory opinion that remedies need not be exhausted if a complainant has been prevented from obtaining adequate legal representation due to indigence or a general fear in the legal community.[22] The complainant has the burden to prove that legal representation was both necessary and impossible to obtain.

The exhaustion of remedies requirement means that in many instances matters will not reach an international tribunal for some years after the matter giving rise to the complaint occurred. To this must be added the delays that all international petition procedures face due to case backlogs, failure of States to respond to petitions in a timely manner, infrequent meetings of treaty bodies, and the usual two-stage process of admissibility and merits. It is not uncommon for decisions to be

---

22 Advisory Opinion OC-11/90.

reached years after the original incident; however, it is also possible for the transmission of a petition to the relevant government to produce an immediate positive reaction or expression of willingness to negotiate a friendly settlement.

Most treaties list other admissibility criteria that may preclude reaching the merits of a complaint. Tribunals may consider a case to be an abuse of the right of petition, frivolous, vexatious or otherwise inappropriate. Forum selection is also required: generally complaints may not be submitted to more than one treaty body or regional mechanism, the aim being to avoid unnecessary duplication at the international level.[23] The HRC and the regional systems have decided that, for this purpose, the Resolution 1503 procedure and complaints to a UN special rapporteur do not constitute such a mechanism.[24] Second, the HRC has taken the view that, inasmuch as the Covenant provides greater protection in some respects than is available under other international instruments, facts that have already been submitted to another international mechanism can be brought under the Optional Protocol if broader protections in the Covenant are invoked. Furthermore, the HRC considers that complaints dismissed by other international mechanisms on procedural grounds have not been substantively examined and they may therefore be brought before the Committee. CERD is the rare treaty that does not consider inadmissible a matter pending before or the subject of a decision by another international procedure.

Regional bodies apply the same rule.[25] The IACHR will not consider a petition if the subject matter is pending settlement in another international governmental organization or "essentially duplicates a petition pending or already examined and settled by the Commission or by another international governmental organization of which the State concerned is a member".[26] However, it will consider the matter if the

---

23 See European Convention Art. 35(1)(b); American Convention Art. 47(d); African Charter Art. 56(7).

24 But see *Peraldi v France*, App 2096/05, ECtHR dec (inadmissible), 7 Apr 2009, in which the European Court declared inadmissible a petition because the brother of the applicant had presented the same facts to the UN Working Group on Arbitrary Detention. For the earlier UN decision, see Working Group on Arbitrary Detention, UN Doc A/HRC/4/40/Add.1 at 11 (2006) (2009).

25 See *Mpaka-Nsusu Andre Alphonse v Zaire*, HRC, Comm No 157/1983, UN Doc Supp No 40 (A/41/40) at 142 (1986), in which the African Commission declared inadmissible a matter already considered by the UN Human Rights Committee.

26 Commission Regulations, Art. 33(1)(b).

other procedure examines only the general situation of human rights in the State in question, and there has been no decision on the specific facts in the petition submitted to the IACHR, or if the other procedure will not effectively redress the violation.

Complaints to the Committee against Torture and CEDAW differ in some respects from the admissibility requirements of other treaties. These two agreements not only bar complaints currently under examination by another procedure of international investigation or settlement, but also declare inadmissible complaints that already have been the subject of a decision by such a mechanism. Several States Party to the ICCPR Optional Protocol have filed reservations to ensure that this rule applies in respect to it as well, in order to preclude "appeals" from unfavourable judgments of the European Court. The CAT Committee's rules of procedure also state that a complaint may be rejected as inadmissible if the time elapsed since the exhaustion of domestic remedies is so unreasonably prolonged as to render consideration of the complaint unduly difficult.

For most human rights bodies the initial screening is done by the secretariat, a necessity given that all such bodies meet only in two to three sessions a year. UN bodies like the HRC, CAT and the CESCR thereafter assign a rapporteur or working group to examine the communications. ILO representations and complaints are submitted to the Director-General of the International Labour Office and a matter is receivable if it is submitted by a proper body and concerns a member State of the ILO; it must concern a convention ratified by the State in question or concern freedom of association. Once the matter is declared receivable, a representation is examined by a special Tripartite Committee appointed by the Governing Body from among the members; complaints on freedom of association are referred to the ILO Committee on Freedom of Association. Other complaints, once sent to the government for its comments, may be considered by a Commission of Inquiry established by the Governing Body.

Although exhaustion of domestic remedies is a prerequisite to filing a complaint, there are urgent actions and precautionary measures that can be initiated where there is an imminent threat of an irreparable injury to an individual or group, without prejudice to any ultimate determination of the merits of the complaint. The rationale lies in protecting the right of petition as well as the rights of those subject to possible harm within the State. In all instances, the State Party may present arguments at any stage of the proceedings on why the request for interim measures should be lifted or is no longer justified. For the Human Rights Committee, the Committee's Special Rapporteur on New Communications may issue a request to the State Party for interim measures with a view to averting irreparable harm before the complaint is considered. Rule 108(1) of the CAT Committee's rules of procedure authorizes interim measures to prevent irreparable harm while the communication is being considered. Most commonly, such requests arise in the context of claims under CAT Article 3 when a deportation is pending and there is a foreseeable risk of the complainant suffering torture in the receiving State. The Committee's Special Rapporteur on New Complaints and Interim Measures decides whether a request for interim measures to the State Party should be made under this rule.

The decision establishing UNESCO's procedure contains ten conditions for admissibility, several of which are matters of form and common to other procedures, others of which are more substantive. They are: no anonymous communications; no abuse of the right of petition; not based exclusively on information disseminated through the mass media; submission within a reasonable time following the violation; and information about efforts to exhaust local remedies. The last mentioned does not actually require that the remedies have been exhausted, only that there be an indication about whether an attempt has been made to exhaust them. The requirements also preclude consideration of any matter settled under another procedure of domestic or international law.

8.5   Friendly settlements

Nearly all complaints procedures include the option of resolving complaints by friendly settlement; some treaties make it mandatory for the treaty body to seek to resolve matters in this way.

UNESCO's procedure is deliberately designed to gather information and reach a friendly settlement in cooperation with the government. Decision 104 EX/3.3 states that "UNESCO should not play the role of an international judicial body". The UNESCO Committee on Conventions and Recommendations handles the procedure, but in practice the process may involve consultations and intercession initiated by the Director-General. In addition, the Committee may recommend specific measures to the Executive Board, including direct confidential consultations with the government concerned in order to reach an amicable solution.

Other treaties allow but do not mandate the procedure. The rules of procedure of the CESCR, for example, provide that at the request of any of the parties, at any time after receipt of a communication and before a determination on the merits has been reached, the Committee shall make available its good offices to the parties with a view to reaching a friendly settlement of the matter said to amount to a violation of the Covenant and submitted for consideration under the Optional Protocol, on the basis of respect for the obligations set forth in the Covenant. Both parties must consent to the procedure. The friendly settlement procedure is confidential and without prejudice to the parties' submissions to the Committee. No written or oral communication and no offer or concession made in the framework of the attempt to secure a friendly settlement may be used against the other party in the communication proceedings before the Committee. Once both parties have expressly agreed to a friendly settlement, the CESCR will adopt a decision with a statement of the facts and of the solution reached. The decision will be transmitted to the parties concerned and published in the Committee's annual report. Prior to adopting that decision, the Committee shall ascertain whether the victim/s of the alleged violation have consented to the friendly settlement agreement. In all cases, the friendly settlement must be based on respect for the obligations set forth in the Covenant. If no friendly settlement is reached, the Committee will continue to examine the communication in accordance with its rules.

8.6 Merits determinations

Once a UN committee decides a case is admissible, it proceeds to consider the merits of the complaint, issuing a reasoned decision for concluding that a violation has or has not occurred under the various articles it considers applicable. The committees consider each case in closed session. Although some have provisions for oral proceedings in their rules of procedure, the practice of most treaty bodies has been to consider complaints on the basis of the written information supplied by the complainant and the State Party. Accordingly, it has not been the practice to receive oral submissions from the parties or audio or audio-visual evidence (such as audio cassettes or videotapes).

Nor do the committees go beyond the information provided by the parties to seek independent verification of the facts. Generally, unlike the regional tribunals, they do not accept amicus curiae briefs. The decision reached, along with any separate or dissenting opinions, is transmitted to the applicant and the State Party simultaneously; it then becomes a public record and is included in the annual report of the tribunal. There is no appeal against committee decisions, which as a rule are final.

The rules of procedure of CERD and the Committee against Torture authorize each of these treaty bodies to seek the attendance in person of one party or the other to provide further clarifications or to answer questions when it considers the merits of a complaint. In practice, such oral proceedings are exceptional.

Most other treaty bodies may obtain any documentation from UN bodies, specialized agencies or other sources that may assist them in considering the complaint. The procedure of the CESCR follows this model, allowing the Committee to consult relevant documentation from other UN bodies, specialized agencies, funds, programmes and mechanisms, and other international organizations, including from regional human rights systems, that may assist in the examination of the communication. The CESCR must afford each party an opportunity to comment on such third-party documentation or information within fixed time limits. As with the HRC, the CESCR sets forth its decision in "Views" on the communication. The Secretary-General transmits the Views of the Committee, together with any recommendations, to the submitter of the communication and to the State Party concerned.

The ILO Tripartite Committees, Committee on Freedom of Association, and Committee of Inquiry all communicate representations and complaints to the government in question, asking for comment and information on the substance of the matter. Commissions of Inquiry may also contact other governments and NGOs for information and hold hearings with representatives of the parties and witnesses. On-site visits are possible as well. When all information is received, the various bodies make recommendations to the Governing Body. The Governing Body then decides whether to close the matter or to publish the proceedings if the matter concerned a representation. For a Commission of Inquiry, a report is sent to the Governing Body and to the governments concerned and the report is published. If the government concerned does not accept the recommendations, it may refer the matter to the ICJ. If the government does not implement the recommendations of the Commission of Inquiry within the time specified, the Governing Body may recommend action be taken to secure compliance. This has rarely happened.[27]

Within UNESCO, if dialogue with the government fails to produce a friendly settlement of the matter, the merits may be considered through written submissions and participation in Committee meetings to provide additional information. In theory, the author of the communication could be present as well, but in practice this has not been done. The process concludes with the confidential report from the Committee to the Executive Board, containing information from its examination of the matter and recommendations. It does not contain a finding that a State has violated human rights.

The judicial decisions of the three regional courts are legally binding on the States appearing before them. In contrast, UN treaty bodies and the regional commissions issue recommendations or other conclusions. The HRC's consideration of individual communications results in "views" forwarded to the parties. The Optional Protocol States this "without explaining how these views shall be reached, for which purpose, and to what effect".[28] In practice, the Committee has acted as a judicial or quasi-judicial body in assessing the evidence and undertaking legal reasoning in its analysis, within the confines of the written procedure established by the Optional Protocol. Over time, the length of the opinions has increased, as have the recommendations on forms of reparation due when the Committee finds a violation.

The final views of treaty bodies, as well as courts, on the merits of complaints have received considerable attention as a source of normative development. The jurisprudence of human rights bodies consists of the application of treaty provisions to specific facts and conclusions about whether or not those facts reveal the violation of a guaranteed right. As such, the decisions and recommendations are instructive beyond the particular State subject of the complaint.

---

27 Art. 33 was used for the first time against Myanmar in respect to forced labour.

28 Torkel Opsahl, *The Human Rights Committee*, in THE UNITED NATIONS AND HUMAN RIGHTS: A CRITICAL APPRAISAL (P Alston, ed., Clarendon 1992), 426.

There is general consensus, however, that the views are not legally binding, at least directly.[29] There are thus no enforcement procedures similar to those conducted by the Council of Europe's Committee of Ministers. Nonetheless, Committee members and many commentators consider the views as "the end result of a quasi-judicial adversarial international body established and elected by the States Parties for the purpose of interpreting the provisions of the Covenant and monitoring compliance with them". As a consequence, they argue that the Committee's views in Optional Protocol cases should be treated as authoritative interpretation of the Covenant under international law.[30] In its 2008 General Comment No 33 on the obligations of States Parties to the Optional Protocol, the Committee explained this position further:[31]

11. While the function of the Human Rights Committee in considering individual communications is not, as such, that of a judicial body, the views issued by the Committee under the Optional Protocol exhibit some important characteristics of a judicial decision. They are arrived at in a judicial spirit, including the impartiality and independence of Committee members, the considered interpretation of the language of the Covenant, and the determinative character of the decisions.

Because of this quasi-judicial character,

13. The views of the Committee under the Optional Protocol represent an authoritative determination by the organ established under the Covenant itself charged with the interpretation of that instrument. These views derive their character, and the importance which attaches to them, from the integral role of the Committee under both the Covenant and the Optional Protocol.

To further support a juridical status for the Committee's views on individual petitions, General Comment 33 cites to Article 2 of the

---

29 C Pappa, Das Individualbeschwerdeverfahren des Falkultativprotokolls zum Internationalen Pact über bürgerliche und politische Rechte (Stämpfli 1996), 316 et seq., argues that they are indirectly binding.

30 R Hansi and M Scheinin, Leading Cases of the Human Rights Committee (Institute for Human Rights, Turku 2003), 22.

31 Human Rights Committee, General Comment 33, The Obligations of States Parties under the Optional Protocol to the International Covenant on Civil and Political Rights, CCPR/C/GC/33, 5 Nov 2008.

Covenant, which obligates a party to provide a remedy to any individual whose rights are violated. According to the Committee, this obligation is triggered each time the Committee makes a finding of a violation after considering a communication under the Optional Protocol. In addition, according to the Committee, the character of the views it issues

> is further determined by the obligation of States Parties to act in good faith, both in their participation in the procedures under the Optional Protocol and in relation to the Covenant itself. A duty to cooperate with the Committee arises from an application of the principle of good faith to the observance of all treaty obligations.[32]

Although the drafting history of the Protocol indicates that States Parties did not intend that the views of the HRC constitute legally binding decisions,[33]

> [n]onetheless any State party will find it hard to reject such findings in so far as they are based on orderly proceedings during which the defendant party had ample opportunity to present its submissions. The views of the HRC gain their authority from their inner qualities of impartiality, objectives and soberness. If such requirements are met, the views of the HRC can have a far-reaching impact.[34]

In the Inter-American system, the I-A Court's view about the legal nature of IACHR recommendations has changed over time. In the early case of *Caballero-Delgado and Santana v Colombia*, the IACHR requested the I-A Court to "declare that based on the principle of *pacta sunt servanda*" the Colombian government had violated the American Convention by failing to comply with the Commission's recommendations.[35] In response, the Court held that:

> In the Court's judgment, the term "recommendations" used by the American Convention should be interpreted to conform to its ordinary

---

32 General Comment 33, para. 15, citing the VCLT, Art. 26.

33 D McGoldrick, The Human Rights Committee: Its Role in the Development of the International Covenant on Civil and Political Rights (Oxford Monographs in International Law) (Clarendon Press 1994), 151.

34 C Tomuschat, *Evolving Procedural Rules: The United Nations Human Rights Committee's First Two Years of Dealing with Individual Communications* (1980) 1 HRLJ 249, 255. See also Nisuke Ando, *The Future of Monitoring Bodies – Limitations and Possibilities of the Human Rights Committee*, 1991–1992 Can Hum Rts YB 169, 172.

35 *Caballero Delgado and Santana v Columbia*, I-A Court HR, Ser C No 22 (8 Dec 1995).

meaning, in accordance with Article 31(1) of the Vienna convention on the Law of Treaties. For that reason, a recommendation does not have the character of an obligatory judicial decision for which the failure to comply would generate State responsibility. As there is no evidence in the present Convention that the parties intended to give it a special meaning, Article 31(4) of the Vienna Convention is not applicable. Consequently, the State does not incur international responsibility by not complying with a recommendation which is not obligatory.[36]

The IACHR reasserted its authority in subsequent cases before the Court[37] and in the *Loayza Tamayo v Peru* judgment, the Court modified its conclusion about the legal weight accorded Commission recommendations. While it reaffirmed that the ordinary meaning of the term recommendations means that they are not legally binding, it added:

> However, in accordance with the principle of good faith, embodied in the aforesaid Article 31(1) of the Vienna Convention, if a State signs and ratifies an international treaty, especially one concerning human rights, such as the American Convention, it has the obligation to make every effort to comply with the recommendations of a protection organ such as the Inter-American Commission, which is, indeed, one of the principal organs of the Organization of American States, whose function is "to promote the observance and defense of human rights" in the hemisphere. (OAS Charter, Articles 52 and 111)

> Likewise, Article 33 of the American Convention States that the Inter-American Commission is, as the Court, competent "with respect to matters relating to the fulfilment of the commitments made by the States Parties", which means that by ratifying said Convention, States Parties engage themselves to apply the recommendations made by the Commission in its reports.[38]

Thus, the principle of good faith requires due regard to the IACHR's recommendations as a matter of applying the structure, object and purpose of the treaty, which confers a monitoring function on the Commission. The Court's analysis could also apply to OAS member States not party to the American Convention, since the Commission

---

36 Ibid., at para. 67.
37 *Case of Genie Lacayo v Nicaragua*, I-A Court HR, Ser C No 30 (29 Jan 1997), para. 11.
38 *Case of Loayza Tamayo v Peru*, I-A Court HR, Ser C No 33 (17 Sept 1997) paras 80–81.

similarly derives a monitoring function from the OAS Charter. The Court now consistently insists on a good faith obligation of compliance with IACHR recommendations.[39] In addition to the Court's reference to *pacta sunt servanda*, the IACHR relies on the principle of *effet utile* to insist that States have a duty to comply with its recommendations.[40] The result is that the Commission considers its reports as valid interpretations of the obligations freely accepted by the States. If a State does not concur with those interpretations it is at liberty to appeal to the I-A Court, in order to dispute the IACHR's conclusions and procedures, although no State has done so.

8.7 Redress

Human rights litigation may serve various purposes. A first aim is largely forward looking, to uphold the international rule of law and bring State laws and practices into conformity with human rights norms. Human rights bodies regularly express their concern with this aspect of the cases before them. The second aim of complaints procedures should be to afford redress to the petitioners. To a large extent, this aim requires assessing the consequences of the violation in order to erase those consequences or to compensate the victims if the harm cannot be eliminated. Redress also aims to uphold the rule of law, but it is foremost concerned with placing the victims as closely as possible to the position they would have enjoyed had the violation not occurred. A third aim, closely related to the first two, is to identify and express condemnation of the violations and the violators. While punishment is not the goal of human rights litigation, the language used by tribunals in their judgments may serve to express condemnation or outrage in the face of particularly serious violations.

As with many other issues in human rights law, remedies are only partly and often vaguely addressed in the basic instruments of regional human rights bodies. Regional courts are granted remedial powers by express provisions in their respective treaties, but no equivalent provi-

---

39 See, for example, *Blake v Guatemala* (Merits), I-A Court HR, Ser C, No 36 (24 Jan 1998), para. 108; *Castillo-Petruzzi et al v Peru* (Merits, Reparations and Costs) I-A Court HR Ser C No 52 (30 May 1999); *Case of Cesti Hurtado v Peru* (Merits), I-A Court HR, Ser C, No 56 (29 Sep 1999), paras 186–7; and *Baena Ricardo v Panama* (Merits, Reparations and Costs) I-A Court HR, Ser C No 72 (2 Feb 2001), paras 191–2.

40 See, for example, I-A Ct. HR, Request for Provisional Measures, Case of the Penitentiary of Mendoza, Order of 22 Nov 2004.

sions exist for the commissions or for UN bodies. The ICJ has held that the power to afford reparations is implicit in jurisdiction to hear a case, as a necessary concomitant to deciding disputes.[41] This power extends to all aspects of reparations.[42] Other courts engaged in dispute settlement and compliance have also assumed that they may award reparations and make related orders.

The remedial powers of international tribunals vary according to the express provisions of the relevant treaties, but the jurisprudence is similar and was the basis for the rules codified in the UN Basic Principles on reparation.[43] International law has long expressed a preference for restitution as a remedy, where this is possible. Some human rights violations, for example, wrongful detention, allow for restitution of the right violated by freeing the person detained. Other rights, like life, cannot be restored once lost and thus require a difficult assessment of the monetary value of the right lost, as a substitute for restitution. Regional tribunals have struggled with the question of assessing compensatory damages as well as the scope of their powers to remedy violations through non-monetary means, often under the heading of satisfaction.

The term "satisfaction" as used in arbitral treaties and in the European Convention draws upon international practice in regard to State responsibility for injury to aliens. In this body of law, satisfaction could require punishment of the guilty and assurances as to future conduct, monetary awards or declaration of the wrong, especially when coupled with an apology from the offending State. Many such non-monetary remedies afforded under the heading of satisfaction in inter-State proceedings are now applied in the human rights context, especially apologies, guarantees of non-repetition and/or punishment of wrongdoers.

The ICCPR's Human Rights Committee, in General Comment 15, summarized the duties of States Parties to afford accessible and effective remedies and to cease ongoing violations. The Committee noted that a failure by a State Party to investigate allegations of violations

---

41 "In general, jurisdiction to determine the merits of a dispute entails jurisdiction to determine reparation". *Military and Paramilitary Activities in and Against Nicaragua (Nicar v US)* 1986 ICJ 14, para. 283.

42 *Corfu Channel Case (Alb v UK)* 1949 ICJ 4, 26 (9 Apr 1949).

43 *Basic Principles and Guidelines on the Right to a Remedy and Reparation for Victims of Gross Violations of International Human Rights Law and Serious Violations of International Humanitarian Law*, UN Doc E/CN.4/2005/59 (2005).

could in and of itself give rise to a separate breach of the Covenant. The obligation to provide an effective remedy, seen as central to the efficacy of domestic enforcement, generally entails appropriate compensation, it may also involve restitution, rehabilitation and measures of satisfaction, such as public apologies, public memorials, guarantees of non-repetition and changes in relevant laws and practices, as well as bringing to justice the perpetrators of human rights violations. A failure to investigate, as well as a failure to bring to justice perpetrators of violations recognized as criminal under either domestic or international law may give rise to a separate breach of the Covenant.

On the regional level, Article 41 of the European Convention denies the European Court the power to annul Member State laws or decisions that are in conflict with the Convention, a power no international human rights court has been granted. The Court's consistent view has been that this provision also serves to deny it the power to direct the State itself to cure the underlying problem. With a rising caseload and repetitive cases resulting from State failure to comply with its obligations, the Committee of Ministers suggested the Court should take a broader approach to remedying violations and indicate the measures the State should take, a practice that is slowly emerging.

The American Convention grants the I-A Court the ability to order compensation and other remedial measures; it has used this power expansively to create an extensive jurisprudence on the issue of reparations. The IACHR may recommend remedies but never quantifies compensation. The African Commission has an uneven record of taking up issues of redress.[44] The African Court has perhaps the broadest remedial powers, being given the authority to "order any appropriate measures" to remedy a violation found.

The Inter-American and African Commissions, lacking express provisions on remedies, have generally recommended in general terms the appropriate action to be taken by a State found to have violated human rights. Neither commission has quantified compensation in any case. In some cases, the African Commission has recommended specific remedial measures that appear close to injunctive orders.[45]

---

44 Gina Bekker, *The African Commission on Human and Peoples' Rights and Remedies for Human Rights Violations* (2013) HUMAN RIGHTS LAW REVIEW 499–528.

45 For Commission decisions calling for cessation of the breach and restoration of the liberty of wrongfully held detainees, see *Constitutional Rights Project v Nigeria* Comm No 60/91 (1996),

In general, human rights bodies appear generally to be attending more to the issue of reparations. The conclusion of the UN's two-decade-long process of drafting Guidelines and Principles on reparations has likely assisted in this evolution, by providing a consensus text of what is required.

8.8 Inquiry procedures and pilot judgments

Human rights law has developed innovative techniques to take up complaints of gross and systematic or structural human rights problems. Some treaties allow the treaty body to initiate an inquiry on its own motion based on information received or on the basis of a complaint. This may result in a formal decision or in a country report with recommendations. To some extent the Resolution 1503 procedure can be considered as this type of mechanism.

States Parties to the ICESCR Optional Protocol may make a declaration accepting the inquiry procedure that is set forth therein. The UN Secretary-General initiates the process, bringing to the attention of the CESCR reliable information indicating grave or systematic violations by a State Party of any of the economic, social and cultural rights set forth in the Covenant. The CESCR thereafter will seek to ascertain the reliability of the information and obtain additional relevant information substantiating the facts of the situation. Based on the information it acquires, the CESCR will determine whether the information received contains reliable information indicating grave or systematic violations of rights set forth in the Covenant by the State Party concerned. If so, the CESCR, through the Secretary-General, shall invite the State Party to submit observations with regard to that information within fixed time limits. Taking into account any observations that may have been submitted by the State Party concerned, as well as other reliable information, the Committee may designate one or more of its members to conduct a confidential inquiry, including making a visit to the State Party with the State's consent, and to make a report. Visits may include hearings to enable the designated member or members of the Committee to determine facts or issues relevant to the inquiry. The report is examined by the CESCR and transmitted, through the Secretary-General, to the State Party concerned, together with any

Comm No 87/93 (1996) and *Center for Free Speech v Nigeria*, Comm 206/97, 13th Annual Activity Report of the African Commission 1999–2000 (calling for the release of detainees).

comments and recommendations. The State Party has six months to submit its observations on the findings, comments and recommendations. After the six-month period, the CESCR may ask the State for additional information on measures taken in response to an inquiry.

The CAT also may initiate an inquiry if it receives "reliable information which appears to it to contained well-founded indications that torture is being systematically practiced in the territory of a State Party". This procedure does not require acceptance by States Parties, but they may opt out (Art. 28); few States have done so.

The European system has faced a growing problem with repetitive cases, indicating an underlying structure problem in several countries. There is no recognition of class actions in complaint procedures, but the Court's overall caseload has become increasingly unmanageable and it has sought to devise innovative procedures to address repetitive cases. One such mechanism is the "pilot judgment", developed in part in response to a resolution of the Committee of Ministers inviting the Court to identify what it considers to be an underlying systematic problem and the source of the problem in judgments finding a violation of the European Convention, in particular when the problem is likely to give rise to numerous applications. Based on its decision in a leading or pilot case, the Court may process large groups of applications concerning the same issue. The first such pilot judgment, *Broniowski v Poland*, led to a change in Polish legislation and a settlement that resolved 167 pending applications before the Court. In 2011 the Court adjourned more than 2,100 applications pending the outcome of a number of leading cases. The pilot judgment procedure could resolve these and other pending applications, but only if the State in question complies with the pilot judgment.

8.9   Follow-up

One indication of the emphasis given to good-faith compliance with pronouncements of human rights treaty bodies is the fact that nearly all of them have now established follow-up mechanisms to evaluate compliance with the recommendations they make. In 1990 the HRC issued a statement concerning measures to monitor compliance with its views, appointing a special rapporteur for this purpose.[46] The spe-

---

46 See A/45/40, II 205.

cial rapporteur ascertains and monitors the measures taken by States Parties to give effect to the Committee's views, by requesting information from the States Parties in respect of all final views with a finding of a violation. In the Inter-American system, the Commission's Rules of Procedure, Article 46, establish a follow-up mechanism based on Convention Article 41.

When a UN treaty body decides that a State Party has committed a violation of rights under the treaty, it invites the State Party to supply information within three (or in some instances six) months on the steps it has taken to give effect to its findings. Even after this, the various committees may request further information about any measures the State Party has taken in response to its views or recommendations or in response to a friendly settlement agreement. In addition to written representations and meetings with duly accredited representatives of the State Party, the Rapporteur or Working Group may seek information from the author/s and victim/s of the communications and other relevant sources. When such a body decides that there has been no violation of the treaty or that the complaint is inadmissible, the process is complete once the decision has been transmitted to the applicant and the State Party.

At the regional level, in theory the European system has the most robust follow-up procedure. Compliance with judgments of the European Court is supervised by the Committee of Ministers, which has the power to take sanctions against States that violate their obligations as Member States. In practice, the Committee keeps open all matters in which there has not been full compliance with the individual measures of reparation to the victim and the general measures necessary to avoid a repetition of the violation. The Committee of Ministers has only once, however, approached a vote on expelling a Member State for gross violations of human rights; the State in question resigned before the vote was taken. Some matters have remained with the Committee of Ministers for decades without full compliance.

Ultimately, compliance with human rights law, like other law, is produced through a process that involves normative development and internalization of the norms, involving a coalition of national and international actors. Coercion, persuasion and acculturation are critical to the process.[47] Over time, human rights bodies have developed

---

47 See R Goodman and D Jinks, *How to Influence States: Socialization and International Human Rights Law* (2004) 54 Duke Law Journal 621.

practices unforeseen by the authors of the treaties, practices now well accepted. The deference shown through State acquiescence can be seen to reflect the authoritative role of treaty bodies, giving rise to even greater expectations of compliance in the future.

In practice, the recommendations, observations and general comments of human rights treaty bodies will have persuasive force insofar as the organs retain their independence, deliver reasoned and consistent opinions using accepted methods of treaty interpretation, and establish a pattern of compliance by States Parties. Such bodies are created precisely to monitor compliance with the obligations of States Parties, so their pronouncements have an authority lacking on the part of NGOs, commentators or other actors. States Parties have the power to reverse the interpretations of treaty bodies through amendment of the treaties; thus far, this has been avoided. In practice, when treaty bodies establish a positive reputation for their work, they garner considerable authority. As it happens, the Human Rights Committee, the IACHR and the African Commission have brought about general acceptance of their pronouncements as authoritative interpretations of the legal obligations under their respective treaties. When domestic authorities, especially courts, incorporate and apply the interpretations, their character can shift from soft to hard law. As more States comply, it becomes increasingly difficult for a single State to ignore the decisions and recommendations of human rights bodies.

9   Enforcement

The enforcement of human rights is first and foremost the responsibility of each State, which is bound to comply in good faith with norms of customary international law and with the treaties in force to which the State is a party (*pacta sunt servanda*).[1] Indeed, the Vienna Declaration and Programme of Action affirmed that "the promotion and protection of human rights and fundamental freedoms is the first responsibility of government".[2] If a State fails, by an act or omission attributable to it, to comply with any international obligation, the law of State responsibility requires that such breach cease and generates a new legal duty to afford reparation for any harm caused by the violation.

The law of State responsibility developed in the context of reciprocal inter-State obligations, the breach of which generally produces an injured State or States to complain of the violation. Such a legal framework is not fully satisfactory when applied to human rights law, however, because another State rarely suffers direct injury due to a State's failure to observe human rights. This lack of reciprocity has led to descriptions of human rights obligations as "unilateral" in nature:[3] that is, obligations directed internally at protecting individuals and groups within the territory and subject to the jurisdiction of the State rather than being obligations performed for the benefit of other States. The doctrine of obligations *erga omnes* serves in part to maintain the framework of State responsibility by establishing that at least some human rights duties are owed to the international community as a whole, obviating the need for an injured State to complain of a

---

1 VCLT, Art. 26 (1969); Human Rights Committee, General Comment No 31, "The Nature of the General Legal Obligation Imposed on States Parties to the Covenant on Civil and Political Rights" UN Doc CCPR/C/21/Rev.1/Add.13 (2004).

2 Vienna Declaration and Programme of Action, 12 Jul 1993, A/CONF.157/23, endorsed by GA Res 48/121 (20 Dec 1993), at para. 1.

3 See, for example, *Austria v Italy*; see also *The Effect of Reservations on the Entry into Force of the American Convention on Human Rights (Arts 74 and 75)*, 2 Inter-Am Ct HR (Ser A) (1983) at paras 29, 33.

violation. In fact, most human rights treaties include the possibility of inter-State complaints among their compliance mechanisms, although such complaints are rarely brought.

International organizations may take measures to enforce human rights obligations should a State refuse to comply with the decisions of monitoring bodies or engage in gross and systematic violations. These measures range from suspension of participation in the organization through economic and other sanctions to the option of using unilateral or multilateral force to intervene in the country.

9.1   Suspensions and exclusions

According to VCLT Article 60, "'A material breach' of a bilateral treaty by one of the parties entitles the other to invoke the breach as a ground for terminating the treaty or suspending its operation in whole or in part". A material breach is "the violation of a provision essential to the accomplishment of the object or purpose of the treaty".[4] For many international organizations, including the UN, respect for human rights is identified as essential to achieving the object and purpose for which the organization was created. Article 5 of the UN Charter authorizes the General Assembly, upon the recommendation of the Security Council, to suspend the membership of a member against whom enforcement action has been taken under Chapter VII; Article 6 permits expulsion for persistent violation. No country has been expelled from the UN for its human rights violations, but on 12 November 1974 the General Assembly voted 91–22, with 19 abstentions, to suspend apartheid-era South Africa from participation in the work of the Assembly's 29th session and the suspension lasted until participation rights were restored on 23 June 1994, following democratic elections in the country. More recently, on 1 March 2011, the UN General Assembly by consensus suspended the participation of Libya in the UN Human Rights Council due to violations of human rights in the country. The decision was taken on the recommendation of the Council and marked the first time that such a suspension had been requested and approved.

Organizations at the regional level often condition membership and/ or participation in the organization on compliance with human rights.

---

4 For further, see Fredrick Kirgis, *Some Lingering Questions about Article 60 of the Vienna Convention on the Law of Treaties* (1989) 22 CORNELL INT'L L J 549.

Membership in the Council of Europe[5] requires European States to conform to the basic principles of the organization – democratic governance, rule of law and respect for human rights. Through the Parliamentary Assembly the Council of Europe seeks specific commitments from applicants respecting human rights and monitors compliance with the commitments made. If the commitments are not forthcoming or the problems are deemed too serious, PACE may recommend that a State not be admitted. The Committee of Ministers may suspend or terminate membership for breach of these same basic principles. In fact, only one State has been denied entry[6] and one State withdrew from the organization[7] rather than face expulsion for violating that State's human rights obligations. Commentators have criticized the Council of Europe for not applying its principles more rigorously,[8] while others maintain that the ability to exercise pressure from within on Member States justifies the absence of more frequent sanctions or withholding membership.[9]

The Organization of American States has taken a somewhat different approach, maintaining State membership in order to insist on compliance with the State's legal obligations, while conditioning participation of the government of that State on respect for democracy, human rights and the rule of law. The Fifth Meeting of Consultation of the Ministers of Foreign Affairs in 1959 adopted the Declaration of Santiago, Chile, which affirms that effective exercise of representative democracy is the best vehicle for the promotion of social and political progress.[10] The resolution made it explicit that "the existence

---

5 Statute of the Council of Europe, Arts 4, 5 and 6.

6 Belarus has been denied entry into the Council of Europe because the Parliamentary Assembly considers the government deficient in commitment to the core principles of human rights, democracy and the rule of law. The Council of Europe also expects observer States to respect these principles.

7 On 12 Dec 1969, the same day the Committee of Ministers was to meet to decide the Greek cases (*Denmark, Norway, Sweden and the Netherlands v Greece*, 1968) and vote on a motion submitted by the Parliamentary Assembly to suspend or expel the government from the Council of Europe due to its human rights violations, Greece denounced the Convention. It later returned, following the restoration of democratic governance.

8 Peter Leuprecht, *Innovations in the European System of Human Rights Protection: Is Enlargement Compatible with Reinforcement?* (1998) 8 TRANSNATIONAL LAW & CONTEMPORARY PROBLEMS 313.

9 See, for example, the debate in the Parliamentary Assembly over admission of Belarus, Council of Europe Doc 9543, Report of the Debate of 26 Sep 2002.

10 Fifth Meeting of Consultation of Ministers of Foreign Affairs, *Final Act*, Doc No OEA/Ser.C/II.5, at 4–6 (1959).

of antidemocratic regimes constitutes a violation of the principles on which the Organization of American States is founded, and a danger to united and peaceful relationships in the hemisphere". This resolution was invoked in 1962 to suspend the government of Cuba from participation. In 2009 the OAS General Assembly rescinded its 1962 resolution excluding Cuba from participating in the OAS, deciding that "the participation of the Republic of Cuba in the OAS will be the result of a process of dialogue initiated at the request of the Government of Cuba, and in accordance with the practices, purposes, and principles of the OAS".[11] In 1992 the OAS adopted the Washington Protocol[12] to the OAS Charter and became the first regional organization to allow suspension of participation in the event that a State's democratically elected government is overthrown by force.

Unlike the Council of Europe, the African Union does not have a provision in its Constitutive Act making membership conditional on respect for human rights, and it is vague on sanctions and enforcement for non-compliance with member States' obligations, although in Article 23(2) it speaks of sanctions for failure to comply with the principles and policies of the AU, mentioning the fields of transport and communications. The AU is free to adopt any measures necessary to respond to a member State's failure to comply with its obligations. In fact, the AU Assembly, as the supreme organ of the AU, has taken some actions in response to human rights violations. During a two-year period, it denied the chairmanship to the Sudan's head of State because of persistent human rights violations in the country.[13] Subsequent institutional changes in the AU have led to even more forceful action in respect to the Sudan and other member States.

A Protocol Relating to the Peace and Security Council (PSC) of the African Union entered into force on 26 December 2003. The AU Executive Council then elected the 15 members of the PSC and adopted Rules of Procedure for the new body. The PSC is based in many respects on the UN Security Council. Article 4(h) of the AU Constitutive Act, repeated in Article 4 of the PSC Protocol, recognizes the right of the Union to intervene in any member State when war crimes, genocide or crimes against humanity are being commit-

---

11 Res AG/RES 2438 (XXXIX-O/09), 9 Jun 2009.
12 Protocol of Washington, 14 Dec 1992.
13 See Afr Union Ass, *Declaration*, Doc No Assembly/AU/Decl.2 (VI) (2006) and Afr Union Ass, *Decision on the Chairmanship of the African Union*, Doc No Assembly/AU/Dec.150 (VIII) (2007).

ted. Any decision to intervene is to be made by the Assembly on the recommendation of the PSC, which also has the power to authorize peace missions, impose sanctions in case of unconstitutional change of government, and "take initiatives and action it deems appropriate" in response to potential or actual conflicts. PSC decisions are binding on member States. Since it first met in 2004, the PSC has taken up crises in the Sudan, Comoros, Somalia, the Democratic Republic of Congo, Burundi, Côte d'Ivoire, Madagascar and Mauritania. It adopted resolutions creating AU peacekeeping operations in Burundi, Somalia and Darfur, and also imposed sanctions, such as travel bans and freezing of assets against persons undermining peace and security, and against those leading coups. The PSC has also moved to establish a "standby force" to serve as a permanent African peacekeeping force.

9.2 Linking foreign assistance to human rights

The OSCE has engaged in linking benefits and obligations since its origin, using the metaphor of "baskets" of commitments in the Helsinki Final Act. To benefit from one basket of commitments, participating States had to comply with the commitments contained in the other baskets. This issue linkage has been particularly successful in promoting compliance with human rights commitments. Participating States periodically convene intergovernmental conferences to undertake a thorough review of the implementation of the provisions of the Final Act. The meetings help focus public attention on the failure of certain States to live up to their human rights commitments.

Several States and the EU now link economic assistance and other programmes to human rights.[14] From the passage of the Jackson-Vanik amendment in 1973, which tied most-favoured-nation status to respect for certain human rights, the issue of utilizing US economic

---

14 See PETER R BAEHR AND MONIQUE CASTERMANS-HOLLEMAN, THE ROLE OF HUMAN RIGHTS IN FOREIGN POLICY (Palgrave Macmillan 2004); Bethany Barratt, *Canadian Foreign Policy and International Human Rights*, in HANDBOOK OF CANADIAN FOREIGN POLICY (Patrick James et al, eds, Lexington Books 2006), 235; HUMAN RIGHTS AND COMPARATIVE FOREIGN POLICY (David Forsythe, ed., UN UP 2000); HUMAN RIGHTS IN CANADIAN FOREIGN POLICY (Robert O Matthews and Cranford Pratt, eds, McGill-Queen's UP 1998); *Japanese Human Rights Policy at Domestic and International Levels* (2003) 15 JAPAN FORUM 287; JULIE MERTUS, BAIT AND SWITCH: HUMAN RIGHTS AND US FOREIGN POLICY (Routledge 2004); HILDE REIDING, THE NETHERLANDS AND THE DEVELOPMENT OF INTERNATIONAL HUMAN RIGHTS INSTRUMENTS (Intersentia 2007).

power to promote the observance of human rights has been contentious. Developing countries in particular object to "conditionality" as an intervention into domestic affairs. Issues of compliance with WTO rules may also arise. At the same time, business as usual is condemned when it serves to prolong the life of a dictatorial regime. US human rights legislation § 502B of the Foreign Assistance Act of 1961, as amended (22 USCA § 2304), and § 116 of the same Act (22 USCA § 2151n) tie the grant of military and economic assistance to the human rights policies of the recipient governments. The underlying policy rationale is articulated in § 502B(a)(1), which reads as follows:

> The United States shall, in accordance with its international obligations as set forth in the Charter of the United Nations and in keeping with the constitutional heritage and traditions of the United States, promote and encourage increased respect for human rights and fundamental freedoms throughout the world without distinction as to race, sex, language, or religion. Accordingly, a principal goal of the foreign policy of the United States shall be to promote the increased observance of internationally recognized human rights by all countries.

Both § 502B and § 116 thus aim to deny assistance to States whose governments engage in activities that reveal "a consistent pattern of gross violations of internationally recognized human rights". That term is defined in § 502B(d)(1) (22 USCA § 2304(d)(1)) as including violations such as:

> torture or cruel, inhuman, or degrading treatment or punishment, prolonged detention without charges and trial, causing the disappearance of persons by the abduction and clandestine detention of those persons, and other flagrant denial of the right to life, liberty, or the security of person.

Section 116(a) uses almost identical language. The phrase "consistent pattern of gross violations" mirrors the language of UN Economic and Social Council Resolution 1503 of 1970. That resolution is at the heart of the UN Charter-based system for dealing with human rights complaints. Over time, the US Congress has adopted additional restrictions on assistance for those engaged in a "consistent pattern of gross violations" or similar standard.[15]

---

15 See, for example, § 403(j)(1) of the Agricultural Trade and Development Act of 1954, 7 USC
    § 1733(j)(1) (providing and financing of agricultural commodities); bilateral debt relief under
    the enhanced HIPC legislation, 22 USCA § 262p-8(c)(4); § 104 (a) of the Africa Growth and

Section 116 also establishes a reporting requirement under which the Department of State must provide an annual human rights status report for all UN member States. Similar obligations are imposed by § 502B. In compiling these annual country reports, the State Department relies on information provided by US embassies as well as on findings of inter-governmental and non-governmental human rights organizations.

Each law contains various exceptions. Thus, economic aid does not have to be terminated if "such assistance will directly benefit the needy people in such country" (§ 116(a)). Moreover, the President may continue security assistance to a gross violator upon certification to the Congress "that extraordinary circumstances exist warranting provision of such assistance" (§ 502B(a)(2)). These and other provisions give the Executive Branch considerable latitude in administering the law with more or less vigour. Ultimately, of course, the question of whether a government is a human rights violator within the meaning of this legislation is a matter of judgment.

In addition to the legislation of general applicability described in the preceding section, the Congress has from time to time enacted so-called country-specific human rights laws to cut off aid to a particular country. Among the States singled out have been Argentina, Burma, Cambodia, Chile, Cuba, Guatemala, Haiti, Iran, Iraq, Libya, El Salvador, South Africa, Sudan and Yugoslavia. This legislation usually has a one-year duration, and may be renewed or extended depending upon the actions of the target government. Sometimes the Congress will also refuse an Executive branch request for security assistance to a country it considers to be a gross violator of human rights. Finally, § 701 of the International Financial Institutions Act of 1977 requires the US government and US representatives to the IFIs to advance the cause of human rights by using their "voice and vote" to prevent development aid from going to countries whose governments engage in gross violations of human rights.[16]

Opportunity Act, 19 USC § 3703(a)(3); § 2(b)(6) and (14) of the Export-Import Bank Act of 1945, as amended, 12 USC § 635(b)(6) and 635i-8(c) (certain functions of the Ex-Im Bank); § 498A of the Foreign Assistance Act of 1961 as amended, 22 USC § 2295a(b)(1) (assistance to the governments of the independent State of the former Soviet Union); and benefits under the Americas Initiative, 22 USCA § 2430b(a)(4).

16 See 22 USCA § 262d(a) (2008).

Within the European Union, in 1991, the Council and the Member States adopted a resolution on human rights, democracy and development that laid down guidelines, procedures and priorities for improving the consistency of development initiatives undertaken with non-Member States. As a result of these guidelines, the EU began including a human rights clause in its bilateral trade and cooperation agreements with third countries. A Council decision of May 1995 extended the human rights clause to all subsequently negotiated bilateral agreements of a general nature. More than 120 such agreements have been signed, the most comprehensive of which is the Cotonou Agreement – the trade and aid pact that links the EU with 78 developing countries in Africa, the Caribbean and Pacific (the ACP group). If any ACP country fails to respect human rights, EU trade concessions can be suspended and aid programmes reduced or curtailed.

The 1993 Treaty on European Union considers as one of the objectives of the Common Foreign and Security Policy the development and consolidation of "democracy and the rule of law, and respect for human rights and fundamental freedoms". A new title in the treaty on development cooperation includes a further direct reference to human rights and democratization: "Community policy in this area shall contribute to the general objective of developing and consolidating democracy and the rule of law and to that of respecting human rights and fundamental freedoms".

A number of guidelines on human rights issues and respect for international humanitarian law have been agreed upon by the Council of the European Union. They cover the topics of the death penalty, torture, human rights dialogues with third countries, children and armed conflict, human rights defenders, the rights of the child, violence and discrimination against women and girls, and international humanitarian law. The EU guidelines are not legally binding, but they represent a strong political signal that these are priorities for the Union. EU actors implement the guidelines through specific actions, such as demarches and statements, and the EU issues its own Annual Report on Human Rights. In general, the EU has favoured an approach based on partnership and cooperation, but it has imposed sanctions on Burma, Zimbabwe and Sri Lanka.

9.3   Trade and financial sanctions

The UN Charter confers upon the Security Council a very broad competence to "determine the existence of any threat to the peace, breach of the peace, or act of aggression" and then to decide what measures should be taken to "maintain or restore international peace and security". The key provision is Article 39 of Chapter VII, which establishes that "[t]he Security Council shall determine the existence of any threat to the peace, breach of the peace, or act of aggression and shall make recommendations, or decide what measures shall be taken in accordance with Articles 41 and 42, to maintain or restore international peace and security". Articles 41 and 42 authorize sanctions ("measures not involving the use of armed force") and the use of force, respectively. Importantly, according to Article 25 of the Charter, the Members of the UN agree to accept and carry out the decisions of the Security Council. Further, Article 103 provides that in the event of a conflict between the obligations of the members of the UN under the Charter and their obligations under any other international agreement, their obligations under the Charter shall prevail.

The first test for the powers of the Security Council to adopt sanctions to protect human rights came in the mid-1960s[17] when, on 1 November 1965, the white minority regime of Ian Smith in what is now Zimbabwe announced its Unilateral Declaration of Independence (UDI) from Great Britain. The following day, the Security Council condemned UDI, calling on all States not to recognize the "illegal racist minority regime" and to refrain from rendering it any assistance.[18] The resolution was adopted by a vote of 10 to 1, with one abstention; France considered the matter an internal UK problem that the Council should not discuss. Later, with the United Kingdom's acquiescence, the Council adopted Resolution 217 (20 November 1965), which called on all States to impose an oil and petroleum embargo and to break all relations with the Smith regime. By December 1966, the UK recognized that the policy of voluntary sanctions had failed, and the Security Council adopted Resolution 232 (16 December 1966), imposing mandatory selective sanctions against Rhodesia pursuant to Article 41 of the UN Charter. It was the first time that such action had been taken in the UN's history. Under Resolution 232, Rhodesia's principal exports were

---

17 Myers S McDougal and W Michael Reisman, *Rhodesia and the United Nations: The Lawfulness of International Concern* (1968) 62 AJIL 1.

18 SC Res 216 (12 Nov 1965).

banned from being imported into any country; also banned was the export to Rhodesia of oil or oil products, arms and military equipment, and aircraft and motor vehicles, as well as equipment or materials for their manufacture, assembly or maintenance. Two years later, the Security Council adopted far more comprehensive mandatory sanctions by Resolution 253 (16 December 1968). Sanctions again were tightened by subsequent resolutions in 1973 (SC Res 333 (22 May 1973)) and 1976 (SC Res 388 (6 April 1976)).

The Security Council members reached agreement on sanctions only once more in the UN's first 45-year history, another case involving racial discrimination: South Africa (1977). Since 1991, in contrast, following the end of the Cold War, the UN has had recourse to sanctions in cases involving human rights violations in Yugoslavia, Haiti, Somalia, Libya, Ethiopia and Eritrea, Liberia, Angola, Rwanda, Sudan, Sierra Leone, Afghanistan, the Democratic Republic of the Congo and Côte d'Ivoire.[19]

The use of economic sanctions, their scope and their targets have evolved considerably. Early multilateral sanctions like those against Rhodesia's Smith regime operated as general trade embargoes, but today's sanctions include targeted measures directed at finances, travel, arms and selective commodities.[20] Furthermore, sanctions target not only repressive governments, but individuals and entities involved in human rights abuses or undermining transitional justice.[21] Beyond UN Security Council enforcement, the EU, the British Commonwealth, and ad hoc coalitions of States have adopted their own measures. In addition, some States impose unilateral sanctions with respect to a particular human rights situation.[22]

---

19 Regarding UN sanctions resolutions, see Andrew Clapham, *Sanctions and Economic, Social and Cultural Rights*, in UNITED NATIONS SANCTIONS AND INTERNATIONAL LAW (Vera Gowlland-Debbas, ed., Kluwer Law International 2001).

20 Richard N Haass, *Sanctioning Madness* (1997) 76(6) FOREIGN AFF 74; DAVID CORTRIGHT AND GEORGE A LOPEZ, THE SANCTIONS DECADE: ASSESSING UN SECURITY COUNCIL SANCTIONS IN THE 1990S (Lynne Rienner 2000).

21 George A Lopez, *Matching Means with Intentions: Sanctions and Human Rights*, in THE FUTURE OF HUMAN RIGHTS: US POLICY FOR A NEW ERA (William F Schulz, ed., U Pennsylvania Press 2008).

22 The five decades of US unilateral sanctions on Cuba have been particularly controversial. The government claims to be enforcing human rights norms, but many see the measures as imposed for ideological reasons, with significant negative impact on rights and the quality of life of the general population. See especially UNITED STATES ECONOMIC MEASURES AGAINST CUBA:

From the beginning various analysts have questioned the efficacy and morality of sanctions.[23] As a result of increasing criticism, the UN Security Council undertook a sanctions review in the 1990s resulting in a shift towards more targeted and specialized economic instruments.[24] In addition, efforts to assess the humanitarian impact of particular UN sanctions have become standard policy[25] since 1995, when the Security Council first appointed a team of independent specialists to investigate sanctions violators and to report on their actions and on how sanctions can be better enforced. These Panels of Experts have helped identify ways of more refined targeting of perpetrators and particular commodities, such as conflict diamonds, that produce large revenues for them.[26] Various States have also taken action to make sanctions more effective by measures to combat money laundering and other practices that undermine financial sanctions.[27]

The new "smart sanctions" take aim at specific companies or individuals that are deemed most responsible for the human rights violations and the particular economic activities that contribute to the violations.[28] They often call on States to freeze financial assets of the government and individual regime leaders, as well as key supporters wherever located; suspend credits, aid and loans; deny access to overseas financial markets; restrict the trade of specific goods and commodities; ban military aid including weapons, computers and related communications technologies; ban travel of individuals or specific airlines and ocean vessels; deny visa, travel and educational opportunities

---

PROCEEDINGS IN THE UNITED NATIONS AND INTERNATIONAL LAW ISSUES (Michael Krinsky and David Golove, eds, Aletheia Press 1993).

23 George A Lopez and David Cortright, *Economic Sanctions and Human Rights: Part of the Solution or Part of the Problem?* (1997) 1(2) IJHR 1; Joy Gordon, *Smart Sanctions Revisited* (2011) 25 ETHICS & INTERNATIONAL AFFAIRS 315.

24 See George A Lopez, *Sanctions*, in OXFORD HANDBOOK OF HUMAN RIGHTS LAW (D Shelton, ed., OUP 2013).

25 THOMAS G WEISS ET AL, POLITICAL GAIN AND CIVILIAN PAIN: ASSESSING THE HUMANITARIAN IMPACT OF ECONOMIC SANCTIONS (Rowman & Littlefield 1997).

26 ALIX J BOUCHER AND VICTORIA K HOLT, TARGETING SPOILERS: THE ROLE OF UNITED NATIONS PANELS OF EXPERTS (Stimson 2009).

27 DESIGN AND IMPLEMENTATION OF ARMS EMBARGOES AND TRAVEL AND AVIATION RELATED SANCTIONS: RESULTS OF THE "BONN-BERLIN PROCESS" (Michael Brzoska, ed., Bonn International Center for Conversion 2001); MAKING TARGETED SANCTIONS EFFECTIVE: GUIDELINES FOR THE IMPLEMENTATION OF UN POLICY OPTIONS (Peter Wallensteen, Carina Staibano, and Mikael Eriksson, eds, Uppsala 2003).

28 See TOWARDS SMART SANCTIONS: TARGETING ECONOMIC STATECRAFT (David Cortright and George A Lopez, eds, Rowman & Littlefield 2002).

to designated individuals; or prohibit access to "luxury items" for the entities and individuals on the designated list.

In some cases sanctions have helped restore and protect human rights, in other cases they have failed to halt abuses, perhaps because the Security Council acted too late or too timidly.[29] The UN failed to take action to prevent ethnic cleansing in Bosnia in 1992 and genocide in Rwanda in 1994. In the Sudan, the Security Council imposed only a weak set of financial asset freezes and travel restrictions against a small number of Sudanese officials. A significant hindrance to stronger action comes from the fact that any of the five permanent members of the Security Council can veto a sanctions resolution or delay adoption until the resolution loses its effectiveness.

It is notable that regional systems have begun to impose their own sanctions in furtherance of human rights. In March 2011, for example, the Arab League for the first time took sanctions against a member State for human rights violations, isolating the government of Libya and calling for the UN to establish a no-fly zone. On 16 November 2011, the League took its strongest action yet, condemning the human rights violations of Syria's government and subsequently imposing sanctions that included freezing the assets of senior officials in the Syrian government, banning visits by those officials to other Arab nations and ending transactions with the Syrian central bank.

Targeted sanctions have raised human rights concerns not only with respect to their possible humanitarian impact, but also because they may be imposed erroneously on the wrong individuals. Throughout the 1990s, the Security Council extended targeted sanctions to terrorist groups and to the State actors and agencies that supported them. After the attacks on the United States on 11 September 2001, the Security Council adopted Resolution 1373,[30] which mandated that UN member States cooperate to remove all means of support for terrorist organizations. A central feature of these new sanctions was a listing of individuals and entities suspected of engaging in terrorism or associating with terrorists, a list compiled at the discretion and unanimous decision of the "1267 Committee". Human rights groups and activists protested that the procedure violated a number of fundamental human

---

29 ALIX J BOUCHER AND VICTORIA K HOLT, TARGETING SPOILERS: THE ROLE OF UNITED NATIONS PANELS OF EXPERTS (Stimson 2009).

30 UNSC Res 1373 (28 Sep 2001) UN Doc S/Res/1373.

rights of the nearly 500 individuals and groups listed by 2008.[31] They condemned the process for its lack of transparency and accountability, failure to afford due process rights, including the right of the accused to confront evidence against them, and absence of the right to appeal or have any judicial review.[32]

In 2008 the ECJ held in the case of *Kadi and Al Barakaat International Foundation*[33] that the UN Security Council could not violate the fundamental rights of individuals. Doing so voided the obligation of European States to implement Security Council targeted sanctions against Kadi and others. The European Union Council reinstated the restrictive measures as a preventive counter-terrorism action permitted under European law, but the ECJ judgment led the UN to undertake reforms of the listing procedure.[34] Security Council Resolution 1822[35] directed the listing committee to review all listed names, produce a clean list, and review each entry every three years.[36]

Scholars give mixed reviews of the effectiveness and legitimacy of sanctions. Social science studies evaluate the success rate of sanctions generally at around 33 per cent and they identify several factors as important to the effectiveness of sanctions.[37] Pre-eminent scholar George Lopez comments that:

> sanctions succeed when decision makers remember that sanctions are only tools – and thus *only one* of the multiple important tools that should be serving a clearly-specified policy goal and broader policy interest. When sanctions become *the* policy, or are maintained for so long that they *de facto* become *the* policy, they are no longer effective.[38]

---

31 INTERNATIONAL COMMISSION OF JURISTS, ASSESSING DAMAGE, URGING ACTION: REPORT OF THE EMINENT JURISTS PANEL ON TERRORISM, COUNTER-TERRORISM AND HUMAN RIGHTS (International Commission of Jurists 2009).

32 See George A Lopez and others, "Overdue Process: Protecting Human Rights while Sanctioning Alleged Terrorists" (April 2009), Report from the Fourth Freedom Forum and Kroc Institute for International Peace Studies www.sanctionsandsecurity.org/overdue-process-protecting-human-rights-while-sanctioning-alleged-terrorists.

33 Joined Cases C-402/05P and C-415/05P *Kadi and Al Barakaat International Foundation v Council and Commission* [2008] ECR I-6351.

34 UNSC Res 1730 (19 Dec 2006) UN Doc S/Res/1730.

35 UNSC Res 1822 (30 Jun 2008) UN Doc S/Res/1822.

36 See Lopez and others (n. 32).

37 George A Lopez, *In Defense of Smart Sanctions: A Response to Joy Gordon* (2012) 26 ETHICS & INTERNATIONAL AFFAIRS 135.

38 Ibid.

Short of military force, economic sanctions are the major enforcement tool available to end systematic human rights abuses by repressive regimes that refuse to comply with their human rights obligations. Blocking access to financial assets allows sanctions to reduce the regime's ability to purchase weaponry and provide incentives to supporters. Targeting the diversity of non-State actors early in an internal war, or as early warning signs of potential atrocities can also perhaps avoid the deterioration of human rights within the State.

9.4   Use of force

"Humanitarian intervention" refers to the use of military force by outsiders for the protection of victims of atrocities. It has a long history, based in "just war" theory, supported by scholars since Hugo Grotius, and followed in practice albeit most often by strong States against weaker ones. Due to its abusive invocation, "humanitarian intervention" became highly controversial and even discredited during the twentieth century as international law increasingly placed strict limits on the right of States to engage in the unilateral use of force. The Covenant of the League of Nations and the Kellogg-Brian Pact (1928), which outlawed war, were followed by the proscriptions in the UN Charter on the use of force except for cases of self-defence or when authorized by the UN Security Council in instances of threats to the peace, breaches of the peace or acts of aggression. The prohibition on the use of force otherwise is expressly stated in UN Charter Article 2(4) and seemingly proscribes any unilateral armed intervention to protect human rights. Despite this prohibition, examples of non-sanctioned humanitarian actions include NATO's intervention in Kosovo and the French in the Central African Republic at the end of 2013. In addition, the UN Security Council has authorized the use of force in several humanitarian actions.

In a number of cases in the 1990s, the UN Security Council endorsed the use of force, with the primary goal of humanitarian protection and assistance: in the proclamation of UN safe areas in Bosnia, the delivery of humanitarian relief in Somalia, the restoration of the democratically elected government of Haiti, and the deployment of the multinational Kosovo Force.[39] After the end of the Cold War, the UN Security Council experienced a spurt of enforcement activity to provide international

---

39 See BRIAN D LEPARD, RETHINKING HUMANITARIAN INTERVENTION: A FRESH LEGAL

relief and assistance to victims of large-scale atrocities from perpetrator or failing States, within civil war contexts.[40] A more activist UN Security Council engaged in de facto intervention in Iraq to protect the Kurds from Saddam Hussein's defeated regime, and Britain, the United States and France enforced a no-fly zone to protect the Kurdish minority in Northern Iraq throughout the 1990s, despite the non-binding nature of the Security Council Resolution 688.[41] The United Kingdom stated its belief that "humanitarian intervention without the invitation of the country concerned can be justified in cases of extreme humanitarian need".[42] Other States contested the legality of the no-fly zones.

When the UN Security Council was unable or unwilling to act, groups of countries sometimes forged "coalitions of the willing" to act without UN authorization. Humanitarian crises in Somalia, Rwanda, Srebrenica, Kosovo and East Timor revealed the split in the UN over civilian protection mandates and capacities. The UN proved unable to act in a timely manner during the genocide in Rwanda in 1994 and the massacre in Srebrenica in 1995. The UN's inaction also led to the use of force by NATO in Kosovo in 1999, reviving debate about Article 2(4) as a prohibition on humanitarian intervention. China, Russia and the Non-Aligned Movement opposed the NATO air campaign and Yugoslavia filed a lawsuit at the ICJ against the NATO States.[43] Belgium argued that the NATO campaign did not violate Article 2(4) because it was not directed against the territorial integrity or political independence of a country, but was rather an action to rescue a suffering population. Many countries disagreed with this interpretation of the Charter.

While the unilateral use of force thus remains highly contentious, the UN Security Council clearly can and does authorize multilateral action to protect civilians, as it did in Libya and Côte d'Ivoire in 2011. But such

APPROACH BASED ON FUNDAMENTAL ETHICAL PRINCIPLES IN INTERNATIONAL LAW AND WORLD RELIGIONS (Pennsylvania State UP 2002) 7–23.

40 THOMAS G WEISS AND DON HUBERT, THE RESPONSIBILITY TO PROTECT: RESEARCH, BIBLIOGRAPHY, BACKGROUND (International Development Research Centre, 2002) 79–126.

41 Washington and London grounded their declaration and enforcement of the no-fly zone on SC Res 688 (5 Apr 1991) UN Doc S/Res/688. But the resolution contains no obvious basis for such a claim and no relevant UN authority ever accepted it.

42 Christine Gray, *The Use of Force and the International Legal Order*, in INTERNATIONAL LAW (3rd edn, Malcolm Evans, ed., OUP 2010), 621.

43 *Legality of the Use of Force (Yugoslavia v Belgium)* ICJ (Preliminary Objections, Judgment of 15 Dec 2004).

action cannot always survive the political process at the UN. China and Russia vetoed draft resolutions on Syria proposed in 2012 and 2013.

Given the uneven history and controversy over humanitarian intervention, States have sought to develop new doctrines and practice that balance sovereignty and peace with the need to protect vulnerable populations from gross and systematic human rights violations. In 2001 the Canadian-sponsored, but independent, International Commission on Intervention and State Sovereignty (ICISS) formulated the concept of the "responsibility to protect" (R2P), to some extent a more developed and nuanced doctrine of humanitarian intervention.[44] UN Secretary-General Kofi Annan appointed a High Level Panel that endorsed the ICISS "responsibility to protect" as a duty of every State.[45] The Panel proposed five criteria of legitimacy: seriousness of threat, proper purpose, last resort, proportional means, and balance of consequences. Annan urged the UN Security Council to adopt a resolution "setting out these principles and expressing its intention to be guided by them" when authorizing the use of force,[46] to provide transparency and induce better compliance with Security Council decisions.[47] The concept was endorsed at the 2005 World Summit by leaders who agreed unanimously that all States have the sovereign responsibility to protect people living within their territory; upon a manifest failure in this sovereign duty, the international community, acting through the UN, could and should take "timely and decisive" collective action in exercise of the international responsibility to protect people from atrocities.[48] Following Kofi Annan, UN Secretary-General Ban Ki-moon appointed a special adviser to develop and refine the R2P principle.[49]

---

44 INTERNATIONAL COMMISSION ON INTERVENTION AND STATE SOVEREIGNTY REPORT, THE RESPONSIBILITY TO PROTECT (International Development Research Centre (IDRC) for ICISS 2001).

45 UNGA "Report of the High-Level Panel on Threats, Challenges and Change" (2 December 2004) UN Doc A/59/565 [201], emphasis in original.

46 UNGA "In Larger Freedom: Towards Development, Security and Human Rights for All: Report of the Secretary-General" (21 Mar 2005) UN Doc A/59/2005 [126].

47 Ibid.

48 UNGA "2005 World Summit Outcome" (24 Oct 2005) UN Doc A/RES/60/1 [138]–[40].

49 UNGA "Implementing the Responsibility to Protect: Report of the Secretary-General" (12 Jan 2009) UN Doc A/63/677; UNGA "Early Warning, Assessment, and the Responsibility to Protect: Report of the Secretary-General" (14 Jul 2010) UN Doc A/64/864; UNGA/UNSC "The Role of Regional and Sub-Regional Arrangements in Implementing the Responsibility to Protect: Report of the Secretary-General" (18 Jun 2011) UN Doc A/65/877-S/2011/393.

Sovereignty thus becomes understood as a functional bundle of rights and duties as R2P attempts to strike a balance between interference and indifference. It preserves to States the right and duty to protect their own populations, but it also strengthens the UN's responsibility for the international community as a whole.[50] Importantly, R2P has a narrow scope; it applies only to four specified international crimes – genocide, war crimes, ethnic cleansing and crimes against humanity – but if such acts are being committed UN responsive actions may engage the full panoply of powers including authorization to use force.

The Security Council invoked R2P during the Libya crisis in 2011, as a basis for action under Chapter VII.[51] After calling on Libya to respect its R2P, human rights and IHL (international humanitarian law) obligations, the UN Security Council passed Resolution 1970, demanding an end to the violence in Libya, which "may amount to crimes against humanity"; imposed sanctions; affirmed Libya's R2P obligations; and referred Gaddafi to the ICC.[52] Subsequently, UN Security Council Resolution 1973 authorized the use of "all necessary measures . . . to protect civilians and civilian populated areas".[53] Resolution 1973 specified the purpose of military action as humanitarian protection and limited the means to that goal. NATO airstrikes nonetheless did not totally eliminate civilian casualties;[54] by the time the conflict ended, up to 30,000 civilians may have died.[55]

The UN responses to massive atrocities since 1991, wavering between action and inaction, suggest that the Security Council will continue to act on an ad hoc and case-by-case, rather than principled and consistent, basis. In the absence of UN action, individual States and coalitions with the capacity and interest to act may still feel the need to intervene to protect victims of atrocities inside other sovereign States.

---

50 Anne Orford, International Authority and the Responsibility to Protect (CUP 2011) 41.

51 For a range of diverse opinions and perspectives on R2P and Libya, see e-International Relations (ed.), *The Responsibility to Protect: Challenges and Opportunities in Light of the Libyan Intervention* (e-International Relations 2011) www.e-ir.info/wp-content/uploads/R2P.pdf.

52 UNSC Res 1970 (26 Feb 2011) UN Doc S/RES/1970.

53 UNSC Res 1973 (17 Mar 2011) UN Doc S/Res/1973, Art. 4.

54 CJ Chivers and Eric Schmitt, "In Strikes on Libya by NATO, An Unspoken Civilian Toll" *The New York Times* (Tripoli, 17 Dec 2011) www.nytimes.com/2011/12/18/world/africa/scores-of-unintended-casualties-in-nato-war-in-libya.html?pagewanted=all.

55 Karin Laub, "Libyan Estimate: At Least 30,000 Died in the War" *The Guardian* (Tripoli, 8 Sep 2011) www.guardian.co.uk/world/feedarticle/9835879.

10 Stock-taking

The initial, critical contribution of the UN was to internationalize the topic of human rights in an organization of universal aim and mandate. As discussed throughout this volume, the very purposes of the UN include promoting respect for human rights and fundamental freedoms for all. Other Charter provisions, notably Articles 55 and 56, also contributed to placing human rights firmly on the organization's agenda. Taken together these provisions made clear that respect for human rights is a matter of international concern, establishing the essential foundation for the development of human rights law at both global and regional levels.

The organs of the UN have given content to the Charter references by adopting a comprehensive set of human rights treaties and other legal instruments, delineating the accepted international minimum standards. This standard-setting has been accomplished through a global political process open to all UN member States. All the main UN organs are concerned with human rights, and separate treaty bodies of independent experts exist for each of the nine core human rights instruments adopted within the framework of the UN. In addition, the UN's legally independent specialized agencies take up human rights issues within the scope of their jurisdiction and expertise. The mandates of all these UN human rights bodies parallel and to some degree overlap each other.

Regional organizations generally provide additional norms and compliance monitoring. The UN was initially sceptical of regional protection of human rights, despite references in regional texts to the UN Charter and the UDHR. According to two leading experts:

> For a long time, regionalism in the matter of human rights was not popular at the United Nations: There was often a tendency to regard it as the expression of a breakaway movement, calling the universality of human rights into question. However, the continual postponements of work on

the International Human Rights Covenants led the UN to rehabilitate, and to be less suspicious (less jealous, some would say) towards, regionalism in human rights, especially after the adoption of the Covenants in 1966.[1]

The human rights instruments adopted by the UN reflect consensus among the States participating in a body of global membership. States from all parts of the world negotiate, conclude, sign and ratify the treaties. In turn, the regional texts and jurisprudence are consistently founded on the universal norms; the most frequent differences appear in the presence of additional rights, rather than in a weakening of global protections.[2]

The regional systems have generally worked well for individual cases but most have grave limitations when it comes to addressing gross and systematic human rights violations. Inter-State cases to address widespread violations are rare and remedies and sanctions that would be adequate to deter abusive governments are extremely difficult to identify. Until recently, the European Court held consistently that it has no power to issue orders to States to correct an underlying law or practice giving rise to violations; its remedies have been limited to declaratory judgments and rather meagre compensation. Although it has initiated some reforms like the pilot judgment and indicated restitution is required in a few cases, it generally has left issues of structural reform to the political Committee of Ministers.

The Inter-American system marked the 60th anniversary of the American Declaration of the Rights and Duties of Man in 2008, as well as the 30th year since the American Convention on Human Rights came into force. In 2009 the IACHR celebrated 50 years of existence and the Court its 30th anniversary. Like the European system,

---

1 THE INTERNATIONAL DIMENSIONS OF HUMAN RIGHTS (Karel Vasak and Philip Alston, eds, Greenwood Press 1982), 451.

2 The influence of universal norms on regional systems has a counterpart in the impact of regional concern with human rights on global human rights guarantees. Indeed, Inter-American regional meetings played a key role in the development of the UN's UDHR. At the International American Conference of War and Peace, held at Chapultepec, Mexico in March 1943, 21 American States asked for a bill of human rights to be included in the Charter of the United Nations. Three of these countries (Chile, Cuba and Panama) were the first ones to submit a draft for such a bill. At the San Francisco Conference they lobbied for inclusion of a bill of rights in the Charter. Other Latin American countries prepared other drafts that became part of the background to the drafting of the Universal Declaration. The text submitted by the Inter-American Juridical Committee was particularly influential. The Chilean draft and the work of the Chilean delegate, Hernan Santa Cruz, were also important.

the history of the Inter-American system has been marked by normative and institutional innovation, as well as by periodic challenges and reforms. The use of country and thematic reports, on-site visits and precautionary measures has been particularly successful in improving the enjoyment of human rights in the Western hemisphere and has begun to have an impact in the African system. However, regional protection of the legally enshrined rights has been undermined by the failures of the member States in the regions in respect to three key matters: (1) a general failure to provide financial resources[3] and personnel to the regional institutions; (2) failure of some States to ratify the normative instruments; and (3) failure of some States to comply with decisions and recommendations of the commissions and courts. Many regions are known for economic inequalities, the presence of vulnerable minorities or indigenous peoples, weaknesses of democratic institutions and chronic instability of governments. The regional "safety net" of human rights institutions is thus particularly important. The promotion and protection of human rights should be a critical component of the parent organizations, but this is not always one of the main purposes.

10.1 Backlash

Widespread criticism of the UN Human Rights Commission led to its replacement by the UN Human Rights Council in 2006. There were high hopes that a Council reporting directly to the General Assembly would have an enhanced status and legitimacy and be more efficient and less politicized. While the Council can point to a few notable achievements since its creation, including adoption of the UN Declaration on the Rights of Indigenous Peoples, it is perceived by many observers to have the same problems as its predecessor. The abolition of the independent Sub-Commission is particularly lamented. The Council's decision to create a weak advisory body is no substitute for the Sub-Commission, despite some overlap in membership,[4] because of the limited powers of the advisory group[5] and the lack of independence of some of the members.[6]

---

3 Human rights work accounts for approximately 5 per cent of the OAS annual budget.
4 Eight former members of the Sub-Commission, including the longest-serving members, from Morocco and Cuba, were elected to the advisory body. Several others worked for the United Nations High Commissioner's office.
5 The advisory body is unable to take any initiative, but can only act on direction from the Council.
6 Ten members of the advisory body come from government, including from the ministries of foreign affairs.

It is probably inevitable that the Council is and will remain a political body. Moreover, it is appropriate that a political body be responsible for standard-setting. The Council, though, has functions beyond those of standard-setting. It is also a compliance body, seeking to ensure that UN member States live up to their human rights obligations. Council procedures are based on existing norms and are designed in part to establish "realistic and effective implementation machinery". A few procedures explore or reflect new human rights concerns that may not otherwise be given sufficient attention. The country-specific mechanisms examine serious human rights situations of non-compliance. All of these have proven their value in the past. For the future, they will remain important mechanisms to respond effectively to widespread violations of human rights treaties and customary law.

Discussion of specific countries was among the most politicized parts of the former Commission's annual agenda and remains so at the Council. No resolution has ever been adopted to criticize one of the permanent members of the UN Security Council. At the same time, those countries that were investigated clearly met the criterion of committing gross and systematic violations. Few if any regional bodies are in as good a position to examine effectively, and respond to allegations of, large-scale human rights violations. The 1503 complaint procedure may be particularly important for significant violations that have not yet received widespread attention and which do not fall within the mandate of the Security Council.

Non-compliance with human rights guarantees remains a critical problem. Unfortunately, the more serious the violations, the less willing or able the rest of the world appears to be to confront those responsible. It should be noted that there are considerable efforts being undertaken to prevent violations from occurring and to engage in closer monitoring through the elaboration of human rights indicators.[7]

Regional systems also face problems of non-compliance and backlash from States, which sometimes seek to "reform" the institutions in response to criticism of governments' human rights records. Initially, reforms were positive. After the European Court began functioning in 1959, the Member States of the Council of Europe adopted a number of protocols to the ECHR that were genuinely aimed at improving and

---

7 See Report on Indicators for Monitoring Compliance with International Human Rights Instruments, HRI/MC/2008/3, 16 May 2008.

strengthening its supervisory mechanisms. In 1998 Protocol No 11 replaced the original Court and Commission, which met a few days per month, with a single full-time Court, enabling applicants to bring their cases directly before the Court. The entry into force of Protocol No 14 in 2010 was less positive for applicants, but was necessitated by the growing backlog of cases, discussed in the next subsection. The Protocol introduced new single-judge formations for the simplest cases and established a new admissibility criterion requiring applicants to have suffered a "significant disadvantage" from violation of their rights; it also extended the judges' term of office to one nine-year unrenewable term.

Three high-level conferences on the future of the European Court have met since 2010 and parliamentary debates have been held in the British Parliament and the Netherlands Senate. The third conference was convened by the United Kingdom, in the context of its Chairmanship of the Committee of Ministers of the Council of Europe. The government organized the Brighton Conference on the future of the Eur. Ct. HR from 19 to 20 April 2012 with the aim of obtaining a political declaration on reforms of the Court. The government has been among the strongest critics of what it views as "judicial activism" on the part of the Court.[8] In particular, British authorities reacted negatively to European Court decisions that condemned its law depriving convicted felons of the right to vote.[9] Outside the UK, the Court's decisions on asylum seekers have produced intense and widespread criticisms, particularly when coupled with extension of economic and social rights to those seeking entry.[10] Critics complain that the decisions interfere with national immigration policies, especially in the light of anti-terrorism efforts.

The outcome of the Brighton Conference was a Declaration and the subsequent adoption of Protocol No 15, which inserts a reference to the principle of subsidiarity and the doctrine of the margin of appreciation into the Convention's preamble; it also reduces from six to four months the time within which an application must be lodged

---

8 See generally: THE EUROPEAN COURT OF HUMAN RIGHTS AND ITS DISCONTENTS: TURNING CRITICISM INTO STRENGTH (Spyridon Flogaitis, Tom Zwart and Julie Fraser, eds, Edward Elgar 2013).

9 David Davis, *Britain must Defy the European Court of Human Rights on Prisoner Voting as Strasbourg is Exceeding its Authority*, in ibid. 65.

10 Marc Bossuyt, *Is the European Court of Human Rights on a Slippery Slope?* in ibid. 27.

with the Court after a final national decision. The Declaration reaffirms the commitment of Member States to the Convention and the right of individual application to the Court.[11] The Declaration also refers, however, to "the fundamental principle of subsidiarity" that should apply to the Court, a reference that indicates the desire of some Member States for greater deference to domestic laws, practices and judicial decisions.

Critics of the European system have commented on the actions of some Member States in respect to the nomination and election of judges, where the domestic processes do not comply with the principles of transparency, fairness and consistency.[12] Some observers claim that the processes have resulted in the nomination and election of candidates who are lacking in the qualifications necessary for the position. Such shortcomings are detrimental for the credibility of the Court and may undermine trust and confidence in its decisions.

As regards the Inter-American system, in June 2011 the OAS General Assembly decided to form a Special Working Group to Reflect on the Workings of the Inter-American Commission on Human Rights "with a view to Strengthening the Inter-American Human Rights System".[13] One key proponent was Brazil, whose government had an unprecedented negative reaction to the request for precautionary measures granted by the IACHR on behalf of indigenous communities in the Río Xingu Basin in Pará. The Commission requested that Brazil suspend construction of the Belo Monte dam, a major development project

---

11 European Court of Human Rights, *High Level Conference on the Future of the European Court of Human Rights, Brighton Declaration* (20 Apr 2013), paras 1 and 2.

12 See Norbert Paul Engel, *More Transparency and Governmental Loyalty for Maintaining Professional Quality in the Election of Judges to the European Court of Human Rights*, 32 HRLJ pp. 448–55 (2012); See also Andrew Drzemczewski, *Election of Judges to the Strasbourg Court: An Overview*, European Human Rights Law Review (EHRLR) 2010, 377.

13 See Record of the meeting of 14 Jul 2011, Doc GT/SIDH/SA.1/11 rev.1, 18 Jul 2011. It states: "This Working Group of the Permanent Council was created at the regular meeting of the Permanent Council of the OAS Permanent Council of June 29, 2011, based on the following 'Statement made by Hugo Martínez, Minister of Foreign Affairs of El Salvador and President of the forty-first regular session of the General Assembly, at its fourth plenary session, following the presentation by Dr. José de Jesús Orozco, First Vice President of the Inter-American Commission on Human Rights': 'The President suggests . . . that it instruct the Permanent Council to deepen the process of reflection on the workings of the Inter-American Commission on Human Rights (IACHR) in the framework of the American Convention on Human Rights and the Statute of the IACHR, with the aim of strengthening the inter-American human rights system, and to present its recommendations to the member States as soon as possible'. (AG/INF.478/11)".

initiated by the government. After the measures were requested, the government reacted by withdrawing its ambassador to the OAS, along with its candidate for a position on the IACHR; it also withheld its annual dues until January 2012, when it paid the US$6 million it owed. Brazil pressed for the Working Group and for its agenda to prioritize a review of precautionary measures. This proposal found support in the Working Group from other States that had been subject to such requests, particularly to protect collective or community rights.

The agenda of the Working Group eventually included the appointment of the Executive Secretary of the IACHR; medium- and long-term challenges and goals; precautionary measures; procedural matters; Chapter IV of the Annual Report; and the work of the rapporteurs. The preparation of Chapter IV of the annual report of the IACHR has been debated for many years. Chapter IV calls attention to countries of particular concern to the IACHR on account of the number or severity of their human rights violations; no State likes to be included therein. Venezuela and Colombia, which have been included in Chapter IV repeatedly in recent years, requested the IACHR to review the methodology and criteria for developing Chapter IV and to reflect on the need for and effectiveness of including such a chapter in its report. Venezuela sought to "reform" Chapter IV by a requirement that the IACHR prepare a report on the human rights situation in every country in the region.

Ecuador recommended that the IACHR introduce a code of conduct to govern the management of the rapporteurships, incorporate all rapporteur reports in a single chapter of its annual report, and allocate the funding it receives in a balanced way to all its rapporteurships. Ecuador further requested that States, observers and other donors make voluntary contributions without specifying their purpose. Ecuador's recommendations were aimed at a single target: the Special Rapporteurship for Freedom of Expression, which has vigorously condemned attacks on freedom of expression in the hemisphere, including in Ecuador.

The members of the Commission and officials from the Executive Secretariat participated in five discussions with the States about the proposed reforms. The Working Group issued its final report and recommendations for the IACHR and for States to the OAS Permanent Council in December 2011, which approved them in January 2012. The section on precautionary measures included more than a dozen recommendations for the IACHR. Many of the recommendations called for the IACHR to do things that it was already doing, such as to "define objective criteria or parameters for determining 'serious and urgent situations' and the imminence of the harm, taking into account the different risk levels" and "clearly establish, in consultation with the parties, a work plan for the periodic review of its Rules of Procedure (Article 25(6)) and practice, including periodic review of precautionary measures". The IACHR had already defined those criteria and also periodically reviews the precautionary measures in effect.

The final document identified the challenges facing the IACHR and outlined a plan of action with strategies to reinforce the IACHR's work for a five-year period. These recommendations included, for example, "Prepare a report on the impact of the non-universality of the American Convention on Human Rights and inter-American human rights instruments, as well as of the recognition of the contentious jurisdiction of the Inter-American Court of Human Rights, on protection and promotion of human rights in the region" and "Prepare a practical guide or manual on friendly settlements to include, inter alia, the status of their regulation in the IAHRS, a compendium of successful experiences and best practices in their use, a list of possible reparation measures, etc". The final report recommended increasing the budget to provide the resources necessary for the proper functioning of the organs of the inter-American system. Recognizing the system's current financial straits, the Working Group recommended that States "gradually increase the resources allocated to the IAHRS organs from the Regular Fund of the OAS". The States also pledged to take concrete steps in this direction.

There followed a year of discussion and reaction by the IACHR and civil society before the process concluded in 2013. On 15 February 2013, the Commission published its draft reforms of the Rules of Procedure, policies and practices and opened a consultation period after which, on 18 March 2013, it approved the new Rules of Procedure, Policies and Practices. In response, on 23 March 2013, the Extraordinary General Assembly of OAS convened to conclude the "strengthening" process, and approved by acclamation a resolution ending the two-year process. Nonetheless, several States, especially those that have been criticized by the IACHR for their human rights violations, continued to press for limiting the powers of the IACHR. Venezuela went further and in September 2013 denounced the American Convention on Human Rights.

The African system also has been the target of criticism and suggestions for reform. It faces many of the same problems that have arisen in other regional as well as global bodies. Regarding the composition of the African Commission, questions have arisen about the independence of some members due to their holding official positions in their State. The Commission is also chronically hampered by a lack of resources from the African Union in order to discharge its mandate. Only two legal officers were paid by the AU in some years, the other lawyers having been paid from extra-budgetary resources. The lack of financial support has resulted in poor terms of service and conditions of work for the staff of the Secretariat, with consequent low morale among the staff. The recourse to outside funding, also done by the IACHR, has led to criticism by States Parties that such contributions affect the independence and credibility of the Commissions. In the case of the African Commission the lack of resources to publish its reports has diminished its visibility and public awareness of its work. Like other bodies, the African Commission has complained of failure by States to comply with requests for adoption of provisional measures under the communications procedure. In addition, the delay of States in replying under the communications procedure has had a negative impact on the speed of consideration of the communication by the ACHPR.

10.2   Backlog

All human rights bodies are struggling with rising caseloads. Without additional resources, which have not been forthcoming, they face an ever-increasing backlog of petitions, increasing the time applicants must wait for a decision. The European system has been particularly hard hit by the exponential growth in complaints, a tribute to its success but also due to the admission of new Member States with little historical commitment to human rights. Regional tensions have emerged due to non-compliance by some of the Members with judgments of the Eur. Ct. HR.

The Court's compulsory jurisdiction over all 47 Member States allows some 800 million individuals to complain of human rights violations. More than 100,000 of them do so each year. The number of cases decided by the European Court during the first semester of 2013 was just under 50,000, representing a 25 per cent increase over the first semester of 2012. Most of the applications were disposed of by a single judge, with just under 43,000 cases rejected. The remaining 7,000 applications were decided by Chambers and Committees. Despite all these dispositions, the number of applications pending on 1 July 2013 was 113,350.

The Court has taken action to deal more strictly with applications. On 6 May 2013 the Plenary Court approved an amendment of Rule 47, effective 1 January 2014, which governs the institution of proceedings before the Court by individual applicants. In so doing, the Court implemented its previously announced intention to take a more formal approach than previously applied to petitions. With a new official form, and with applicants required to present their case in a clear and succinct way, accompanied by all necessary supporting documentation, Registry staff are supposed to determine straight away the nature and scope of each new application received, saving time and effort. Paragraph 5 makes clear that failure to observe the necessary formalities will as a rule mean that the application will not be submitted to judicial examination. The rule is not inflexible, however, and provides for three exceptions: "(a) the applicant has provided an adequate explanation for the failure to comply; (b) the application concerns a request for an interim measure; (c) the Court otherwise directs of its own motion or at the request of an applicant".

The European caseload crisis is largely linked to compliance. Ninety-two per cent of the repetitive cases in 2013 came from seven countries: Italy (24 per cent); Serbia (18.5 per cent); Turkey (17 per cent); Ukraine (14 per cent) Romania (8.5 per cent); United Kingdom (5 per cent); Russia (5 per cent). The Court and some scholars have mentioned the possibility of a default judgment procedure as a response to the huge number of repetitive cases on the Court's docket. Repetitive cases now form the biggest category of pending applications before the Court. Even with the tools offered by Protocol No 14 and with the pilot judgment procedure, the Court has not managed to reverse or even contain the rise in the number of such cases. The Court has repeatedly insisted that this problem must be remedied by the States directly concerned, and by the Committee of Ministers in its supervisory role.

Another measure to deal with the backlog in the European system is Protocol No 16, which will allow the highest domestic courts and tribunals to request the Court to give advisory opinions on questions of principle relating to the interpretation or application of the rights and freedoms defined in the Convention or the protocols thereto. Protocol

No 16 is optional, but if accepted may allow a greater number of matters to be resolved in domestic courts.

In addition to the problems raised by the quantity of complaints, the court is facing qualitatively different complaints, in other words, those alleging widespread and serious violations, including summary executions, disappearances, torture and prolonged arbitrary detention. Many of these cases require the Court to engage in extensive fact finding, because the systematic State practices causing the violations mean that the government has not investigated the violations nor allowed domestic remedies to function. The Court's ability to engage in fact finding is limited by resources and expertise, leading a few defendant governments to question the credibility of the Court's findings. As a result, while compliance with the Court's judgments, backed by the Committee of Ministers, has historically been high, there is a risk that those governments engaged in the most egregious violations will be unwilling or unable to halt and remedy the violations being committed.

At the UN level, Manfred Nowak has expressed well some of the concerns of those who work on or with human rights bodies about their present effectiveness and future viability:

> the proliferation of UN human rights treaties with different but overlapping reporting obligations and with separate treaty monitoring bodies working on an unpaid, voluntary and part-time basis, together with a trend towards universal ratification of these treaties, has led to an unmanageable and deeply frustrating situation for all involved. Governments complain about the high number of reports they are obliged to draft periodically, and which often are examined many years after their submission, and the expert bodies complain about the lack of discipline among governments and the limited time they are given to examine the numerous reports. [O]nly a major structural reform can help to solve the ongoing crisis.[14]

Nowak's comments can be extended to the complaints procedures and other compliance mechanisms discussed herein. All human rights bodies, global and regional, are faced with expanding mandates and limited resources. The UN Office of the High Commissioner for Human Rights functions because of outside contributions; only 20 per cent of its funding comes from the regular UN budget. This is repli-

---

14 Manfred Nowak, UN Covenant on Civil and Political Rights: CCPR Commentary, 712–53 (2nd edn, NP Enge 2005), at 718–19.

cated in regional institutions: some 55 per cent of the funding for the IACHR comes from governments and other entities outside the OAS, which contributes only 5 per cent of its budget to human rights. The lack of political will to create effective compliance bodies and procedures is evident not only in the limited funding afforded, but also in sporadic attention given to compliance with recommendations, decisions and judgments of human rights bodies.

Treaty-monitoring bodies have moved towards more effective compliance mechanisms, with optional protocols either adopted or being negotiated for several major human rights instruments to allow the filing of individual petitions. Other mechanisms involve early warning and on-site inspections. Legally, the importance of their concluding observations and general comments or recommendations is undeniable, even as their precise legal character remains debated. The functions of treaty bodies all began with periodic reporting by States Parties. It is a procedure that could easily have become mired in self-serving reports with little check on accuracy or completeness. In practice, however, the independent members of the treaty bodies developed, to varying degrees, robust systems for questioning and reviewing State reports. It is clear, however, that States at the global level remain wary of creating any judicial mechanism or binding right of petition for victims asserting that their rights have been violated.

10.3   Conclusion

Despite continuing controversy over the aims, normative content and powers of global and regional institutions, human rights law can be said to have restrained many dictatorial powers and established the criteria for transition to democracy and the rule of law. It also succeeded in challenging many totalitarian and authoritarian governments, although it cannot claim sole credit for democratization over the past two decades. Successes in human rights can be attributed to several linked factors. First, unlike many global issues, human rights is aided by its moral and ethical dimensions and the innate desire of every human being for protection from abuse. The very idea of human rights as a legitimate claim of every individual, founded in theology, morality and philosophy, is thus a powerful governance tool. Second, civil society has insisted on the right to participate in the development of international human rights law and structures. Non-state actors, particularly human rights NGOs, have played an essential role at every stage of the human rights movement. NGOs represent actual or potential victims of human rights violations who are concerned with preventing governmental actions that are contrary to human rights guarantees. NGOs are often the first to focus attention on new issues. They may take the lead in developing the content of specific human rights and pressing States to make them law; in some instances they bypass the States altogether, writing human rights standards to govern key non-State actors. They provide legal assistance to victims of human rights violations, gather evidence and bring cases before international tribunals. Their roles as watchdogs and whistle-blowers are crucial to the effectiveness of human rights guarantees. Any State that is concerned with domestic or international political support cannot afford to ignore broad-based NGOs.

Of course there have been failures to prevent or halt many situations of massive abuses, including genocide. The reasons are many. First, there are legal restraints. Human rights has been hampered by traditional concepts of State sovereignty and domestic jurisdiction, as well as by the consent-based nature of international obligations that prevents enforcement of norms against non-consenting States. This legal barrier is reinforced by the conflict of interest inherent in a system where those violating human rights participate in standard-setting, compliance monitoring, and enforcement. At an extreme, this leads to challenges to the normative basis of human rights governance from ruling elites who seek to retain power by invoking cultural relativism. They challenge the universality of human rights despite their participation in drafting normative instruments guaranteeing such rights and their subsequent voluntary consent to them through treaty ratification.

Second, and more generally, most States exhibit a reluctance to criticize others for human rights violations, unless there are independent political reasons to do so, such as ideological conflicts or unfriendly relations. In many cases, the reluctance stems from concern about reciprocal complaints – there being no State free of human rights problems – but it also derives from the multifaceted nature of international relations. States usually must balance, and often subordinate, consideration of human rights issues to other international concerns, including trade, military and strategic policy, and foreign investment. When human rights does become a cornerstone of bilateral and multilateral relations, particularly on the part of a powerful State or a group of States, it can have a significant positive impact on compliance with human rights norms.

Finally, human rights governance is limited by its own design, which had in mind restraining powerful government agents. It has not succeeded in addressing the massive violations that occur in weak or failed States where anarchy and civil conflict prevail, because violations by non-State actors that cannot be controlled by a State generally fall outside the scope of most human rights law. Humanitarian law and international criminal standards concerning crimes against humanity and war crimes cover non-State actors, but these topics are usually, if mistakenly, treated separately from human rights in international law.[15] International human rights institutions and systems are seen to lack the power to step into failed States and have been so far unable to develop new institutions and procedures to prevent or remedy violations in anarchical States or those in which internal armed conflicts are occurring. Even where there are functioning States, deregulation and globalization have created powerful non-State actors outside the governance structure. The future of human rights will need to address all these issues to maintain the progress achieved over the past centuries.

The goal of human rights law is to end violations of rights and prevent future violations. Each critique should lead to a more effective legal system. The international human rights law system is clearly not responding to some of the most serious violations today. Human rights machinery must be improved to ensure that attention and resources are devoted to those situations most requiring a response. The problem is political and is likely to remain political.

While there are many causes for concern, the overall picture remains positive. The proliferation of regional human rights systems into new regions brings additional institutional mechanisms and support for human rights where it has been lacking or marginal. The affirmation of universal norms in this process is also a cause for celebration. Finally, the support of many States and governments for global and regional mechanisms to assist the States in fulfilling their primary obligations to promote and protect human rights is real. It will probably always be a struggle to maintain progress and avoid backsliding, but there can be little doubt that international human rights law and institutions have brought improvement to the lives of millions of persons throughout the world.

---

15 D Bethlehem, *The Relationship between International Humanitarian Law and International Human Rights Law in Situations of Armed Conflict* (2013) 2 CAMBRIDGE JOURNAL OF INTERNATIONAL AND COMPARATIVE LAW 180–95.

Bibliography

Alexy, R. A Theory of Fundamental Rights (OUP 2002).

Alston, P. (ed). Labour Rights as Human Rights (OUP 2005).

An-Na'Im, A.A. et al. (eds). Human Rights and Religious Values: An Uneasy Relationship (Eerdmans 2005).

Arai-Takahashi, Y. The Margin of Appreciation Doctrine and the Principle of Proportionality in the Jurisprudence of the ECHR (Intersentia 2002).

Arnold, R. (ed). The Universalism of Human Rights (Springer 2013).

Bagchi, S.S. and Das, A. (eds). Human Rights and the Third World: Issues and Discourses (Lexington Books 2013).

Baik, T. Emerging Regional Human Rights Systems in Asia (CUP 2012).

Bantekas, I. and Oette, L. International Human Rights Law and Practice (CUP 2013).

Bates, E. The Evolution of the European Convention on Human Rights (OUP 2010).

Baxi, U. The Future of Human Rights, 3rd edition (OUP 2012).

Beitz, C.R. The Idea of Human Rights, 3rd edition (OUP 2009).

Bellamy, A.J. Responsibility to Protect: The Global Effort to End Mass Atrocities (Polity 2009).

Bisaz, C. The Concept of Group Rights in International Law: Groups as Contested Right-Holders, Subjects and Legal Persons (Martinus Nijhoff 2012).

Bloed, A. The Conference on Security and Co-operation in Europe: Analysis and Basic Documents 1972–1993 (Kluwer Academic Publishers 1993).

Brysk, A. (ed). Globalization and Human Rights (U California P 2002).

Burgorgue-Larsen, L. and De Torres, A.U. The Inter-American Court of Human Rights: Case Law and Commentary (OUP 2011).

Carozza, Paolo G. 'Subsidiarity as a Structural Principle of International Human Rights Law' (2003), 97 *American Journal of International Law*, 38.

Charron, A. UN Sanctions and Conflict: Responding to Peace and Security Threats (Routledge 2011).

Christofferse, J. Fair Balance: Proportionality, Subsidiarity and Primarity in the European Convention on Human Rights (Martinus Nijhoff 2009).

Christou, T.A. and Raymond, J.P. (eds). European Court of Human Rights: Remedies and Execution of Judgments (British Institute of International and Comparative Law 2005).

Clapham, A. Human Rights Obligations of Non-State Actors (OUP 2006).

Conte, A. and Burchill, R. Defining Civil and Political Rights: The Jurisprudence of the United Nations Human Rights Committee, 2nd edition (Ashgate 2009).

Corradetti, C. (ed). Philosophical Dimensions of Human Rights: Some Contemporary Views (Springer 2012).

Cortright, D. and Lopez, G.A. Sanctions and the Search for Security: Challenges to UN Action (Lynne Rienner 2002).

Craven, M. The International Covenant on Economic, Social and Cultural Rights: A Perspective on its Development (OUP 1995).

Da Costa, K. The Extraterritorial Application of Selected Human Rights Treaties (Martinus Nijhoff Publishers 2013).

Davis, H. Human Rights Law: Directions, 3rd edition (OUP 2013).

De Greiff, P. (ed). The Handbook of Reparations (OUP 2006).

De Wet, E. and Vidmar, J. (eds). Hierarchy in International Law: The Place of Human Rights (OUP 2012).

Diemer, A et al. Philosophical Foundations of Human Rights (UNESCO 1986).

Donnelly, J. Universal Human Rights in Theory and Practice, 3rd edition (Cornell UP 2013).

Dupuy, P.M., Francioni, F. and Petersmann, E.U. (eds). Human Rights in International Investment Law and Arbitration (OUP 2009).

Durham, W.C. Jr and Brent G.S. Law and Religion: National, International and Comparative Perspectives (Aspen 2010).

Ernst, G. and Heilinger, J. (eds). The Philosophy of Human Rights: Contemporary Controversies (De Gruyter 2012).

Evans, G. The Responsibility to Protect: Ending Mass Atrocity Crimes Once and For All (Brookings Institution Press 2008).

Faúndez, L.H. The Inter-American System for the Protection of Human Rights: Institutional and Procedural Aspects, 3rd edition, (Inter-American Institute of Human Rights 2008).

Fenwick, C. and Novitz, T. (eds). Human Rights at Work: Perspectives on Law and Regulation (Hart 2010).

Finnis, J. Natural Law and Natural Rights (Clarendon Press 1992).

Fitzmaurice, M. and Merkouris, P. (eds). The Interpretation and Application of the European Convention of Human Rights: Legal and Practical Implications (Martinus Nijhoff 2013).

Føllesdal, A., Peters, B., Ulfstein, G. (eds). Constituting Europe: The European Court of Human Rights in a National, European and Global Context (CUP 2013).

Gewirth, A. The Community of Rights (U Chicago P 1990).

Gómez, I.F. and De Feyter, K. (eds). International Human Rights Law in a Global Context (Deusto UP 2009).

Gomien, D. (ed). Broadening the Frontiers of Human Rights: Essays in Honour of Asbjørn Eide (Scandinavian UP 1993).

Goodale, M. (ed). Human Rights: An Anthropological Reader (Wiley-Blackwell 2009).

Goodhart, M. (ed). Human Rights: Politics and Practice, 2nd edition (OUP 2013).

Goodman, R. and Jinks, D. Socializing States: Promoting Human Rights Through International Law (OUP 2013).

Green, L.C. The Contemporary Law of Armed Conflict, 3rd edition (Manchester UP 2008).

Griffin, J. On Human Rights (OUP 2008).

Hannum, H. 'The Status of the Universal Declaration of Human Rights in National and International Law' (1995–1996), 25 Georgia Journal of International and Comparative Law, 287–397.

Hanski, R. and Scheinin, M. Leading Cases of the Human Rights Committee, 2nd revised edition (Åbo Akademi University 2007).

Hanski, R. and Suksi, M. An Introduction to the International Protection of Human Rights, 2nd edition (Åbo Akademi University 1999).

Harris, D., O'Boyle, M. and Warbrick, C. Law of the European Convention on Human Rights, 2nd edition (Butterworths 2009).

Harrison, J. The Human Rights Impact of the World Trade Organization: Studies in International Trade Law (Hart 2007).

Hellum, A. and Aasen, H.S. (eds). Women's Human Rights: CEDAW in International, Regional and National Law (CUP 2013).

Henkin, L. The Age of Rights (Columbia UP 1990).

Hersch, J. (ed). Birthright of Man (UNESCO 1968).

Hestermeyer, H.P. et al. (eds). Coexistence, Cooperation and Solidarity: Liber Amicorum Rüdiger Wolfrum, 2 volumes (Martinus Nijhoff 2012).

Holder, C. and Reidy, D. (eds). Human Rights: The Hard Questions (CUP 2013).

Ingelse, C. The UN Committee Against Torture: An Assessment (Martinus Nijhoff 2001).

Ishay, M.R. The Human Rights Reader (Routledge 1997).

Joseph, S. Blame It on the WTO: A Human Rights Critique (OUP 2011).

Joseph, S., Kinley, D. and Waincymer, J. (eds). The World Trade Organization and Human Rights: Interdisciplinary Perspectives (Edward Elgar 2009).

Joseph, S., Schultz, J. and Castan M. The International Covenant on Civil and Political Rights: Cases, Materials and Commentary, 2nd edition (OUP 2004).

Kamminga, M. Interstate Accountability for Violations of Human Rights (U Pennsylvania P 1992).

Keane, D. and McDermott, Y. (eds). The Challenge of Human Rights: Past, Present and Future (Edward Elgar 2012).

Keck, M.E. and Sikkink, K. Activists beyond Borders: Advocacy Networks in International Politics (Cornell UP 1998).

Keller, H. and Stone-Sweet, A. (eds). A Europe of Rights: The Impact of the ECHR on National Legal Systems (OUP 2008).

Keller, H. and Ulfstein, G. (eds). UN Human Rights Treaty Bodies: Law and Legitimacy: Studies on Human Rights Conventions (CUP 2012).

Kovács, P. International Law and Minority Protection: Rights of Minorities or Law of Minorities? (Akadémiai 2000).

Kramer, M.H., Simmonds, N.E. and Steiner, H. A Debate over Rights: Philosophical Enquiries (OUP 1998).

Kretzmer, D. and Klein, E. (eds). The Concept of Human Dignity in Human Rights Discourse (Kluwer Law International 2002).

Landman, T and Carvalho, E. Measuring Human Rights (Routledge 2010).

Langford, M. et al. (eds). Global Justice, State Duties: The Extraterritorial Scope of Economic, Social and Cultural Rights in International Law (CUP 2013).

Lauren, P.G. The Evolution of International Human Rights: Visions Seen, 3rd edition, (U Pennsylvania P 2011).

Leuprecht, P. Reason, Justice and Dignity: A Journey to Some Unexplored Sources of Human Rights (Martinus Nijhoff 2012).

Lyons, G.M. and Mayall, J. (eds). International Human Rights in the 21st Century: Protecting the Rights of Groups (Rowman & Littlefield 2003).

MacDonald, R.S.J., Matscher, F. and Petzold, H. (eds). The European System for the Protection of Human Rights (Martinus Nijhoff 1993).

Madsen, M.R. and Verschraegen, G. (eds). Making Human Rights Intelligible: Towards a Sociology of Human Rights (Hart 2013).

Martinez, J.S. The Slave Trade and the Origins of International Human Rights Law (OUP 2012).

Maxwell, J.A. and Friedberg, J.J. Human Rights in Western Civilization 1600–Present (Kendall/Hunt Publishing Company 1991).

Mayer, A.E. Islam and Human Rights: Tradition and Politics (Westview/HarperCollins 1995).

McGoldrick, D. The Human Rights Committee: Its Role in the Development of the International Covenant on Civil and Political Rights (OUP 1994).

Méndez, J.E. and Wentworth, M. Taking a Stand: The Evolution of Human Rights (Palgrave Macmillan 2011).

Menuge, A.J.L. (ed). Legitimizing Human Rights: Secular and Religious Perspectives (Ashgate 2013).

Meron, T. (ed). Human Rights in International Law, 2 volumes (Clarendon Press 1984).

Meron, T. 'On a Hierarchy of International Human Rights' (1986), 80 *American Journal of International Law*, 1.

Moeckli, D., Shah, S. and Sivakumaran, S. (eds). International Human Rights Law (OUP 2010).

Möller, J.T. and De Zayas, A. The United Nations Human Rights Committee Case Law 1977–2008: A Handbook (NP Engel 2009).

Moyn, S. The Last Utopia: Human Rights in History (Harvard UP 2010).

Muntarbhorn, V. Unity in Connectivity? Evolving Human Rights Mechanisms in the ASEAN Region (Martinus Nijhoff 2013).

Murphy, T. Health in Human Rights (Hart Publishing 2013).

Nirmal, C. Human Rights in India: Historical, Social and Political Perspectives (OUP 1999).

Nowak, M. UN Covenant on Civil and Political Rights: CCPR Commentary, 2nd edition (NP Engel 2005).

Odello, M. and Seatzu, F. The UN Committee on Economic, Social and Cultural Rights: The Law, Process and Practice (Routledge 2012).

Orford, A. International Authority and the Responsibility to Protect (CUP 2011).

Pasqualucci, J.M. The Practice and Procedure of the Inter-American Court of Human Rights (CUP 2003).

Perera, L.P.N. Buddhism and Human Rights (Karunaratne 1991).

Perry, M.J. Toward a Theory of Human Rights: Religion, Law, Courts (CUP 2007).

Provost, R. and Sheppard, C. (eds). Dialogues on Human Rights and Legal Pluralism (Springer 2013).

Ramcharan, B.G. Contemporary Human Rights Ideas (Routledge 2008).

Ramcharan, B.G. The UN Human Rights Council (Routledge 2011).

Reus-Smit, C. Individual Rights and the Making of the International System (CUP 2013).

Risse, T., Ropp, S.C. and Sikkink, K. (eds). The Persistent Power of Human Rights: From Commitment to Compliance (CUP 2013).

Risse, T., Ropp, S.C. and Sikkink, K. (eds). The Power of Human Rights: International Norms and Domestic Change (CUP 1999).

Robertson, A.H. and Merrills, J.G. Human Rights in the World: An Introduction to the Study of the International Protection of Human Rights, 4th edition (Manchester UP 1996).

Roht-Arriaza, N. (ed). Impunity and Human Rights in International Law and Practice (OUP 1995).

Rosenbaum, A. (ed). The Philosophy of Human Rights: International Perspectives (Greenwood 1980).

Runz, J., Martin N.M. and Sharma, A. (eds). Human Rights and Responsibilities in the World Religions (Oneworld 2003).

Sachedin, A. Islam and the Challenge of Human Rights (OUP 2009).

Saeed, A. (ed). Islam and Human Rights (Edward Elgar 2012).

Seiderman, I. Hierarchy in International Law: The Human Rights Dimension (Intersentia 2001).

Sen, A. The Idea of Justice (Allen Lane 2009).

Sharma, A. Hinduism and Human Rights: A Conceptual Approach (New York: OUP 2004).

Shelton, D. Remedies in International Human Rights Law, 2nd edition (OUP 2006).

Shue, H. Basic Rights: Subsistence, Affluence and US Foreign Policy (Princeton UP 1980).

Sieghart, P. The International Law of Human Rights (Oxford: Clarendon Press 1983).

Sigg, A. International Human Rights Law, International Humanitarian Law, Refugee Law: Geneva from Early Origins to the 21st Century (Swiss Federal Department of Foreign Affairs 2003).

Sikkink, K. The Justice Cascade: How Human Rights Prosecutions are Changing World Politics (Norton 2011).

Sisay, A. The Justiciability of Economic, Social and Cultural Rights in the African Regional Human Rights System: Theory, Practice and Prospect (Intersentia 2013).

Sklar, K.K. and Stewart, J.B. (eds). Women's Rights and Transatlantic Antislavery in the Era of Emancipation (Yale UP 2007).

Sohn, L.B. and Buergenthal, T. International Protection of Human Rights (Bobbs-Merrill 1973).

Stearns, P.N. Human Rights in World History (Routledge 2012).

Steiner, H.J. and Alston, P. International Human Rights in Context: Law, Politics, Morals, 2nd edition (OUP 2000).

Sussman, R.W. and Cloninger, C.R. (eds). Origins of Altruism and Cooperation (Springer 2011).

Swindler, A. (ed). Human Rights in Religious Traditions (Pilgrim Press 1982).

Thakur, R. The Responsibility to Protect: Norms, Laws and the Use of Force in International Politics (Routledge 2011).

Tuck, R. Natural Rights Theories: Their Origin and Development (CUP 1979).

United Nations Educational, Scientific and Cultural Organization. Four Statements on the Race Question (UNESCO 1969).

United Nations. Report of the United Nations High Commissioner for Human Rights, Trade and Investment (2 July 2003) UN Doc E/CN.4/Sub.2/2003/9.

United Nations, Office of the High Commissioner for Human Rights. The Corporate Responsibility to Respect Human Rights: An Interpretive Guide (United Nations 2012).

Van Dijk, P. et al. (eds). Theory and Practice of the European Convention on Human Rights, 4th edition (Intersentia 2006).

Van Roosmalen, M., Vermeulen, B., Van Hoof, F. and Oosting, M. (eds). Fundamental Rights and Principles: *Liber Amicorum* Pieter Van Dijk (Intersentia 2013).

Viljoen, F. International Human Rights Law in Africa, 2nd edition (OUP 2012).

Weiss, T.G. Humanitarian Intervention: Ideas in Action (Polity 2007).

Weschler, L. A Miracle, A Universe: Settling Accounts with Torturers (U Chicago P 1990).

Westbrook, R. (ed). A History of Ancient Near Eastern Law, 3 volumes (Brill 2003).

Wheeler, N. Saving Strangers: Humanitarian Intervention in International Society (OUP 2000).

Wilson, E.O. The Social Conquest of Earth (Norton 2012).

Wilson, R.A. and Mitchell, J.P. (eds). Human Rights in Global Perspective: Anthropological Studies of Rights, Claims and Entitlements (Routledge 2003).

Index